MANAGING PEOPLE

MANAGING PEOPLE

The Art and Science of Business Management

A. Dale Timpe

Series Editor

Facts On File®
New York · Oxford

This is volume six in Facts On File's series "The Art and Science of Business Management," each volume of which provides a broad selection of articles on an important business topic of our time.
Volume one: *Motivation of Personnel*
Volume two: *The Management of Time*
Volume three: *Leadership*
Volume four: *Creativity*
Volume five: *Performance*

Managing People

Copyright © 1988 by KEND Publishing

Library of Congress Cataloging-in-Publication Data

Managing people / A. Dale Timpe, series editor.
    p. cm.—(The Art and science of business management : v. 6)
    Bibliography: p.
    Includes index.
    ISBN 0-8160-1901-0
    1. Personnel management.   I. Timpe, A. Dale.   II. Series.
HF5549.M31357 1988
658.3—DC19   88-3187

Printed in the United States of America

10 9 8 7 6 5 4 3 2 1

CONTENTS

PART III: A BASIS FOR COMMITMENT: COMMUNICATION AND PARTICIPATION

PART IV: WORK DESIGN AND EMPLOYEE SATISFACTION

PART V: CAREER PATHING: DEVELOPMENT, PROMOTION, AND PLATEAUS

PART VI: BEHAVIOR, CONFLICT, AND DISCIPLINE

PREFACE

Rarely has the management of employees received more attention than it does currently. By choice and by default, a new era of human-resource-management practices and philosophy is emerging.

The transformation to a service economy, the information explosion, advances in technology, and the intensely competitive global and domestic markets have created enormous pressure on corporations to change not only *what* they do but *how* they do it as well. This fundamental transition has affected every level and every aspect of companies' operations.

Corporate cultures and values are also in transition, requiring a new breed of employee with new skills. Accordingly, employers now find it imperative to train workers in the new skills that the workplace demands.

The composition of today's work force has changed. The workers are generally better educated, not as committed, and have higher expectations than their predecessors. Thus, traditional values and behavior are being challenged.

For generations the prevailing work mode has been that managers make plans and give orders and that workers execute the plans and produce. No more. The most profound dimension of the new human-resource philosophy is the willingness of management to give employees at every level a greater voice in company operations. In almost every case, an increase in employee participation ultimately fosters stronger employee commitment to the company and its business objectives.

As a consequence, the power and status of middle managers and first-line supervisors are being squeezed as companies delegate decision making to lower levels of the corporate hierarchy. Managers are realigning their priorities and are spending less time on policy and financial matters and more time interacting with employees. Thus, there is a greater need for executives to understand and develop good relationships with employees. Progressive human-resources efforts are concentrating on personnel effectiveness rather than on control, procedures, and productivity.

Managing People provides access to a broad spectrum of practical knowledge, research, and theory relating to the subject. The diversity of insights, experiences, and theoretical concepts presented here offers many solutions for human-resource planning, superior/subordinate relationships, effective communication, employee participation, and career development techniques. The sources represent a wide range of professional publications, including a number not readily available to most executives. For those wanting a more detailed discussion on a particular aspect, the bibliography provides a valuable resource tool.

A. Dale Timpe
Series Editor

ACKNOWLEDGMENTS

The articles are reprinted with the permission of the respective copyright holders and all rights are reserved.

Aiello, Robert J. "They Hear You . . . But They're Not Listening" by permission from *Public Relations Journal*, © 1983.

Axline, Larry L. "Strategic People Planning" from *Management World* by permission of the Administrative Management Society, © 1984.

Addams, Lon H. "Up to Speed in 90 Days: An Orientation Plan" by permission of *Personnel Journal*, © 1985.

Baer, Walt. "Employee-Managed Work Redesign—New Quality of Work Life Developments" from *Supervision* by permission of The National Research Bureau Inc., © 1986.

Beer, Michael and Spector, Bert A. "Managing Human Assets—It's Time for New Thinking" from *Office Administration & Automation* by permission of Dalton Communications, © 1985.

Boyd, Losana E. "Why 'Talking It Out' Almost Never Works Out" from *Nation's Business* by permission of the U.S. Chamber of Commerce, © 1984.

Bucalo, John P., Jr. "Successful Employee Relations" from *Personnel Administrator* by permission of The American Society for Personnel Administration, © 1986.

Buchanan, W. Wray, Hoy, Frank and Vaught, Bobby C. "Any Development Program Can Work" by permission of *Personnel Journal*, © 1985.

Cameron, Dan. "The When, Why and How of Discipline" by permission of *Personnel Journal*, © 1984.

Day, Charles R., Jr. "Do Your Managers *Really* Manage" from *Industry Week* by permission of Penton/IPC, © 1985.

Discenza, Richard and Smith, Howard L. "Is Employee Discipline Obsolete?" from *Personnel Administrator* by permission of The American Society for Personnel Administration, © 1985.

Farrant, Alan. "Proper Handling of Subordinate Problems" from *Supervision* by permission of The National Research Bureau Inc., © 1985.

Flamholtz, Eric G., Randle, Yvonne and Sackmann, Sonja. "Personnel Management: The Tone of Tomorrow" from *Personnel Journal*. This article represents an adapted version of the article entitled "Future Directions of Human Resource Management from 1985 to the Year 2000: An Environmental Scan Overview," from the UCLA Institute of Industrial Relations' publication *Future Direction of Human Resource Management*, edited by Eric G. Flamholtz, Yvonne Randle, and Sonja Sackman by permission of the Regents of the University of California, © 1986.

Gannon, Martin J. "Managerial Ignorance" from *Business Horizons* by permission of the Foundation for the School of Business at Indiana University, © 1983.

Goddard, Robert W. "The People Focus" from *Management World* by permission of the Administrative Management Society, © 1984.

Greenhalgh, Leonard. "Managing Conflict" from *Sloan Management Review* by permission of the Sloan Management Review Association, © 1986.

Hagedorn, Homer J. "'Everybody into the Pool'" from *Across the Board* by permission of The Conference Board and Homer J. Hagedorn, © 1984.

Hanna, John B. "Assessing Your People Potential" from *Management World* by permission of the Administrative Management Society, © 1984.

Hatcher, Larry and Ross, Timothy, L. "Gainsharing Plans—How Managers Evaluate Them" from *Business* by permission of the College of Business Administration at Georgia State University, Dr. Larry Hatcher and Timothy L. Ross, © 1986.

Hiller, E. A. Sturgis, Jr. "Personnel—Every Manager's Responsibility" from *Management World* by permission of the Administrative Management Society, © 1983.

Hollingsworth, A. T. and Hoyer, Denise Tanguay. "How Supervisors Can Shape Behavior" by permission of *Personnel Journal*, © 1985.

Kelly, James F., Jr. "Coping with the Career Plateau" from *Personnel Administrator* by permission of The American Society for Personnel Administration, © 1985.

Kornreich, Jerome S. "Myths" by permission of *Personnel Journal*, © 1985.

Lasden, Martin. "Prima Donnas: Living with Them when You Can't Live Without Them" from *Computer Decisions* by permission of BaetechPublishing Company L.P., © 1984.

Leigh, David R. "Business Planning Is People Planning" by permission of *Personnel Journal*, © 1984.

Linder, Jane C. "Computers, Corporate Culture and Change" by permission of *Personnel Journal*, © 1985.

Muczyk, Jan P. and Reimann, Bernard C. "Has Participative Management Been Oversold?" from *Personnel* by permission of American Management Association, © 1987.

Napier, Nancy K. and Peterson, Richard B. "Putting Human Resource Management at the Line Manager Level" from *Business Horizons* by permission of the Foundation for the School of Business at Indiana University, © 1984.

Near, Janet, P. "Reactions to the Career Plateau" from *Business Horizons* by permission of the Foundation for the School of Business at Indiana University, © 1984

Pascarella, Perry. "Plugging in the 'People Factors'" from *Industry Week* by permission of the U. S. Chamber of Commerce, © 1985.

Patterson, William P. "Managing the Maverick" from *Industry Week* by permission of Penton Publishing, Inc., © 1987.

Pilla, Lou, McKendrick, Joseph and Mason, Janet. "The Challenge to Middle Managers" from *Management World* by permission of the Administrative Management Society, © 1984.

Quible, Zane, and Hammer, Jane N. "Office Automation's Impact on Personnel" from *Personnel Administrator* by permission of The American Society for Personnel Administration, © 1984.

Rand, James F. "Negotiating: Master the Possibilities" by permission of *Personnel Journal*, © 1987.

Reynolds, Peter C. "Corporate Culture on the Rocks" from *Across the Board* by permission of the Conference Board and Peter C. Reynolds, © 1986.

Rosenberg, Sheila. "The Power of Team Play" from *Management World* by permission of the Administrative Management Society, © 1983.

Sanders, Larry W. "Help Your Subordinates Grow" by permission of *Personnel Journal*, © 1984.

Schuler, Randall, S., Galante, Steven P. and Jackson, Susan, E. "Matching Effective HR Practices with Competitive Strategy" from *Personnel* by permission of American Management Association, © 1987.

Sears, David L. "What Do Employees Want?" from *Management World* by permission of the Administrative Management Society, © 1984.

Sherman, Ethel C. "Your Attitude Is Your Altitude" from *Supervision* by permission of the National Research Bureau, Inc., © 1985.

Skeegan, Sam. "Six Steps to Hiring Success from *Management World* by permission of the Administrative Management Society, © 1985.

Slocum, John W., Cron, William, L., and Yows, Linda C. "Whose Career Is Likely to Plateau?" from *Business Horizons* by permission of the Foundation for the School of Business at Indiana University, © 1987.

Thiel, Carol Tomme. "Training Starts With Top-Down Accepetance" from *Infosystems* by permission of Hitchcock Publishing Company, © 1984.

Tobias, Lester L. "Hiring for Excellence" from *Industry Week* by permission of Penton Publishing, Inc., © 1987.

Wallach, Arthur E. and Jackson, Lauren Hite. "Getting an Answer to 'How Am I Doing?' from *Personnel* by permission of the American Management Association, © 1985.

Wilkinson, Roderick. "Who Gets the Promotion" from *Industry Week* by permission of Penton/IPC, © 1985.

Zey, Michael G. "Mentor Programs: Making the Right Moves" by permission of *Personnel Journal*, © 1985.

MANAGING PEOPLE

Part I
THE WORKPLACE: PEOPLE AND THE CULTURE

1.
PLUGGING IN THE 'PEOPLE FACTORS'

Perry Pascarella

> Most companies pay more attention to return-on-investment calculations on their capital assets than on their human assets. A business plan may be "blindsided" by unforeseen costs—related to hiring more people or increasing training programs on the upside, or layoffs and severance pay on the downside.

A manager creating a business proposal generally tries to be as analytical as possible—systematically including all of the factors that have to be studied, and quantifying them whenever possible. All the factors, that is, except the human ones.

There, the manager often trusts his intuition as to whether he has included what needs to be considered. And quantification is a rarity.

But the best of business plans can be "blindsided" by unforeseen cost—related to hiring more people or increasing training programs on the upside, or layoffs (with accompanying severance pay) on the downside. Or by the torpedoing of morale through actions that employees perceive as a breaking of trust.

Even a well-intentioned company like Xerox Corp., where concern for people is a tradition, can—because of its size and complexity—overlook some of the human-resource ramifications of business moves. The negative effects on employees can not only hurt morale—as was the case at Xerox when the firm was forced to impose layoffs a few years ago—but can also result in costs that turn potential winning proposals into expensive propositions.

The lesson sank in at Xerox, which had developed a new management "tool" to assess, in advance, the impact of business decisions on human resources—and to anticipate how the people consequences of those decisions will affect business prospects.

Though some things defy measurement, the device is practical enough to suit even the most bottom-line-oriented manager. It is being used by the

Customer Services Organization (CSO)—the largest part of Xerox's Business Systems Group (BSG)—to "take the intuitive and the gut feel out of human-resource implications and put it into a business-planning process," says Brain O'Connell, personnel manager for BSG marketing operations.

A simple-looking 34-page booklet leads the manager preparing a business proposal through the human-resource considerations that should be taken into account. He determines which ones need study and quantification. He may do the job in three minutes, or he may spend weeks doing the research. But there is no "maybe" when it comes to filling out the last page—the impact statement—and incorporating it into his business proposal. William Blair, former senior vice president of CSO, headquartered in Rochester, N.Y., made it clear that he would review only those business proposals that include human-resource impact statements.

HOW IT WORKS

The booklet begins with a page of "focus" questions covering five areas:

1. Head count—additions, reductions, and reassignments.
2. Changes in employee costs—compensation, benefits and indirect forms of compensation.
3. Relocation of people and/or facilities.
4. Conformance to the company's industrial-relations principles.
5. Impact on other functions or operations in the company.

Next, there is an overview sheet indication where assessments should be made. This shows, for example, that if additional employees are needed, the manager should examine needs related to hiring, training, career paths, job security, and affirmative action. (See Figure 1.)

Then a section of more-detailed questions follows for each of the five focus questions. In the "additional employment" portion of the head-count section, for example, the manager has space to list the number of people needed, types of positions, employee types (full time, part-time, contract), sources, timetable, and cost to hire. There are sections, too, on the availability of employees from protected classes (to meet affirmative-action requirements); type, timetable, and cost considerations for training; newly defined positions and career paths; how long the new positions will last; and their impact on other groups.

The next-to-last section of the booklet takes the manager through the financial and non-financial impacts with a provision for showing dollar amounts and recommended actions.

The last page, perforated for inclusion in the business proposal, allows for a general statement, pros, cons, and recommendations.

Figure 1.
Xerox's Assessment Road Map

Skill Requirements/Mix	Hiring	Training	Redeployment	Grade Changes	Area Differentials	Salary/Direct Compensation	Indirect Compensation	Career Paths	Job Security	Turnover	Affirmative Action	Disruption	Health & Safety	Environmental Review	Geographic Review	Legal Review	Personnel Support	Management Credibility	
	A	A					A	A		A									**1. Head Count** — a. Additions
										A	A					A	A		b. Reductions
A			A				A	A		A									c. Reassignment
			A		A					A	A			A					**2. Employee Costs** — a. Compensation
											A			A			A		b. Benefits
						A						A							c. Other Indirect
		A	A				A		A				A						**3. Relocation** — a. People
												A	A						b. Facilities

4. Industrial Relations Principles

A careful review should establish that:

a. The proposal has been rigorously checked to ensure consistency with industrial relations principles.

b. Any inconsistencies/conflicts have been explicitly identified.

c. The resulting costs, risks, etc., have been specified, along with satisfactory contingency plans and/or business justification.

5. Other Xerox Functions

A careful review should establish that:

a. Identification of other Xerox function(s) impacted is realistic.

b. Cooperation/agreement was obtained from responsible individuals in the affected functions.

▪ This adaptation of the "analysis overview" page in the Xerox Human Resource Assessment/Impact Analysis booklet indicates key areas to explore in conjunction with broad "focus" questions. The capital As stand for "assessment recommended."

The personnel department stands ready to provide assistance to managers for making the assessments. "It's not the role of Personnel to stand in the way of business proposals," believes Mr. O'Connell; it should, instead, help line management manage the human resources. And it should assist in assessing the impacts on human resources that can make or break plans and policies.

BROKEN PATTERN

When times got tough for Xerox in the recession years of the early '80s, the former glamor company looked for new ways to control costs and become more competitive. Management put itself through "competitive benchmarking" to understand better how other leading companies' costs and processes compared with its own—and to instill more quality into all its operations. It did some pulling back in compensation and benefits. It was forced to lay off workers. The cumulative effect was that people began to think that Xerox was "no longer the people-oriented company they had joined," recalls Mr. O'Connell.

Top management, in turn, realized that it had unintentionally, "broken the psychological contract" with employees. Mr. O'Connell wanted to "develop a tool that would be built into the management process to increase the accountability of line management for human resources."

In early 1983, Mr. O'Connell, then personnel manager for CSO, approached Ernie Glickman of Harbridge House, Inc., a Boston-based consulting firm. "Is anybody taking a disciplined approach to dealing with the human-resource factors in its business planning?" he asked.

Mr. Glickman did a literature search and conducted telephone interviews with a number of leading companies. Several of these companies were selected for personal interviews conducted by Robert Seurkamp, then employee and industrial relations manager, and a Harbridge House consultant. Xerox also conducted a legislation search to take stock of the many developments affecting personnel matters. The findings pointed to the lack of a disciplined approach in avoiding personnel pitfalls. Then the trio turned to Xerox's management. Everyone in senior management saw the need to formalize the human-resource evaluation process, Mr. Glickman says. They recognized that "we can do it intuitively, but there is probably a better way."

His research—and experience at other companies—led him to conclude:

- Most companies develop strategies and then intuitively assess the impact on their people.
- Executives assume that their people will implement the strategy, "but that doesn't always happen."
- Most companies are "more comfortable with the return-on-investment

calculation on their capital assets; they do not calculate the return on their people or give it as much weight."

CRITERIA

What, then, should be this tool that management seemed to want—and what should it be able to do? The answers, says Mr. Glickman:

1. Through an earlier assessment, attain higher-quality strategies of proposals to produce better bottom-line results.
2. Reestablish certain operating principles in order to regain employee commitment.
3. Improve the business-planning process.
4. Make human-resource assessment an integral part of business planning and operational decision-making.

By February 1984, a draft of the assessment booklet had been prepared. Top management of CSO was supportive: Mr. Blair issued a memo insisting that, beginning in March, all business proposals would have to include a human-resource impact statement.

The draft immediately underwent a real-world test: gaging the impact of a proposal to close a Xerox distribution center. The end result? "We avoided a layoff," says Mr. Seurkamp. "We forced the focus on the fact that laying off people was going to cost money. We found assignments for the people involved and avoided the costs of severance pay, and so on."

Mr. Blair implemented the process with the vice presidents who reported to him at the time. They, in turn, have conducted orientation meetings with their staffs and the process has cascaded two levels. Other managers who want to use the process are welcome to do so.

Mr. Seurkamp, now a program manager in Xerox's national service organization, says: "What we were trying to do was to get people to understand that even though we have to take tough actions and we have to bring costs down, that doesn't mean we don't care about our people." In effect, says Mr. O'Connell, "we are reestablishing certain values" regarding people that have to emanate from the top.

The developers of the human-resource assessment were not trying to give workers a "warm fuzzy" feeling, says Mr. Seurkamp. "We wanted to demonstrate to management that you need to understand the cost of what you're doing and what impact it has on people. There are a number of impacts on people and almost every one of them costs money somewhere." "We're telling management: 'We know you have to become more cost-effective; let's try to do it an even better way.'"

BOTTOM-LINE DIFFERENCE

Analyzing human-resources costs can sometimes show that a promising business proposal is really a bad one. At one point, for example, CSO studied the suggestion that company cars be eliminated. It seemed to offer significant year-to-year savings. But after the proposal was run through the human-resources assessment, it looked like more dollars in *added* costs.

If a business proposal were to precipitate a union-organizing attempt, management may have to spend weeks trying to turn the situation around. Just the direct and easily quantifiable costs of pulling people in from the field for meetings, and management's time, add up to big dollars.

The human-resource assessment will not often cause a proposal to be scrapped, Mr. Seurkamp points out, but it may lead management to alter the way it handles the decision—as was the case in the closing of the distribution center.

This assessment process helps mangers determine how their business proposals impact not only their own manpower situations, but other functions as well. In that case, says Mr. Seurkamp, "you must go to the manager of that function and essentially do a human-resources assessment of that function.

"If marketing wants to make pricing-plan changes, will it require retraining for administrative employees? Will it require new positions within the administrative group? It's the responsibility of marketing to meet with administrative management to determine what the human resources implications will be."

In any company, marketing may want to launch new products, but the service department may not have enough trained technicians in the right parts of the country. Or marketing may expect that a price cut will stimulate sales, but there may not be enough service people to handle the added volume.

The assessment process has become an integral part of the business-proposal process within CSO. In the months ahead it will be reviewed at the BSG senior staff level for expansion to other units. It would not be surprising to see other companies emulate this process. But, warns Mr. Glickman, managers have to feel a sense of ownership—they have to realize that it is not something that the personnel department is imposing on them.

It is more than just another paperwork burden. It is a tool to foster better management decision-making.

Perry Pascarella is executive editor of Industry Week.

2.

THE PEOPLE FOCUS

Robert W. Goddard

For generations the prevailing work mode has been that management plans and gives orders and workers execute plans and produce. That rigid division is now being replaced by a management style encouraging employee involvement. Employee participation has become the responsibility of managerial leadership.

Over recent years, as the decline in the North American workforce's productivity has become a highly publicized issue, three myths have emerged relating to the productivity problem. The first is that there was once a "golden age" of the North American worker. The second is that the soft factors of production, such as worker dedication, are not primary to improved productivity. The third is that the emphasis on encouraging worker participation is just a passing fad.

The success of the Japanese in managing U.S. firms, the growing legion of companies instituting quality-of-worklife programs, and a flurry of recent research studies contradict each assumption. The evidence is mounting: the North American worker is O.K., but the work culture is not.

1) THE GOLDEN AGE

The productivity of the United States is the highest in the world and is still increasing, although at a declining rate. There is nothing wrong with the current workforce that modern tools and improved management wouldn't cure. A 1978 U.S. Chamber of Commerce survey of U.S. employees concludes, "there is a large reservoir of positive attitudes that managers might utilize more effectively to improve performance and increase productivity."

Opinion Research Corporation (ORC) has been monitoring employee attitudes since the 1950s. Their most recent survey of managers, professionals, clerical and hourly workers indicates that employees are losing their *incentive*—rather than their will, need, or ability—to work. They are becoming increasingly dissatisfied with their companies, management and supervision, career opportunities, rewards, and input into decision making.

Surprisingly, this growing unhappiness with the work setting has not diminished job satisfaction. Independent research studies conducted by ORC, the Work in America Institute, the University of Michigan's Survey Research Center, Sentry Insurance Company, and the U.S. Chamber of Commerce indicate that our work *ethic* is thriving, while our work *behavior* falters. Findings of these research studies include the following:

- 75 to 80 percent of all workers are satisfied with their jobs;
- 78 percent have inner need to do the very best they can regardless of pay;
- 84 percent would work harder and do a better job if they were more involved in decisions relating to their work;
- 75 percent would prefer to go on working even if they would live comfortably without working for the rest of their lives;
- 60 to 65 percent are highly committed to their companies and would return if beginning their careers again;
- 74 percent would accept work reassignments wherever help is needed in their company if they were convinced their sacrifices would help achieve higher productivity; and
- 63 percent would agree to have their salaries linked to higher personal productivity.

A large body of experimental data supports these findings. Psychologist Raymond Katzell, for example, has reviewed 103 experiments designed to test whether an improved incentive system, including both money and greater control over one's work, would lead to high individual productivity. It did in 85 of the experiments.

We have a basically sound workforce. The Japanese who manage U.S. plants with U.S. workers concur that U.S. workers are well trained and relatively well motivated.

The real problem, said Daniel Yankelovich, chairperson of the social research firm of Yankelovich, Skelly, and White, is that "the leaders who run our institutions do not really understand today's workforce: tens of millions of well-educated Americans, proud of their achievements, zealous of their freedoms, motivated by new values, with substantial control over their own production, and ready to raise their level of effort if given the proper encouragement."

2) HARD VS. SOFT

To illustrate "hard" vs. "soft" factors, an example is the Japanese experience in this country. The Japanese distinguish between the "soft" factors of production (the dedication of the workforce) and such "hard" factors as technology, capital investment, and research and development. They recognize that the soft factors are just as important as the hard ones and that, indeed, the two are interdependent. They have a better grasp of how to capitalize on our work ethic than we do.

The proof is not hard to find. In 1974 Matsushita Electric took over a Motorola TV factory in Illinois. With new management, but virtually the same employees, the number of defects in the factory's TV sets decreased from 1.5 to 0.03 in four years—a 50-to-1 improvement.

Sanyo Electric took over a unionized Arkansas television factory in 1976, and in less than a year reduced the retail failure rate of its TV sets from 10 percent to less than 2 percent. In San Diego, Sony's plant absenteeism and turnover rates are 25 percent to 50 percent below those of other electronic companies in the area. Output per labor unit is 22 percent higher than that of a U.S. counterpart.

"Japanese companies that have established subsidiaries in the U.S.," said Hirotake Takeuchi of the Harvard Business School, "are as committed to people building and team building as they are to product quality. They are finding that American workers are responding very positively toward concerns for quality improvements and human resources development."

The most telling argument that the human element is the major factor in productivity comes from U.S. workers themselves. For a number of years the University of Michigan asked a sample of workers to keep a diary of activities on the job. An analysis of these diaries revealed that between 1965 and 1975 the amount of time employees actually worked declined by more than 10 percent.

More significantly, in a recent survey conducted by Opinion Research Corporation, people from all labor categories indicated that they perform at only 65 percent of their capacity. If extrapolated to all American workers, the researchers say, these two factors alone, quite apart from such considerations as insufficient investments and aging equipment, could account for the slowed tempo of productivity growth.

This finding raises a disquieting issue. A 1981 Gallup study for the U.S. Chamber of Commerce indicates that only 40 percent of business executives assign top rank to worker's attitudes and abilities as a factor that could increase overall company production. Furthermore, only 20 percent of them believe that efforts at the worker's level (the soft factors of production) can make the greatest contribution to improved productivity.

3) PARTICIPATION FAD

We are beginning to see a change in some of the historic assumptions about work roles and rules. For generations the prevailing work mode has been that management plans and gives orders, and workers execute plans and produce. That rigid division is now seen by many as outmoded. "A management style encouraging employee involvement and participation has become an accepted responsibility of U.S. managerial leadership," said William M. Batten, chairperson of the New York Stock Exchange.

Today nearly 50,000 companies and several million managers and employees are partially or deeply involved in some kind of worker involvement scheme. These programs have taken many forms, such as Ford's Employee Involvement (EI), GE's Bring Quality to Life (BQ2L), and Westinghouse's quality circle program.

The philosophy behind this participatory and humanistic approach to management is that, given time and the proper work structures, most people, no matter what their level in an organization, *want* to work smarter and more responsibly. All they need is a work environment that recognizes employees as intelligent and trustworthy, provides the necessary tools, encourages participation and input in decision making, and creates a sense of self-esteem, self-fulfillment, and community.

Quality circles have become perhaps the most popular manifestation of the emphasis on employee involvement and the successes it can bring. For example, 15 teams at Lockheed Missiles and Space Company saved their company almost $3 million from problems solved during a two-year period. Ten teams at Honeywell facility improved assembly productivity by 46 percent over two years.

More to the point are the quality-of-worklife (QWL) committees established by such companies as AT&T, General Foods, Honeywell, the Continential Group, and General Motors. The concern of these "productivity" teams extends far beyond cost reduction and product quality to such specific areas as facilities, safety, and recordkeeping.

Unlike their Japanese counterparts, these QWL efforts are strictly an American invention—voluntary, informal, advisory, and positioned outside traditional work structures. Structurally, their chief focus is on organizational "oughts," or potential opportunities for betterment, not just the daily "is" of operational life.

Ted Mills, chairperson of the American Center for the Quality of Work Life, has been monitoring QWL programs since their advent in the early 1970s. "When properly introduced and implemented," he said, "QWL has proved to be demonstrably effective, in both human and economic terms."

In 1982 the nonprofit Public Agenda Foundation examined American attitudes toward work. A huge majority of the respondents (82 percent) stated that they had some degree of discretion and control over the effort they gave to their job. An even larger majority (88 percent) said they had control over the quality of the work or service they performed.

These findings illuminate a little-noted fact about the modern workplace. "Most working Americans," said Daniel Yankelovich, "have it in their power to decide whether they will satisfy only the minimum requirements of their job or exert the extra effort that makes the difference between ordinariness and high quality, between adequacy and excellence."

In the battle for improved productivity—and the profits that go with it—technology and capital are important weapons. But only human beings can determine the victor.

Robert W. Goddard is director of publications in the personnel development department of Liberty Mutual Insurance Companies, Boston, Massachusetts.

3.

THE CHALLENGE TO MIDDLE MANAGERS

Lou Pilla
Joseph McKendrick
Janet Mason

By all indications, middle managers are very aware of the challenges they face in the future. They understand that complacency is the ticket to a quick demise of their careers, and that staying abreast of management techniques and updating their skills are the keys to executing their broadening responsibilities.

From Texas to Toronto, from California to New York, middle managers are facing a challenge. It is a challenge bigger than any that they, as a group, have experienced before. It is not limited to any one industry, size business, or location. And it is a challenge that strikes at the heart of every middle manager's dreams, hopes and goals for the future.

This challenge has been brought on by a variety of forces changing not only middle managers' jobs, but the jobs of every North American manager and employee. Three forces stand prominently above the others. First, the economic recession has caused many organizations to cut staff. Often, these cuts have been made in middle-management ranks, which, over the years, have grown into many levels. Middle managers have found themselves, in some ways, victims of an overblown corporate structure.

Second, the penetration of automation into the office is causing business to take a hard look at its existing staff and management structures, with an eye toward how automation can eliminate labor-intensive work processes and make *management* more productive. Managers are being called upon to implement new office technologies to boost their own productivity as well as that of their employees.

Third, today's workforce has come to be comprised of employees whose values, goals and behaviors differ radically from those of their predecessors. Their loyalty to the company is tenuous and conditional, not assumed and expected; their goals are often short-, not longterm; and what motivates them is not, in many cases, what inspired earlier workers toward greater output.

The challenge to middle managers, then, is to refocus, update and integrate their skills to deal with these new forces and the tough new business environment they have engendered.

PARING THE RANKS

One study of over 100,000 managers, conducted by management consultants SMC Hendrick, Inc., based in Framingham, Massachusetts, affirms that a major change in job structures and responsibilities is now taking place at middle-management levels. The study found that, on the average, companies are paring their middle-management positions by one-third and will alter remaining middle-management positions within the next few years.

Middle management has been "growing at an alarming rate ever since World War II," says Charles K. Rourke, president of SMC Hendrick. "Companies are now starting to reach the critical mass of excess middle managers and are beginning to do something about it." The actual number of middle managers will increase in coming years, Rourke predicts, as organizations expand into global markets, although their percentage will decline.

"There is definitely a crisis situation facing middle management," asserts Richard H. Jacobson, vice president of administrative services with Blue Cross & Blue Shield of Wisconsin in Milwaukee and International President of the Administrative Management Society (AMS). He emphasizes that all companies, not just the Fortune 500, are thinning management levels and adding new responsibilities to remaining managers.

The structural changes affecting middle management are nothing new, says Robert Zager, who first wrote on the subject in 1961. Zager, who is vice president—policy studies of Work in America Institute, Inc., based in Scarsdale, New York, states that until they are faced with challenges such as foreign competition, organizations are complacent toward the efficiency of their management ranks.

The participative management movement is also affecting middle management, Zager notes. "There is more attention to pushing responsibility down the line. As these managers sense greater attention to the shop floor, they feel squeezed in the middle."

AMS members in many locations and sizes of companies indicate that they are feeling the current restructuring of middle management. According to Douglas R. Aitken, administrative officer for engineering and construction with Manitoba Hydro in Winnipeg, and president of the Winnipeg chapter of AMS, his engineering and construction group has been affected by a restructuring of all management levels. Further south, Maryann Gilmore, branch manager of corporate field administration for Honeywell, Inc., in

Charlotte, North Carolina, and first vice president of the AMS Charlotte chapter, notes a new focus in her division on re-evaluating open management positions before they are filled with new personnel. And although his own position hasn't come under fire, V. Richard Chiarilli, C.A.M., office manager at Lancaster Stone Products Corp. in Williamsville, New York, and first vice president of the AMS Buffalo Chapter, says middle managers in Buffalo are "hanging onto the arms of their chairs a little tighter than they normally would be."

INSTANT INFO

Taking on new responsibilities is a major part of the current challenge to middle managers. This is brought on by a number of factors, including fewer managers performing jobs that used to be distributed over a greater number of people, calls for greater productivity, and, perhaps most important, the arrival of office automation.

"The whole reason for the pyramidal or hierarchical structure is control," according to Rourke of SMC Hendrick. "Now computers are diminishing the need for this hierarchical structure, as information can be transmitted instantaneously, not passed through the layers of hierarchy. Organizations will become flatter because of computers."

The introduction of computers to management jobs is, in fact, the *only* major change affecting middle management, says Robert Half, president of Robert Half International Inc., headquartered in New York City. Taking a contrary position, Half maintains that the discussion of the middle-management crunch is "artificial," and that there has been no serious change in middle management. Managers will have to be more knowledgeable, however, according to Half, as they will be overseeing more sophisticated employees, such as data processing personnel.

Amy Wohl, president of Advance Office Concepts Corp., in Bala Cynwyd, Pennsylvania, confirms that office automation presents a major challenge to middle managers. "Office automation makes middle managers more effective and consequently fewer middle managers are needed," she states.

Wohl feels that computer skills are becoming essential management tools. "We will very quickly get to the point where if managers don't have basic computer skills and are unwilling to learn, companies won't hire them." However, Wohl notes, learning computer skills isn't as foreboding as it once was. Today, computers are becoming easier to use and training programs are more effective.

According the AMS International President Jacobson, managers will have to demonstrate botton-line results, and should prepare themselves with computer literacy skills and an awareness of financial management principles. New entries in the U. S. Department of Labor job listing are all technician related, states Jacobson, indicating that middle managers will have to be generalists surrounded by technicians.

Jane Seeley, C.A.M., personnel director at VISA, USA, Inc., in San Francisco and an AMS international director-at-large, concurs that there is a need for managers to develop computer skills. Currently, she has found it helpful to be knowledgeable about computers so she can instruct programmers. However, she has no present need to perform hands-on computer applications.

This new mandate of acquiring computer skills is hitting close to home for Chiarilli of Lancaster Stone. Not only is he presently involved with a feasibility study for the acquisition of a new minicomputer, which he hopes to have operating in a few months, but his firm is now revamping its telecommunications system as well, targeting a new setup for installation at about the same time. Chiarilli no doubt feels the weight of the upcoming computer decision, in that his company recently had to get rid of a poorly designed computer, and because the new computer will be his responsibility.

Aitken of Manitoba Hydro could empathize with Chiarilli. His office just received its first small business computer, which he will be sharing with other managers and support staff. Although he has worked with a terminal tied to a mainframe computer, Aitken, a 20-year company veteran, notes that this will be his first experience with the new, smaller device.

Gilmore's experience with office automation is equally compelling. A 22-year employee of Honeywell, she has, over the past two years, been involved with implementing word processing and having her office become part of a nationwide computer message network.

THE HUMAN DIMENSION

Despite the emphasis on developing computer skills, managers cannot live by technology alone. "Managers must also be able to blend human dimensions of their jobs with technology," AMS International President Jacobson stresses. People skills will be paramount as management is confronted with a changing workforce which will be more knowledgeable, better educated, and more responsive to psychological incentives and alternative work patterns. The status quo will no longer be tolerated, Jacobson adds, and managers will have to pursue opportunities to broaden their knowledge.

Gilmore of Honeywell notes that, when it comes to advancing, automation and people skills "are being constantly intertwined," but asserts the "need to constantly keep up on the human relations side" of management.

"We are dealing more and more with individuals than with policies and procedures," says Seeley of VISA. Five years ago, companies dealt more with the financial aspects of business than with employees. Now, she says, business has to change.

One of the bright spots in what has been a trying time for middle managers is the new power that goes along with new responsibilities. Middle managers, according to Jacobson, will take on greater freedom and authority to make decisions, and will need to be more innovative in finding ways to increase corporate profitability. "Managers will be more accountable for their work and they will have to demonstrate results," he emphasizes. "There are fewer jobs and those who will keep their jobs are the ones who hone their skills and become even more professional." The installation of fewer management levels at Manitoba Hydro, according to Aitken, "probably has resulted in a somewhat greater range of authority for myself."

Rourke of SMC Hendrick also predicts a new role for middle managers in the coming years—they will be multifunctional, not specialized. "We're not going to see the very narrow range of responsibility that we have in the past," he says. Management training will play a significant role in meeting the challenge. "Major companies will adopt management development and technical opportunities for their employees," states Jacobson. "I see a time when employees will spend 40 percent of their on-the-job time in development and training programs." Wohl agrees that training is important and urges managers to learn something about office automation as soon as possible.

As one who has been taking seminars and workshops to strengthen her current skills, Seeley emphasizes that managers must develop abilities outside of their specific areas to increase their chances of staying competitive.

By all indications, middle managers are extremely aware of the challenges they face in the future. They understand that complacency is the ticket to a quick demise of their careers, and that staying abreast of management techniques and updating their skills are the keys to executing their broadened responsibilities. As Douglas R. Aitken affirms, the new mandate for managers is to keep current with new technologies—and not to be happy with just "sitting in my comfortable pew."

Lou Pilla is editor of Management World *and* Impact: Office Automation. *Joseph McKendrick is news editor of* Management World *and editor of* The Generalists, AMS International Leadership Report, *and various other AMS newsletters. Janet Mason is assistant editor of* Management World, *and public relations assistant with the Administrative Management Society, Willow Grove, Pennsylvania.*

4.
PERSONNEL—EVERY MANAGER'S RESPONSIBILITY

E. A. Sturgis Hiller, Jr.

> Why every manager must accept that people management can no longer be shouldered only by the personnel department and that the organization's people should receive as much attention as its other assets. If this is done in a conscious, orderly way, rather than in haphazard and occasional bursts of enthusiasm, the results can be astounding.

The main principle of good management, in its simplest form, can be stated as follows: "Do unto others as you would have them do unto you."

Personal failures in an organization are seldom the result of the individual alone—far too often they are failures in leadership, which can be prevented. To prevent failure, the leadership of every organization must accept full accountability, and be committed to the positive actions necessary for successful human resources management.

The success of an organization depends on having an adequate number of people in the right job at the right time, all producing at their highest capacity. Managers cannot, then, expect intelligent human relations to develop spontaneously while most time and effort is devoted to consideration of tasks and resources.

It complicates things significantly when a struggle is necessary to place human resource activities on the same level of importance in the minds of managers as material resources. Whenever consideration of the human element is of less than primary importance in management circles, ultimate success of the organization is in question.

Management has been defined in very simple terms as "getting things done with and through the efforts of other people," and that function breaks down into two major responsibilities, planning and control.

Planning consists of deciding what you want your people to accomplish. This involves the careful determination of needs, the establishment of objectives, the outlining of procedures that will attain those objectives, and the proper assignment of responsibility to individuals or groups of individuals.

Control requires the use of various methods which will stimulate the people in the organization to work in accordance with the plan. There are at least two

19

control factors that require attention: organization structure and supervision.

Unless the organization structure is simple and all who are part of it understand it, it will defeat its own purpose, which is to enable people to work together in groups as effectively as they would work alone. There should be no misunderstanding about individual or departmental authority and responsibility, or about interrelationships between individuals and organizational units.

The function of supervision is to close the gaps between desired performance and actual human performance. If the mere issuance of policies and instructions would cause people to do what they are supposed to do, supervision would not be necessary.

Having divided the activity of management into the two basic elements of planning and control, it is simple to arrive at a statement of the primary executive function—to determine what you want people to accomplish, to find and train people competent for such accomplishment, to see that methods are developed by which they will perform more effectively, and to check periodically on how well they are accomplishing it.

Management, then, is the development of people—not the direction of things. If this fact is accepted, many management difficulties disappear. The manager who says that he or she would rather exhaust him or herself doing things correctly than expend the time and patience necessary to get other people to do them correctly is admitting that he or she cannot manage.

Thus, management and human resources administration are one and the same, and should never be separated. Management *is* human resources administration.

Since management requires staff and line activities, it is natural to divide human resources functions between staff personnel and line executives. Line managers have complete and final responsibility and authority for human resources matters. Staff personnel managers are expected to advise, help, and be of service to the line in the fulfillment of these responsibilities. There is an important place for both in any organization.

What complicates this relationship is the desire on the part of some line managers to delegate all human resources responsibility to a staff personnel manager or department, as well as the tendency of some personnel managers to seize such responsibility. If this is permitted, the human resources cannot receive proper consideration.

Good human relations within an organization is the most important contributing factor to a successful business. To build sound human relations, your dealings with the people in your organization must involve their perfectly natural motives and desires. Consider, then, a few of these natural interests. If you agree that they would apply to you personally, you can be sure that they apply to employees you supervise.

- When an individual is seeking new employment, he or she wants to be treated courteously and made to feel at ease.
- A new employee wants to be welcomed to a job rather than thrown into it.
- The employee would like to receive simple and intelligent instruction in what he or she is expected to do and what constitutes a job well done.
- Everybody likes to work for someone they can respect and in whom they can have confidence.
- Everybody wants someone to recognize their importance.
- Many people like to feel their daily work is of service to others.
- People want realistic recognition of a job well done.
- There are few people who will not work hard and long for incentive. Special recognition always inspires greater effort.
- Everybody likes to work in an organization in which there is universal confidence in the ability and fairness of top management.

The foremost responsibility of *every* manager is essentially the same, regardless of his or her level in the organization, regardless of the organization's size, whether it is in the public or private sector, whether it is operated as a profit or non-profit institution, and whatever its product or service. That responsibility is to create an environment or climate which encourages each individual to contribute positively to the purpose, the goals and the objectives of the organization.

If one were to summarize all the different ways of ensuring good management, the list would run into the hundreds.

Consider, then, just the seven simple steps that follow. If followed carefully and with reasonable attention to sequence, they will ensure adequate management attention to the way in which operations are conducted and human resources are developed. With both old and new employees and in both old and new situations, application of these recommendations will bring about improvement in human performance.

1) Develop a simple outline of the functions to be performed. This can apply to an individual job or to a complete unit of an organization. It should include an understandable statement of what people are to do, what authority they have in doing it, and what their relationships with other people are.

2) Develop a simple statement of performance expectations. There are many activities for which, at first, it seems impossible to develop standards of performance. However, a sincere attempt to develop standards will often produce very definite and acceptable objectives. If a job can't be measured, then it should not exist.

3) At regular intervals (at least quarterly), check actual performance against the standards that have been set. If management is to plan its activities, it must know how big a gap there is between what is being done and what should be done. This should be checked in terms of individual and group performance.

4) Make a list of corrective actions necessary to improve performance where such improvement is needed. Individuals cannot develop into better employees unless they are continuously increasing their skills, gaining knowledge, changing their habits, and assuming constructive attitudes. A manager should know where improvement is needed.

5) Select the best sources from which employees can obtain help and encouragement. Sources can be divided into four categories: the immediate supervisor; other individuals in the organization; people outside the organization who could be brought in; and outside sources of help to which the individual could be referred.

6) A time should be set aside in advance for supplying the help and encouragement that are needed. If we do not plan in advance, the time can be made available only through disrupting the functioning of the organization. It makes no sense to go to all the trouble of deciding what should be done, analyzing what has been done and determining what action is needed, if no action is taken.

7) Assure a mutual understanding of what constitutes a fair days's pay for a fair day's work, as well as what other incentives are worth working for. On a firm base of fairly administered financial and other incentives, a climate can be developed that will cause people to stay with you rather than go elsewhere for more money.

The people in the organization should receive as much attention as material things. If this is done in a conscious, orderly way, rather than in haphazard and occasional bursts of enthusiasm, the results can be astounding. A person reacts quickly and favorably to understanding, fairness, and consideration. If you approach your management activities with that idea in mind, much of the frustration which you now experience will disappear.

The greatest single reward that any manager can receive is to have his or her subordinates say that they are better workers because of the manager's leadership. Such an attitude builds morale and loyalty, and these will accomplish the impossible.

An organization will reach its full potential when management has established a climate that assures recognition of the needs, goals, and achievements of each of its employees.

A manager is successful only when the employees of the organization are an integral and contributing part of its success.

Every manager and supervisor is accountable and their performance can and must be measured by the way in which they fulfill their responsibilities in human resources management.

E. A. Sturgis Hiller, Jr., is a human resources consultant based in Merritt Island, Florida.

5.
WHAT DO EMPLOYEES WANT?

David L. Sears

The most important lesson of this ongoing study comes from looking at 30-year trends. While there are some changes (type of work overtaking security as the number-one priority for men, for example), the real trend is stability. While managers may be tempted to jump on the bandwagon of motivational fads, employees' concerns may be more basic and constant.

What do people value most about work? Answering this question is the first step in motivating them. Goals and preferences—the things that people want—play an important role in directing their work efforts and accomplishments. If the rewards from work are in line with these preferences, and if rewards are in turn linked to employee performance, then employees are very likely to be motivated.

However, if managers misread these preferences, the opposite can occur. If work "rewards" don't line up with preferences, they are not rewards at all, or at least not the most effective rewards.

So the question facing management is: What do people value about their work? Money (the obvious answer)? Advancement? Security?

Many managers are familiar with the "hierarchy of needs" described in Abraham Maslow's theory of motivation. Maybe you've even tried to use this hierarchy, which describes the priorities of people's needs. At the lowest level of this hierarchy are physiological needs—food, water and air. At the top are the so-called "self-actualization" needs—needs to realize one's potential and achieve self-fulfillment. In theory, once people have satisfied their physiological needs, they shift their efforts up through the hierarchy, moving from needs involving physical comfort and safety to those involving social relationships, esteem and finally, at the top, self-actualization.

The problem with trying to apply this hierarchy in the workplace is that the needs are presented in very general terms and extended well beyond the confines of work to the personal needs and aspirations of employees. The revelant

24

question for the manager is more specific: What *workplace* needs—needs that management can respond to—are most important to employees?

Many companies try to answer this question by conducting employee attitude surveys. These surveys are time consuming and costly, so they tend to be one-time projects rather than ongoing pursuits. They also tend to be organizational "snapshots," limited to one employee group and to a set of specific and probably transient issues. As a result, data on diverse groups, collected over a period of time, is rarely available to managers, making it difficult to determine employee needs.

LONG-TERM INSIGHTS

One job-performance questionnaire, however, administered by Minnesota Gas Co., headquartered in Minneapolis, provides just such long-term data, and supplies some interesting and useful insights into the question of the priorities of employee needs.

The questionnaire asks people to rank 10 common job factors according to the importance they attach to them: a "1" is placed next to the factor felt to be *most* important, and a "10" placed next to the factor felt to be the *least* important.

While the questionnaire's design is simple, it deals with work issues of continuing importance. More important, use of the questionnaire has provided a wealth of data about the attitudes and preferences of employees versus what managers think they are. Minnesota Gas has used the questionnaire for over 30 years and has collected data from 57,000 people: job applicants and employees; managers and subordinates; older and younger workers; men and women; the highly educated and the barely educated.

The results of the actual administration of the preference questionnaire are displayed in Figures 1. and 2. They outline a variety of employee wants ranging from pay and working conditions to advancement. If, like most people, you predicted a number of differences between your own priorities and those of others, some of the results may be surprising. For the most part, predicted differences are exaggerated. Employees' preferences are actually quite similar to managers'. The predicted importance of pay is especially off-target. Managers on average predict it to be foremost among employee priorities, when actually it ranks fifth. Benefits and hours are predicted to have moderate importance, when actually they rank low. In contrast, company and co-workers rank higher than expected.

DIFFERENT PREFERENCES

Using questionnaire results, researchers at Minnesota Gas have analyzed the different preferences of men and women, of people in different occupations

Figure 1.
What Are Your Job Preferences?

	Managers' Preferences	Managers' Predictions of Employees' Preferences	Actual Employee Preferences
Advancement (Opportunity for promotion)	1	3	3
Type of Work (Work that is interesting and well liked by you)	2	4	2
Company (Employment by a company for which you're proud to work)	3	7	4
Security (Steady work, no layoffs, sureness of being able to keep your job)	4	2	1
Pay (Large income during year)	5	1	5
Supervisor (A good boss who is considerate and fair)	6	9	7
Co-workers (Pleasant and agreeable fellow workers)	7	10	6
Benefits (Vacations, sick pay, pensions, etc.)	8	5	8
Working Conditions (Comfortable, clean workplace; no excessive noise, heat, cold, odors, etc.)	9	8	10
Hours Good starting and quiting time, good number of hours per day or week, day or night work, etc.)	10	6	9

and age groups, and of different education levels. Also, researchers outside Minnesota Gas have administered the same questionnaire to employees in private companies (Minnesota Gas is a public utility). Below are some of the results of these studies.

- Men consider job security to be most important, and working conditions the least important. Women rank type of work first, and benefits last. Men's ranking of type of work has moved up over the years. The importance of security to women has, on the average, decreased over the years.
- The importance of pay and benefits has been increasing for both men and women, while the importance of advancement has been decreasing.
- For younger workers, short-term factors (co-workers, hours, pay and working conditions) seem to be of primary concern. Older workers are more concerned with long-term factors (advancement, benefits, and security).
- Single men's preferences closely match those of young men, and differ from married men. On average, there are few differences between the preferences of married and unmarried women or between older and younger women. The preferences of widowed and divorced women, however, take predictable turns; an increased concern for advancement, benefits and security.
- Predictably, as one's level of education increases, the importance of security decreases and the importance of type of work increases. Employees with an eighth grade education rank security first and type of work fifth. In contrast, employees with advanced degrees rank security seventh and type of work first.
- Compared with job applicants, employees give a higher priority to pay, benefits, working conditions and advancement. Employees give a lower priority to company than do job applicants.
- Differences between public and private company employees are relatively minor, at least for the categories of employees studied. Employees in retailing ranked hours and company higher than did Minnesota Gas employees, and ranked pay and security lower. Employees in a private data processing firm rated type of work as more important, and hours and security less important, than did Minnesota Gas employees.

What conclusions and lessons can be drawn from Minnesota Gas Co. data?

- Be careful when making assumptions about the needs that motivate employees. Don't guess at priorities—find out what they actually are. Don't automatically figure that the needs of your subordinates are different than yours, especially when it comes to the importance of providing them with meaningful and fulfilling work.
- Income security rather than high income seems to be the more significant money issue, especially for men and employees with moderate and lesser levels of education. This is hardly surprising—most managers predicted that security needs would be high—but it is something that mangers tend

to lose track of. Attending to issues of security can be important in work motivation.

- Men and women do have some different work priorities. However, as this ongoing study has found, the differences seem to be more a matter of circumstances than sex. If females are breadwinners, their priorities are likely to be the same as male breadwinners.
- Expect the priorities of applicants to differ from those of employees. Evidence from the Minnesota Gas questionnaire indicates that work "intangibles" such as interesting and diverse work and work climate figure heavily in applicant priorities. These factors can be used to the advantage of a company's management in mapping recruitment strategy to gain new employees.
- Perhaps the most important lesson of this ongoing study comes from looking at 30-year trends. While there are some changes (type of work overtaking security as the number-one priority for men, for example), the real trend is stability. While managers may be tempted to jump on the bandwagon of motivational fads, employees' concerns may be more basic and constant.

Thus, the results of this ongoing study point to the need for all organizations to strive for truly understanding employee needs, and to align their motivational efforts with the needs that employees express as important to them.

David L. Sears is a human-resource consultant based in New York.

6.
STRATEGIC PEOPLE PLANNING

Larry L. Axline

> Growth is usually not a smooth process but occurs in waves. The very
> real impact of management skills cannot be denied, as human resources
> are the lifeblood of an organization. Be sure your organization does not
> put so much emphasis on profits that the flow of good people—and ex-
> ercise of good management judgment—is constricted.

Although businesses plan for growth, human resources are often taken for
granted or held in reserve until the numbers and financial targets are crunched
and finalized. With such inadequate attention to the people, or "soft skills" of
management, it seems that some businesses exist in spite of themselves.

There is a need to combine the human resources of business with its other
operations. As a starting place, managers must ask themselves what they want
to accomplish, how large they want the company to be, and where the
necessary capital and people will come from.

Of course, finance and capital are important to business. Top management
must determine the cash-flow requirements and identify where this money will
come from. They must also anticipate the financial structure of the organization which will be necessary in the next two to three years.

However, it takes people to translate dollar projections into reality. The
whole idea is to squarely address the issue of translating the volume of growth
into the types and numbers of people needed to support the volume. Managers
must recognize that a growth crisis will happen if they don't plan now. Planning
doesn't need to be elaborate, but is must be timely, and clearly ahead of the
need.

If human resources are critical to the continuity of an organization, why do
some almost systematically tend to drive high achievers away? Consultants
frequently sit down with company presidents and ask them where they want to
be, what their expectations are for the organization, and especially their expectations of performance for the key people. Then the key employees, away

from the presidents, are asked these same questions. This extremely simple procedure usually yields some amazing results—it often seems as though the president and key employees are working for different organizations.

Following are the three most common concerns employees have about management expectations: 1) "nobody around here tells me what is going on"; 2) "what's my future and career path with this organization?"; and 3) "how are you keeping score on me?" The individual must also play a significant role in resolving these issues and must avoid the temptation to place all the burden and blame on management.

ACCELERATING CAREERS

When working with executives and managers in their career acceleration programs, human resource development professionals request that each individual objectively assess the advantages and disadvantages of the present position and its future prospects. In addition, he or she is asked to state clearly, in writing, personal strengths and weaknesses, as well as short-term objectives for money, position, and the balance of job with family life.

By considering the list of objectives for the longer term (3 to 10 years), and identifying alternatives and career paths, the individual is often able to determine the most likely course of action to meet his or her professional objectives. If those objectives are closely aligned to the organizational objectives, the company is far less likely to lose an extremely valuable employee. Also, the employee is far more likely to perform at a high level.

Commonality of expectations is often the key to successful organizational planning, and is clearly a soft skill of management which has a hard impact on the financial results. The following steps are necessary to start and develop an organizational plan:

- a statement about the company, its corporate philosophy, thrust, and direction—this should define what business it is really in, and what it intends to accomplish;
- an analysis of current customers, industry practices, and market potential—this should define the trends, the profit potential, and the primary competitors;
- an analysis of what people are needed to accomplish the given objectives—if the employees are not already in the organization, management must decide where employees can be recruited from and at what time;
- after the capital equipment replacement program and expansion needs are analyzed, the sources, and types should be defined; and
- the foregoing sections may be combined into a statistical overview in which capital and people requirements are identified in terms of timing and need.

The plan must be monitored and recycled each year. This should be done in the spirit of management effectiveness and not to please others. The plan should not become simply a public relations and credit acquisition tool.

PLANNING'S "SOFT" CRITERIA

In addition to the initial questions asked which were, 1) what are we trying to accomplish? 2) how big do we want this company to be? and 3) where will the necessary capital and people come from?, the following criteria are added. These are, 1) will the plan work over the long term? 2) can we live with it in the short run? and 3) what impact will the plan have on our people and what needs to be done?

Only when these soft criteria have been specifically evaluated by top management is it possible to develop a realistic and workable plan. These criteria cannot always be measured, but their importance cannot be overstated.

The computer, especially with the advent and availability of microcomputer software packages, can assist in business forecasting and planning. However, management judgment must prevail in the final analysis. Years of seasoned management experience must be applied to computer-assisted planning and models to assess their reasonableness within the limits and reality test of time, money, and people constraints.

Thorough and systematic planning is essential to the growth, continuity and future health of the organization. A good organizational plan is an unrecorded asset. Inability or unwillingness to develop a realistic plan may result in a significant unaccrued liability and the eventual demise of the organization.

For most companies, there is a gap between objectives and organizational performance. However, there is no substitute for effective planning and foresight. It is essential that companies begin to think in terms of longer-range planning horizons they should also consider precisely what is necessary to achieve the goals they tell their competitors, customers and bankers that they are going to achieve. To do anything short of realistically testing these assertions may simply be an exercise of "talking to ourselves, about ourselves." Many unhealthy companies fall into this category.

There are many reasons for developing an organizational plan. One is to accelerate growth and to improve profitability. Equally important is establishing realistic and achievable objectives, based upon a thorough analysis of the market potential and the necessary people and capital to realize those objectives. There is often a vast difference between what a company *could* do and what it *can* do based upon organizational resources.

Organizational planning develops a commitment on the part of managers. It provides them with a road map and directions. They function with more complete understanding of overall objectives—even when they encounter the inevitable detours in their personal and organizational plans.

Inevitably, all people will have phases in their lives when they feel out of balance vocationally. Frustrations, changes, and pressures will pile up. At those times, a written personal audit and alternative analysis may help to focus on the sources of pressures and available options. We must remind ourselves that it is not *who* is having vocational problems or facing career decisions, by *when* will it happen to me? Similarly, the question is not *which* resource-stretched, aggressive companies will encounter the growth crisis, but *when* will it happen to us? Few of us go through life without some illness.

Growth is usually not a smooth process—it occurs in waves. The hard impact of the soft skills of management cannot, and should not, be denied, as the flow of human resources is the lifeblood of an organization. Be sure your organization does not put so much emphasis on profits that the flow of good people—and exercise of good management judgment—is constricted and restrained. Profit expediency must not be permitted to occur at the expense of the people in the business, for it is people that are crucial to the long-term health and stability of the organization.

Larry L. Axline is founder and president of Management Action Planning, Inc., Boulder, Colorado.

7.
PERSONNEL MANAGEMENT: THE TONE OF TOMORROW

Eric G. Flamholtz
Yvonne Randle
Sonja Sackmann

> Developments in human resources management are usually evolution-
> ary, and managers often find themselves dealing with issues only after they
> have become problems and problems after they have become crises.
> Tomorrow's crises are already taking shape, but they can be mini-
> mized—and possibly avoided.

Developments in human resources management are usually evolutionary, rather than revolutionary. Because of that, practitioners often find themselves dealing with issues only after they have become crises.

Tomorrow's crises are already taking shape, but they can be minimized—and possible avoided—if human resources executives take the time to observe the evolutionary path of today's work-related issues.

These issues are only pieces that must, like a jigsaw puzzle, be assembled to create a clear picture. Given what we know and understand about the changes taking place today and those anticipated in the next 15 years, it is possible to construct an accurate facsimile of tomorrow's workplace.

EXECUTIVES MUST MANAGE KNOWLEDGE, SKILLS AND TALENTS

Effective use of human resources may be defined as the effective use of employees' knowledge, skills and talents. In the future, effective use of people will depend upon human resources managers' abilities to: recognize the increasing diversity of workers; provide opportunities for worker participation in decision making; design jobs to meet worker needs for personal growth; match worker skills with job requirements; and design and allocate work to better match changes in the business environment with changes in the work force composition.

Diversity of the work force. Because the future work force will include distinct sub-groups, there is a growing demand for organizations to be able to accommodate a variety of individual needs. That accommodation will necessitate organizational systems—such as management, planning and control—that are responsive to a work force diverse in gender, lifestyle, age and ethnic background.

The diversity of lifestyles and households will necessitate changes in current patterns of employment, compensation and benefits. Male and female workers will continue to seek somewhat different forms of compensation and the increased number of women in the work force (and particularly working mothers) will necessitate greater recognition of such specific needs as child care and flexible schedules.

The more diverse age range of the work force in the coming years will require changes in the allocation and use of the diversity of skills, talents, needs and expectations. For example, younger employees tend to be more satisfied by pay, greater responsibilities and time off; job security, medical and retirement benefits are generally more important to older people.

Finally, the growing ethnic diversity of the work force may demand increasing recognition and opportunities to fulfill ethnic-based needs and to minimize such ethnic-based differences as language and educational background.

Employee involvement in decision making. Opportunities must be developed for employees to become actively involved in making work-related decisions since more of the population will want to participate in decisions affecting them.

Research has shown that the development of these opportunities can have a positive impact on organizations because such involvement may increase satisfaction and performance outcomes.

Employee personal growth. In the future, employers must be concerned with redesigning jobs in order to meet individual employee needs for personal growth, autonomy and recognition. People are increasingly seeking jobs in which they can use and be recognized for their individual talents, skill and knowledge.

The need for changes in existing job designs is suggested by the current decline in job satisfaction revealed in a recent survey.[1] This decline may indicate that current job designs and rewards systems are not meeting employee needs.

Matching job skills with requirements. Based on trends in the international economy and increasing competition, matching employee skills with appropriate jobs will be a continuing problem.[2] The increasing turbulence in the economy and in technology will create needs for skills that many companies' existing work forces do not currently have. At the same time, these changes will make other skills obsolete.

Improving the situation will require frequent evaluations of required and existing skills and of ongoing training intended to give employees the needed knowledge and skills.

Work allocation and the environment. With an increasingly turbulent business environment, the changing nature of the work force, and the increasing convergence of technology, work must be allocated and designed differently in the future. New technologies may help this endeavor.

The changing composition of the work force, the changing nature of U.S. households, and the changing nature of social values, combined with faster economic cycles in the business environment, will require a more flexible allocation of work. Possible solutions include part-time work, job sharing, job transfers between couples, flextime or on-call schedules.

New technology (such as data processing, video teleconferencing, computer-assisted design and so forth) will demand new designs to accomplish tasks and projects. Smaller divisions, autonomous work groups and overlapping groups are structural answers to the availability and use of new technologies.

Flexibility of middle management. The shift from an industrial to a service-based economy, the changing nature of social values, faster economic cycles in the business environment and increasing innovations in technology will require a role change for middle managers. There will be a new focus on information management and on planning and coordinating activities.

In the future, managers must be more flexible in terms of the leadership style they use. For example, highly educated and skilled segments of the work force will seek help facilitating their work, while those less skilled will require more instruction and direct coaching.

RECRUITMENT AND TRAINING EFFORTS MUST BE EXTENDED

Recruitment is the effective search for needed employees; selection is the appropriate choice among job applicants to fill an open position; and training provides employees with the skills and knowledge needed to perform a certain job effectively.

In the future, companies will need to be concerned with extending their recruiting efforts, developing careful screening procedures, training employees to help them adapt to change, providing appropriate and sufficient educational programs, and accounting for their investment in recruiting, selecting and training employees.

Extend recruitment efforts. Changes in the geographic distribution of the population will require an expansion of recruiting efforts for firms in some areas of the United States. This particularly applies to those employers in the

Northeast and North Central states who may face spot shortage and therefore require more extensive recruiting campaigns as people continue to migrate to the South and West.

Select more carefully. A greater diversity in the values and needs of the work force, combined with the changing requirements of the work itself, will necessitate more careful screening of job applicants to reduce costs associated with training and turnover.

Given a stronger identification of workers with certain personal, work-related and ethic values, companies must be more concerned with identifying workers whose values correspond to their own. A careful screening of those attitudes and values that are emphasized in a given company may reduce costs associated with turnover.

Companies can reduce training costs by exercising greater care in screening for those skills they anticipate needing in the future. In general, people must be recruited who have a high learning capacity, are adaptable to change and tolerate ambiguity.

Provide training. Given the variety and rate of change in the business environment, there will be an increasing need to help people adapt to continuous change.

Technological changes, demographic changes in the work force composition, changes in the legal and regulatory environment, changes in social and cultural values, and trends in the economic and international sphere will increase the need for organizations to help personnel adapt to constant changes and learn skills.

Training programs that help workers adapt to continuous change will increase organizations' ability to continue to function effectively.

Increase investments in education. In a world in which the pace of technological innovation has quickened and economic conditions are becoming more turbulent, it will be important to provide a variety of educational programs to employees. These include cross-training, retraining, continuing education, management development and interpersonal skills.

Retraining will be necessary in those cases in which workers are displaced by increasing use of computer-assisted design and manufacturing and other innovative technologies. In this retraining, intellectual skills (rather than manual skills) will be emphasized because, in the future, such skills will be required to design, operate and manage automated systems in factories, on farms and in offices.

To avoid obsolescence of skills and thus reduce the need for retraining, continuing education programs are needed to update worker skills. These programs allow those in the technical professions to stay abreast of state-of-the-art knowledge and the use of new and converging technologies.

Along with providing technical skills training, companies must be concerned with providing appropriate management development programs for employees of the future. These programs will need to include, for example, interpersonal skills training that will allow managers to successfully supervise diverse groups of individuals who may differ in their needs, attitudes, expectations and motivations.

In addition, the growing number of women joining the work force may create a need for work-related interpersonal training in male/female relationships, for both employees and their families.

Practice human resources accounting. The shift from an industrial-based economy to one based on knowledge and information will require designing ways to account for investments in people's capabilities. There will be a growing need to account for the investments that organizations are making to recruit, select and train their employees.

With systems to account for human resources, organizations will be better able to decide if training ("making" people) or recruiting ("buying" people) is more cost effective. Human resource accounting methods are currently being developed and tested.[3,4]

Take legal precautions. The increasing number of lawsuits filed because of alleged unfair termination will make it increasingly important to involve legal services in recruiting, selection, hiring and termination procedures. This advice can be valuable in designing procedures to avoid possible litigation and in identifying and correcting problems within existing systems.

To avoid litigation, companies must be especially concerned that promises made to employees are fulfilled. Job advertisements must be formulated in ways that preclude promises of permanent employment. Recruiters must be made aware of how statements made to future employees about their employment security can be phrased in a manner that will prevent lawsuits.

Written documents, such as employment contracts and employee handbooks, need to be carefully screened for implied promises of permanent employment.

Companies will also need to become concerned with creating practices that are objective and impartial. In this regard, employee evaluation procedures must be reviewed and redesigned so they are based on observable data.

Employees should also be given the chance to review and comment on their evaluations before they are finalized and evaluations should be kept on file so they can be reviewed by employees upon request. Supervisors must also be trained in performance evaluations and in dealing with poor performance issues to avoid legal problems.

COMPENSATION AND BENEFITS MUST BE MORE FLEXIBLE

Compensation and benefits are the means by which employees are recognized and rewarded for their work efforts. They are also the means through which employees satisfy their physical and psychological needs.

The new generation of employees will weigh salary and benefits packages against their personal needs and values. Therefore, compensation and benefits packages must offer greater flexibility in order to meet individual needs.

Individualize compensation and benefits. In an attempt to meet the needs and expectations of individual employees, companies must offer a range of compensation and benefits components from which employees can design their own packages.

These components include health care benefits for families, child care, life insurance, time-income trade-off options, opportunities for sabbaticals and educational leaves, flexible compensation schedules and alternatives to retirement.

Under such a flexible system, it might be expected that younger workers would demand larger current cashflow and reimbursement in the form of additional time off or unpaid vacations. Older workers, on the other hand, may prefer deferred income payments or higher medical and retirement payments.

To meet the increasing need for child care (resulting from the growing number of two-income and single parent households) and to counter child-related absenteeism, companies may have to provide child care services directly or offer flexible schedules that give employees the opportunity to meet this need themselves.

In terms of retirement plans, workers in the future will seek alternative plans because of the problems with the current Social Security system. Corporations may, therefore, want to offer alternative retirement packages, as well as retirement counseling so the chosen packages will best meet individual needs.[5]

Prepare for more retirees. More people will retire and more will retire earlier. This trend will require preparing for sufficient funding of pension plans. Companies may also want to invest in designing alternatives, such as partial retainment or using employees after retirement age on a consulting basis.

The increasing number of women in the work force, meanwhile, will require several changes in the business environment traditionally dominated by white males. Areas of concern include issues of equal compensation between women and men, policies regarding discrimination and sexual harassment, and provision of special services, such as child care.

Address the issue of equal compensation. Companies will need to be concerned with providing benefits, compensation and services that meet the needs of both women and men, and that reward individuals based on equal pay for equal work.

Companies will have to provide adequate wages and promotion opportunities to women since these aspects of compensation are prominent in satisfying women's concerns. Such provisions, however, cannot be made at the expense of opportunities for men.

Attractive benefits for women include special services, such as child care and the opportunity for flexible work schedules that ease the integration of their professional roles with their family lives. For men, one of the most attractive benefits appears to be increased leisure time.

Formalize discrimination policies. As pressure to eliminate workplace discrimination based on sex, race, physical ability and age continues to increase, companies will need to develop formal policies that specify what constitutes discrimination and sexual harassment to avoid lawsuits. Employee awareness must be raised about the issue, and special grievance procedures to review complaints may have to be included in company discrimination policies.

In an effort to avoid involvement in discrimination suits, employers should seek input from employees and be responsive to claims of discrimination.[6]

Another way to avoid litigation is to create valid management systems for job and performance evaluations to assess the job qualifications and performance levels of candidates.

HEALTH, SAFETY AND UNIONS WILL CONTINUE TO BE ISSUES

Trends in the business environment indicate that companies need to pay more attention to the issues of employee health, safety and legal rights.

In the future, companies must provide better information on workplace health and safety issues to employees, design methods to help employees deal with stress, be more sensitive to job security issues, design special contracts for knowledge workers and find ways to combat increasing health care costs.

Companies also cannot overlook unions. Several environmental trends indicate that the basic composition of union membership will change and that unions' futures will depend on how well they will serve members' needs. It may become increasingly difficult, for example, to organize employees who favor individualism.

Major implications for human resources managers include the need to be sensitive to unionization and the problems unions will face, the need to be concerned with gainsharing and employee stock ownership plans and the need to increase the use of joint labor-management teams.

Provide information on health and safety. Employers must be more responsible in providing information to employees on workplace health and safety, including potential health hazards and safety regulations.

This need is ongoing. As technological advances are introduced into the workplace, there will be a need to evaluate them in terms of potential health hazards. Environmental monitoring committees composed of both workers and management may be established to jointly evaluate the workplace for health hazards and search for solutions to alleviate identified hazards.

Providing adequate information and increasing employee involvement in monitoring the workplace could reduce the number of lawsuits filed by employees in an effort to protect their "right to know" about hazards.

Be prepared for increasing stress. The existing level of stress and frustration is likely to increase among parts of the work force in the future. Causes of this stress will include increased competition for the same jobs (especially middle management positions) among members of the baby boom generation.

Single parents and people who are members of dual career families will also experience stress as they try to balance a career with the needs of their families. Increased stress will also be placed upon those workers who must obtain new skills because technological innovations have made their jobs obsolete. Workers will increasingly be forced to relocate, to learn new skills, to adapt to new jobs, to adjust to lower paying employment and to interact with a more diverse group of people.

Each of these changes will place increasing stress upon individual workers. Therefore, organizations may want to increase their awareness of potential sources of stress, reduce or try to avoid them and provide stress reduction programs for their employees.

Be more sensitive to job security issues. Policies regarding company hiring, firing, layoffs and performance issues will have to become more sensitive to legal liability since the number of court decisions to protect the job security of workers is expected to increase. The courts may favor the notion of mutual loyalty and life-long employment, rather than employment at will.

In an effort to reduce the possibility of law-suits resulting from claims of unfair termination, employee handbooks must be carefully screened for false promises of long-term employment, and interviews that may imply life-long employment.

Be sensitive to unionization and union problems. In an effort to attract new members and to retain old ones, unions can be expected to become involved in new issues of interest to workers and to oppose efforts of individualization. Companies that provide predominantly low-paying jobs with little advancement and/or learning opportunities are likely targets for future unionization.

A continued decline in the proportion of workers represented by unions is expected, but it is unclear what actions unions will take to preserve their status. Unions should concentrate their efforts on addressing the impact of any of the environmental trends, including worker's increased desire for participation in decision making, concerns about workplace health and safety issues, changes in worker satisfaction, or introduction of new technologies into the workplace that may replace workers and individualize the labor force.

An awareness of ongoing union issues and joint labor management bargaining efforts is the best strategy to avoid problems with unions in the future.

Be concerned with gainsharing and employee stock ownership plans. In the future, bargainers will need to be concerned with issues of risk, gainsharing and employee stock ownership. Gainsharing arrangements may eliminate the need for renegotiation as workers' pay is increased or reduced based on profitability.

Increase the use of joint labor/management teams. Companies will need to increase the use of quality circles and joint labor-management participation teams since doing so may reduce the likelihood of strikes. The tradition of co-determination in European countries may lead to a similar trend in the United States, which will result in greater cooperation between unions and management.

None of these issues or concerns, of course, is new. What is new is a growing recognition that successful human resources management now depends on anticipation of the future of such issues as much as managing them today. In a predominantly service-based economy, the service potential of human resources can be considered the only competitive advantage in the long term.

Other resources, such as appropriate finances and technology, are mobile and culture-neutral; they can be transmitted, sold and moved across companies and national boundaries. The adaptation and effective use of new technology by competitors occurs so quickly that technological advantages are beginning to mean less and less. Attention to human resources will, therefore, become increasingly important for companies that hope to stay competitive.

References

1. Opinion Research Corporation, *Strategic Planning for Human Resources: 1981 and Beyond.* October 23, 1980.
2. Ehrbar, A. F., "Grasping New Unemployment," *Fortune.* May 16, 1983, pp. 107-112.
3. Flamholtz, E. G., *Human Resource Accounting.* San Francisco, CA: Jossey-Bass Publishers, Inc., 1985.
4. Flamholtz, E. G., *Management of Human Resources* (edited by Y. Tsurumi). Tokyo: Heim International's Modern Management Series, 1985.
5. Kovach, K. A. "New Directions in Fringe Benefits," *SAM Advanced Management Journal,* Summer 1983, pp. 55-63.
6. Linenberger, P., and Keavenly, T., "Sexual Harassment and Employment," *Human Resource Management,* Spring 1981, pp. 11-17.

Eric G. Flamholtz is professor of management at the Graduate School of Management, UCLA, and assistant director of the ULCA Institute of Industrial Relations, where he heads the Center for Research on Human Resource Management. Yvonne Randle is a research assistant at the Graduate School of Management and the Institute of Industrial Relations, UCLA. Sonja Sackmann is a visiting lecturer and a research associate in the behavioral and organizational sciences at the Graduate School of Management, UCLA.

8.

'EVERYBODY INTO THE POOL'

Homer J. Hagedorn

> What makes corporate culture powerful is the presence of common
> values expressed in the same way at the same time. This shared vernacular
> makes communication easier, which in turn makes organized activity
> feasible.

For all the talk of "culture" in corporate boardrooms and executive suites, there are still skeptics—lots of them. Many top managers see such discussions as a sort of hobby, an amiable exercise that is not really very helpful in the battle to keep the bottom line black and the shareholders off their backs.

In fact, the notion of corporate culture addresses real human issues that often impinge on the success of a business. The most dramatic recent example is the case of Continental Illinois National Bank, whose near collapse captured headlines throughout the summer of 1984. More than one of the Continental Illinois surviors ruefully admitted that the corporation's leadership had shown a remarkable disregard for reality, and had proceeded under the assumption that "we're too big and too important to go under."

The origins, workings, and likely outcomes of such an attitude are possibly more compreshensible to the student of group behavior than to the banking expert, who could see the profound danger in Continental Illinois's stockpile of unsecured loans, and wonders why the company's officers could not. This situation was hardly unprecedented. One of the features of corporate culture is that the beliefs and habits of the company's leaders can anesthetize them against problems that from the outside are painfully apparent. The corporate culture—like the culture of some remote Indian or South Seas tribe—may not permit the prudent warrior to offer warning to the council of elders.

In my direct experience with corporate cultures—I have worked with more than 100 companies over the last half-dozen years alone—I've usually been able to search out the prudent warrior who can list the critical symptoms. Those symptoms may be far more subtle and less evident to the trained eye than a portfolio bulging with bad loans. Any culture is a web in which each part is related to all the others and to the whole. A love affair between a senior executive and a member of his staff, an epidemic of gambling in office pools, even a remark about the arrogance of a company's salesperson may reveal a deeper disturbance in organization or leadership.

Culture in particular companies is easy to describe if you know what you are looking for and how to find it. The systematic approach is a cultural profile, which begins with a little detective work but consists mainly of asking a sample of experts (people who live and work in the culture and know it well) to answer a set of open-ended questions; a skilled profiler then interprets the responses. Some questions are direct: "What does the company do best?" Some are evocative: "If you remember the founder of the company, what sort of a person was he, and what did he expect of people?" Some take advantage of the current culture fad: "How would you characterize your corporate culture?"

With skilled interpretation, the responses help reveal the internal patterns that are unique to a particular company. The profiler is looking for the most candid statement possible of what a company stands for, and what it can't stand. In many cases these subjects have never been expressed, or have been stated only as pieties.

The following cases are composites, based on my experience as a management consultant at Arthur D. Little. In some of the examples, facts have been changed so that clients won't recognize themselves in the story, In some cases I have clarified the situation for easier observation, removing the internal resistance and preoccupations that make profiling a corporate culture such an inexact science.

CASE 1: TENNYSON'S TIGERS

The Problem at Tennyson Togs Inc. The CEO is concerned about turnover among talented young managers. Within the past six months, three of the company's five most promising young executives have left. Two of them have gone to work for Tennyson's chief competitor. One of those two left on the verge of a major client presentation, and took key notes and materials with him. There has been attrition in earlier years, but the loss of three key people at once suggests that something is wrong, and that others may join the exodus.

The Basic Detective Work. The CEO calls in Holmes and Mead, consultants in corporate culture, to conduct an initial inquiry. Holmes knows that companies that experience heavy and steady losses of high-potential young executives commonly fall into one of two categories. The "proving-ground" company throws all of its "young tigers" together into a pit, and employs a survival-of-the-fittest philosophy, advancing the most aggressive into higher levels of management, discarding the rest. The "training-ground" company brings in more young executives than will fit into the available spaces higher up, fosters the development of all of them, but eventually encourages some to depart at the appropriate juncture.

Holmes finds that of the three departed young tigers, only one expressed gratitude at having had the opportunity to "begin my career at Tennyson Togs." The other two were bitterly surprised about the shortage of room at the top and the intensity of what they saw as an artificially induced struggle. One actively sought a position with Tennyson's key competitor. And one not only sought a position with the competitor, but contrived to carry a project and client along with him—in retaliation against Tennyson's "deceit." Holmes asks the CEO to meet with his partner, Mead, who specializes in cultural profiling.

The Cultural Profile. Mead says to the CEO, "Holmes's conversations with several former Tennyson managers reveal a culture that clearly tolerates one-upmanship, and honors those who launch 'preemptive strikes'—that is, who shift blame to others or criticize those who are likely to attack their work. Your culture encourages internal competition, but it also believes strongly in need to attract and train bright young people."

Mead conducts a series of interviews with key executives and with relative newcomers who are perceived as high fliers. These interviews contain a number of loaded questions:

- Do higher-level managers resent the mutual aggressiveness they've had to put up with, or do they accept it as a fact of life and glory in the toughness that has enabled them to survive?
- Do managers regard insufficient teamwork and collaboration as a problem—or is there no mention of this as an issue?
- Since aggressiveness seems to be so highly valued by the company, what is it supposed to accomplish for Tennyson Togs?
- When asked why Tennyson Togs hires too many tigers, do employees, customers, and competitors consistently give the same answer, or are there a variety of different explanations?
- Why don't the tigers know what's in store for them before they come to work at Tennyson?
- What other traits are attributed to one-uppers and preemptive strikers? Are these people viewed as the heroes, the leaders, and the builders? If so, in what sense are they perceived to be "building"? If this isn't so, then who *are* the acclaimed heroes of Tennyson Togs, and what are the characteristics that make them heroic?
- Is it considered bad form to mention one-upmanship when discussing the training of new recruits at Tennyson? If so, what values support this sort of unspoken law?
- Is this culture bad for Tennyson Togs?

As Mead gathers answers, she discerns that the company can move away from the proving ground and toward the training ground if management and governing groups agree. But she also wants a clear reading on how hard such a change would be. So she presses for a more complete description of the Tennyson Togs culture, and for a better understanding of how the culture serves the firm's profitability.

The Outcome. Mead's culture profile confirms a yearning for less aggressive internal competition among most people in middle and upper management. But changing, she knows, is almost out of the question unless top management wants it, too. And the very top people at Tennyson Togs remain devoutly committed to the value of the fittest surviving. Since the company has clearly prospered through aggressive selling, Mead is inclined to agree with the CEO that internal competition is still serving its desired purpose.

She informs the CEO that there are three choices, one of which (change the culture) is precluded by top management's own faith in internal competition and the values that support it. But the company *can* cut down on the number of tigers it hires every year. Or Tennyson can warn its promising managers that most of them will be leaving within five years, and will have to insist on the training they think they need while they stay with Tennyson.

CASE 2: EVERYBODY INTO THE POOL

The Problem at Chlorine International. Several senior managers are concerned that office pools for sporting events seem to be proliferating among the staff. They have no strong objections to this sort of sociable gaming, but the practice appears to play a major role in the company's daily life. Work doesn't truly begin on Monday until the weekend's games have been complied, compared, and discussed. It's as though these pools provide many supervisors and department heads with their main reason for coming to work.

The Basic Detective Work. First, Holmes tries to find out whether the office pools really are taking up a lot of many employee's time. Once he has determined the scope of the pool epidemic, he wants to know whether some external element has infiltrated the company solely for the purpose of creating a gambling enterprise.

He concludes that there are a lot of pools, but no mastermind. Something, he tells his client, is causing this recreational gambling activity to thrive and spread at Chlorine International. It's part of the corporate culture.

The Cultural Profile. "Contrary to popular belief, people won't habitually goof off on the job unless something in their company's values encourages it," says Mead. "This case clearly calls for a cultural profile, just to find out what those values are at various levels of the company. My bet is that we will find that senior management is unwittingly abetting the bettors."

The Outcome. Mead's cultural profile demonstrates one of the ills of industrial maturity. Chlorine International is a company in an old-line smokestack industry with no substantial ownership interest either on the board or in senior management for more than a generation. Senior management controls all board appointments and management incumbency. As profitability declined throughout the industry as a whole, a new attitude arose. Its first traces showed up in a CEO with a penchant for limousines, lavish office furnishings, and the outward trappings of power. A management culture followed this example. Managers now openly act out the belief that "this place exists for our enjoyment." In turn, lower level managers regard recreational gambling pools as their right. They see no harm in these activities and insist there's no reason to give them up as long as the upper-level executives insist upon their own far costlier "fun," including what the middle-level people describe as mutually awarded bonuses, lofty titles, and management retreats held semiannually in exotic resorts.

"The company is perceived as a way of life," Mead tells her clients, "a place to live, a place to be, rather than as a business. The company's longevity reinforces this value. Nobody can believe that it would ever cease to exist. But I can tell you now that Chlorine International will almost certainly go out of business."

Chlorine International's top managers react with alarm and disbelief. Almost in unison, they reply: "How do you know that?"

"It's simple," says Mead. "No client in a position like yours is prepared to listen to what I have to say, and to deal with it. Ladies and gentlemen, your actions are the source: your employees' activities are the symptoms. Unless some of you are truly prepared to deal with a situation that, by now, implicates everyone with the power to change it, this consultation can serve no further purpose."

CASE 3: THE RIGHT OF
THE FIRST NIGHT

The Problem at Great Gadgets Inc. The chairman of the board has gotten wind of a love affair between two company executives. Although this relationship was discreet at first, it has lately erupted into several emotional scenes during working hours. Worse, the chairman has begun to hear rumors that other love affairs between employees have occurred, leading him to suspect that this is fairly common.

The Basic Detective Work. Holmes finds that the two lovers are a fairly senior male executive and a younger female protegee. "A classic case," Holmes tells the chairman. "You must remember that the dynamics in this sort of relationship are usually not just personal and sexual—though the lovers many profess it to be so limited. It also has to do with power." Holmes reminds the chairman of the simple and traditional solution. "If your foremost concern is to clean up this particular mess," he says, "do the usual thing: Move the man, fire the woman."

The chairman says, "No, I'd like to find out whether this dalliance is a symptom of a deeper problem within the company." Thus commences the cultural profile.

The Cultural Profile. Mead warns the chairman, "When these things happen regularly, they suggest something in the company's shared values that encourages people to exploit each other. Besides what these affairs can do to your firm's reputation, you might have some other problems that have to do with too many people living by the belief that 'All's fair in love and war.'"

Mead begins to probe among the Great Gadgeteers. To what extent are they willing to accept exploitation in their midst? Is the level of exploitation already high? In what ways is it helpful, and to whom? In her investigation, Mead uncovers a pattern of affairs between senior men and junior women. It has become so institutionalized that it reminds her of the medieval "Right of the First Night," which permitted a feudal lord to deflower a peasant girl on the eve of her wedding. This extraordinary level of exploitation has generated considerable cynicism but also no little tension and confusion with the company. What role does a young woman play at Great Gadgets, for example, if she is *not* approached romantically by her boss? Or if she refuses the offer?

Nevertheless, this is an accepted pattern in the company, and it even serves some of the junior partners in these liaisons—usually women— as a route to advancement. A complex set of unspoken rules perpetuates the practice.

The winners in this culture are the younger people, who are attractive to powerful older people and have the wit, the strength, and the aggressiveness to take the risk of exploitation. They turn it back on the older people, seeking to get as much out of the transaction as they have to put in. The losers are the hard-working people of all ages with blinders on. These people can't win because those willing to comply with the exploitation get the special assignments, the inside information, and the early promotions.

The Outcome. Holmes and Mead report on the extent of sex-related exploitation within Great Gadgets' culture. Mead stresses that this sex-power connection does not exist in isolation. "By U.S. standards," she tells the chairman, "You have a general pattern of domination by senior managers (most above the age of 45) that is unusually intense. The pattern of responsive submissions by junior women here at Great Gadgets is also exceptional—again by U.S. standards."

Mead makes a related observation: Great Gadgets uses high-cost metals in nearly all its product lines, and the company has shown an exceptional ability to cope with periodic crises in supply of the metals. Since the early 1960s, Great Gadgets has responded to scarcity of these materials, which the company hasn't been able to keep in inventory in significant quantities because of high cost, by sending youthful managers of both sexes scurrying hither and yon to fill the shortages and trim the prices—regardless of sacrifice to their personal lives. The chairman realizes he's hearing about two different problems. He had started by wrestling with moral and ethical issues raised by office sex, but he now begins to wonder whether ambitious young executives aren't going too far in their responsiveness to superiors' demands. He wonders whether his junior managers have been trained not to question authority even when it would be wiser to do so. This training could apply equally to a metals-supply crisis or a proposition from the boss.

The chairman congratulates Mead on having brought these issues together and putting them clearly in focus. "The thing we really have to settle here, among ourselves," he says, "is what kind of company we want to be. We've seen exploitation and submission lead to a crisis and we can't let it continue."

The chairman realizes that some old values must be retired or seriously modified. To a limited extent, guided by Mead's restraining hand, the chairman accomplishes this objective physically—by retiring the most feudal of his executives (exploiters and exploitees) and transferring a number of others.

He also initiates a management-development project that will eventually reduce Great Gadgets' dependence on exploitation of juniors by seniors, by giving juniors the right "contract"—that is, by making more explicit, when they are hired, the demands that will be made on them and the cost to their personal lives.

Even with these changes, the chairman understood that some desired new values will be very slow in developing. Before Mead departs, she and the chairman have drawn up a set of measurable objectives that will mark Great Gadgets' progress toward a less exploitative corporate culture. The chairman learns in advance the potential obstacles to these changes. He even has a set of management guidelines that will help him phase in the desired changes while meeting a minimum of resistance.

CASE 4: THE MCENROE SYNDROME

The Problem at Uppity Products. Word has gotten back to the president of the company that he has arrogant employees. At a recent Chamber of Commerce meeting, he happened to overhear two local merchants expressing a grudging admiration for Uppity's management people in terms often used to describe John McEnroe: "These guys can be a real pain in the neck, but they're so good at what they do, I guess they really don't have to be nice guys."

The Basic Detective Work. Holmes agrees with the president that arrogance is never an appropriate attitude for businessmen, especially in relation to customers. Holmes probes and finds out that very few of the local Chamber of

Commerce people are potential Uppity customers. Of these customers who are local, most share this negative perception, while professing their loyalty to Uppity. Holmes finds the negative perception less prevalent in Uppity's out-of-town customer group, but determines that it does appear in a significant number of cases.

Holmes notes that those who see Uppity as arrogant have difficulty providing specific evidence to support their feelings. It seems to come down to statements by salesmen that "the one best way to do things is the Uppity way," and that customers are free to leave Uppity for other suppliers if they don't want to take things the Uppity way. But this is rarely said directly and never heatedly.

Holmes informally interviews a number of the "arrogant" managers and salespeople identified in his research. He finds them neither aware of their impression on the public nor apologetic when told of it.

The Cultural Profile. The cultural profile reveals a company that deeply believes in its tradition. For many years, its proprietary technology and production techniques have made Uppity the industry leader. The company has been able to set its prices as much as 20 percent above what competitors charge and still turn away business. More recently, however, other companies have begun to erode the Uppity niche. Although respondents to the cultural profile readily acknowledge that the Uppity advantage is not what it used to be, they continue to express confidence in the "basic assets of Uppity, its superior people."

The Outcome. A select management group convened by the president has a little trouble accepting Mead's interpretation. She wants them to ponder whether employees really believe that they're better than anyone else, and that being at Uppity proves it. Mead convinces the managers of the importance of "the superiority value" in their culture. Now they can face up to some correctable problems in hiring and orienting new people, and in managing the sales force. No longer will they hand so much of the credit for past and present success to personnel superiority. They will also credit the good luck in having stumbled into a narrow and defensible place in the market.

"Trying to explain the inexplicable is a burden most people cannot bear." Mead tells them. "Most Uppity people have neither believed basically in their own superiority nor been able to accept that they could survive in the corporation if they admitted to anything less than superiority. Furthermore, they were stuck with the fact that Uppity traditionally has gotten the business it wanted at a premium price. Maybe somebody actually was superior. But what Uppity Products really had was a bunch of people covering up their insecurity when they never needed to feel insecure in the first place.

"Active management can dispose of this problem readily, now that you're clearly aware of what it is. You have to make results—not superiority—your prime deliverable. One easy first step is to get everybody talking about how the good fortune inherited from earlier times has given Uppity a head start on the job that lies ahead."

CASE 5: THE DEHYDRATED MARINER

The Problem at Albatross Enterprises. A feature story in the state's largest newspaper carries capsule descriptions of the state's major corporations. Part of the summary describes Albatross as "an ancient mariner whose water has dried up." The board of directors is appalled at this perception of the company and demands changes. The chief executive gets the ultimatum.

The Basic Detective Work. Holmes's initial investigation of Albatross shows that the plant looks as it did 50 years ago, as does the company's all-WASP, all-male upper management. Nevertheless, Albatross is still paying its stockholders handsome dividends, and a number of innovations have kept the company at the leading edge of its industry.

"Do you want to defend your company against the ancient-mariner charge?" Holmes asks the CEO.

"Of course," says the CEO.

The Cultural Profile. In this case, a cultural profile provides the basis for an excellent defense. Mead enlists the cooperation of the Albatross director of public relations. As expected from a cursory inquiry, Mead finds corporate values that perpetuate a devotion to detail, product integrity, tried-and-proven methods, commitment to customer service, and loyalty to longstanding clients. These values genuinely represent the "flip side" of the dehydrated mariner. "If you're going to defend yourself," Holmes and Mead say to the CEO, "you're best off understanding in considerable depth what you're defending."

The point of this self-examination, Mead tells the CEO, is to be certain that the image sought is consistent with Albatross's unspoken values. The company can't present itself as a bright-eyed, bushy-tailed entrepreneurial go-getter if that image isn't true, even though bright-eyed entrepreneurs and embryonic high-tech firms are the darlings of the day.

But Mead does find a problem. Because it has served the stockholders well, changelessness has become a religion at Albatross Enterprises. Albatross management has worked hard to downplay innovations—although there have been some, and dramatic ones at that. The employees, whose unguarded remarks prompted the newspaper's characterization, feel left out of modern times. Notwithstanding their collective pride in Albatross's accomplishments and their job security, they sense that their leaders are ashamed of the company's new technology and afraid of introducing new blood into the executive suite.

The Outcomes. With cultural profiles in hand, the Albatross public-relations chief has the ammunition to go to the newspaper with "new information," facts that present Albatross in a new and positive light. His opportunity comes when the newspaper follows up its capsule summaries of leading companies with a series of extended features. Armed with a credible rejoinder to the dehydrated-mariner characterization, he gains Albatross an early placement in the series.

Externally, the image-building effort succeeds because it is based in the solid conservative reality that is, in fact, Albatross. At the same time, the board was awakened to the need for substantial *internal* public relations, to engage more actively the employees' pride and loyalty. Mead suggests that the first step should be a number of seemingly trivial architectural improvements: a new, more inviting entrance to the plant, more windows, and a more forthright presentation of the company's latest innovation.

These hypothetical cases are like many that surface in the executive suite. Symptoms are often concrete and compelling in themselves, but they can be misleading. The investigative process, including cultural profiling, provides the troubled business leader with guidance on how to take action. In the majority of these examples, a cultural profile was not actually the first or only choice of our fictional consultants, Holmes and Mead. But there are two sets of circumstances in which any sizable company ought to seek to understand its culture in a systematic, detailed way: 1) When a major merger or acquisition is in the works, and 2) When a company knows that it must make difficult or far-reaching changes in strategy, operations, or products.

If a synergy-seeking merger happens *before* the·big differences between two participating organizations' values are addressed, months—or years—of depressed productivity can result. Poor decisions on staffing, strategy, and organizational structure are almost guaranteed. Problems will be painfully apparent, but their sources will be elusive. Management that does not understand the source of such problems will either ignore them or deal with them in ways that only saints or master statesmen could get away with. Floods of refugees will exist to attest to the allegedly cold and heavy-handed methods by which an "honorable merger" turned into a "hostile takeover."

By the same token, major changes in a company's strategy, operations or products are matters that require consensus. This consensus need not be a vote, nor even a spoken understanding of what's going on. But such changes are impossible to implement if they are not introduced in a way that is compatible with the prevailing or emerging corporate culture. If a change in corporate culture is necessary, it must happen before or during the changes in strategy, operations or products—not afterwards.

To be useful, culture must consciously leave behind the parts of the past that have died, and it must join in actively creating the future.

PROFILING THE CORPORATE TRIBE: BASIC TERMS

As defined by the nondilettante, corporate culture comprises the values that companies—and parts of companies—live by. To a large extent, culture is: 1) What we think of what we do, 2) How we do it, 3) What we think most important to get done, and 4) Why it's so important. Culture also includes our expressions of the kind of management we want (or think we deserve), what we think we are really good at as a company, and what we think we can't do successfully but wish we could.

What makes corporate culture powerful—and characterizes a "strong culture"—is the presence of identical values in a lot of heads, expressed in the same way at the same time. This common vernacular makes communication easier, which in turn makes organized activity feasible.

But culture is not the only way in which employees express feelings about their organization. Whenever I begin to work with a corporate culture, I accumulate data that mix culture values, propositions reflecting organizational climate, and expressions of morale. As an abstract definition each of the three is easy to distinguish. In practice, though, one needs skill and patience to tell the difference.

"Morale" is the way people feel about how well the last battle was fought, combined with expectations for the next battle. "Organizational climate" measures how well management is controlling the internal environment to meet people's expectations. "Culture" embodies the underlying shared values that shape people's expectations for themselves and for one another.

Homer J. Hagedorn is a management consultant at Arthur D. Little Inc.

9.
CORPORATE CULTURE
ON THE ROCKS

Peter C. Reynolds

> The idea of a single corporate culture that characterizes all levels of the
> organization is both naive and undesirable. A corporation, by its very
> nature, brings together disparate subcultures—engineers, financial
> analysts, copywriters and cooks—and not only is it inevitable that these
> people will have differing conceptions of appropriate social action, but
> their jobs require it.

For a 15-month period during the early 1980s, I worked at a company I will
call the Falcon Computer Company, a start-up manufacturer of microcom-
puters in the heart of Silicon Valley. When I joined the firm, a year after its
founding, the future looked very bright, and during my time there the company
quintupled in size to more than 250 employees. It was featured on the covers of
important trade publications, and even *Time* magazine singled out Falcon
Computer as one of the rising young stars of Silicon Valley that investors
should be watching—possibly another Apple.

The company did indeed bear scrutiny, but not in the way *Time* had intended. Just two and a half years after its founding, it closed its doors for good,
with a stunning loss of more than $32 million of investment capital and a debt
of millions more. How 250 people can lose such a large amount of money in
such a short period of time is an interesting story in itself, but a meteoric rise
followed by a sudden descent into oblivion is not uncommon in the computer
industry; the most unusual aspect of the Falcon debacle is that a professional
anthropologist happened to be on the scene to record it.

I am an anthropologist by training, not a businessman or a computer
scientist, so I view the computer industry from a very different perspective.
Before taking a job in Scilicon Valley, I did field work among hunters and
gatherers in the Malaysian rain forest, studied the stone tool-making of
Australian aborigines, did frame-by-frame analysis of films of social communication, and videotaped folk technology in Papua New Guinea. I was an
experienced observer of human interaction and technical processes long before
I began my business career, and it was not too difficult to keep accurate notes of

what went on at Falcon. At meetings, I would offer to take the minutes, and I made it a point to memorize interesting conversations, writing them down in my journal the same day. But I had been hired not as an anthropologist but as a software trainer through an executive-recruiting firm, so my observations were never confounded by people in the company playing a role for the benefit of the visiting scientist. Even those who knew I had a doctorate in anthropology thought that anthropologists studied only savages, and that therefore my previous interests and experience had nothing to do with them.

Falcon Computer's infatuation with its own corporate culture, the subject of this article, is not a hothouse creation conjured into existence by the bright lights of anthropological scrutiny. To the contrary, as a recently returned expatriate I was embarrassingly out of touch with the mega-trends of American life, and I first learned the term "corporate culture" from the natives themselves. In fact, shortly after joining the company, I was told by one of the managers that the president and vice presidents met periodically in closed session to develop a "Falcon culture," and that they had hired a management-consulting firm to help them define it. One goal, the manager said, was to preserve the atmosphere of a start-up even after Falcon became a big company. The manager referred to these sessions as "culture meetings," but later on they were officially designated "values meetings."

To an anthropologist, the conscious creation of a culture by management is amusing, because all human groups have culture by nature, and these systems of values and beliefs are shaped by experience, tradition, class position, and political circumstance—all powerful forces that are extremely refractory to directed change, particularly by occasional committee. Nonetheless, behind closed doors, with middle management and nonmanagerial staff excluded, the president and his executive staff created a document called "Falcon Values" that expressed the culture of the company. This document was then distributed to all of the company's managers, who met, again in closed session, to further discuss and refine the premises of the corporate culture. By the time this document was ready for dissemination to middle management, I had been promoted to manager myself, reporting to the vice president of marketing, and this gave me a front-row seat at all subsequent cultural deliberations. At one of the meetings I attended, the president of the company and most members of the executive staff were present, so I was able to observe the deliberations of the upper echelons of the company, as well as those of middle management. In fact, since the tables at culture meetings were always arranged in a circle, unlike all other meetings in the company where the tables formed a rectangle, my vantage point on this issue was as good as the president's.

The Falcon Values document was two pages long, too long to examine in detail here, but it summarized such things as attitude toward customers and colleagues, the style of social communication, the desiderata of decision-making, and the working environment that the company wanted to create. Yet one of the most interesting things about it, from an anthropological field-workers point of view, was the disparity between the statements that were written down on paper and the social reality that produced the document in the first place. For example, in the values document under "customer orientation" one found: "Attention to detail is our trademark; our goal is to do it right the first time. We intend to deliver defect-free products and services to our customers on time."

Yet even as this policy was being adopted in executive session, it was generally known that defective computers were being shipped to customers—and I was told by two company sources that the decision to send the new computers, despite evidence of defects, had been made at the highest level in order to squelch growing industry rumors that Falcon would miss its announced release date. As I did not witness the decision, I cannot ascertain the validity of what I was told, but there were reliability problems that were certainly known to the executive staff. I was able to confirm the dismal state of the product for myself when I obtained permission to borrow some computers from the shipping room to use in a training class I was asked to organize. These were brand-new units, already packed in their printed cartons, and because so few machines were coming off the production line, only by great bureaucratic effort was I able to divert them from their intended destinations as customer machines. Yet only two of the four machines started up correctly when the start-up disk was inserted, and I only got them running because I happened to have a technician on my payroll.

In another example of the disparity between the official culture and the actual, consider this statement from the values document: "Managing by personal communication is part of the [Falcon] way. While we recognize the importance of group sessions, we encourage open, direct person-to-person communication as part of our daily routine."

"Open communication" was in fact a buzzword at Falcon, often used by software engineers to pry information out of management, but the culture creation process was nonetheless done in secret, strictly following the chain of command. The executive staff developed the initial document without consultation of middle management, middle managers were asked to affirm an existing document under the guise of "discussing" it, and the rank-and-file employees were told about open communication only after it had already been adopted by the company. Interestingly enough, democratic decision-making was also a written value: "We believe that rapid and sound decisions are the key to [Falcon's] success and that they should take place at the lowest common level. We encourage open discussion and honest feedback about the decisions that have been or will be made."

Even from these few examples it is clear that there was considerable disparity between the written culture and the behavioral culture observable in day-to-day social relations. From an anthropological perspective, this disparity was neither unusual nor unexpected. A century of field work in non-Western societies has shown that cultures are not homogeneous like carrots but layered like onions, with context-sensitive rules governing even widely held values. Who among us thinks that the injunction "Thou shall not kill" applies to soldiers on the battlefield or to policemen confronting violent felons? Thus it is not surprising that the Falcon Values document encoded one system of values while the shipping room implemented another. Although we may deplore such moral hypocrisy, the decision to ship defective machines to large customers also fails by a worldlier standard, best epitomized by Antoine Boulay de la Meurthe's judgement of the murder of the duke of Enghien: "It is worse than a crime; it is a blunder."

Human beings, of course, are well aware of the disparity among systems of value, and the Falcon Values document did not fool very many employees into thinking they would get promoted by espousing open communication or blowing the whistle on defective products. In fact, skepticism about the Falcon values was itself an ethnographic fact, well documented in many field notes. For example, the vice president of software engineering seemed genuinely interested in the concept of open communication, and he circulated an initial draft of the values document to all of the people on his staff, asking them to comment. Many programmers took the opportunity to compare Falcon with other companies where they had worked, and many of these written replies, which were given to me after the company went bankrupt, reveal an undisguised skepticism about the possibility of legislating a culture. "You can't create values," wrote one engineer. "The way 'culture' is used at [Falcon] is pretty simple-minded, compared to say anthropology," another responded.

The general impression one gains from reading these remarks is that most members of the software engineering staff were unimpressed by the Falcon Values document, and some went so far as to compare it to archetypal examples of corporate stupidity—such as the executive charged with keeping desks neat at the Intel Corporation, known as Mr. Clean.

Cultures are shared models of social relations, and almost everyone knew that the operative values at Falcon were hierarchy, secrecy, and expediency, regardless of what the official culture said. My field notes, in fact, preserve a number of statements that can be interpreted as realistic models of the social relations, and these present a very different picture from that of the values document. "Make sure that training does not becomes a gating item for the software," the product marketing manager told me. Translation: Make sure that delays in software development cannot be attributed to delays in the training program. "I've seen this before," he continued, "Bill [a fictional name for the vice president of engineering] is going to kick the ball upstairs and try to say that Sam's group and marketing are not ready—to get himself off the hook."

In computer companies, the sales department will normally tell the customer what he wants to hear, or even try to sell him products that do not exist, whereas engineering is expected to hold the line on truth. At Falcon, roles were reversed. As the manager of customer support reflected over lunch, "Sales is the conscience, while engineering is living on fantasies."

The Falcon Values document was both a model of the culture and a part of the culture, but it was so at variance with reality that few people took it seriously. Even some of the official communications seemed to contain ironic humor.

For example, the vice president of finance and administration used Falcon culture to justify the institution of employee badges as a security measure. Although security badges are commonplace in the computer industry, probably few companies have ever presented this tactic to their personnel as an example of open communication. Yet at Falcon, the directive establishing this practice stated that employee badges would contain only first names, "in keeping with our casual culture."

The skepticism toward the official corporate culture was commonplace enough to be commented upon by members of the executive staff. For example, the vice president of marketing reported to the values meeting that he had conducted an informal survey among his own staff on the perception of Falcon Values. He said there were three main categories of responses:

1. It's all motherhood and apple pie.
2. So what?
3. Boy! Is this place becoming bureaucratic.

Clearly, a model of the culture must be close enough to the truth that it can be referred to without eliciting smirks, but this is not to say that ideal models of social relations are irrelevant to day-to-day life, or that cultural ideals are generally treated with skepticism by a society's participants. Human beings, in corporations as anywhere else, live in a moral universe, and the most interesting thing about the official Falcon culture is how little credence it gave to the moral standards already operative in the company. In reviewing my notes, I have come to the conclusion that people at Falcon did, to a large extent, hold the values of defect-free products and democratic decision-making; and, when among themselves, employees were not shy about evaluating the company by their own standards of right and wrong when corporate behavior was perceived as unjust. For example, a software engineer told me: "Basically, if some people have to work the Labor Day weekend, then everyone should. Since the software had to be ready on the 6th, then everyone should work one weekend, or say the last three weekends in August—everyone in the company."

Not only were there official ideals, encoded in the values document, and unofficial ideals, expressed by employees in informal conversation, but there were also officially sanctioned ideals that never made it into writing at all—except in the anthropologist notebook. Each communicative channel in a complex social organization has a cultural system of norms that goes along with it, and the verbal ideal is different from the written ideal. Consider, for example, the dos and don'ts encoded in the following fragment of conversation: "At this morning's meeting, Winfield [fictional name for the company president] used the word 'mind set' and Zeke [pseudonym for the chief design engineer] said, 'We're not supposed to use that word; I've heard it twice in two days.' At the beginning of [Falcon] they decided never to use the word 'committee' or 'mind set'—it was a reaction against buzzwords."

As the company's fortunes began to decline, about two and half years after its founding, the disparity between the values meetings and the everyday culture became more and more grotesque. At a time when the public-relations department was claiming "volume shipments of products to key accounts," the manufacturing division was essentially producing hand-crafted machines. The mother board on the Falcon computer, the circuit board containing the central processor and other important logic elements, had a design flaw that required the hand-soldering of jumper wires during the manufacturing. These hand fixes were so expensive that they absorbed all the economies of scale that mass manufacturing is supposed to provide, and they were so time-consuming that production slowed to a trickle.

At this point in the company's history, when a state-of-the-art manufacturing line was turning out handicrafts, when the mother board would take a minimum of six months to redesign, when a manager at Procter & Gamble reportedly shouted to technical representatives that he never wanted to see a Falcon computer again, and when financial reserves were hemorrhaging at the rate of $2 million a month, the disparity between the actual and the official culture came to be expressed as sardonic humor.

In the irreverent asides of the now irrevocably cynical staff, the manufacturing division was dubbed "Research and Development." The more knowledgeable the people, the more devastating their remarks. The service manager told me: "We do have a zero-defect program: Don't test the product and you'll find zero defects." The manager of customer support gestured at the closed doors of the marketing conference room: "The sales meeting is taking so long because they're trying to get the regional sales managers to agree to the impossible—to sell the product as it exists."

The values meetings, however, gathered steam even as the company itself was rapidly losing pressure, and personnel asked all departments to begin a series of regular meetings to discuss the values document and to devise plans for its implementation. The vice presidents, and sometimes the president himself, attended the values meetings organized for departmental staff, and these kickoff meetings lead to a series of round-table discussions that were just getting under way when the first big layoffs reduced the staff by a third. Several competing computers appeared in the marketplace, and the investment companies, which had floated three refinancings largely on the strength of the president's promises, finally lost patience and moved to slow the "burn rate" of their venture capital by cutting expenses as extensively as possible. The executive staff took the opportunity to find a scapegoat for all that had gone wrong, and they fired the vice president of marketing in the middle of the night, broke up his department, and allocated his staff among themselves by the time the sun came up. The next morning, the company was abuzz with stories, in spite of the official blackout imposed by the advocates of open communication. The marketing department secretary, now working for sales, asked me what I thought about the events of the night before. I told her I thought they were sleazy even by Falcon standards. She nodded, and then said, with ill-disguised anger, "It makes you realize what bullshit Falcon values are."

Fifteen months of participant observation at a microcomputer company confirms the importance of the concept of culture for understanding the structure of the modern corporation, but it also shows that "culture" is not the official system of values promulgated by management. It is a whole range of shared models of social action, containing both real and ideal elements, each layer cued by the social context and the channel of communication: the observed behavior, the official document, the things said at meetings, the things said when alone with one's boss, the things said to one's boss when the boss's boss is present, the situation that is said to be real, the verbal expressions of what the situation should be, and humorous renderings of all of the above. Will the real corporate culture please stand up?

When I began my research, I shared one of the assumptions of the Falcon executive staff—that an effective company requires a homogeneous corporate culture. But having had an opportunity to look more carefully at functional specialization, it is clear to me that the idea of a single corporate culture that characterizes all levels of the organization is both naive and undesirable. A modern corporation, by its very nature, brings together disparate subcultures within a single organizational framework—engineers and financial analysts, copywriters and cooks—and not only is it inevitable that these people will have differing conceptions of appropriate social action, but, most importantly their jobs require it.

Therefore, it makes sense to accept cultural diversity as a fact of life and ask instead how it facilitates or impedes the larger goals of the organization. Does the public-relations department's desire for good press facilitate the production of reliable products by manufacturing, or does it lead to the premature shipment of defective machines? Does the model of the social organization held by middle management match the model used by the executive staff, or do these levels of organization work at cross purposes because of differing conceptions of social reality?

If corporations are collections of subcultures, does this mean that departments and divisions have nothing in common that can be construed as the corporate culture—the system of values and social traditions that characterizes the management style? No, for there are also company-wide values that crosscut the subcultures, and this was true of Falcon as well. At Falcon, however, the overall corporate culture was most clearly revealed in the disparity between the official and the actual, in the mismatch between the real and ideal cultures. Although probably all societies have a disparity between idealistic and realistic models of social relations, because people are ethical animals and the world is imperfect, at Falcon the falsification of realistic models was sanctioned and encouraged by the social organization. Falcon culture was expressed not by the ethical ideals presented in the values meetings, but by the great intercultural disparity between the ideal and the real: The implicit premise of Falcon culture was that there was no truth to the official documents. For example, a marketing manager, in charge of developing production schedules for the delivery of the software, penned in some dates in the product plan that even I could tell were overly optimistic. She must have interpreted the expression on my face, for she smiled ironically, and said, "The *schedules* are the theology."

Was higher management itself aware of this disparity between the ideal and the real? Was the Falcon Values document an idealistic program that went wrong or a cynical use of rhetoric by people who communicated to their subordinates a far different model of acceptable behavior? Questions of motive are always the most difficult to answer, but the official development and production schedules relayed up the managerial hierarchy as attainable goals not only were meaningless but were known to be meaningless by all the participants in the review cycle—except, perhaps, the venture capitalists on the board who dug into their pockets for three rounds of financing.

Culture is not an ideological gimmick, to be imposed from above by management-consulting firms, but a stubborn fact of human social organization that can scuttle the best of corporate plans if not first taken into account. If the venture capitalists had known that the key element in Falcon computer's culture was disparity between the official version and the actual situation, would they have continued to fund the company for as long as they did? In this case, the failure to apply even the rudiments of the anthropological methods can be measured in tens of millions of dollars.

Peter C. Reynolds is a principal of Intermedia Inc. of Sausalito, CA, a media production firm specializing in the translation of technical concepts into video images.

Part II
MANAGING THE PEOPLE FACTOR

10.
ASSESSING YOUR PEOPLE POTENTIAL

John B. Hanna

People are the key to an organization's success. Management must take the lead in obtaining the optimum effectiveness from employees—in the form of efficiency, loyalty, productivity, creativity, and enthusiasm. These objectives necessitate more innovative and productive ways to manage people.

When an organization creates an environment where employees can achieve company goals and personal goals simultaneously, efficiency, loyalty and job enthusiasm are bound to be high.

This, according to M. Scott Myers, noted behavioral psychologist and author of the book, *Every Employee a Manager*, is what human resource management should achieve. He, like other behavioralists, such as Herzberg, Maslow, Argyris and McGregor, has provided substantial insights into people management. Employee motivation and effectiveness is determined by the manner in which employees are managed.

Each manager's perspective of human resource management will vary depending upon his or her work experience and knowledge of the discipline. Just as "every employee is a manager," it is essential that every manager be a good manager of people. Managers must have a sensitivity to the discipline of human resource management. There is a strong correlation between one's management effectiveness and human resource management skills.

Human resource management provides direction to the management of the organization to meet both the objectives of the organization and the needs of the employees. And, time and time again, it has been proved that the one method for achieving people effectiveness is *discipline*.

To illustrate, the manager's task can be compared to that of a coach of an athletic team. Both are measured by certain standards of performance. In both cases, one of the key ingredients of success or failure is discipline. It is the substance that binds together the talents of the individual members into a successful organization.

Discipline can be defined as a means to provide training that is geared to achieving individual growth. The teaching and development aspect of discipline must be based upon an affirmation about people, or the "Theory Y" of management as described by Douglas McGregor. In his classic theory, a manager's style of managing reflects his or her assumptions about people. The Theory Y (developmental) manager assumes that people prefer to discipline themselves through self-direction and self-control. In contrast, the "Theory X" (authoritarian) manager assumes that people need authority or discipline administered as a control, coercion or punishment to motivate them to perform. The recognition of employee attributes such as integrity, hard work and the desire to assume responsibility to achieve and succeed are essential. To meet business objectives, management must be diligent in the pursuit of discipline.

All organizations must achieve certain objectives for profit and self-perpetuation. Organizations face a dilemma when investing in human resource programs. To do so may require reducing profit or changing pricing strategies for the short term to eventually achieve the growth or perpetuation objectives. However, these are decisions management must make to attain long-term gains.

Managers generally take pride in knowing their people and knowing how to get the job done. The skill management uses to integrate the needs of people to support the organization's objectives will determine, to a great extent, business success or failure. Thus, employees' needs—*motivation and maintenance*—must be met.

According to behavioral psychologist Myers, effective job performance depends on the fulfillment of both the employees' motivation and maintenance needs. Motivation factors focus on the achievement of company and personal goals. Maintenance factors have little motivational value, but they help job satisfaction. An environment rich in opportunities for satisfying motivation needs leads to motivation-seeking habits. Conversely, a job situation sparse in motivation opportunities encourages preoccupation with maintenance factors.

The management tools or skills essential to human resource management are comparable to those of a doctor performing an operation. Without the programs, policies and resources, human resource management will not be effective. Therefore, to manage a human resource program, special skills are needed to establish the design, development, implementation and maintenance of the necessary programs or management tools. The human resource management functions are listed below.

- *Policy formulation*, which provides for the establishment of human resource management standing plans of action and assuring governmental compliance.
- *Employee relations* is engaged with developing morale programs that include communication programs, maintaining an effective work environ-

ment, grievance and labor relations administration, performance appraisals and attitude surveys.

- *Organization planning* requires the establishment of appropriate structure, span of management, organization levels (staff and line relationships), management system (planning, goal setting, action planning and periodic reviews), long-range plans and the development of management strategy.
- *Training and development* is accomplished from an organization needs assessment in such areas as employee orientation, technical development, management skills (technical, human, conceptual), on-the-job programs and career pathing (establishing individual growth opportunities, such as job posting).
- *Compensation administration* includes wage and salary administration and job evaluation (determining job or position values) and compensation plans (sales commissions and management incentive bonuses).
- *Employee benefits and services* include worker's compensation, Social Security, unemployment, group insurance, payment for time not worked, employee bonuses, perquisites and personnel services (social and recreational programs).
- *The planning* function involves the determination of sources to recruit people (short- and long-range needs), and staffing needs from inside and outside the organization (costs for placement and turnover), pre-employment selection, interviewing and testing (techniques, aptitude, skill and psychological test selection), personnel data retention systems and outplacement (exit interviewing, counseling and job placement).
- *Safety and health* deals with providing a safe and healthy work environment through the establishment of accident prevention programs (accident-cause analysis), workers' compensation administration, pre-employment physical assessments and other employee health programs.

The human resources management questionnaire (Figure 1) deals with organizational issues pertaining to motivation, communication, organization structure, staffing and development. How do you evaluate your organization's human resource management needs and philosophy? You may want your business associates, staff and boss to respond to these questions after you have completed the questionnaire to determine their perception of your company's human resource management environment.

The challenge of management is to increase human resources management effectiveness. The theory that people oppose work, that they must be closely supervised, that they avoid responsibility, and are best managed by authoritarian leaders is giving way to a more participative style of leadership. People want and will continue to gravitate toward organizations that provide opportunities for them to become involved with the success of their business. This includes the freedom to grow in their jobs, opportunities to participate in

Figure 1

Is Your Company Receptive to Human Resource Management?

Respond to the following statements and place your score of 1 (almost never) to 10 (almost always) in the column on the right. A space is provided in the event you want to encourage others to participate.

	Your Score	Other Score

MOTIVATION

1. The environment in our organization encourages and releases the individual motivations of employees.

2. Our organization deals effectively with the following needs:
    A: Defines employee job responsibilities thoroughly by providing answers to these questions:
    1) What do you want me to do?
    2) How do you want me to do it?
    3) What constitutes a good job?
    B: Encourages employee growth opportunities through promotions and training and development programs.

3. Our organization fosters a climate of trust between individuals and groups necessary to achieving the goals of the employee and the company.

4. Our organization frequently and willingly evaluates its objectives, goals and decision-making processes with those responsible for their fulfillment.

COMMUNICATIONS

5. Communication in our organization is timely, accurate, open and two way.

6. Our organization provides a process of self-criticism.

7. Work groups in our organization interact effectively without destructive conflict.

8. Changes in technology, administration or personnel are accomplished with effective planning and in a timely manner.

ORGANIZATION STRUCTURE

9. Our organization's internal structure is readily adaptable to changing conditions.

10. Procedures facilitate the business operations, and when they get in the way of productive work, changes are made.

11. Our organization deals effectively with both the needs of the employees and the business objectives.

STAFFING AND DEVELOPMENT

12. Our organization has an effective recruitment program for obtaining competent people.

13. Our organization has an effective program for the training and development of competent people.

14. Our organization has an effective system to promote employees.

Scoring the Questionnaire

Motivation (Questions 1-4)
0-10   points   poor

Motivation (Questions 1-4)

11-25	points	unsatisfactory
26-40	points	good
41-50	points	excellent

Communications (Questions 5-8)

0-8	points	poor
9-20	points	unsatisfactory
21-32	points	good
33-40	points	excellent

Organization Structure (Questions 9-11)

0-6	points	poor
7-15	points	unsatisfactory
16-24	points	good
25-30	points	excellent

Staffing and Development (Questions 12-14)

0-6	points	poor
7-15	points	unsatisfactory
16-24	points	good
25-30	points	excellent

An overall assessment of the organization climate based on your answers to the questions would be as follows:
0-30 points = poor; 31-75 points = unsatisfactory; 76-120 points = good; 121-150 points = excellent.

---

the decision-making process and an atmosphere of trust and open communication perpetuated by a management willing to deal with their concerns.

A sound human resources management should provide direction in meeting the objectives of the organization while at the same time meeting the needs of the employees. People effectiveness is the key to an organization's success. Management must take the lead to obtain the optimum benefits that are to be realized from employees in the form of efficient performance, loyalty, higher productivity, creative approaches, and enthusiasm. The answer to this challenge of getting more from the total compensation costs must come from more innovative and productive ways to manage people.

John B. Hanna, is president of Personnel Services, Cherry Hill, New Jersey.

11.

BUSINESS PLANNING IS PEOPLE PLANNING

David R. Leigh

Discover how Robbins & Myers tied human resources planning to its business plan—and the lessons they learned. Their experiences will straighten your path to a successful human resources program.

For strategic business planning to succeed it must be tied to human resources planning. Conversely, for human resources planning to succeed, it must be tied to strategic business planning.

The purpose of the following article is to describe how we at Robbins & Myers designed and installed a viable and workable human resources planning process tied to our strategic business plan.

Although different organizations with different businesses and in different situations may require a different approach, there are some basic principles that apply to all human resources planning.

We give our experiences to help straighten your path to a successful human resources program. We found that our successes were inevitably the result of following some basic principles. Our failures were—for the most part—related to forays into the frills of human resources planning.

AN OVERVIEW OF ROBBINS & MYERS

Robbins & Myers is a multi-division, multi-product manufacturer, who in the last fiscal year had sales in the range of $200 million and a work force of approximately 2,500 employees.

The company operates in a somewhat autonomous, decentralized setting with four major divisions: three within the industrial products area and a fourth in consumer products.

The growth rate has been approximately 20% compounded per year. Top management places a strong emphasis on the business planning process.

KNOW WHERE YOU ARE GOING AND WHY

Planning is very difficult, especially if it's about the future. The very nature of the job of strategic human resources planning involves a process of anticipating a future which is uncertain and making assumptions to support that uncertainty. Planners need to keep the following in mind.

Have clear goals. It is imperative that at the beginning of the planning process someone establish appropriate objectives for the system and verify that those objectives relate to the organization.

These goals should certainly include some kind of realistic and objective timetable for the implementation of the total system. This time frame, as we have found, is significantly more than one year.

Clarify your assumptions. Organizations are individual in terms of their positions in time, culture, leadership style, marketing goals, growth objectives, etc. So, write down those assumptions related to your own individuality to make human resources planning valid.

These assumptions should not be used to hedge your bets, but rather as a rationale for launching or postponing any human resource planning efforts. Once written they need to be viewed for accuracy against top management's business strategy.

Some of our assumptions were:

- Robbins & Myers continues to grow at a rate faster than the economy
- human resources could be a greater constraint to growth than capital availability
- major national, global and environmental changes would not have a greater impact on our company than business in general
- each strategy center was responsible for developing its own human resources rather than depending on other parts of the organization to provide future leadership

Some of these assumptions would later prove to be correct; others were not so valid.

HEED THE LESSONS WE LEARNED

While human resources planning can evolve into a cult within itself, there are some basic guidelines which we found to be true in developing a strategic plan.

Do your research. Research means talking to people in the company early, finding out what they see as needs, and determining what problems they're having that might be helped by human resource planning.

It also means reading the books, talking to the consultants, and visiting other companies—but taking what you read and hear with a grain of salt. You may find, as we did, there are many sources to tell you how to do human resources planning, but there are relatively few who have successfully installed human resources planning in an integrated and systematic way.

Keep it simple. In all the research we conducted, it became quickly apparent that it would be easy to go overboard on this project. Therefore the rule that leaped forward was: keep it simple in the beginning.

Advanced computer models, Markoff modelling, and exotic demand and forecasting techniques may have a place, but not in the initial phase of human resources planning.

Know the business strategy. If the key human resource planner doesn't know the business strategy, don't bother with strategic human resource planning.

We must tie our human resource planning to the company's business needs and to the real problems the company is facing. Otherwise, the plan won't be used or seen as useful by line managers.

Forge a link between the business planning cycle and human resource planning. One of the most important factors in our success was our initial decision to tie human resources planning to our existing business cycle.

In doing so, we accomplished several things. First, line managers were encouraged to address human resource planning at the same time they were thinking of business planning.

Second, we piggybacked on an accepted process that was ingrained as a basic tenet for success in our organization. Third, we formed relationships with the corporate business planning manager working with him to develop an appropriate approach.

Finally, we used the annual strategic business planning manual as the vehicle to introduce human resources planning for the organization.

All these decisions turned out to be fortuitous. It boils down to one basic concept: strategic human resources planning must be tied to business planning to make sense.

Make human resource planning a corporate objective. With our human resource planning system, the president recognized that continued growth of Robbins & Myers might well be constrained by our inability to provide needed human resources for growth.

Since he saw this as more limiting than financial, marketing or production constraints, development of a human resources plan for each division was adopted as a key corporate objective for the fiscal year.

This one decision had more to do with human resources planning getting the attention it needed than any other single decision.

To support this corporate objective, divisional objectives were developed which in turn were included in the objectives for both strategy center managers and human resources managers within the divisions.

Establish a planning horizon. How long is a reasonable time frame for strategic human resources planning?

We chose three points in time: 1) where we are now; 2) where we expected to be in two fiscal years (approximately 30 months); and 3) where we expected to be at the end of the coming fiscal year.

In larger organizations with stable businesses and where staff turnover is more predictable, longer time frames might be appropriate.

Set a realistic completion date. We probably tried to accomplish too much in too short a time period. More importantly, we did not provide enough face-to-face education to accomplish idea acceptance and commitment for a full response in the early stages.

On the other hand, the rapid growth rate of the organization provided significant logic and reason for the fast start-up.

Get the organization's attention. How do you get attention? From the beginning, it's a question of ownership. Whose program is this?

To the extent possible, your preliminary research contacts and foundation building should attempt to minimize the image of a "personnel department" or "corporate" program, if at all possible.

To eliminate it altogether is neither realistic nor pragmatic; but to the extent possible, minimizing a corporate image is an important part of the process.

Get support from all areas. To get strong support from the operating areas, organize the process to give line managers something they want. The challenge here involves timing the introduction of human resources planning with visible needs.

For example, you might tie the project into a request for related information from a line manager or division president.

Next is support from the top. Is there any personnel-related proposal that does not say support from the top is essential for success?

The top person in the organization must have an appreciation and see a need for human resources planning. We had this support, and it was invaluable.

The top person must also have a high respect for the human resources function and its previous contributions to the organization. If your group is seen as a personnel department whose primary job is that of record keeper, forget any broad human resources planning effort for the moment. It is imperative that the department's past history demonstrate support and contribution to the business success of the company.

Get key people involved in the process. Considerable efforts were taken to involve the individual plant human resources managers in the continuing process of developing and implementing the human resources system.

Although initial design was done primarily at the corporate level, there was a great deal of communication with the division human resource managers. In making this decision, we placed our human resources eggs in the baskets of our field human resources people for implementation. In most cases, this worked well. In a few, it did not.

Also built into the system was the inclusion of the local human resources manager in the business planning process. Where this had not been done previously, the human resources plan was instrumental in getting the person in this position involved in business planning.

Our program was most successful in those areas where the local human resources people were significantly involved in the business planning process.

However, by not sufficiently involving vice presidents and line managers, we may have made some initial mistakes. The corporate group funneled most of the information concerning the plans to the local human resources persons and initiated relatively little direct contact with line management.

This approach was in keeping with a more decentralized approach. But, if we were starting again, we might place additional emphasis on initial face-to-face contact with key line managers.

Provide sufficient structure and detail. The question of how much structure should be in the initial plan was raised frequently during the whole process.

Because this was our first attempt at corporate-wide strategic human resource planning, we elected to provide considerable detail during the first year. This decision was based primarily on the assumption that many of the managers involved had little or no formal exposure to human resources planning principles.

Our decision to provide significant detail was defensible on the basis of the need for direction and information. However, this decision also created a problem situation for the more autonomous and creative managers who challenged the degree of structure in the system.

The degree of structure was modified for the second year to allow more freedom for those managers who wished it.

OUR STEPS IN THE PLANNING PROCESS

So what did we do? Our planning model is on an annual cycle starting in September, the first month of our fiscal year. At that time, material is sent to the human resources managers and key line managers and included as a separate chapter in the strategic planning manual.

These materials provided each of the strategy center managers with background material, assumptions, objectives, and a human resources calendar defining each section of the program, what was to be accomplished and the due dates. (See Figure 1.)

We then identified the following steps to be taken in developing the human resources plan in accordance with the business plan:

Identify the strategic human resources issues. The first basic step in the process was the identification and analysis of the strategic human resources issues that related to the accomplishment of the business plan.

We provided sample issues on both a national and local basis. It was the responsibility of the strategy center manager to develop the relevant issues that would either constrain or possibly enhance the achievement of the business plan *before* it was formally proposed and approved.

Conduct and organizational analysis. The basic premise was that the form should follow function. Any change in the strategic direction for the business could well include organizational changes.

Thus, the second step in the program was an organizational analysis and the development of an organizational plan for one and two future fiscal years. These plans were developed by the strategy centers based upon the changes in organizational structure seen as appropriate according to their strategic plans.

Forecast staffing requirements. Once additional slots and positions were identified in the organizational analysis, the next step included forecasting and staffing.

Each location made a basic forecast of *new* positions based upon probability and those positions that had probabilities of more than 70% turnover.

In the first year we did not attempt to forecast normal turnover for two reasons. One, we were placing our emphasis on key positions that were highly predictable, and two, normal turnover is hard to predict accurately when you have small numbers of people in most classifications and strategy centers.

Once key staffing needs were identified, staffing tables were developed at both discipline and organizational levels to show the total number of people needed to fulfill the projected business plans.

Following the submission of the organizational and forecasting material, the corporate human resources staff analyzed projections, raised clarifying questions and summarized the data.

Develop succession plans. From that point, the managers developed individual succession plans for the key positions. This involved identifying replacements for the replacements

Identify training requirements. Training managers also analyzed organizational and operational problems in light of the training requirements for the future.

Training proposals were presented by each group, and this information was

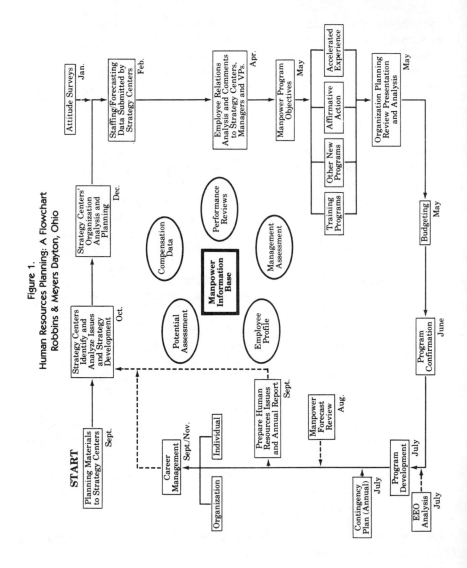

Figure 1.
Human Resources Planning: A Flowchart
Robbins & Meyers Dayton, Ohio

then used at a corporate level to help establish training objectives and develop programs, including accelerated experience and affirmative action programs.

Identify individual development plans for key people. A final segment provided by the human resources staff was the identification of individual development plans for the key people who had been singled out in the succession planning process.

These individual development plans were presented in writing and then monitored throughout the year. Individual plans were limited to key people during the first year and were kept to a maximum of 5-to-10% of the exempt work force.

Present the plan for organizational review. The organizational review is the key end point in this planning process. Each division president makes a presentation to the president of the organization, the vice president of human resources, and the manager of corporate management planning and development.

In this presentation, the division president summarizes the human resources plan, including the issues, organizational changes, relevant forecasting information, and individual development plans for key personnel.

The organizational review is an opportunity to clarify and question the proposed plan. The manager's planning process is then confirmed so that he or she may proceed.

Develop a budget. After the organizational review, a budget is developed. If complete organization staffing tables have been prepared by location management, the staff budgeting becomes an easy process.

The budgeting of programs and other expenses at the corporate level is then done much more appropriately and accurately than in the past. Development programs can then be budgeted at local and corporate levels.

Conduct a follow up. During June and July, prior to the September start of the fiscal year, program confirmations are made; development starts for the following year; EEO plans are developed; and manpower forecasts made the previous February are reviewed for accuracy. Thus, recruiting plans can be developed for both college and corporate-level recruiting systems.

The plan then recycles so that the following September or October, the whole process is repeated again in sequence with the business planning cycle.

One note should be made. During the first year, the career management section was not implemented. At the time it was felt that adding that additional element to the implementation of the program was well beyond the capabilities of the system.

In the second year of the program, we implemented the career management section on a division basis with each division selecting appropriate career management elements to fit its particular business cycle.

The model also includes a database that feeds information into the various elements of the program and becomes the source for determining what decisions are made at various points in the process.

REVIEWING OUR INITIAL RESULTS

What do we feel we achieved? First, we identified a human resources system that was a logical outgrowth of the business planning cycle. We established in the minds of management that human resources planning is a continuing process that develops from the business plan.

Secondly, we implemented a system that worked surprisingly well for a first effort. Finally, we were able to modify elements of the program based on line management's experience and provide an improved process for the second year.

David R. Leigh is manager of Corporate Management Planning & Development, Robbins & Myers, Inc., Dayton, Ohio.

12.
HOW SUPERVISORS CAN SHAPE BEHAVIOR

A. T. Hollingsworth
Denise Tanguay Hoyer

> Behaviors change in gradual stages, not in sweeping motions. An individual masters one component, moves on, modifying the next stage, and so on, until all the components are mastered and a new complex behavior is "shaped."

"Yes, that's a good idea, but it won't work in my department. I won't get anyone to go along with me and make it work."

If you're a personnel manager or a trainer, you've heard these arguments before, but you can do something to counter this defeatist and unproductive attitude. You can help your managers and other trainees learn to "shape" the behavior of their subordinates, peers, and, sometimes, superiors to make the implementation of new ideas, techniques and procedures work in their departments.

You are responsible for seeing that employees not only learn new concepts, but that they are also able to implement these new concepts on the job.

The training process can be divided into three distinct phases:

1) The introduction of new concepts or techniques. The introduction of new concepts is the obvious reason that trainees attend development programs. This facet of the programs offers new ideas or different approaches to problems facing managers and provides some problem-solving ideas.

2) The acceptance of these new concepts or techniques by training participants. Trainers must demonstrate how these new concepts can be used to enhance departmental productivity and effectiveness and improve managerial performance. Trainees must be convinced that the new ideas and techniques can, in fact, aid them.

In order to do this, trainers rely on examples of role play situations, experiential exercises and other simulations that allow the trainees to see the usefulness of implementing the new concepts.

3) The development of creative strategies for implementing these new concepts or techniques on the job. Finally, trainers must assist employees in developing creative strategies to use in implementing the new ideas in their own, individual work situations.

Trainees must be prepared to deal with resistance to new ideas and have flexible strategies to overcome this resistance.

PLAN HOW TO IMPLEMENT NEW IDEAS ON THE JOB

This third phase is an important, but often neglected, responsibility of the personnel department, and therefore merits an in-depth look.

Personnel managers should be aware of the management development concepts that are being taught to trainees in both in-house and outside training programs.

This will allow the personnel manager to assist trainees in the application of new managerial concepts and to encourage them when barriers arise. It will also give trainees a "sounding board" for creative applications before actually using them in the job situation.

The initial step in the implementation phase of training is to address all the "yes-but" responses to training concepts. The personnel manager should have a meeting of all training participants. (This may be the final segment of an in-house training program or *immediately* following an outside program.)

Essentially, each individual, on an independent basis, evaluates each concept and formulates strategies for using it. This strategy development should be done with an emphasis on "brainstorming" (or creative development of ideas) without stressing the immediate viability of each idea.

After each individual has done this, the results are presented and discussed. Finally, a group consensus can be developed highlighting the application methods with the highest probability of success.

The meeting should not last for more than two hours. Creativity and momentum tend to be lost when meetings drag on.

Anyone who manages people realizes that there is an art to working—not for or against—but *with* people. In order to fully develop and enhance employees, certain behaviors must be "shaped."

To gain the maximum results from any training situation then, trainees must be prepared to modify not only their behavior but also the behavior of others in the job situation.

There are 10 steps in this process.

1) Accommodate the process of behavioral change. Behaviors change in gradual stages, not in broad sweeping motions. An individual masters one component, moves on, modifying the next stage, and so on, until all the components are mastered and a new complex behavior is "shaped."

In order to direct this shaping process then, you as a trainer, must approach behaviors in segments—assigning priorities to each aspect and rewarding each in sequence. Although this takes time, the results are certainly well worth it.

The rewards can take the form of verbal praise, posting of successes, time off, job changes or promotions, or anything else that is meaningful to people.

2) Define new behavior patterns specifically. The key here is *specificity*. State what you wish to accomplish in explicit terms and in small amounts that can be easily grasped. A good example was provided by a group of salespeople recently told to be more courteous to potential clients. The directive was not effective until "courteous" was defined and broken down into manageable components, such as: how to greet clients, how to gain their interest, how to introduce products, and, finally, how to close the sale.

3) Give individuals feedback on their performance. In most cases, individuals *are* interested in how well they are performing. They want to know how they have done and whether or not they have achieved their goals.

A once-a-year performance appraisal is not sufficient. This absence of feedback often allows mediocre behavior to appear, if not acceptable, at least tolerable—which it is not.

Daily output reports, though perhaps the opposite extreme, provide the recipients with a continuing opportunity to compare their records to some standards or behavior expectations or even to their own past performances. Merely understanding the results of their behavior and will often motivates employees to improve on their own.

4) Reinforce behavior as quickly as possible. Inform your subordinates that you are aware of their behavior as soon as it happens. If an individual comes to work on time, the timeliness should be praised or recognized. Tardy individuals should likewise be notified.

This reinforcement should take the form of attention, recognition and praise, all of which can be given very quickly and serve as quite effective rewards.

5) Use powerful reinforcements. In order to be effective, rewards must be important to the employee—not to the manager.

The reinforcement must also be strong enough to both elicit new behaviors and maintain correct ones.

For example, if managers constantly give praise but never a raise, praise may lose its effectiveness.

The rewards available must be carefully explained. If organizational policies constrain economic rewards, a special effort will be needed.

6) Use a continuous reinforcement schedule. The key word here is consistency. New behaviors should be reinforced *every time* they occur. This reinforcement should continue until these behaviors become habitual.

With complex behaviors, each component is rewarded until the complex behavior is finally mastered.

7) Use a variable reinforcement schedule for maintenance. Do not allow behavior to lapse because of lack of reinforcement. Even after behavior has become habitual, it still needs to be rewarded, though not necessarily every time it occurs.

8) Reward teamwork—not competition. Zero-sum games—in which one individual can only win at the expense of others—produce only losers in the long run.

A helping relationship is a must for developing a team spirit and the reward system should foster this. Group goals and group rewards are one way to encourage cooperation in situations in which jobs and performance are interdependent.

By conducting group problem-solving sessions everyone can be involved in teamwork and high performance.

9) Make all rewards contingent on performance. In order to learn, employees need to know why they are being rewarded or, in some cases, not being rewarded.

For instance, raises given once a year merely inspire curiosity—it is never quite clear *why* a raise was given—not motivation.

Tie all rewards (attention, praise, recognition, raises, and so on) directly to behaviors that you want repeated.

10) Never take good performance for granted. Ensure that high performers realize that they are recognized as high performers and are rewarded appropriately.

Even superior performance, if left unrewarded, will eventually deteriorate. Once performance has been improved, motivational techniques need to be "freshened"—not stopped.

The true sign of a training program's effectiveness is improved performance back on the job. This is only possible if the trainee returns to the work situation armed with both new skills and a creative plan for implementing these skills and techniques.

These 10 guidelines should be kept in mind when developing any strategy for the implementation of new ideas. Remember, the way people act toward you today is often a result of the way you trained them yesterday.

A. T. Hollingsworth is professor of management and chairman of the management department at the University of North Carolina, Asheville, North Carolina. Denise Tanguay Hoyer is assistant professor of industrial relations and management at James Madison University, Harrisonburg, Virginia.

13.

DO YOUR MANAGERS
REALLY MANAGE?

Charles R. Day, Jr.

Too often, managers duck decisions and neglect people as they shuffle papers and crunch numbers. Too few are held accountable for their actions, critics say. And too many fear responsibility.
Is the company to blame?

The episode had been forever branded in Robert Grasing's memory. A management consultant, Mr. Grasing had presented his corporate client with 15 specific recommendations to improve its operations. After reviewing them, a senior executive agreed that at least ten were sound ideas.

"But he quickly made it clear that he wasn't about to adopt any of them, because they would require taking some risks," recounts Mr. Grasing, vice president of Robert E. Nolan Co., Simsbury, Conn. He vividly remembers the executive telling him: "I got where I am today by not making mistakes. I survived."

Surviving, though, isn't managing. Neither is the paper shuffling and the number crunching that fill many a managerial agenda. And when confronted with the broader question—*Are managers really managing today?*—the response of a host of respected critics is all too crisp:

No.

"Obviously, they are not, and you know that as well as I do," snaps Dr. Ray O. Werner, professor of economics at Colorado College, Colorado Springs. "What's needed today are managers who can ask: *what do people want? How can you deliver it? And what happens if you don't?* We don't have managers who ask that," he insists.

Not everyone is guilty as charged, of course. The dozen experts who addressed the issue can readily point to shining examples of executive action. All told, though, their appraisals stand as compelling evidence that too many managers today aren't worthy of the title. The ineffective managers stand accused of:

- Lacking the skills necessary to motivate, train, and communicate with people.
- Failing to fully understand their business operations.
- Perpetuating and responding to an outdated reward system that discourages innovation and risk-taking.
- Wallowing in oceans of data that seldom tell managers what they really need to know.

INSUFFICIENT

The technical skills and "staff expertise" that managers possess is widely praised, but that's not enough, contends Dr. Warren Bennis, professor of management at the University of Southern California, because the emphasis on such skills has given birth to a "generation of incrementalists—people who are good at the routine. But they fail to motivate people to do better." he says.

Dr. Bennis, who has advised the last four administrations in Washington, conducted a study of chief executives of 90 major U. S. companies. He concludes that "no more than 20% are truly leading their companies."

To charge managers with failing to get the best out of their people is a stinging indictment. After all, motivating employees is their premier task. Yet, of some 125 shortcomings identified by Industry Week sources, 77 (over 61%) are people-related. (The others have to do with organizational problems, technical skills, and the tendency to seek quick fixes.)

One cause of this problem stems, perhaps, from a shift in the nation's workday collars from blue to white. For example, the auto industry's white-collar staffs doubled from 1950 to 1980, while the number of production workers fell 16%. David Kearns, president and CEO of Xerox Corp., Stamford, Conn., suggests that managements have neither recognized nor responded to the attitudinal changes—toward work, organizational life, and bosses—extant among better-educated workers.

As a result, managers face a decidedly different workforce today, one that often challenges traditional managerial axioms. Workers' unwillingness to blindly follow orders is but one reflection of the difference. Thus, veteran managers are simply being overwhelmed, while younger ones schooled in specific disciplines—law, finance, technology—are not much better equipped.

But some leaders, aware of the problem, are attempting credible solutions. One, a direct result of mushrooming white-collar employment, is the two-career ladder. "It's a professional ladder" which serves as an alternative to the traditional management ladder, explains Richard D. Calmes, vice president for personnel and industrial relations at American Motors Corp., Southfield, Mich. Technical and professional employees climb it by honing their skills and increasing their knowledge, earning recognition, and sometimes pay, equal to that in management.

Not long ago, for instance, Mr. Calmes asked a young personnel analyst to present a study to the automaker's board. "Just doing that was a big thing for that individual. It brought him recognition, helped his career, and stimulated others," he says. "And it didn't cost [the company] a nickel."

However, too many companies neglect the recognition factor, and cling to the notion that money alone motivates people. In truth, money may not even be No. 1. The former co-director of the White House Conference on Productivity, L. William Seidman, determined that the leading motivator is personal satisfaction—not dollars.

TOO LITTLE PARTICIPATION

Bringing employees into the decision-making process is one method that some managers are using as a motivational tool. Yet, many others "make decisions beforehand, and seek opinions afterwards," laments Paul R. Sullivan, senior vice president, Harbridge House, Inc., a Boston-based consulting firm. There was sad evidence of that long ago in Detroit when an eager executive was admonished that "people get ahead in this company by waiting to hear what their supervisors think, then working to support that decision."

That tack just won't fly anymore, nor should it, reasons Lee Iacocca in his autobiography. Employees, he reminds, strive "to help achieve goals they helped shape." Yet, he says, "too few executives let their people run with the ball."

Adds Mr. Seidman, now Dean of Arizona State's College of Business Administration: "There are still too many companies that see workers as either the enemy or a commodity item. That's simply the wrong approach."

Both individual managers and their organizations must shoulder the blame for the malaise they find themselves in today, contends Mr. Sullivan. "Many managers fear responsibility," he states flatly. "They don't understand how their decisions will impact other facets of the business because they don't fully understand the business itself."

Colorado College's Dr. Werner, who heartily concurs, holds graduate business school faculties responsible, castigating them for drumming nothing into their students.

Dean Seidman also fears that too little attention has been paid to such functions as "purchasing, logistics, materials handling, and the like, which tie up a bundle of money." And Harold Geneen, the former legendary—if controversial—CEO of ITT Corp., faults business schools for spending too much time on mechanics and too little on the "emotional values of good management."

For whatever reason, failure to grasp the entire corporate picture often paralyzes managers. They delay decisions or "delegate them 'up' to a higher level, when, in fact, the decisions should be made then and there," says Harbridge House's Mr. Sullivan.

Managers are afraid to make mistakes, adds Robert MacAvoy, partner with Easton Consulting Inc., Stamford Conn., in part because "they aren't allowed to be wrong very often, if at all." This stems, he believes, from the unfounded notion that management is a "science." According to that approach, he says, "anything not in the equation is ignored. And when things don't go the way they are supposed to on paper, someone is blamed."

OF LITTLE FAITH

Unwillingness to take risks is often a sign that the organization lacks trust in its managers and won't let them manage, Mr. Sullivan also believes. Moreover, senior executives often are reluctant to delegate "because they feel they must be involved in many decisions, so they can report to *their* bosses." In turn, second-guessing flourishes, adds Mr. MacAvoy.

The budgeting ritual is a case in point, consultant Mr. Grasing says. Managers are annually expected to present accurate budgets, "after which they are told by others not close to the situation to cut them by 15%. So budgeting becomes a game in itself," he concludes. "Yet, even after a budget has been approved, managers still have to undergo more scrutiny for any expenditure over a given sum of money." Why? The answer escapes him. "If the budget has been approved, why does there have to be yet another set of controls?"

One answer, theorizes Mr. Sullivan, may be found in the history of the U. S. space program. "Major contractors have to live in a 100% failure proof environment. There was absolutely no room for error," he points out. "For many, I suspect, it looked like a good way to run *any* business."

Another reason why managers are stifled: there are too many of them. Xerox's Mr. Kearns notes that the U. S. has by far the highest ratio of managers to workers. "Business always tries to solve problems by throwing more managers at them," he says. "What's needed is not more, but better."

Building layer upon flabby layer of management has squeezed innovation out of corporations and clogged communications channels. "To succeed today, you must be able to articulate clearly your goals throughout your organization," stresses Edward I. Rosen, co-founder, president, and CEO of Ziyad Inc., a Denville, N. J., manufacturer of computerized office products. Multilayered managements make that terribly difficult, if not impossible—and they waste money.

Not only do these layers swell operating costs, but they also give rise to what USC's Dr. Bennis calls the *Pinocchio effect*. Just as storyland's Geppetto crafted the marionette Pinocchio, uncertain of what he would look like upon completion, creators of ideas seldom recognize the final results—simply because communications become tangled.

"Not only that," says Colorado College's Dr. Werner, "many ideas are never even acted upon, because someone along the line thinks the short-term costs aren't worth it."

SOUR SYSTEMS

Rewards systems themselves, critics further charge, continue to beget "short-term thinking" and decisions, despite vows to the contrary. Compensation systems based on the "bell curve," for instance, typically allow a manager to properly reward only a select few employees, says Mr. Grassing. "To take care of other equally deserving people, he has to create overtime, or concoct other devices, which everyone can see through."

Other pay systems, like those based on a manager's "span of control" (i.e., the number of workers reporting to him), discourage managers from streamlining operations. "A manager may be able to cut the number of positions he controls and still achieve the desired results—to improve profits and productivity," he explains. "But that will effectively cut his compensation, so he doesn't."

Results themselves are another sore spot with management's critics. Too often, managers aren't held accountable when goals aren't attained mainly because "nobody makes them do it," chides Mr. Geneen in his book, *Managing*, published by Doubleday in 1984. "Explanations and rationalizations are too readily accepted," he says. "Indeed, they are even expected." Thus, companies set lofty goals even though everyone knows that hitting just 80% of them will be acceptable. "Even if someone exceeds that 80%, sales will be hidden so they can be used next year," Mr. Geneen observes.

Ziyad's Mr. Rosen believes that such practices are counterproductive. "People will respond to high targets and respect each other more when they are held to them."

The lack of good "qualitative measures" of managerial performance is lamented by others. At the very least, appraisals should consider the long-term effects of executive decision, but almost none do. Too few managers, in fact, accept the idea that there even are qualitative aspects to an evaluation, consultant Mr. MacAvoy believes.

That reflects, in part, poor corporate recruiting efforts, contends Colorado College's Dr. Werner. Industry is not getting the talent it needs, he says. Instead, it just accepts what it is getting. He suspects that company recruiters don't know what top management really wants. He recalls a recent visit by a U.S. Steel Corp. recruiter to his campus. The recruiter refused to talk with anyone except business administration majors. "But those types are too narrow to deliver the broad-based skills and understanding that business now needs," Dr. Werner believes.

Corporate recruiting and promotion practices are weak, agrees consultant

Mr. Grasing. But weaker still are the training programs available to managers once they're hired, if they're available at all. "In too many cases," Mr. Grasing says, "managers are put in a position and its is simply hoped that they will do well."

NEGLECTED TASK

Some observers suspect that business is putting far too much faith in M.B.A. degrees and college training, while managers themselves "misunderstand" their responsibilities as teachers, says Harbridge House's Mr. Sullivan. "I remember an engineering executive who felt that he had no time for people concerns, that his job was purely a technical one. The truth is, his job was to make sure he had the right people on board doing the right things to get the technical job done."

Managers might have more time for people if they weren't, as Mr. Iacocca says, "so weighed down with information."

That's one of the real problems, Dean Seidman believes. "We are measuring everything today, but we have to better manage the ability to gather information. Measures alone are just a barometer." The sheer volume of information today, adds USC's Dr. Bennis, "often obscures the meaning."

Xerox CEO Kearns blames management as a whole for the numbers glut. "There is no clear purposed or sense of mission in the office." he says. "Offices are not organized to produce or manage information in a meaningful way." (Lest one think that Mr. Kearns has a particular ax to grind, he also stresses that automation for its own sake leads to disaster.)

Even Mr. Geneen, who possessed a capacious appetite for numbers, says numbers themselves aren't important. Their real value is what they reveal about the business and what needs to be done.

At some point, states Mr. Iacocca, managers have to put numbers aside "and take that leap of faith." They have to act.

Mr. Geneen puts it another way—forcefully: "Managing means to manage! You must be in control of your operations. If something goes wrong, you probe until you find the cause, and if one solution does not work, you try another, and another and another . . ."

A story told by Mr. Geneen about an ITT European manager makes one wonder if the same initiative and common sense would have prevailed in a U.S. manager. The overseas manager was struggling to rein in soaring inventory cost. After a variety of sophisticated measures had failed, the manager appointed someone to stand at the company loading dock. His instructions were simple and non-computerized: Reject any item that had not been ordered.

It worked like a charm.

14.
PUTTING HUMAN RESOURCE MANAGEMENT AT THE LINE MANAGER LEVEL

Nancy K. Napier
Richard B. Peterson

Perhaps one of the biggest mistakes that many companies make is to delegate much of the HRM accountability to the personnel department. The personnel staff typically has the expertise in this area, but line management is top management's key representative to employees and in the best position to implement the programs.

It is time to make good human resource management a reality. We have long had the techniques, skills, and tools to do this, but too often the skills and tools have been the domain of personnel specialists, not line managers. Line managers should be the principal "human resource managers" of any corporation. As implementers of policy they are in a position to practice good management of human resources. Human resource specialists should act as consultants to line managers, providing information about various techniques or suggestions about policies and ways to implement them.

Line managers can be the total point of good human resource management. In many cases, a manager needs additional guidance from top management or training from personnel specialists. In other cases, the manager should take the time to consider more carefully the repercussions of his or her actions. In all cases, however, the line manager is in the critical position of influencing the way employees view the organization and its human resource approach. The article has three sections. We first discuss some of the possible reasons for human resource mismanagement. Then we show typical cases or vignettes of human resource mismanagement and possible ways to remedy the situations. The vignettes come from our own experiences and contact with private and public sector organizations. Finally, we identify actions that top management might take to improve line managers' handling of human resources.

WHY DO WE MISMANAGE EMPLOYEES?

There are at least ten reasons contributing to human resource mismanagement in organizations. While many of the reasons are understandable, they also result in costs to the organization. If the frequent claim that "people are our most important asset" is valid, why does it often seem that organizations convey the opposite message? Is it possible that the corporate leaders don't really believe that managing human resources on a daily basis contributes to the bottom line? For all the rhetoric concerning the importance of human resources, constructive action may well be the exception rather than the rule. How is this situation possible? Let's look at a number of explanations.

Poor Training In Managing Human Resources. Unfortunately, in all too many cases, an employee recently promoted into management is not given proper training in effective behavior relating to interviewing, compensating, and motivating members of his or her staff. For example, the company or division may have held a skills course in performance appraisal for managers two years ago, but such training would not be available again for managers until the next time the course if offered. And yet, a new manager may be required to conduct several performance appraisals shortly after taking the job. Could we realistically expect the new manager to have the necessary skills when this was never part of his job before?

The problem is compounded if the new manager 1) assumes that managing people is only "common sense" or 2) is hesitant to admit lack of knowledge or skills in conducting such performance appraisals.

Limited Options. Much of the managerial literature assumes that managers have considerable flexibility in handling their employees. The reality is that important organizational and personal constraints exist. The managerial philosophy that permeates the company represents one important constraint. While most American executives are uncomfortable with the idea of corporate philosophy, much research on organizational climate and human resource theory shows that many firms can be identified with specific models of how employees are viewed. Raymond Miles wrote a book in which he identified three basic models: Scientific Management (employees as "units of production"), Human Relations ("concern with employee needs"), and Human Resources ("employees as long-term 'investments' in and 'contributors' to the firm").[1] While it is doubtful that every firm falls neatly into one of these three models, it is possible to use similar classifications. Most observers would agree that there is an overriding philosophy at such firms as IBM, General Electric, and General Motors. Much of the managerial value system derives from the role of past chief executives as Thomas Watson, Sr., or Alfred Sloan.

The philosophy of top management undoubtedly limits manager's options in dealing with employees. If top management views the employment relationship primarily as one of economic exchange, long-term employee development approaches may be discouraged. An exchange relationship such as Human Resources, which meets employee and organization needs, may be the most appropriate approach, but it is currently rare. Alan Fox, in his book *Man-Mismanagement*, shows how management philosophies such as coercion, scientific management, human relations, and participative decision making, some of them similar to Miles' approaches, have all failed to elicit real employee commitment. Fox believes that much of the blame for the failure of these managerial approaches is due to the low trust that most managers place in their subordinates, whether they be research scientists, keypunch operators, or machine operators.[2]

Time Demands. One of the most common reactions managers have to requests to spend more time working with their staffs is that they don't have time. The production superintendent may feel overwhelmed by demands to cut the scrap rate to 1.3 percent. The regional sales manager may be under considerable pressure to increase product sales by 15 percent in spite of economic recession and tougher price competition. The cost accounting manager may argue that she doesn't have time to establish a long-range training program for her staff because her section is obliged to complete the same number of reports with 12 percent fewer staff members.

In such situations, managers find it hard to believe that good management of human resources may, in the long run, contribute to making their jobs easier. Although it is difficult to prove a direct correlation between effective human resource management and success in reaching sub-corporate goals, anecdotal and case-by-case evidence suggests that properly trained and motivated employees do perform effectively.

Short-Term Payoffs. For years business commentators have decried the short-term focus of many American companies. Managers frequently get the message that their unit, division, or plant needs to focus on short-term profit or efficiency indicators. The latest monthly or quarterly figures become the report card. Such timing of accountability doesn't lend itself to concern for long-term goals such as developing human resources. Rather building a top-flight investments department becomes a matter of showing how the firm increased its return on investments by 7 1/2 percent last month over earlier years' figures. An investment manager may find that spending time on human resources today helps only his successors since he may be transferred or promoted out of the job within a year or so. If managerial self-interest is strong, it's much easier to relinquish responsibility for managing human resources. Managers quickly learn top management's priorities and place their energies accordingly.

Lack of Bottom-Line Accountability. Few companies provide bottom-line accountability for managing human resources. Rarely is there a major emphasis in a managerial performance appraisal form on assessing a manager's skills in identifying top applicants, earmarking particular training needs of subordinates, and so forth. It's not really surprising, then, that many managers don't take management of human resources very seriously. The test of whether "people are our most important asset" is the attention given to human resource management in managerial performance reviews.

Even when some attention is accorded to line management's responsibility for improving utilization of their employees, the standards are often quite vague. That makes it difficult for the line manager to show effective behaviors in this area. The more important question is what concrete steps can be taken to improve managerial performance in the area.

Assumption About Effectiveness. Top management often assumes that if a manager looks good on the bottom line, then he or she must be effective in motivating his or her staff. This may be an incorrect assumption. The manager may be placing unreasonable pressures on the employees to produce. In some cases, where there is an unreasonably high employee turnover or an inordinate number of employee requests for transfers out of the department, we find later that the manager was really ineffective. Higher managerial ranks rarely have a conduit to the informal employee network, so they may not realize that the individual manager has a problem until it's too late.

Secretiveness in Personnel Matters. Secretiveness represents a key problem area for line management in dealing with employees. In some cases the line manager gets a sense of power from withholding key information from his or her subordinates regarding compensation policy and practice performance appraisal ratings, affirmative action plans, and training opportunities. However, in other situations line management believes, or has been told, that top management doesn't wish them to share much information with their staff. Thus, when employees inquire about such matters as how their ratings compared with other employees doing similar work, the information is not forthcoming.

Faddism. Human resource, like any other area, is subject to the latest fads, whether it be MBO, sensitivity training, job design, behavioral observation scales, or labor-management committees. Flitting from one fad to another may suggest that top management doesn't have a long-term approach to managing human resources. Even the managers after some time question whether the company has a comprehensive and consistent set of policies and practices in the areas of selection, performance appraisal, compensation, training and development, affirmative action, and labor relations. Employees often feel that they are unwilling participants in the latest gimmick.

Delegation to the Personnel Department. Perhaps one of the biggest mistakes that many companies make is to delegate much of the human resource management accountability to the personnel department. The personnel staff typically has the expertise in this area, but really isn't in the best position to implement the various programs. Line management, not the personnel department, is top management's key representative to employees in most organizations. The personnel department should establish key policies, practices, and programs as well as advising line managers regarding the implementation; however, management would be remiss if the line organization didn't become centrally involved in the process. First of all, by delegating many of the activities to the personnel department, line management may well be conveying the idea that managing employees isn't all that important, or that the line manager is not qualified to handle such issues. Second, such delegation deprives line management of an important role in motivating the employee staff.

Discomfort of Line Management. Managerial discomfort may well be the most important reason for mismanaging human resources. Managers may feel more at ease in situations where clear-cut solutions exist. An accounting manager can feel comfortable with nationally approved accounting principles that reduce the ambiguity of the job. A production manager may receive a relatively "clean" report of how his work unit performed last week. However, in the area of managing human resources, clear-cut solutions rarely exist. The necessary human resource techniques may exist, but there are no panaceas when it comes to a line manager's explaining why a given employee received a low salary increase this year. If the communication is bungled, it's often impossible to go back and rectify the situation with that employee. There aren't a lot of second chances in this area. The less comfortable the line manager feels, the greater the likelihood that the unpleasant situation will be handled badly.

Can line managers improve their skills in managing their staff? We think so. The next section provides examples and possible approaches to reducing mismanagement of human resources.

MISMANAGING HUMAN RESOURCES

Let us begin by assuming that most managers and supervisors wish to deal with their employees in a fair manner, and to help their subordinates in carrying out their job responsibilities. No doubt, there are many instances when positive results ensue. In such cases we are likely to find a fairly high level of trust has developed between the superior and subordinate. In the best sense of the word, reciprocity has taken place. On the one hand, the employee understands and accepts the manager's expectations regarding behavior and job performance. On the other hand, the manager is clear in stating the job expectations, honest and forthright in dealings with the subordinate, and willing to view the employee as more than a "commodity" and the work relationship as more than merely as economic exchange. However, we can find many examples from our own employment experience where the organization's or individual manager's mismanagement led to employee disappointment, anger, and ultimately distrust.

The following vignettes are based upon real examples of poor human resource management. We are not arguing that the manager intentionally mismanaged, but rather that the resulting action damaged the supervisory relationship and the accomplishment of organizational goals. In some of the cases both the organization and the participants lost.

The following examples encompass the breadth of human resource management activities in most large corporations in the United States. Each scenario illustrates a failure in line management's managing of its human resources. We'll begin by looking at employee selection.

PROMOTION

A Problem. The vice president of the engineering department, Jim Nesbitt, had been informed by Tom Heward, one of his section managers, that Tom would be resigning in three weeks to take a position with another company. The next day the grapevine was at work speculating about who might be chosen as a replacement. Most of the engineers expected the position to be filled by promotion. Two or three names were mentioned as the most likely successors. Each of them worked in the same section where the vacancy existed. Yet, nothing seemed to happen—it appeared almost as if everything was in limbo.

Tom Heward left, and the position stayed vacant. Finally, two weeks later, a notice posted on the section's bulletin board announced that the job was to be filled by Bill Downs, a production department member who had some managerial experience. The frontrunners for the position were shocked and disappointed at the selection process. It came out later that no one in the engineering department had even been given the opportunity to be considered. There was no open job posting, no listing of skill or of experience requirements, no explanation from Jim Nesbitt about why Bill Downs had been chosen. Bill didn't seem to have the background for the job. Did management have a "hidden agenda"? Wasn't there anyone better qualified for the position within engineering? What about Jim Nesbitt's recruiting pitch about favoring promotion from within? Did top management really care about their employees?

A Solution. Several problems are evident. First, there was a lack of communication from Jim to his staff about how the position would be filled. Second, there was no clear job description defining the duties and requirements. Finally, there was apparently pressure to fill the position without taking sufficient time or getting enough information to do it carefully. Jim, his subordinates, and others could have worked to alleviate some of the confusion and misunderstanding.

We don't know what information Jim received from the department manager. He could have asked for a description of what the position had included, whether it needed changes, and if any of the manager's subordinates could fill it. The section manager may have been grooming someone for the position. Either Jim was unaware of that or was unresponsive to the manager's comments. Whether he talked to the manager or not, once Jim had information about the position, he could have shared it with some or all of his staff by posting it or by meeting with potentially interested employees. If the position could not be filled internally, that information should have gone to the staff.

Before the position was filled, staff members could also have taken the responsibility of asking about the job, and seeking information from Jim rather than waiting. Jim had other problems in addition to filling this department manager's position. It seemed department members spent much time fretting without letting Jim know of their interest.

The actual promotion process excluded section members and other managers. Jim might have included key managers who would be peers of the new managers and perhaps some subordinates in the interview process. That would have eased the introduction of change and helped increase staff members' commitment to a new manager.

Once Bill Downs was chosen, Jim should have introduced him personally. Without Jim's clear backing, it is likely that the new manager will be blackballed by some of his subordinates. If so, his job will become more difficult and the section may spend several weeks or months getting its footing.

The human resource department could also have helped in this situation. Once the department manager announced his upcoming departure, the human resource specialist might have approached Jim to see if he wanted assistance in defining the job, finding candidates, and the like.

Finally, it is unclear whether Jim was responding to top management directives to fill the position from the outside. If so, giving Jim the latitude to explain the requirement to staff members may have eased some of the tension.

PERFORMANCE APPRAISAL

The Problem. Supervisors at a mid-sized manufacturing firm were expected to fill out performance appraisal ratings on each non-exempt employee every six months for merit pay purposes. Many of the supervisors were frustrated with the process because, with the exception of a few measures like number of units produced in a given time period, very few objective standards could be used. It was hard to relate quality to an individual worker's contribution. Most of the supervisors relied on absentee and tardiness records or on some gut-level sense of inter-personal skills. Few supervisors were comfortable with these "soft" measures, and they were even less happy when workers asked why they hadn't received merit pay increases. It appeared that management had done little to help the supervisors understand the process or to show how they could learn to identify and rate appropriate job behaviors. Where was the training back-up? Why wasn't performance appraisal given more attention by higher management? How could the supervisors defend the system when they realized its fallacies?

A Solution. As the vignette illustrates, managers who are unable to articulate clear expectations and standards for subordinates' performance are, unfortunately, all too common. Several steps might have helped rectify this particular situation. First, the supervisors should not have had to carry out the performance appraisal without some training and guidance. If training was not provided, or provided only irregularly, supervisors should have asked for help. If managers were reluctant to request help, perhaps the human resource specialists should have periodically touched base and asked how they could assist managers in the process.

Training for supervisors or first-line managers might have included, for example, how to define a job, its criteria, and its standards for performance; how to give feedback (positive or negative) so the employee can use it to improve performance behavior; and how to help employees set goals. It was not enough to assume the employees knew what their job entailed, how to do it, or what should be accomplished over the long run. Managers and employees often need assistance in planning and carrying out these tasks.

In the appraisal interview, supervisors and subordinates together could determine job criteria and standards. It takes time initially, but should save time later. Establishing standards and criteria jointly may encourage a subordinate's commitment to achieving goals and carrying out tasks involved in the job. To develop together an agreement of what a job entails and what needs to be done is a major step in better performance appraisal, communication, and trust.

The line manager could seek an indication from top management on the role of performance appraisal: how much time should managers devote to the activities and what outcomes should result. Management can imply that performance appraisal is important yet appear to negate it by not providing incentives for managers to perform appraisals carefully. Managers need some indication from top management of the priority it places on appraisal.

Employees also could have played a role in improving performance appraisal. Subordinates could have requested information on standards and expectations for their jobs. Employees have the responsibility for understanding their job's requirements, and mangers could have encouraged employees to assume that responsibility. One way to encourage employee responsibility might have been to have employees compile information for their own performance appraisals. Each subordinate could have developed a file of information pertaining to his or her performance during the previous period. Subordinates and supervisor could review the information and negotiate future actions during the employee's performance appraisal. Compiling information would have allowed the employee to give input that he saw as relating to job performance and could have increased the chances of the employee's commitment to the job tasks.

COMPENSATION

The Problem. Several years ago employees in one company became angry and confused with the apparent inconsistency between the firm's compensation policy and practice. Year after year top management communicated the message that pay raises were based solely on merit—the better the job performance, the higher the annual pay increase. Seniority and showing up for work wouldn't be enough to qualify for merit increases. One year, after twelve months of double-digit inflation, employees compared their raises and discovered that almost everyone had received an 8 percent "merit increase." How could top management and their immediate supervisors call that a merit increase when it was less than the rate of inflation, and almost every employee had received the same amount? How could one put any trust in his or her boss? How did managers feel when they told their best performing employee that the 8 percent was a merit increase?

Another illustration shows how organizations suffer by such mismanagement. In this case, management rewarded 80 to 90 percent of managers and employees with bonuses even though they doubted whether that high a percentage of non-unionized employees were performing their jobs at better than satisfactory levels. Was the firm's compensation practice consistent with good management?

A Solution. The vignette illustrates the basic problem of linking compensation and performance. Most organizations like to claim they link the two. Too often, however, employees see inconsistencies, like blanket merit increases or widespread bonuses.

Frequently, firms can give employees more salary and wage-setting information than they do. Line managers should understand the salary policy and explain the process in general to employees. Knowing the general policy might begin to quell fears of inequity and potential dissatisfaction.

Most firms cannot show direct performance-pay relationships because of the many contributing factors, such as economic conditions. However, the firm in the vignette might have given employees more information, especially about the financial situation of the firm, the relationship between the firm's performance and employee rewards, the firm's future, and steps that are being taken to improve performance of the firm. Such information as salary ranges within job classes might also be offered.

Providing information is one way to stave off employee dissatisfaction but often other actions may be useful. In a situation where there is little salary distinction between outstanding and average performance employees, other forms of recognition may be in order, such as free tickets, dinners, weekend trips, or club memberships.

Line managers can perform the useful function of transferring information concerning subordinates' confusion and disappointment about the compensation program to top management and human resource specialists. Understanding how employees view a compensation program may help in future structuring.

Rather than depend solely on the information human resource specialists and managers wanted to give, employees could have asked for more detailed compensation information. They might have requested such information as, "Where do I stand relative to others in the group? What specific actions do I need to take to receive a raise of a certain percent?" While managers often cannot give specific information on increases, such questions force both the employee and managers to relate performance appraisal to the compensation process. The result should be to clarify job criteria and standards, thereby better integrating compensation and performance appraisal. Such questions also encourage line managers to go back to their managers and human resource specialists for information on what can be offered. It can begin a discussion of how much openness the firm can provide and whether making contracts with employees for certain levels of performance output and compensation is feasible, given certain economic and financial conditions.

TRAINING

The Problem. One afternoon Jane Shipes was called into her boss's office. After some small talk, she was told that the company would sponsor her in a night MBA program at the local public university, and that classes would begin the middle of the following month. The firm would pick up the cost of tuition and books. Jane hadn't asked to be sponsored. She hadn't even been aware that she was being considered. Immediately after delivering this message, the boss said that he had another important meeting and ushered her out. Jane was left to wonder, "Why me? Isn't my B.A. in Computer Science enough background for the job? Is the firm just trying to show commitment to affirmative action by sending me instead of Tom Sales? Should I be pleased or scared? What is the real message?" Finally, there was anger: "Why didn't the manager give me the chance to react? Don't I have the right to say whether I want to go or not?"

In this situation, many people would conclude that the company-paid MBA was a clear case of positive feedback to Jane Shipes. However, would the same hold true if the manager told Jane that she was to attend a supervisory skills course, an organizational development session or a programming course without explaining why?

A Solution. Two problems are evident here. First, Jane was selected for an MBA program without having a chance to say whether or not she wanted to go.

Second, she received almost no clue about the reasons behind her selection. Had her manager handled the situation differently, Jane's attitude toward the program and future training opportunities might have been more favorable. He would have alerted Jane earlier that she was being considered for the program. At that point, he could have given reasons for her consideration and could have had a reading from Jane on whether she wanted to go. Sending her unwillingly may be more expensive in the long run.

If it was impossible to alert Jane before her selection, the manager still could have presented the opportunity differently. To lessen Jane's fears and answer questions, he could have given background on the selection process and described how the course could enhance her skills and future job opportunities. Finally, the manager could have suggested she talk to others at the firm who had also attended the program.

In conjunction with planning her own career, Jane might have looked at various MBA or other training programs. She could have initiated a discussion with her boss on which program she wanted to pursue and why.

If she had found herself "trapped" in the MBA program she could have 1) refused to pursue it, possibly damaging future opportunities, 2) used the program to increase her skills and identify future opportunities within the firm, or 3) used it to identify opportunities outside the firm.

Managers and employees can receive lists of training options and programs from the human resources department staff. Once managers, and presumably employees, have decided some training may be called for, selecting the program jointly increases employee commitment and responsibility for making the program successful.

JOB DESIGN

The Problem. The top management of a large plant of a nationally known consumer goods corporation had decided to implement a job redesign program in its largest production department. Sessions were held with managers and supervisors affected by the job redesign both in the department and in related departments. The factory employees, all of whom were non-union, heard only secondhand reports about the contemplated change. One day there was an announcement on the employee bulletin board that the job redesign would begin taking effect the beginning of next month. Plant management expected that the affected employees would prefer the new system to the traditional method. There was some consensus that some jobs would be upgraded, resulting in higher wages for approximately one-third of the affected employees. However, no promises were made.

The workers in the unit were not consulted much regarding their ideas concerning the job redesign. However, within three months there was a great deal of give-and-take between the workers and the two supervisors in the unit. By the end of the first year, production was up 15 percent, rejects were down 35 percent, and overall costs were only 3 percent higher than under the old production system unit. The workers were happy since their jobs seemed more interesting. Furthermore, most of the employees had learned new job skills, and 40 percent of the workers in the unit received higher pay than they would have had under the old system. While the results after another year were somewhat less impressive, there were no pressures to discontinue the program.

Then, two months ago the key production manager in the unit was promoted to corporate headquarters. His replacement, though very competent, was less committed to job redesign than his predecessor. Principally, he was unconvinced of the long-run payoffs and wanted to increase short-run gains more rapidly. Last week the new manager announced that in February that unit would return to doing the work in the old way. The employees weren't consulted before the change. Some of them felt that they had been sold out. There was even talk of organizing a union since they seemed to have no power. Why weren't they consulted? Why didn't they have any input? Where was justice when management could turn off the spigot so abruptly? Comments like "Why try to help the company—they don't seem to care!" were commonly heard among the workers.

A *Solution*. Any new program treads a tenuous path for its first few months. The job redesign program described in the case is a perfect example of the fragility of many such programs.

Once a program is established, discontinuing it might be very damaging. The managers, both new and old, could have prevented the employee's frustration and potential unionization. Rather than arbitrarily removing the job redesign program, the incoming manger could have consulted employees and the departing manager. Even if the new manager decided the program should go, employees would have had the chance to give input and receive information about the decision process.

If there was a real commitment to such programs, rather than following what might be perceived as the latest human resource fad, why was there no cost-benefit assessment before its establishment or at the stage of its elimination? The firm's management likely had little information on the costs of program start-up, maintenance, or elimination. Why make another move—ending the program—without determining its impact?

Finally, employees had a responsibility to make the new manager aware of their concerns and attitudes about keeping or eliminating the program. When the new manager arrived, employees did little to indicate to him their commitment to the program. If the program was, in actuality, improving production and morale, the departing manager and the employees could have used such information to make a case for keeping the job redesign program. With some evidence from employees on the program's benefits, the new manager may well have seen the value of keeping the entire program, or at least parts of it.

Again, in this case, there was little evidence of top management's long-term commitment to the job redesign program. When the new manager wanted to eliminate the program, the top management "response" was to go with whatever the new manager decided. In a situation of reciprocity, top management assumes line managers and employees can interpret a policy and implement it. To do so, though the policy or attitude must be visible. Without a clear statement, each manager decides independently whether to pursue a program, such as job redesign.

CAREER PLANNING

The Problem. A lot of attention has been devoted to individual career planning but, unfortunately, many large American companies have not established organization-level career planning operations, as is illustrated by the following case.

Ted Ramsey had an MBA degree from a major Pac Ten university with a concentration in finance. For seven years he worked for a medium-sized bank—the last three of these years in the International Banking Department. He received yearly merit increases and last year he was promoted to assistant vice president where he supervised four employees.

A friend gave Ted the book *What Color Is Your Parachute* for his last birthday. He read it thoroughly, completing the various exercises designed to help him learn more about his interests, strengths, weaknesses, and so forth. He felt very good about his skills, but became concerned about whether his career aspirations were compatible with opportunities at the bank. Ted realized how little knowledge he had of how he fit into the bank's plans.

He decided to set up a meeting with his boss to discuss career planning. He briefly told his boss that he would like to share some information concerning his own career planning efforts, and receive some feedback on where the bank saw him going. An hour was set aside for the conference. After talking about his personal efforts and goals for twenty minutes, he asked his boss what kind of planning the bank did concerning career steps. Ted asked if the bank routinely conducted manpower and succession planning. What appeared to be the various career ladders or paths for someone with his background and experience? How might he find out the skills that he needed to improve if he was to be promoted? What was the probability of job change or promotion in the next three to five years? His boss rather sheepishly admitted that the bank's manpower planning system was somewhat rudimentary. There was no systematic basis for forecasting job movement in the organization. The boss had read an article or two on career paths, but no one had ever thought to chart job movement over the years as a way of helping employees and lower managers identify lateral or vertical steps from one job to another in the bank. Finally, Ted's boss said that employee development was not a strong part of the performance appraisal process. When there was an opening, several vice presidents compared notes and then selected someone for the job. Within thirty minutes the conference was over. If Ted wanted more information, his boss advised him to check with the personnel department. Ted was disappointed as he left his boss's office.

Three months later Ted Ramsey started work at a rival bank where formal manpower planning, career pathing, and succession planning programs were in place and were used. Ted felt lucky to find an employer who gave more attention to future movement of its employees and managers. His new boss had already informed him how the career planning system worked. Also the boss mentioned that the two of them would meet yearly to discuss how Ted's performance was being "read" by the bank and what were the specific steps to reach some of Ted's goals for his career.

A Solution. Ted Ramsey left one bank for another partly because his boss could give him no career guidance or information. The bank he left lost what seemed to be a good employee because it did not plan for its future human resource needs or how it could use its current resources in the future. Ted, his boss, and the bank management could have taken steps to avoid the situation. Given his former bank's stance on career planning at the time he approached his manager, Ted took the best way out for him: he left the bank.

Ted put his manager on the spot regarding the bank's career planning policies. The manager could have persuaded Ted to let him ask about the bank's future plans for such activities. If career planning policies were close to being implemented, Ted might have stayed. If they were not, the manager could have raised the issue with the human resource department or top management to develop a plan regarding 1) how to determine what kind of and how many people it would need in five years, 2) how the firm's plans for change (growth, retrenchment) would mesh with its human resources, 3) who would move to various slots, or 4) what types of career paths would be available for various employee groups and individuals. In general, the human resource department should have been keeping Ted's boss apprised of basic policies in the career planning area.

LAYOFFS

The Problem. The year 1982 was a grim one for many firms and their employees. Large-scale layoffs in auto, steel, wood products, and commercial airline firms had devastating effects in Michigan, Illinois, Ohio, Washington, Oregon, and a host of other states. Declining business meant high unemployment, declining tax revenues, and family and personal stress. The employees laid off for lengthy periods often found themselves with very limited alternate job possibilities. Even when laid off employees were willing to move elsewhere, they often couldn't sell their homes because of the poor employment situation and high interest rates. A lot of the newly unemployed felt themselves caught, "between the devil and the deep blue sea." Many of the unemployed would have seriously considered temporary wage cuts, short work weeks, or leaves of absence without pay if they still had their jobs. As one person said, "It's hell being out of work."

In one company, some lower-level mangers asked if their firm's top management would be willing to explore a variety of options short of layoffs to deal with the depressed business conditions. If top management was open to the idea, some scenarios would be prepared concerning the costs and benefits of the various alternatives. One company's experience[3] had suggested that the true economic costs to the firm of layoffs are typically understated. Where feasible, short work weeks, periodic unpaid leaves, and even pay cuts might be preferable to putting the employees out the door.

Top management wasn't convinced that there was a better, quicker way to reduce costs other than laying off staff. They didn't relish the idea of layoffs, but that was a way the company had cut expenses before, so managers were at least familiar with the process.

Morale was hard to maintain under such circumstances. A good share of the company work force felt a sense of helplessness. No options were provided for spreading the work around. One was either employed or out on the street. Did company management really care? Even if business picked up in the industry, would there ever be the same feeling the employees had had about the company? After all, many of the old timers had previously believed the firm had been a good employer. Would it be in the future?

A Solution. One of a manager's hardest tasks is to determine whom to lay off or fire and how to carry out the decision. Line managers can approach such a situation in at least two ways. First, as the vignette suggests, they might ask about, or even suggest, alternatives to layoffs. Shorter work weeks, sharing work, transferring people to other departments—all these options should be considered by top and line managers. The costs of layoffs, such as the economic (unemployment compensation) and social (more unemployment, health, marital problems) ones, may be much greater than the cost of alternative methods.

If top management insists on layoffs, managers should request guidance on such issues as what criteria to use in making the decision, how to handle the employee interview, what reactions to expect from employees, and what technical information about benefits, alternative job possibilities, and so on they need to provide to employees.

In any impending layoff situation, rumors and poor morale can sap a highly productive atmosphere. Certain factors can help ease the agony of the situation. First, the more information employees have about what will happen, how decisions will be made, and what assistance the organization can provide, the more their fear and concern will be alleviated. Even an unpleasant experience is more tolerable if it is understood.

Secondly, the process should occur as quickly as possible without rushing decisions. The waiting time is "lost" productivity, so the sooner the employees learn what will happen, the better.

Finally, managers must attend to the remaining employees. For those employees, the initial fear of layoff is over. There may be future cuts, though, which cause continuing anxiety. Also, remaining employees may be affected by seeing co-workers leave. All parties, the victims and the observers, will have to acknowledge the decision and its implications. Managers should be aware of the implications to employees and should help them work through the effects of the decision on each of them.

These vignettes raise several issues. One is that line managers are the critical players in practicing good human resource management. To accomplish their task, however, managers must have the support of others. Several parties must be actively involved and assume a certain degree of responsibility for the human resource management process to be truly effective. There should be an exchange of information and responsibility between human resource management staff, top management, line management, and subordinates. Line managers cannot be more open to employees, give more feedback on performance, or provide more information on top management policies if they do not have the information or if employees are not primed to receive it. Managers must be able to provide information, but employees must also be willing to ask for information and must assume a certain amount of responsibility in using the information to improve their own performance.

While line managers are in a crucial position to practice good methods of managing human resources, they sometimes need support and guidance. Top management should provide the direction and fundamental policies that underlie human resource management within a given firm. If the guidance is not clear, line managers should seek it out. In addition, managers sometimes need sounding boards of additional expertise on human resource management. They should have access to and use experienced managers or human resource management specialists. Asking for advice is not an admission of an inability to manage human resources. Every manager attests to the difficulties of human resource issues. So why do managers avoid seeking assistance? They seek out help when developing a new product, designing advertising campaigns, or buying a computer system. Why not draw on persons in-house, or outside, who may have additional expertise in managing human resources?

References

1. R. C. Miles, *Theories of Management: Implications for Organizational Behavior and Development* (New York: McGraw-Hill, 1975).
2. A. Fox, *Man-Mismanagement* (London: Hutchinson, 1974).
3. Dan L. Ward, "The $34,000 Layoff," *Human Resource Planning*, January 1982: 35-41.

Nancy K. Napier is an Assistant Professor and Richard B. Peterson is a Professor in the Department of Management and Organization at the University of Washington in Seattle.

15.
MANAGERIAL IGNORANCE

Martin J. Gannon

Although managers as a class are obviously intelligent, research suggests that the job-specific knowledge bases of many executives are substandard, which may well negatively influence an organization's performance. Four major causes of this problem, and possible solutions to each, are presented: ineffective selection of managers, unfocused management training, inappropriate organizational rewards systems, and information overload.

It is common knowledge that the United States is experiencing serious problems in the area of lagging productivity. Many explanations have been offered for this situation, but one plausible explanation may well help to explain a large part of the problem: the ignorance of managers. Not their stupidity. Managers as a class are anything but stupid. But there is evidence that the job-specific knowledge bases of many, and perhaps most, executives are quite substandard. In turn, low knowledge bases may lead executives to make decisions that are less than optimal—and sometimes not even satisfactory.

THE EVIDENCE

Perhaps the best available evidence of job-specific managerial ignorance is provided by Henry Mintzberg's well-known profile of managerial work.[1] According to his study, the classical profile of the manager as a rational planner who systematically, sequentially, and proactively plans, organizes, directs, and controls is incorrect. This classical profile stresses the primacy of proaction and planning. Mintzberg's profile, however, suggests that the manager is relatively passive until a problem confronts him. Hence his style of management is reactive rather than proactive. He is more a firefighter than a planner.

Mintzberg argues that the reactive mode dominates because managers work long hours at an unrelenting pace, at fragmented, varied, brief, and discontinuous activities. Under such conditions it is difficult, and perhaps impossible, to be a proactive planner. In his own study of five CEOs, Mintzberg found that the average amount of time they spend on any one activity during a day is nine minutes, and the longest amount of time is about two hours. Further, these harried managers dislike any information that they must acquire through reading and serious study. They favor "live" information that can be acquired through face-to-face communication, either on an individual basis or in a group. In particular, these manager dislike the "dead" information provided by computerized management information systems, as such information is usually dated and of little value by the time it reaches them.

One study of managerial knowledge revealed that some personnel executives seemed to know much less about their field than a typical undergraduate who had completed only one course in this area.[2] The researchers gathered this data by mailing a questionnaire containing job-specific items to 281 personnel executives who were members of the National Society of Personnel Administration. These managers held very responsible positions: more than one-third worked in personnel divisions directly influencing at least a thousand individuals. In addition, they possessed high levels of formal training: 79 percent were college graduates, 33 percent had completed some graduate work, and 28 percent had received at least a master's degree.

To test for job-specific information, these two researchers selected two introductory textbooks which effectively summarized the current research in personnel and used them to construct twenty-two items, nine of which conformed to the research evidence and twelve of which did not. The respondents were requested to either agree or disagree with each statement.

The results of this study were disheartening. Only 19.7 percent of these managers made decisions which conformed to the evidence of research even 70 percent of time; 41.1 percent scored 59 percent or less, and 39.2 percent scored between 60 and 69 percent. Some of the results were startling. For example, 60.7 percent of these executives believed that high job satisfaction is directly related to high productivity, even though research studies have failed to establish such a clear relationship. Moreover, researchers confirmed this lack of a relationship well over thirty years ago.

Similarly, 33.4 percent believed that the optimal span of control is in the range of ten through fifteen, although research indicates that the optimal span is dependent upon such factors as type of technology, educational level of the work force, geographical separation of subordinates, and so forth. Also, 49.4 percent said that the interview is the best method of employee selection, even though research indicates that interviewing is fraught with all types of biases and stereotypes, thus leading to the selection of unqualified candidates in many instances. In fact, research demonstrates that the best predictor of future performance is past performance, which should logically lead to a de-emphasis of interview data. An actual measure of job performance—for example, asking a candidate for a sales job to make a presentation—is typically the best method of employee selection.

A related study of managerial ignorance asked forty-five recognized researchers to identify the most important books and articles in the field of organizational behavior. The researchers then surveyed 200 top-line officers who could conceivably implement such research in their own organizations in order to increase organizational performance. The researcher arrived at the following dismal conclusion:

"The most startling and distressing aspect of these executives' replies is that only a small portion of them *have even heard* of many of the articles and books nominated as 'most significant' by the research or practice in industrial psychology. Even fewer have any firsthand knowledge of the specific nature of the contributions, and only a negligible number state that the contributions have significance for the actual conduct of business."[3]

In short, given the validity of Mintzberg's profile, we should not be surprised that many managers can be judged to be substandard in the area of job-specific knowledge. Admittedly the line manager should not be expected to possess as much expert knowledge of particular areas as the staff manager. Still, the fact that there are very wide gaps in his job-specific knowledge base generates an uneasy feeling as to whether such a manager should be making major organizational decisions.

There are many reasons why managers lack job-specific knowledge. Four of them are: the way managers are selected, the way managers are trained, organizational rewards systems, and information overload.

MANAGERIAL SELECTION

The selection of managers generally appears to be a haphazard process. As indicated above, the research evidence on selection indicates that the best predictor of future performance is past performance. However, research on the selection interview indicates that the interviewer makes up his mind about whether to hire a job candidate within the first three to five minutes.[4] Further, if he changes his mind, the change tends to be from positive to negative. These results occur partly because the interviewer is heavily influenced by stereotypes, preconceived notions about people used in making decisions.

At least partly for this reason, measures of past performance are frequently accorded much less weight by the hiring interviewer than are such extraneous measures as the height, clothes, and attractiveness of the job applicants. H. Steinberg dramatized the importance of such extraneous factors by dressing a young man applying for a managerial position in two contrasting styles: an adequate but nondescript middle-class style, and an elegant upper-middle-class style.[5] In the nondescript style of dress, the job applicant was usually rejected for the job, and sometimes he could not even get by the secretary to obtain a job interview. In the elegant style, he experienced no problems in obtaining a job interview, and almost always received a job offer.

Sadly, business executives and authors actually demean measures of past performance which would encourage the strengthening of job-related knowledge bases and the improvement of individual and organizational performance. For example, J. Livingston studied a sample of graduates of the Harvard Business School, and concluded in a widely-cited article that those with the higher grades were *less* successful in their careers.[6] He ignored, however, a substantial body of research evidence indicating that there is a low but statistically significant positive correlation between grades in school and career success. We would expect such a result, given the concept that past performance is the best predictor of future performance, and grades represent one category—but only one—of past performance. Moreover, the graduates of the Harvard Business School constitute a select group, and there is not a sufficient amount of variance in Livingston's study upon which meaningful generalizations can be based.

MANAGEMENT TRAINING

A related cause of managerial ignorance is management training. James Hayes, President of the American Management Association, had estimated that over 500,000 managers receive some form of management training every year in the United States. Approximately $100 billion is spent annually on both employee and managerial training in the United States.

However, the types of managerial training programs currently available stress the importance of behavioral sensitivity to others and general decision-making ability. Much less common is the management training program that summarizes the research and current issues in a particular area, such as accounting or finance, and reviews new analytical techniques. This movement away from job-specific training increases as organizational level rises.

The failure to update periodically the knowledge bases of executives is particularly glaring since the knowledge acquired in undergraduate or MBA programs quickly becomes dated. Moreover, the problem of updating knowledge bases seems to be becoming more serious. An engineer's education in 1970 had a half-life of about five years; that is, half of what is learned in college becomes obsolete in five years.[7] In 1940, this half life was twelve years. While the length of time before obsolescence occurs may be greater in the functional fields of business than in engineering, managers overseeing activities is these areas would still greatly benefit from a periodic updating of their knowledge bases.

REWARDS SYSTEMS

Why has managerial ignorance become such a problem? The advantages associated with the periodic updating of knowledge bases are obvious. One possible answer is provided by Mintzberg, who has argued that managers don't really have much time for such activities, which require some study and effort.

A more plausible explanation, however, is that American organizations have constructed punishment-oriented reward systems in which the acquiring of knowledge is of much less importance than many other activities, particularly sheer survival. An archetypal American success story revolves around the top manager who is hired from outside to shape things up. He immediately fires a large number of the managers in the organization. Given this pattern of behavior, which is described at least once a week in major business publications, it is almost impossible for managers to believe in such ephemeral concepts as company loyalty and organizational commitment.

As so many commentators have pointed out, the opposite situation exists in Japan. Approximately 35 percent of all managers and workers in Japan are guaranteed lifetime employment until the age of 65. In this setting the concepts of organizational commitment and loyalty take on substantive meaning, allowing the managers to spend more time developing knowledge bases and less time worrying about their job security, power relationships among managers, or conflict. In fact, the American firms that effectively guarantee lifetime employment, such as IBM, are noted for having committed managers and workers.

Additionally, the use of punishment-oriented reward systems may account for the well-known penchant of American managers to take a short-run perspective on problems, focusing on yearly and sometimes quarterly changes in the company's stock market value as the prime measure of performance. Some observers argue persuasively that American companies would rather serve existing markets than create new ones, to follow rather than to lead, and to buy existing companies rather than to develop a superior product or process technology.[8] This pattern of behavior requires much less knowledge than a bold, long-term strategy, since the manager does not need to be on top of the latest developments when this approach is used. Thus a vicious cycle may well be created. Punishment-oriented reward systems force the manager to focus on the short term, which requires much less of a knowledge base. In turn, this failure to develop the knowledge base can easily lead to making decisions that are poor in the long run because the managers fail to take into account key variables.

Further, if authors such as Michael Maccoby are to be believed, a large number of managers spend an excessive amount of time worrying about such issues as power and how to acquire it.[9] From our perspective, at least a part of this time could be more fruitfully employed updating job-specific knowledge bases.

Maccoby's descriptive phrases serve as a case in point. He profiles various types of managers, many of whom are devious and untrustworthy *jungle fighters* motivated primarily by the desire to dominate other managers. Others are *gamesmen*, an emerging type of manager who approaches the managerial job as if it were a game, with his or her source of motivation the contest itself. Maccoby does point out that some managers are *craftsmen* who are motivated by an intrinsic interest in their work and the desire to do a good job. However, while Maccoby does not provide any figures, he suggests that the number of managers who are gamesmen and jungle fighters is increasing. By implication, then, the number of managers interested in updating their job-specific knowledge bases periodically is also decreasing.

INFORMATION OVERLOAD

At least one additional cause of managerial ignorance needs to be addressed: the explosion of knowledge and the information overload that accompanies it. Managers are drowning in paper, and they experience great difficulty trying to make sense of all the information available. They are not alone, as almost everyone in modern America experiences this problem. Lewis Lapham, former editor of *Harper's*, makes the following observation on this point:

"Who now can make sense of the surfeit of information? Even a middle-level executive at a middle-level brokerage firm receives 500 household advisories a week (not to mention subscriptions to trade journals, the daily and financial press); dossiers of equivalent bulk circulate at every level of authority within the corridors of any American institution large enough to boast of its presence in the twentieth century. What then must be the data base provided for the officials holding the higher places in the bureaucracy the size of the State or Treasury departments? Who has the time to read what they have to read?

"The more people know, the less they know. To the extent that society as a whole expands and complicates its acquisition of knowledge, so the individual members of society find less and less to say to one another on any level of meaning beyond the reach of Mike Wallace."[10]

It is little wonder that managers dislike reading and reflection and prefer live information that can be obtained through face-to-face contacts. Still, managers at all levels in an organization are involved in planning, and planning requires some study and reflection which I hope is accompanied by a thorough understanding of the problems facing the organization. Such a thorough understanding presumes a well-developed knowledge base periodically updated. These, then, are the four major causes of the problem of substandard managerial knowledge bases. Fortunately, there are some possible solutions to the problem.

BETTER WAYS TO SELECT AND TRAIN

One of the most ambitious attempts to improve the selection process, undertaken by the life insurance industry, recognizes both the glaring weaknesses associated with the selection interview and its absolute necessity in most hiring decisions. This industry developed a three-day workshop designed specifically for training interviewers who hire life insurance agents. The workshop itself revolves around the work performed by life insurance agents and the development of a profile of a successful life insurance agent. More important, this interview format has been validated; that is, the decisions made in accordance with the criteria specified during the training sessions tend to result in the hiring of successful life insurance agents. Conceivably, this type of selection strategy could be used to hire managers.

A related approach is the use of an assessment center. Over 20,000 companies now use some form of an assessment center designed to evaluate the managerial career potential of job candidates. Although practices vary widely, almost all assessment centers involve some exercises that measure the individual's ability to function under pressure, such as having the candidates discuss a problem in a group while being observed by psychologists and experienced managers. Similarly, some assessment centers employ the in-basket training exercise in which the individual is informed that he must assume the responsibilities of his superior, who has been hospitalized. Usually a telephone is available, as is a list of phone numbers that the candidate can call as he attempts to solve the problems given him.

In recent years, assessment centers have been used not only for selection but managerial development. Periodically a manager will return to the company's assessment center to identify weaknesses that he must overcome during the next phase of his career.

However, assessment centers do not directly address the issue of job-specific knowledge that a manager requires. Normally there are no sessions devoted to updating the manager's knowledge base.

One solution is to incorporate into the assessment centers some traditional methods of training such as the lecture, which are very effective in conveying information, or to use these methods independently. However, managers typically dislike this type of traditional training because of its passive nature. As an alternative, managers could be required to read an introductory textbook or a series of articles prior to the training and to analyze cases tailored to their own organizations whose solutions would be directly related to this reading. Ideally, each case would describe an actual organizational problem and the manner in which the manager completing the training solved it. In addition, the presentation of each case would be *incomplete*: all participants would be given *only* the xeroxed problem description, and they would propose solutions before each presenter would discuss his solution after which the participants would critique this solution. Hence the training would be simultaneously highly interactive and focused on the acquisition of knowledge.

An alternative approach that some organizations use is to sponsor periodic "new concepts" seminars throughout the year. Such seminars can be held early in the morning or during lunch hours, and they can be repeated to ensure that managers who must miss one session have a chance to attend the same session later. Each session should be kept relatively short, approximately one or two hours.

As part of the "new concepts" seminars, or independent of them, outside speakers can be invited. However, management should ensure that these outside speakers are on the frontiers of their respective fields, or at least have something meaningful to say. There are several celebrated speakers who are quite entertaining, many of whom have built their reputations on the develop- ment of relatively simplistic theories that researchers have disproven or never really taken seriously. In some cases, the theory has been considered invalid for several years, and organizations which implement it on the advice of an entertaining speaker are doing themselves a grave disservice. Conversations with their own staff, the staff of other organizations with solid research reputations, and academic researchers should help management to identify significant opinion leaders who could serve as effective speakers. Alterna- tively, corporations could complete questionnaire surveys periodically similar to the survey conducted by Dunnette and Brown described above, focusing specifically on significant books and articles as judged by recognized researchers. Authors of the most significant research studies could then be in- vited to make a presentation.

Receptions after these seminars can serve the dual purpose of increasing in- teraction among organizational members and providing an opportunity for them to discuss informally the concepts to which they have been exposed.

Additionally, training can be patterned after the "great books" training programs that were popular during the 1950s. The original "great books" programs featured the reading of "classics" by such writers as Plato and Aristotle. However, attendees at these programs were actually more anti- business after the training than before it, an understandable outcome given the anti-business bias of many classical writers. But it should be possible to develop a "great books program in management" that would feature both serious read- ing and group discussions.

Finally, it is possible to attach job-specific managerial ignorance by stressing self-training. Management can make available books, articles, and programmed tests for executives to read. Significant readings can be identified by the periodic surveys of recognized researchers described above, and managers can be encouraged to be familiar with them.

Unfortunately, most business firms and government agencies make minimal efforts in this area, and at best operate a small library that is frequently placed in a virtually inaccessible room in a large office building. Such libraries could be supplemented by small reading rooms distributed throughout the managerial working areas. The cost of this undertaking, when compared to the upkeep of a library, is quite reasonable, and makes it easy for managers to read during lunch breaks, before work, and at any other time they find convenient. At the same time, top management sponsorship of such reading rooms would directly indicate its concern about the updating of managerial knowledge bases.

As part of self-training, management can encourage executives to learn from one another by providing opportunities for them to interact frequently. As suggested above, receptions following seminars help achieve this. Some universities sponsor daily afternoon coffee hours within each department or professional school. When ever feasible, business firms might move in this direction, which can be a welcome alternative to managers taking coffee alone at their desks.

REWARDS AND INFORMATION OVERLOAD

As suggested previously, American firms tend to reward short-run managerial success. A manager comes into the organization, shakes it up through terminating many long-term and loyal executives, and produces short-term profits. In the long-run, however, the organization may well be destroyed, because the managerial work force is demoralized by such behavior, and the best performers often leave. Such a shake-up manager tends to leave before the true magnitude of his errors is discovered, and goes on to compound them in another organization.

There have been some radical suggestions for eliminating this problem. For example, Lester Thurow has argued that managers should not be able to exercise company stock options for ten years after leaving a company. Others are working on more conservative approaches.

From our perspective, both long-term and short-term behavior should be rewarded. As we have argued, a manager would be more interested in new developments and increasing his job-specific knowledge if he realized that he could not succeed by employing only short-term tactics, which are less taxing and require much less knowledge than long-term strategies. Some organizations have begun to move in this direction and, at the same time, to apply modern psychological theory to their reward systems. For example, Black and Decker does not give all of its executives a yearly bonus, since such fixed rewards do not constitute an effective motivational strategy when managers come to expect them. Rather, a top level committee at Black and Decker meets periodically and identifies the managers who will receive bonuses for their outstanding performance. It is possible to receive no bonus for several years, and then to receive two bonuses within six months. In this fashion Black and Decker communicates to is managers its concern with both the short run and the long run.

Perhaps the most formidable cause of job-specific managerial ignorance is information overload. We have already suggested some solutions, such as "new concepts" management training and reading rooms. There are others, including speed reading and writing or communication courses and the publication of a newsletter summarizing the latest developments, articles and books. However, these methods involve the managers only passively. Hence it is relatively easy for a harried manager to justify his failure to take advantage of such reading.

Still, it is quite possible that managers themselves will begin to grapple more effectively with the problem of information overload if organizational rewards systems reflect the importance of possessing job-specific knowledge. As the psychological literature has shown, one of the most common methods, if not the most common method, of handling a major problem is escape, which is how managers seem to be responding to information overload. If organizations actually want managers to possess a wealth of knowledge, they should emphasize this fact through alterations of organizational reward systems. Even though managers will always face the problem of information overload, alteration of organizational reward systems should provide additional time for increasing knowledge bases that had previously been allocated to wasteful or less essential organizational activities.

The problem of updating knowledge bases constantly confronts managers. There are no easy solutions. If, however, organizations begin to address the problem, or at least recognize it, the benefits can be enormous, not only for the organization but for the individual manager and his career.

References

1. H. Mintzberg, *The Nature of Managerial Work* (Englewood Cliffs, N.J.: Prentice-Hall, 1980).
2. M. Gannon and J. Noon, "Management's Critical Deficiency," *Business Horizons*, January-February 1971: 49-56.
3. M. Dunnette and Z. Brown, "Behavioral Science Research and the Conduct of Business," *Academy of Management Journal*, 1968: 177-188.
4. E. Webster, *Decision Making in the Employment Interview* (Montreal: McGill University, Applied Psychology Centre, 1964).
5. H. Steinberg, "Your Wardrobe Is Your Weapon," MBA, 1975: 45-49.
6. J. Livingston, "Pygmalion in Management," *Harvard Business Review*, July-August 1969: 81-89.
7. G. Dalton and P. Thompson, "Accelerating Obsolescence of Older Engineers," *Harvard Business Review*, September-October 1971: 57-67.
8. R. Hayes and W. Abnerathy, "Managing Our Way to Economic Decline," *Harvard Business Review*, July-August 1980: 67-77.
9. M. Maccoby, *The Gamesman: The New Corporate Leader* (New York: Simon and Schuster, 1977).
10. L. Lapham, "Gilding the News," *Harper's*, July 1981: 31-39.

Martin J. Gannon is a Professor of Management and Organizational Behavior at the University of Maryland in College Park.

16.

MATCHING EFFECTIVE HR PRACTICES WITH COMPETITIVE STRATEGY

Randall S. Schuler
Steven P. Galante
Susan E. Jackson

> To effectively compete in today's demanding marketplace, a company must develop a clear-cut strategy buttressed by coordinated HR practices. The best competitive strategy will fail unless an organization has a blend of the right skills and practices to make it work. This happy combination is never a coincidence; it demands foresight and planning.

When companies want to gain an advantage in the marketplace, they generally use one of three competitive strategies: cost reduction, quality improvement, or innovation. These strategies are most effective when they are systematically coordinated with human resources management practices. Put simply, different competitive strategies call for quite different skills and behaviors from employees.

It is our contention that employers continuously determine what characteristics their employees will exhibit by making decisions about an array of highly specific human resources practices. (Whether they make these decisions consciously or not is another matter.) These practices include personnel planning, staffing, appraisal, compensation, training and development, and labor relations. It is our belief that companies can improve the environment for success by making choices about these human resources practices that are consistent with and support their chosen strategy. The process will be facilitated, moreover, if the human resources director—the personnel manager of yore—is admitted into the circle of strategic planners and "deputized" to be an agent of change in the company.

This article first looks at the link between the three competitive strategies and human resources practices. Then it describes a framework for assuring that the two are made compatible. Finally, it illustrates the process by showing how one $20 million business wrestled with these issues until it found the right fit between strategy and human resources management.

A TRIO OF CHOICES

A company or corporate division makes its strategic choices to gain a competitive advantage over rivals, but each strategic choice has broad implications for human resources practices.

A *cost-reduction strategy* is typically an attempt to gain the upper hand by becoming the industry's lowest-cost producer. Tight controls, overhead minimization, and economies of scale are hallmarks of this strategy. Productivity is the primary goal. Translated into HR terms, this strategy often involves payroll reductions. Since 1980, the labor force has shrunk 17% in textiles, almost 30% in primary metals, and 40% in steel. Chrysler, Ford, and even AT&T have taken this painful approach to cost reduction.

Lower costs can also be achieved by lowering wage rates. One way to do this is to relocate plants to states with cheaper labor. Whirlpool, Electrolux, and other makers of household appliances have taken this route. Another approach is to negotiate wage concessions from unionized workers; Continental and Eastern have done this in the airline industry. Altogether, by trimming the workforce and lowering wages, American manufacturers have improved their productivity an average of 4.1% annually over the past four years, compared with a 1.2% average annual improvement in the rest of the economy.[1]

The strategy of *improving quality* achieves two aims simultaneously: It helps a business 1) establish a reputation for reliability and quality among customers and 2) improve its operating efficiencies by minimizing scrap and "redos." To carry out this strategy, an employer must foster among employees a commitment to continually improve quality. This implies obtaining suggestions from employees and, even more, letting employees know their suggestions are welcomed and heeded.

At Corning Glass Works, for example, good ideas for product improvement often come from employees. To carry out those ideas, Corning lets its workers form short-lived "corrective action teams." Corning also encourages workers to submit written "methods improvement requests" to their supervisors. These are more than suggestion-box offerings; Corning makes sure these requests get prompt, formal replies so that employees aren't left in the dark about the fate of their proposals. In terms of HR practices, Corning's policies imply the need for feedback systems. Teamwork must be permitted and facilitated. Decision making and responsibility must be part of everyone's job description. And job classifications need to be flexible.

The third possible strategy, *innovation*, is designed to set a company's products or services apart from those of its competitors. Because the imperative in this strategy is to produce a unique product, conditions for creativity and innovation (essentially, for internal entrepreneurship) must be created. These conditions can be created either formally—through official corporate policy—or informally.

Campbell Soup is an example of a company that has taken formal steps to promote innovation. Under the directions of President R. Gordon McGovern, the company was split into some 50 independent business units, each with a charter to develop new products. The results are impressive. In a 5-year period, Campbell introduced 334 new products—far more than such larger competitors as Beatrice, Nestle, or General Foods. A less systematic, although no less successful, effort to foster innovation is 3M's informal doctrine of allowing employees to bootleg 15% of their time to work on their own projects.

An innovation strategy has a number of implications for HR policies. Employees must be given more discretion to act on their own. Controls must be flexible. There must be ample investment in human resources, including the provision of resources for experimentation. Failure must be allowed and even occasionally rewarded.

STUDYING THE MENUS

The above examples provide only the barest outlines of some links between strategies and HR practices. In fact, there is a systematic way to meld the two. It begins by recognizing that there are many HR choices to be made, and that at various times some are more appropriate than others. Decisions about human resources management can be viewed as making selections from six HR practice "menus." As Exhibit 1 shows, each menu concerns a different aspect of HR management: planning, staffing, appraising, compensating, training and development, and labor/management relations. In each of these areas, a company (or corporate division) must make a number of decisions. Notice that each of the choices runs along a continuum. Most of the options are self-explanatory, but a rundown of one of the menus will illustrate how the process works. Let's look at staffing, for example.

The first choice on the staffing menu involves deciding on the source from which to recruit applicants. At one extreme, companies can rely on the internal labor market—e.g., other departments in the firm and other levels in the organizational hierarchy. At the other extreme, companies can rely exclusively on the external labor market. Although this distinction may not be significant for entry-level jobs, it is a very important one for most other jobs. Recruiting internally essentially means a policy of promotion from within. This commits a firm to providing training and career-development opportunities if the promoted employees are to perform well.

The next decision is whether to establish broad or narrow career paths. The broader the paths, the greater the opportunities for employees to acquire skills in many functional areas and to gain exposure and visibility throughout the firm. Both of these consequences enhance an employee's opportunities for promotion. However, the time frame for this skill-acquisition process is likely to be much longer than that required for the acquisition of more limited skills. Thus promotion may be quicker under a policy of narrow career paths, yet they may limit an employee's career opportunities more over the long run.

Exhibit 1
HR Management Practice Menus*

Planning Choices

Informal ←⟶ Formal
Short term ←⟶ Long term
Explicit job analysis ←⟶ Implicit job analysis
Job simplification ←⟶ Job enrichment
Low employee involvement ←⟶ High employee involvement

Staffing Choices

Internal sources ←⟶ External sources
Narrow career paths ←⟶ Broad career paths
Single ladder ←⟶ Multiple ladders
Explicit promotion criteria ←⟶ Implicit promotion criteria
Limited socialization ←⟶ Extensive socialization
Closed procedures ←⟶ Open procedures

Appraising Choices

Behavioral criteria ←⟶ Results criteria
Purposes: Development, Remedial, Maintenance
Low employee participation ←⟶ High employee participation
Short-term criteria ←⟶ Long-term criteria
Individual criteria ←⟶ Group criteria

Compensating Choices

Low base salaries ←⟶ High base salaries
Internal equity ←⟶ External equity
Few perks ←⟶ Many perks
Standard, fixed package ←⟶ Flexible package
Low participation ←⟶ High participation
No incentives ←⟶ Many incentives
Short-term incentives ←⟶ Long-term incentives
No employment security ←⟶ High employment security
Hierarchical ←⟶ Egalitarian

Training and Development Choices

Short term ←⟶ Long term
Narrow application ←⟶ Broad application
Unplanned, unsystematic ←⟶ Planned, systematic
Individual orientation ←⟶ Group orientation
Low participation ←⟶ High participation

Labor/Management Relations Choices

Traditional ←⟶ Nontraditional

---

* Adapted from R. S. Schuler, "Human Resource Management Practice Choices," in R. S. Schuler, S. A. Youngblood, and V. L. Huber (eds) *Readings in Personnel and Human Resource Management,* 3rd ed., West Publishing, 1987.

Another staffing choice to be made is whether to establish one or several promotion ladders. Establishing several ladders increases the opportunities for employees to be promoted within a given technical speciality without having to assume managerial responsibilities. Establishing just one promotion ladder enhances the relative value of a promotion and increases the competition to get it.

Part and parcel of a promotion system are the criteria used in deciding whom to promote. The criteria can vary from very explicit to very implicit. The more explicit the criteria, the less adaptable the promotion system is to exceptions and changing circumstances. What the firm loses in flexibility, however, the employee gains in clarity, although this clarity may benefit only those who fulfill the criteria exactly. The more implicit the criteria, the greater the flexibility to move employees around and develop them more broadly.

Once a firm has hired or promoted an employee, it must decide how extensive the socialization will be. With minimal socialization, firms convey few informal rules and establish few procedures to immerse employees in the cul-

---

Exhibit 2
Twelve Employee Characteristics
for Strategy Execution*

1. Highly repetitive, ⟷ Highly creative,
   predictable behavior   innovative behavior
2. Very short-term ⟷ Very long-term focus
   focus
3. Highly cooperative, ⟷ Highly independent,
   interdependent   autonomous behavior
   behavior
4. Very low concern ⟷ Very high concern
   for quality   for quality
5. Very low concern ⟷ Very high concern
   for quantity   for quantity
6. Very low risk ⟷ Very high risk taking
   taking
7. Very high concern ⟷ Very high concern for
   for process   results
8. High preference to ⟷ High preference to
   avoid responsibility   assume responsibility
9. Very inflexible to ⟷ Very flexible to change
   change
10. Very comfortable ⟷ Very tolerant of am-
    with stability   biguity and unpre-
    dictability
11. Narrow skill appli- ⟷ Broad skill application
    cation
12. Low job (firm) ⟷ High job (firm)
    involvement   involvement

* Adapted from R. S. Schuler, "Human Resource Management Practice Choices," in R. S. Schuler, S. A. Youngblood, and V. L. Huber (eds) *Readings in Personnel and Human Resource Management*, 3rd ed., West Publishing, 1987.

ture and practices of the organization. Although it is probably easier and cheaper to do this than to provide maximum socialization, employees will likely feel a weak psychological attachment and commitment to the firm.

A final choice is the degree of openness in the staffing procedures. The more open the procedures, the more likely there is to be job posting for internal recruitment and self-nomination for promotion. To facilitate a policy of openness, firms need to make the relevant information available to employees. Such a policy is worthwhile, since it allows employees to select which jobs they want. This is critical to a successful job/person fit. The more secret the staffing procedures, the more employee involvement is limited in selection decisions, but decisions can be made faster.

THE RIGHT FIT

Employees obviously exhibit a wide variety of work-related characteristics. Exhibit 2 identifies 12 characteristics that we believe to be most influential in deciding whether strategies succeed or fail. Notice that they are not either/or in nature but, like the menu choices, range along a continuum.

The strategically driven company must instill in and elicit from its employees the characteristics that best support its chosen strategy. It can achieve this by choosing the human resources practices that provide the best "fit" with that strategy. Exhibit 3 shows which employee characteristics and human resources management practices provide the best fit for each of the three strategies.

The cost-reduction strategic fit. Companies pursuing a cost-reduction strategy, for example, need employees whose behaviors are relatively repetitive and predictable. Employees must focus on short-term results, and they must work primarily autonomously. Their workstations are typically discrete units—i.e., assembly-line positions. The workers should focus primarily on quantity of output and secondly on quality. They should not be risk takers, and they should be disinclined to seek greater responsibility. They should be attracted to job stability and less interested in change. Their skills must be narrowly focused. Finally, significant psychological commitment to the job or company is not required.

What do these desired employee behaviors imply for HR practices? Several things are immediately obvious: An employer should opt for low levels of employee participation in activities such as writing job descriptions, doing performance reviews, and determining salary adjustments. Both job criteria and career paths should be narrowly focused. The company should stress short-term and results-oriented criteria when doing performance appraisals. HR needs to set up only minimal employee training and development since repetitive and predictable behavior is primarily required. Little attention to job security is needed.

Exhibit 3
Matching HR Practices and Employee Characteristics With Competitive Strategies

Cost Reduction Strategy	Quality Improvement Strategy	Innovation Strategy
Employee Characteristics	*Employee Characteristics*	*Employee Characteristics*
Predictable, repetitive behavior	Predictable, repetitive behavior	Creative, innovative behavior
Short-term focus	Intermediate-term focus	Long-term focus
Relatively independent behavior	Some cooperative behavior	Cooperative interdependent behavior
Modest concern for quality	High concern for quality	Modest concern for quality
High concern for quantity	Modest concern for quantity	Modest concern for quantity
High concern for results	High concern for process	Modest concern for process
Low preference for responsibility	Preference for responsibility	Preference for responsibility
Low flexibility to change	Modest flexibility to change	Flexibility to change
Low tolerance of ambiguity	Modest tolerance for ambiguity	High tolerance of ambiguity
Narrow skill application	Modest skill application	Broad skill application
Low job involvement	High job involvement	Modest job involvement
HR Practices	*HR Practices*	*HR Practices*
Low participation	High participation	High participation
Explicit job criteria	Explicit job criteria	Implicit job criteria
Mostly internal sources	Some external sources	External sources
Narrow career paths	Narrow career paths	Broad career paths
Results criteria	Mostly results criteria	Process and results criteria
Short-term criteria	Mostly short-term criteria	Long-term criteria
Mostly individual criteria	Some group criteria	Some group criteria
Little employment security	Some employment security	Some employment security
Few incentives	Some incentives	Many incentives
Hierarchical pay	Egalitarian pay	Egalitarian pay
Little training	Extensive training	Extensive training
Traditional labor/ management relations	Cooperative labor/ management relations	Cooperative labor/ management relations

The quality-improvement strategic fit. A strategy that stresses quality improvement dictates a separate set of employee characteristics and different choices about human resources practices. The major difference will obviously be in employee orientation toward quality. Quality will become significantly more important than quantity. To achieve quality, employees need to be highly aware of the process by which the company makes or delivers goods and services. In addition, employees must have a moderate interest in assuming greater responsibility, as well as a significant degree of psychological identification with the company. There is also a greater need for employees to work cooperatively and interdependently. And their focus must be on the intermediate term, which is when quality begins to yield results.

As a result, a company's HR practices, including a measure of job security, must foster employee identification with and participation in corporate affairs. For example, employees should be involved to a significant degree in writing job descriptions, doing performance appraisals, making compensation decisions, and the like. They should also be provided with extensive training in job and group-process skills. Training in group dynamics, for instance, hastens the establishment and effectiveness of quality circles. Incentives should be provided to encourage both individual and group suggestions for all quality improvements that are made.

The innovation strategic fit. Companies pursuing an innovation strategy need employees that are highly creative and flexible to change. The employees must be tolerant of ambiguity and unpredictability; after all, innovation means they are treading on unchartered ground. They need to be risk takers, and they should prefer to assume responsibility. A broad range of skills is important. The newness of the tasks at hand will require employees to work cooperatively and interdependently. They will also need a moderate level of psychological involvement with their jobs and the firm. Employees must also be moderately concerned with both quality and quantity of production. The focus should be equally on the process by which the company generates its product or service and on the achievement of results. Finally, because the results of innovation are often not immediately visible, employees must have a long-term focus.

HR management in an innovative environment must give employees broadly written and even somewhat ambiguous job descriptions. The firm must encourage high levels of employee participation in areas such as personnel planning and appraisal. Because cooperation and interdependence are desirable, HR should use both individual and group-focused performance criteria and compensation incentives. The company will want to establish broad career paths to reinforce the development of a broad range of skills. And performance appraisal criteria must be long term and based on both process and results.

THE EXPERIENCE OF FROST INC.

One company that has made an exactingly conscious effort to match competitive strategy with HR management practices is Frost Inc., a Grand Rapids, Michigan, manufacturer with sales of $20 million. Frost, founded in 1913 as a maker of furniture hardware, shifted after World War II to producing overhead conveyer trolleys, primarily for the auto industry. Charles D. "Chad" Frost, the great-grandson of the founder, acquired control of the business in the 1970s.

Concerned about depending too heavily on one cyclical industry, Chad Frost made several attempts to diversify the business, first into lawn mower components and later into material-handling systems, such as floor conveyers and hoists. "It was a total failure," Frost says. "Every time we'd try to make a new product, we screwed up." The company engineers didn't know how to design unfamiliar components, the production people didn't know how to make them, and the salespeople didn't know how to sell them. Frost diagnosed the problem as inflexibility. "We had single-purpose machines and single-purpose people, including single-purpose managers."

Frost decided automating production was the key to flexibility. The company decided to replace its 26 old-fashioned screw machines on the factory floor with 11 numerical-controlled machine tools paired with 18 industrial robots. It decided to design and build an automated storage-and-retrieval inventory control system, which Frost would later sell as a proprietary product. And it decided to completely automate the front office to reduce indirect labor costs. It formally launched the program in late 1983.

What at first glance appeared to be a hardware-oriented strategy turned out to be an exercise in human resources management. "If you're going to reap a real benefit in renovating a small to medium-sized company, the machinery is just one part, perhaps the easiest part of the renovation project," says Robert McIntyre, head of Amprotech Inc., an affiliated consulting company Frost formed early in the automation project to provide an objective, "outside" view. "The hardest part is getting people to change."

Frost was clearly embarking on a strategy of innovation. As it turns out, many of the choices the company made about human resources practices encouraged the employee characteristics we have identified as being crucial to the success of an innovation strategy.

For example, Frost immediately set out to increase employee identification with the company by giving each worker 10 shares of the closely held company and by referring to them henceforth as "shareholder/employees." The share ownership, which employees can increase by making additional purchase through a 401K plan, is also intended to give employees a long-term focus—another behavior important to a successful innovation strategy. Additional long-term incentives consisted of a standard corporate profit-sharing plan and a discretionary profit-sharing plan administered by Chad Frost.

Frost's compensation package was also restructured to strike a balance between employee concern for results—i.e., productivity—and the process by which goods get manufactured. In Frost's case, the latter was a significant consideration, since the production process was at the heart of the company's innovation strategy. The company instituted a quarterly bonus that is based on companywide productivity and established a "celebration fund" that managers can tap at their discretion to reward deserving employees.

By making the quarterly bonus dependent on companywide productivity, Frost is encouraging cooperative, interdependent behavior. The celebration fund, meanwhile, is used to reward and reinforce innovative behavior. (Even the form of the celebration can be creative. While most rewards are as simple as a lunch with Chad Frost or, at most, a weekend for an employee and spouse at the local Marriott Hotel, one employee was granted his unusual request to have a belly dancer perform in the office!)

Frost encourages cooperative behavior in a number of other ways as well. Most of the offices have no doors in order to foster communications. For example, Chad Frost's "office" is simply a large open area at the end of the hallway. This allows employees easy access. Most executive perks have been eliminated, including reserved parking spaces and getting paychecks two days before other workers. All employees are trusted with access to the company's mainframe computer (with the exception of payroll information) via more than 40 computer terminals scattered around the front office and factory floor.

Vital to any innovation strategy, in our view, is getting employees to broaden their skills, assume greater responsibilities, and take risks. Frost encourages employees to broaden their skills by paying for extensive training programs, both at the company and at local colleges. But Frost goes even further by identifying the development of additional skills as advancement in its own right. This is partly out of necessity, since Frost has compressed its eleven previous levels of hierarchy into just four in order to speed decision making. This makes it harder to reward employees through traditional promotions. Now, Frost employees are challenged to advance continuously by adding skills, assuming more responsibilities, and testing the limits of their abilities.

ALL IN THE EXECUTION

When fitting HR practices to a firm's competitive strategy, several key points must be kept in mind. The first is that human resources practices, if they are to be changed, should be changed and implemented all at once. Failure to invoke one practice implies that another is being invoked (perhaps unwittingly or unintentionally), and this is likely to stimulate and reinforce employee characteristics that are incompatible with the selected strategy. The results are conflict, ambiguity, and frustration.

Needed here is a human resources director to monitor the fit between competitive strategy and human resources management practices. This person should combine the strategic role with the role of change agent. Because of its attendant uncertainty, most change in organizations is not easy to effectuate. Having a human resources director skilled in the change process can enhance the transition from one set of human resources practices to another.

Does all this really work? Yes it does. Firms that successfully implement competitive strategies, however, have recognized and respected individual differences. Not all employees desire to change or are willing to accept change. For these employees, effective firms provide outplacement assistance.

Successful firms also place their strategic imperative above the hierarchical imperative. That is, they make decisions about selection, recruitment, compensation, and appraisal practices for strategy-related reasons; they do not permit differences in these practices to exist primarily for status or collar-color reasons.

Finally, in strategically successful companies, top management stands behind the attempt to gain competitive advantage and believes that people matter in determining success or failure. This belief was nicely captured by former Citibank CEO Walter Wriston, who said: "I believe the only game in town is the personnel game . . . My theory is if you have the right people in the right place, you don't have to do anything else. If you have the wrong person in the job, there's no management system known to man that can save you."

Reference

1. *Business Week*, Nov. 17, 1986.

Randall S. Schuler is professor of the Graduate School of Business, New York University. Steven P. Galante is a staff reporter on The Wall Street Journal. Susan E. Jackson is associate professor in the Department of Psychology at New York University.

17.

UP TO SPEED IN 90 DAYS: AN ORIENTATION PLAN

H. Lon Addams

> His or her first weeks on the job are management's best opportunity to set the tone for a worker's entire period of employment, but the opportunity is often overlooked. Use this complete 90-day program to open lines of communication that can improve morale, productivity and employee/management relations.

How many times has an employee thrown up his or her arms in disgust and exclaimed, "I never knew I was supposed to do it that way!"

Chances are that the exclamation is only the final outburst in a series of frustrating incidents that began the day the employee started the job.

Employee performance is often directly related to attitude, and therefore shaping a positive attitude must begin on the first day of work and continue throughout the first few months.

The first weeks on the job are the best opportunity management has to set the tone for a worker's entire period of employment, but the opportunity is often overlooked.

Invaluable lines of communication can be established at the outset. What are the potential results? Consider the following:

- Improved employee morale
- Improved relations between employees and managers
- Fewer employee errors on the job
- Improved understanding of company policies and procedures
- Better customer service
- Better understanding of company benefits.

As appealing as these results may be, they are not easy to achieve. Effective orientation programs depend on clear, concise explanations of the basics: essential company policies, employee benefits, corporate procedures, organizational structure.

This process is best illustrated by outlining an orientation program that has proven to be successful.

PEOPLE ARE CRUCIAL TO SUCCESSFUL ORIENTATION

An effective orientation program depends heavily on three people: the new employee, his or her supervisor, and a personnel department representative.

Successful programs also depend on adequate time. The best programs feed information to new employees in stages—over the course of several weeks.

Unsuccessful programs often cram employee brains with detail after detail, usually during the first hour of the first workday. Orientation information is best understood if dispersed over time, in segments.

First day. On the first day, the new employee should meet for approximately three hours with the personnel department representative. This is an informal This is an informal session; the format might be something like this:

- The personnel department representative welcomes each new employee individually.
- Employee forms are completed and returned to the personnel department.
- A supervisor checklist is briefly discussed and given to each new employee to give to his or her supervisor.
  This checklist helps the supervisor remember specific items to be discussed during his or her portion of the orientation activities.
- A brochure outlining immediate concerns (such as pay) is briefly discussed.
- The company's organization chart and map of department locations is reviewed.
- A recent company newsletter is given to the new employee.
- A performance review form is discussed.

Next, the personnel department representative takes the new employee to lunch and subsequently helps locate his or her supervisor.

The employee's supervisor then spends whatever time is needed to review the supervisor checklist form. The nitty-gritty everyday procedures are discussed.

This is the time to begin building rapport between the new employee and his or her supervisor. Following their discussion, the supervisor and the new employee both initial the supervisor checklist form, which is then returned to the personnel department.

Next, the supervisor should conduct a tour of surrounding company facilities. Having already determined an appropriate "buddy" the supervisor implements the buddy system by introducing the new employee to his "friend."

· This buddy congenially answers questions and introduces the new employee to other key employees who many be interacting with the new employee.

Second day. The second day is a prime time for the supervisor to answer questions that arose the first day. The supervisor should sit down with the new employee, listen, and answer questions thoughtfully.

The other dimension of this interview involves the performance review form. Together, the supervisor and employee discuss the employee's expected performance.

At this time, the supervisor should note the mutually agreed upon goals and expectations on the form. After 30 days, and again after 90 days, the employee's actual performance should be outlined on the form, which should then be returned to the personnel department.

The purpose of the form is to acquaint the employee with supervisor expectations and to prompt the supervisor to articulate those expectations. Thus, there should be *no surprises* at the end of the typical 90-day probation period.

Two weeks. After the employee has been aboard two weeks, he or she should attend an all-morning formal session with the personnel department representative and other new employees.

The purpose of this session is to acquaint new employees with company policies and employee benefits not previously discussed. The best approach is to use a slide/sound program.

Slides can be updated; a movie cannot. A good slide/sound presentation can be interesting, informative and relaxing. Of equal importance is the fact that an effective presentation should leave the employee with the message, "We [management] care about you. We made this a professional presentation—you're worth the time and money it took."

This formal presentation should emphasize that the new employee is very much a part of a viable organization. Such "family spirit" can be achieved in several ways. For example, the personnel department representative can:

- Build company spirit by explaining interesting company history and the importance of company products and/or services.
- Introduce top management and the various department managers within the company. Invite the president to personally share company philosophy with the new employee.
- Emphasize the essential role of the individual employee in the organization.

Much can be covered in this formal orientation session, but don't overdo it. Some topics—such as insurance—need only cursory coverage at this point. Possible goals and topics for the orientation include:

Building pride in the organization. Help the employee feel proud of his or her new company by explaining corporate history, purpose (products and/or services), goals, and the importance of each employee. The latter point can be emphasized using a company organization chart.

Outlining company policies and procedures. Provide basic information on such company responsibilities as payroll, overtime compensation, performance evaluations, advancement opportunities, salary increases, working schedules and training.

At the same time, corresponding employee responsibilities, such as attitude and performance, attendance and punctuality, dress code and related policies, and maintenance of company property, should be discussed.

Communicating employee benefits. Employee benefits should also be discussed. Specific topics to address include holidays, vacation, sick leave, health and accident insurance, dental insurance, life insurance and disability plans, and pension and profit-sharing programs. Any corporate "extras," such as company discounts, educational assistance or a company newsletter, should also be noted.

Explaining employee recognition programs. Finally recognition programs, such as awards for attendance or performance, or suggestion system awards, should be explained.

A copy of the employee handbook should be distributed to each person. The book should be kept at the employee's work station.

The personnel department representative should briefly review the contents and discuss questions with the group. Key company policies and the reasons for them should be emphasized. With a reasonable explanation, employees will more willingly accept a company policy or procedure. Future problems can be averted by discussing such matters at the outset.

The representative should emphasize the importance of knowing the information in the handbook. Many time-consuming questions to supervisors and to the personnel department can be eliminated if the new employee reads and understands the contents of the handbook.

As an incentive to help employees read the handbook, the representative should explain that a brief questionnaire on the handbook contents will be completed by each new employee in two weeks.

This must be mentioned in a positive manner to avoid negative connotation of a quiz.

One month. After an employee has been on the job one month, a personnel department representative should informally visit the new employee. The intent is that he or she can answer any questions the new employee might not feel comfortable asking of the supervisor.

The personnel staff member should administer a written questionnaire to the new employee. This questionnaire simply checks to see if the employee *understands* key policies, procedures, and employee benefits contained in the employees handbook. Any incorrect answers should be discussed.

Lastly, the personnel department representative should pick up the completed 30-day performance appraisal from the supervisor.

This informal meeting is an excellent time for the personnel department representative and the supervisor to communicate about the new employee's performance to date.

Once again, the caring attitude must be reinforced.

Three months. After the new employee has been working three months, the personnel representative should visit the new employee again. Informally, the representative should answer any questions, pick up the 90-day performance review, and determine if the new employee is no longer "new" but "at home."

In many companies, 90 days is considered the employee probation period. Following this model, both the personnel department and the supervisor have hard data to consider.

The 30- and 90-day appraisals tell a great deal about the employee's completion of work goals and about his or her attitude.

Having interacted with the employee several times, the representative can help the supervisor determine how well the new employee has adjusted to the company environment. This two-way communication between the representative and supervisor can substantially reduce the number of "gut instinct" terminations.

The supervisor and personnel department must work together to see that each is up-to-date on the status of the new employee. Each has a different perspective, but both play an integral part in helping new employees feel good about their jobs, the people around them, and the company's management.

Naturally, new employees must do their part in their attitude-building. They must effectively listen, read (company materials, handbooks), ask questions, and act appropriately.

But it's a mistake to expect a new employee to simply "fit in" and adjust to company norms, policies and supervisory expectations without an organized, effective orientation program.

Management that sincerely cares about its employees needs a well-designed orientation program. The model suggested in this article can be tailored, with minor alterations, to help achieve two time-worn company objectives: high employee morale and productivity.

H. Lon Addams is an associate professor in the department of management at Weber State College, Ogden, Utah.

18.

PRIMA DONNAS: LIVING WITH THEM WHEN YOU CAN'T LIVE WITHOUT THEM

Martin Lasden

> They can be both gloriously gifted and abominably abrasive. Because prima donnas are easily bored, in high demand, and notoriously independent, the relationship between them and those they supposedly serve is bound to be an uneasy one, even under the best conditions.

Not all geniuses are jerks. But if you happen to be a jerk, genius can be a tremendous asset. When you can contribute so much to an organization, a multitude of sins is likely to be overlooked. You can be rude and repeatedly see your rudeness go unchallenged; you can be tactless and see your tactlessness go unchecked.

Life can be easy on the gifted or truly brilliant. But, as prima donnas seem to be governed by a different set of rules, life becomes extremely difficult for managers who are responsible for keeping these characters in line. And, while frazzled managers might find comfort in reminders that no one is indispensable, having a supercharged brain on board can be addictive. These pros have the potential to save the irretrievable and solve the inextricable. And, after all, your employees are a reflection on you. Doing what ordinarily can't be done is good for your career, even if more than occasionally you rely on a brilliant subordinate. It can be tough to relinquish a prima donna's formidable talents.

Richard Sorken, vice president of development services for the Bank of California, San Francisco, remembers the time a major software-development project was going down the tubes, plagued by seemingly insurmountable technical problems. That was when, at the 11th hour, he called on Hal, considered the organization's programming genius, to save the day. Many also thought Hal to be opinionated and abrasive, with a knack for alienating co-workers. But, God, was he brilliant—with a mind that could leap through stacks of technical minutiae in a single bound. "Hal turned that project around within 48 hours," Sorken recalls. "He worked 20 hours the first day and 16 hours the next. The users were ecstatic. I can tell you, he'd have to tick off an awful lot of people before I'd get rid of him."

Such is the stuff of ecstasy. But for these moments of ecstasy, how many hours of agony and assaults on staff morale should a good manager bear? Robert Jirout, vice president of information services at the Chicago Board of Trade, puts a limit on the amount of guff he'll take from a prima donna. He remembers how ornery one of his technical hotshots was. "In a single day he could get 2 1/2 times more work done than anybody else," Jirout says, "but he strutted around like he was a god of the technical world. And when he disagreed with you, he'd let you know about it—over and over again." When the superstar caused embarrassment by protesting an internal policy in front of a prospective client, however, he'd gone too far. "I walked him right to the door and took away his key," Jirout recalls. "At that moment, I didn't care how difficult he would be to replace."

Riding on the horns of this dilemma, managers have three options.

There is, first of all, the preemptive approach—tailoring employee selection methods in such a way as to prevent prima donnas from ever being hired in the first place. James Tunis is probably typical of those who advocate this approach. As vice president of corporate services at Lincoln National Life Insurance Co., Fort Wayne, Indiana, Tunis has been burned one too many times. "Too often," he says, "I've essentially been blackmailed. Projects would get to a critical point, and then the prima donna in the group would say, 'Either do it may way or it won't get done.' For a manager, that's a terrible spot to be in."

To guard against this, Tunis now does a lot of what he calls "inoculation" during job interviews. "I do my share of selling," he says, "but I also make it a point to tell prospective employees about the crummy side of the job. I'll tell them the work is not all creative, or traveling is involved, or programs need to be written in Fortran once in a while." Such honesty discourages the most troublesome geniuses from ever getting on the payroll, Tunis says.

That's not to say that all geniuses are rejected. But when it comes to the best and the brightest, Tunis expresses a distinct preference for the very young, and, in fact, actively recruits gifted college students for part-time winter and full-time summer work. "They're just as smart as the prima donnas," he asserts, "but unlike prima donnas, they're hungry, highly motivated, and haven't yet learned just how indispensable they might be."

For managers who are more dazzled by brilliance than fearful of turmoil, the second obvious alternative to keeping prima donna out is to welcome them abroad and then work with them to smooth their roughest edges. Douglas LaBier, a psychoanalyst and senior fellow at the Washington-based Project On Technology, Work and Character, observes that all too often managers unwittingly reward the sadistic and/or grandiose behavior of their hotshots because they are too afraid to call them on it. But attacking the offensive behavior head-on with diligent counseling, LaBier insists, can bring about meaningful improvements.

A case in point occurred at a large computer company LaBier worked with recently. There, a female manager had under her charge a technical wizard with an extremely autocratic manner. After an extended period of uncooperative behavior, she decided to take the initiative by stressing the need for teamwork: If people didn't work together, the work just couldn't get done. Because the manager expressed this message often and stridently enough, the star performer became markedly more cooperative, LaBier reports.

But even under the best conditions, behavior modification is a tenuous proposition—especially if the behavior in question is deeply rooted in the offender's personality—the product, perhaps, of years of conditioning. Exploring the inner workings of the abrasive mindset, psychologist Harry Levinson has suggested that just beneath the bravado of the prima donna, there likely is a terribly insecure person—a perfectionist whose lack of self-esteem is constantly reaffirmed by his or her inability to attain out-of-reach goals. In an article entitled "The Abrasive Personality,"[1] Levinson wrote:

"If a person is always pushing himself toward impossible aspirations and is never able to achieve them, there are two consequences for his emotions. The greater the gap between his ego ideal and self-image, the greater will be both his guilt and anger with himself, for not achieving the dream. And the angrier a person is with himself, the more likely he is to attack himself or drive himself to narrow the gap between his ideal and his present self-image. Only in narrowing the gap can he reduce his feelings of anger, depression, and inadequacy.

"However, as the unconscious drive for perfection is irrational, no degree of conscious effort can possibly achieve the ideal, or decrease the self-punishment such a person brings down on himself for not achieving it. The anger and self-hatred are never-ending, therefore, and build up to the point where they spill over in the form of hostile attacks on peers and subordinates, such as treating them with contempt and condescension.

". . . In fact, the abrasive person's need for self-punishment may be so great that he may take great, albeit neurotic, pleasure in provoking others who will subsequently reject, that is, punish him. In effect, he acts as if he were his own parent, punishing himself as well as others. In the words of psychiatrist Anna Freud, he becomes a good self-hater."

Needless to say, the person Levinson described has serious problems; unless you're a trained psychotherapist, the prospects for reforming such an individual are not promising. This suggests a third option. Not to ban or change the hotshot, but rather to very carefully select assignments where he or she can do the most good while causing the least harm. In other words, what you want to do is isolate the superstar.

"The ideal is to put your prima donna in a separate building, preferably one without heat or water," says Herbert Halbrecht, a Stamford, Conn., headhunter who has dealt with his share of technical geniuses. "They thrive under harsh conditions," he notes. "And when you put these people together, they attack problems with an almost fanatical determination. They're crazy! They're consumed by their creative talent."

Such vacuum-sealed environments, however, are not easy to come by, and often difficult to create. At the First National Bank of Boston, Senior Vice President William Synnott talks about the time he tried, and failed. "I never could find a niche for this one particular fellow," he recalls. "This guy could do almost everything. He had a great mind. But he was extremely rutted in his opinions and during meetings he would try to ram those opinions down people's throats. I tried to isolate him by having him report directly to me, but in the end I had to let him go. He grated on too many people's nerves. My own managers didn't want to deal with him. I couldn't protect him."

For bosses to protect their socially inept geniuses, certain conditions must be met. One area of concern is organizational structure. Is there a way to work around these prima donnas so that they cause the least possible offense? At Digital Equipment Corp. (DEC), in Maynard, Mass., Al Crawford, director of corporate planning, accomplishes this by creating small special task forces set apart from the rest of the organization. The key, Crawford says, is to establish an organizational "buffer"—a structure that is effective all the way down to the infrastructure of specific jobs. Where a certain job might ordinarily entail user contact, for example, if there's an asocial prima donna involved, bosses would be well-advised to break up that job so that user contact is delegated to someone else.

Another critical question to consider here is: When you need a genius to get a job done, who should be the genius' teammates? The best is other geniuses. It works out this way because, as Confucius observed over 2,500 years ago, equals make the best partners. Unequals, on the other hand, tend to get on each other's nerves. Specifically, when hotshots work closely with ordinary mortals, you're likely to see their impatience run up against mortals' exhaustion, their condescension against their co-workers' resentment.

As Bank of California's Sorken affirms: "The genius' standard of excellence is different from everybody else's. And when a project gets to those critical stages when tension naturally builds, the clash between the gifted and not-so-gifted can really start to get on everybody's nerves. It just doesn't work out." Thus, if your genius really needs company, by far the best way to provide it is to hire other masterminds.

A TIGER BY THE TAIL

And then there's the whole question of supervision. Do you need to be a technical hotshot to manage one? Not necessarily, say those who have done it. What certainly is needed, though, is enough managerial experience and self-confidence to be able to keep your authority intact.

"Never let your geniuses engage you in a discussion that you can't understand," warns Geno Tolari, vice president at Informatics General Corp., Palo Alto, Calif. His warning underscores the point that, if you're not careful, the brilliance that can work for you can work against you as well. Allowing a subordinate's mastery of technical particulars to confuse and undermine your sense of purpose is one clear example of this.

To be sure, they can be an intimidating lot, these wizards with strange looks in their eyes, who, given the slightest provocation, will start chanting unintelligible computerese. And it's certainly understandable that managers confronting such powerful magic day in and day out could be prone to miscalculation, and under- or overreaction. Either way, the consequences can be most unfortunate. In the former case, there is the prospect of seeing a total breakdown of authority—the prima donnas running amok. In the latter, there is the danger that the bosses themselves will fall into a knee-jerk mentality; fighting battles that need not be fought, and eventually—for the wrong reasons—driving the gifted away altogether.

The tension often comes to a head when those with exceptional abilities start to demand extraordinary privileges, including, but not limited to, inflated salaries. There are demands made for plush offices, new equipment, flexible hours, trips to esoteric, if not remote, seminars, and work-at-home privileges. The prima donna may actually be worth it all. But there's more involved here than just the value of one individual. There's the integrity of carefully laid corporate policies to consider. How can any rule continue to be respected if visible exceptions are made?

William Harrison, the data processing director at The Hartford (CT) Insurance Co., is inclined to take a tough stand on this issue. "It's wrong to tailor policies to specific individuals," he declares. "It's just too disruptive, and I can't ever remember doing it."

Managers like Chuck Oldenburg, however, are of a different mind. "We have set pay scales and job descriptions around here," says the general manager of computer services at Standard Oil of California, San Francisco. "But where do you find a job description for a genius? I can't give away cars, limousines, or golf-club memberships. So what I try to do is satisfy their special interests."

Sometimes, Oldenburg admits, that does mean breaking the rules. For example, there is one brilliant designer of programmer-productivity tools at Chevron who has a private office. At his level, he's not supposed to have a private office, but he demanded one, and because he was so good and saved the company so much money, he got it. A similarly gifted hotshot comes to work only four days a week. Again, it's against the rules, but working at his terminal at home, he actually puts in the equivalent of a seven-day work week.

Oldenburg acknowledges that management was fearful that such special treatment would stir up resentment among the rest of the staff. "When we allowed this guy to come in four days a week," he says, "we feared the worst: that his colleagues would be lining up at my door. But it didn't happen. People recognized that he was a genius and that he got twice as much work done as anybody else." In all, Oldenburg counts about a dozen among his 1,200-person staff who are gifted enough to be eligible for such privileges.

But perhaps the most precious corporate asset the prima donna puts a claim on is the manager's time. Remembering one particularly talented and troublesome subordinate, Robert Umbaugh, vice president at Southern California Edison Co., Rosemead, Calif., says: "I spent half my time managing data processing, and half my time managing him." Umbaugh includes in that estimate all the time it took to counsel the star, chastise him, and smooth the feathers he continually ruffled. For Umbaugh, this went on for several years. The prima donna finally resigned after he was not chosen to fill a managerial position.

Looking back on it now, Umbaugh wonders whether it was all worth it. "You have to do a sort of cost-benefit analysis," he says. "If you have someone who's doing the work of eight people, but burns nine others to the point where they can't do their work anymore, then you'd have to say that person isn't worth it."

But, was Unbaugh's departed star worth it? Umbaugh ponders the question. "I think he was truly indispensable," Umbaugh says. "He had a more thorough knowledge of computers than anyone I've ever known. But I have to say that when he finally left, the department was better off in the long run. The disruptive element was removed and the vacuum in expertise was eventually filled."

Another executive at a West Coast bank is more blunt. Still burning with the memory of a certain prima donna who abandoned him at a project's most critical moment, he decries: "Prima donnas keep reinforcing this perception that they're indispensable. But when you come right down to it, they're like a cancer. Their obnoxious attitudes contaminate your whole team!"

And yet, despite everything—their mischief, their orneriness, their lack of loyalty—despite it all, it still isn't easy to dismiss the contributions some prima donnas make. Chevron's Oldenburg certainly can't. He cites the recent case of some homegrown software-development tools that the company wanted converted to a different operating system. Effecting this conversion would enable Chevron to take advantage of a greater number of networking opportunities. Chevron took the problem to IBM, which, after a lengthy study, concluded that 12 workers would need a year to do the work. Instead, Oldenburg turned to four of his hotshots, and within six months, the conversion was completed. "They thought of ways to speed the process that the IBM people hadn't even anticipated," Oldenburg says.

Like drilling for oil in a mine field, soliciting the services of a prima donna can as easily end with a disaster as with a payoff. But when you hear stories like the one that Oldenburg tells—and there appear to be lots of others—even cautious executives are obliged to take note and ponder the prospects for bringing such brilliance under control for constructive use.

Because prima donnas are easily bored, in high demand, and notoriously independent, the relationship between them and those they supposedly serve is bound to be an uneasy one, even under the best conditions. There are aspects of the prima donna's personality, however, that managers can take heart about, like the overwhelming need to know, solve, get things done, and, just as significantly, the need for constant praise and recognition. For, unlike the average employee with an ordinary range of outside interests, prima donnas are the sort of people who tend to keep all their eggs in one basket.

Being as good as they are, their self-esteem, sense of purpose, and joie de vivre are all wrapped up in their jobs; this puts a tremendous amount of pressure on that job to deliver satisfaction. Managers can't change that situation, but they can defuse it with as simple a gesture as a pat on the back, a trophy, or—as in the case of one manager—a monogrammed necktie.

"I think it meant more to him than if I gave him a $1,000 bonus," says a Midwest Management Information Systems manager who recently rewarded one of his top performers with a $12 red tie emblazoned with the corporate initials. What this fellow had done was invent a programming tool to aid on-line system development that's so good, IBM has decided to market the product (with, of course, the appropriate royalties reverting to the company).

"I have to tell you that I like them," says Anne Ashley, manager of the Performance Evaluation Center at Amdahl Corporation, Sunnyvale, Calif. On several occasions, Ashley has successfully utilized the talent of reputed geniuses with whom other managers couldn't get anywhere. "What I have found is that you have to take the time to know them a little bit. You have to coach them, listen to them, get to know them as individuals. If you give them the feedback they need and the recognition they deserve, they can be real pussycats."

Of course, not all troublesome geniuses can be made to purr, and there may well come a time when good sense compels you to kick out the most irascible of the litter. "I don't do any complex cost-benefit analyses," says the president of a Midwest computer-services company. "My stomach tells me when I've had enough."

Reference

1. "The Abrasive Personality" by Harry Levinson, *Harvard Business Review*, May-June 1978.

19.
MANAGING THE MAVERICK—
Or . . . How to Get a "Wild Duck" to
Fly in Formation

William P. Patterson

A maverick is someone who is independent—an outsider, unbranded by the group and essentially belonging to no group. The unusual behavior of mavericks makes for good stories, but trying to manage someone who thinks and acts differently has driven many an otherwise adroit manager right up the wall.

"I want more wild ducks in this company, people who don't respect tradition for tradition's sake," challenged a computer company president.

Buoyed by the challenge, a young manager once again presented his boss with a proposal to merge two departments, He had been with the company for only six months, but it was obvious that such a move would save significant dollars and increase efficiency.

The boss hit the ceiling. He splintered a pencil between his fingers and scoffed, "It's a wild duck idea!"

"But the president . . . he want more wild ducks," retorted the young man.

"Yeah!" shouted the boss, "but wild ducks who fly in formation.!"

A senior manager at a consulting firm returned to headquarters late one afternoon just as the side door was being locked for the evening. The guard smiled, gesturing to the executive to use the front door. Instead, the executive picked up a large rock and hurled it through the glass door. Reaching inside, he unlocked the door and marched with great dignity to his office, the sound of alarm bells screaming down the corridor.

At a manufacturing company a top executive was highly valued for his ability to quickly get to the root of a problem and propose an unusual, but successful, solution. However, his indictments of co-workers were just as stinging as his achievements were brilliant. He always left a trail of "psychic blood" behind him. He would openly tell people exactly what he thought of them, berating them for their lack of initiative—when they saw themselves as simply trying to maintain a sense of system and order.

RIGHT UP THE WALL

Though the unusual behavior of mavericks makes for good stories, trying to manage someone who thinks and acts differently has driven many an otherwise adroit manager right up the wall.

The usual set of corporate controls, power, and rewards just don't work with a maverick. "What makes a maverick," observes Lester Tobias, a partner in Nordli, Wilson Associates, Westborough, Mass., a consulting firm of business psychologists, "is his vision and values. Mavericks fundamentally don't see the world the way most people do."

Says Homer J. Hagedorn, senior analyst for organizational behavior at Arthur D. Little, Inc., Cambridge, Mass.: "Mavericks neither respect nor disrespect control and power. They don't need it; aren't cowed by it. It simply doesn't touch them."

There are many types of mavericks but they are difficult to categorize. They exist at the periphery of a group and, as Mr. Hagedorn points out, "they don't crop up as a major model of any psychological or sociological taxonomy, but as bits and pieces of subcategories."

THE ORIGINAL

The word "maverick" itself shows why. The story is told that in 1845 Samuel Maverick received 400 head of cattle in lieu of a debt. He neglected to brand the calves, and ever after the stray calves and, later, wild longhorn cattle have been known as "maverick." Psychologically, then, a maverick is someone who is independent—an outsider, unbranded by the group and essentially belonging to no group.

As such, they are little understood. Most people are ambivalent about them, but some sing their glories.

"I say hurrah for mavericks," says Edward Mandt, vice president-personnel for Maccabees Mutual Life Insurance Co., Southfield, Mich. "Organizations need people like that. To keep on your toes you need someone who has enough clarity and force to break through the ongoing groupthink."

"What the maverick does is insist on analyzing, criticizing, and getting at the basic underlying assumptions of the group," comments Mr. Hagedorn. "He can sometimes prod members of the group into re-seeing the situation. He's a catalyst for change."

"Mavericks generally are very forceful," says Nordli, Wilson's Mr. Tobias, "and they have developed a strong character because of the courage to speak their minds regardless of opposition. They easily galvanize a group's energy."

Brian Moore, general manager of Hewlett-Packard Co.'s Manufacturing Systems Group, Cupertino, California, believes a maverick has to do more than just criticize. "What we want is not only people who see the world differently and question the status quo, but also 'champions'—people who come up with a new solution and will champion it within the company."

However, the maverick, he believes, has to be capable of climbing on board once the direction has been decided. "You don't want disruption in the execution phase," advises Mr. Moore. "Mavericks have to be able to play with the team. Otherwise, they don't last too long."

FLYING IN FORMATION

Being able to fly in formation upon request does not come naturally to the maverick. His belief in himself and his perception of reality are usually too strong to admit to easy compromise. "Mavericks usually have great self-confidence," comments Mr. Tobias. "Usually their mothers have taken a strong interest in them (they tend to be firstborn). She has nurtured their importance and rewarded their creativity." Deep down, he says, there may have been some childhood trauma that emotionally isolated them. "They get the feeling that they can't depend on anyone—that they have to do it all alone," he says.

The maverick, at the edge of the group, lives in the shadow of rejection. Married more to his ideas than to his relationships within others, he is not likely to have a network of friends to protect him within the company. What he bets on is the strength of his ideas—their originality—to carry him through. Observes Richard Borough, a Palo Alto, California, psychologist who has treated many Silicon Valley mavericks: "He tends to feel enough personal security that whether he is liked or disliked does not matter to him very much. He is concerned with outcomes rather than invitations to dinner. Still, he is always walking among psychological mine fields; he never knows when things will blow up."

EASY SCAPEGOATS

Mavericks are useful to companies needing agents of change. But they also make useful scapegoats when things aren't going right. The group can easily turn on him because the maverick is, by nature, an outsider. The maverick tends to engender unease among the group. "People just plain don't enjoy having to cope with the unusual," notes Arthur D. Little's Mr. Hagedorn.

The unconscious tendency of the group is to establish balance by what Nordli, Wilson's Mr. Tobias calls "delegitimizing the other's strength." If someone has a strength we don't share, then we will see it as shallow. Conformists see the nonconformist as silly, naive, and adolescent, while the nonconformist sees others as shallow.

It then becomes a vicious circle. The group isolates the maverick and/or he distances himself from the group. If he tries to air his viewpoint, the group will give passive resistance. The maverick then gets louder, more self-justified, and even obnoxious, which further turns everyone off.

"This is the kind of environment where you really have to stand up and be counted," says Gail Quinn, who works in the employee counseling and development department of the National Broadcasting Co., New York. "One way to do that is by being different of course. But then you have to know the boundaries. What do we do with people who don't? We get rid of them!"

Robert M. Bramson, president of Bramson, Parlette, Harrison & Associates, Berkeley, California, business consultants, says, "Most mavericks are too good to fire, but they're very hard to live with. Still, without them, executives tend to hire 'for comfort'—they hire staff that thinks the way they do; they all see the same world. The problem is they leave out a whole piece of the world, and their decisions become too biased and narrow."

THE DOWN SIDE

Dr. Douglas LaBier, a Washington psychoanalyst and a senior fellow at the Project on Technology, Work & Character, a nonprofit organization, has just completed a seven-year study of successful careers in large corporations. In his book, *Modern Madness: The Emotional Fallout of Success*, published by Addison-Wesley, he examines the hidden, negative cost of success that employees pay in the form of a range of emotional and value conflicts. Persons with a fundamentally different point of view (there are neurotics who only play at being different) are especially prone to inner as well as outer conflict. "Mavericks appear to be on the increase in corporations," Dr. LaBier declares. "And the workplace itself is undergoing a tremendous change, a revolution in itself, what with the introduction of computer technology, the entry of women into management and (despite all the talk) a growth in bureaucracy."

Uncertainty abounds in the modern corporation. The corporate-identity crisis, coupled with the need for change to compete in the global marketplace, so seems to be jarring the traditional mind-sets that the value of mavericks is more appreciated. But ironically, it comes at a time when, Dr. LaBier points out, "The workplace is increasingly focused on interdependency and teamwork. So the question remains: How to integrate the maverick's orientation with the team's?"

James March, professor of organizational behavior at Stanford University, Palo Alto, California, sees the need for mavericks in terms of "getting more variability within the organization." But he admits: "We don't know how to do that very well. We mostly manage to prevent deviations. We try to build buffers between control systems and mavericks, hiding them out in the Skunk Works or whatever. This has adverse consequences for discovering exciting new things. That, I presume, is the basis of all the interest in mavericks and not just an infatuation for their 'aesthetic beauty.'"

THE UP SIDE

If he's labeled as a "deviation," the maverick understandably calls a lot of negative association onto himself. And psychologists can trace a line of development that runs from maverick to scapegoat to rebel to martyr; all words that are unconsciously given a negative coloring. "We forget that—to the English—the Founding Fathers of this country were all mavericks, rebels, traitors," notes Dr. LaBier. "Thomas Jefferson even advocated revolution periodically to cleanse government of its weaknesses."

Exclaims Maccabees Mutual's Mr. Mandt: "The true maverick is our intellectual conscience, maybe our social conscience, too."

Nordli, Wilson's Mr. Tobias counters: "Just the same, one person's creative, stimulating thinker is another's pushy pain in the neck."

"Mavericks are like castor oil," claims Arthur D. Little's Mr. Hagedorn. "You take it because it is good for you. It's never palatable and always leaves an aftertaste."

Mr. Mandt wonders: "Where would the world be without Issac Newton? Einstein? Picasso? Freud and Jung? Darwin? And on the business side there is a whole slew of people like H. Ross Perot and Steve Jobs in computers, Clement Stone in insurance . . . They all turned the world to their way of thinking."

"Its true," says Mr. Hagedorn. "In supporting a maverick in your organization you may be nurturing the new wave of the future. Companies need mavericks to shake them up or they may become buggy whip manufacturers."

MANAGING A MAVERICK

So while there is consensus in favor of the employment of mavericks, the questions remains: How to manage a maverick?

One perennial hotbed of maverickdom is consulting and research firms. SRI International Inc., Menlo Park, California, is a good example. "Around here, maverick behavior is prized," notes Gary Bridges, SRI's training consultant. "Our culture is very embracing of that type of individual."

People are always defined from a given context, and at SRI "the zone of acceptability is very wide," Mr. Bridges observes. "We don't have any mavericks, in that sense. But we do have a lot of creative people motivated by an inner sense of values, an inner calling."

But naturally there are difficulties. "Many people here want to do leading-edge research. When the client has given us $40,000 and it's all spent, how to you persuade someone to stop?" asks Mr. Bridges. Sometimes they just have to cut the money off, but before that, Mr. Bridges says, he tries to get to know the researcher to "hook up in some way with his ideals and values."

He spends a lot of time with that person, asking open-ended questions, paraphrasing what he hears to build a sense of mutual understanding. Once a rapport has been achieved and perhaps some compromises reached, it is much easier to act without inflicting unnecessary ego-damage.

"The big bugaboo in managing a maverick is people assuming everyone is just like they are, except they are a little defective," points out Mr. Bramson, a consultant and the author of *Coping with Difficult People*, published by Doubleday. "I'd say it accounts for 75% of all human problems."

Managing, in Mr. Bramson's terms, is to get to know what he considers the three strongest influences on behavior: thinking styles; roles repertoire (the different roles a person plays); and motivational preference (what rewards and context spark an employee to do his best).

In his book he examines five different styles of thinking. These are realist, analyst, pragmatist, idealist, and synthesist. Mavericks, he believes, tend to have a "high loading" in synthesis thinking.

The synthesist orientation, he believes, is based on a "world view that there is no such thing as basic agreement among people about facts. What is important are the inferences that people make from the data they get, and the way those people feel about them." Therefore, the synthesist believes he must first distill the subject down to some basic values that everyone acknowledges as the essence of the issue. "Synthesists," he writes, "tend to be challenging people, curious, restless, and creative. They are motivated to understand, but not necessarily control, the world and are much concerned that others see them as competent and worthy of admiration."

"With the synthesist," explains Mr. Bramson, "the manager must go through a tremendous effort of value clarification. And, beware, he is a marvelous debator." But if a basic understanding and a level of trust are established, then he is a much easier person to manage, Mr. Bramson says.

OPPOSITES ATTRACT

Mavericks always attract their opposites in any organization. These opposites are control-dominance and power-oriented people. "The maverick has a difficult time with this kind of co-worker or boss," explains Arthur D. Little's Mr. Hagedorn. "Each type makes the other very defensive. The control person is 'triggered' in his negative feelings for his fear of losing control. The maverick, by nature, is not controllable. Both need to realize that they are implicated in the relationship. It does take two to tango."

Mr. Tobias at Nordli, Wilson views the situation differently. He sees the maverick as likely to be an intuitive and opportunistic thinker, one who keeps the question open and allows the situation itself to speak to him. In contrast, the linear thinker is focused on facts, moves a step at a time, and is not easily diverted. He also wants to impose his ideas and attitudes on the situation—to force it into something he can deal with through rules and statistics. So he advises giving the maverick enough space in which to explore. But, at the same time, he wants to let the maverick know that there are needs in the other direction—the need to reach conclusions, to make decisions, and to clarify the bottom line.

Mr. Tobias chuckles and says, "It's a really dynamic situation. The maverick can't be excellent if he allows himself to be forced into a linear mode of thinking and behaving. The linear thinker believes people are crazy unless they proceed linearly. He needs the security of knowing, and the maverick embraces not knowing. A real odd couple."

Managing a maverick—or any type of employee, for that matter—is an opportunity to "understand" in the broadest sense of the term. In reaching outside his given mind-set to see the subordinate as a person and not as a label or an image, the manager must question not only what he is seeing but also what his own attitudes and values are. This is certain to make him a better manager. And it is likely to build a better and more productive relationship with the person he managers.

For the maverick, it offers a chance to mature and grow.

"Once a maverick, always a maverick," declares Mr. Tobias. "We can't change who we are. But the level of maturity, of constructiveness—this is what varies. A seasoned maverick who knows his, and the company's, limits can be a powerful asset."

Part III
A BASIS FOR COMMITMENT: COMMUNICA-TION AND PARTICIPATION

20.
GETTING AN ANSWER TO "HOW AM I DOING?"

Arthur E. Wallach
Lauren Hite Jackson

The Organization Climate Assessment combines features of both survey and group-meeting programs, yet is unlike either. Chances are good that this combination of quantified data, group involvement and a positive atmosphere will improve employee relations in any organization.

Regardless of the size of the payroll, the number of plants, or the variety of the product line, an organization depends on groups of employees in separate units to get its work done. One of the manager's challenges, then, is to encourage his or her group to work as a team, rather than as a set of individuals concerned only with their own chores. And one of the human resources department's challenges is to help managers build this team atmosphere by providing them with timely, detailed, and practical analyses of employee attitudes, concerns, and creative suggestions.

The problem is that the tools currently available to human resources professionals to elicit and measure employees' feelings and perceptions are not able to provide this kind of information. Large-group surveys, which measure such broad areas as employee satisfaction with pay and supervision, are a workable tool for large and diverse operations. They provide employees with an opportunity to give opinions on issues they feel are important while providing management with the statistically valid information it needs to set policy, define objectives, and measure progress. Typically, however, the administration and analysis of these surveys take a long time, and results cannot be attributed to specific performance groups. In short, the broad scope of these surveys limits their usefulness to long-range planning and general policy matters.

On the other hand, small-group methods—like the Nominal Group Technique, Delphi, and Ideawriting—have been used successfully at the work-unit level to collect data about a topic of specific interest or to solve a well-defined problem. But because of the small size of the participating group, the narrow scope of its interest, and the lack of a valid measurement instrument, these methods have never been particularly reliable indicators of general attitudes.

Rather than live with the limitations of existing techniques, the human resources group of BFGoodrich Tire Group decided to develop a process that would match the accuracy and reliability of a highly structured instrument—such as a formal survey—with the rich, qualitative data typically obtained through interviews or small-group techniques. It wanted to give accurate, timely, and practical attitude information to local (as opposed to corporate) management. The result was the Organization Climate Assessment (OCA).

A step-by-step process, the OCA combines features of both survey and group-meeting programs, yet is unlike either. It has been tested for several years throughout the BFGoodrich business and found successful in administrative and production environments, with clerical and supervisory employees, and at domestic and offshore facilities.

THE OCA PROCESS

The OCA process begins with a "preactivity" meeting between the manager taking part and a trained human resources professional. This meeting draws their shared commitment to each step in the process—including the planning and implementation of policies that respond to employee attitudes and ideas. The manager typically outlines concerns in this meeting and discusses problems he or she has identified. A time schedule is set up, and specific responsibilities are assigned.

Following this, the human resources professional distributes a preliminary questionnaire so that all employees in the group—not just a sample—have the opportunity to give their opinions in the eight areas listed and defined in Exhibit I. Most of the 31 items in the questionnaire (whose reliability, computed by coefficient alpha, is estimated at .88) are statements with which respondents rate the strength of their agreement on a scale from 1 to 5. Several are multiple-choice questions, though, while two are open-ended and let employees identify and comment on issues not covered in other parts of the survey.

No doubt, distributing 31 survey items to individual employee groups cannot give the depth of information that a comprehensive, companywide attitude survey offers, but the OCA survey has several benefits. First, because it involves all employees within one unit, it gives the human resources department the opportunity to compare one area's morale with morale in other business segments at the same location, in similar units at other locations, in the entire corporation—even in other companies, as indicated by national norms. In addition, the limited range of issues on the survey ensures that the manager and

Exhibit I

The Organizational Climate Assessment

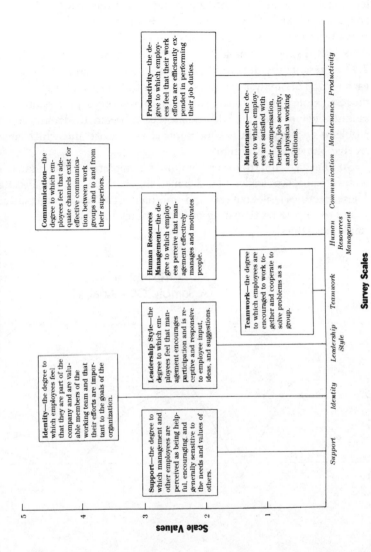

Survey Scales

Scale Values

employees will focus their attention on eight traditionally important concerns. (Importance has been validated through follow-up activities with various methodologies that confirmed a correlation between the OCA survey finding and more detailed research.) Also, this limited scope allows human resources personnel to analyze and graph the data overnight.

Exhibit II shows a sample analysis of the survey. You can see that a value of 2.75 represents the dividing line between satisfaction and dissatisfaction for each area. This analysis serves as the basis for and directs the next step in the process: group discussions. The human resources professional uses these rankings before meeting with employees to begin to determine where real problems and opportunities for improvement exist and which areas should receive immediate attention.

On the day after the questionnaire's completion, the human resources professional acts as leader for group meetings with 8 to 12 employees at a time. These meetings last about one-and-one-half to two hours, and participation is voluntary. If the participating unit has more than 50 people, a sampling of employees attends.

Exhibit II
A Sample OCA Analysis

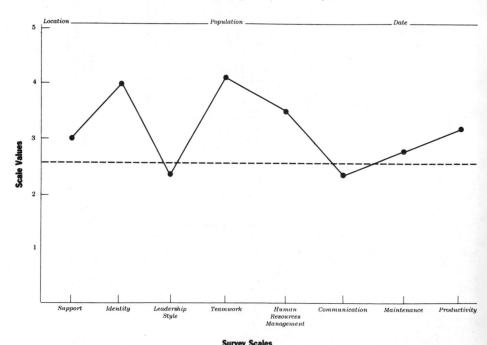

This analysis reveals that employees in the sample group identify strongly with the company and have little difficulty working together to solve problems. But they feel that communications could be better. Poor communications may be why they also believe that the manager is not always receptive and responsive to their ideas. (This interpretation was, in fact, confirmed during the group sessions.)

As these first meetings begin, the leader gives a narrative presentation of the general results of the survey—without discussing specific features of the scaled scoring. For the rest of these sessions and during several subsequent meetings, he or she stresses the positive findings—there are always some—and encourages employees to make suggestions to improve these areas even more. Only after a positive atmosphere has been established and highly rated areas explored will the leader direct the discussion toward weaknesses that the questionnaire revealed, again looking for suggestions that will bring improvement.

For example, he or she may open the discussions by saying, "Most people indicated that communications here are really good. What's good about them?" Responses may range from "The supervisor's always willing to listen when there's a problem," to "We have weekly meetings to go over problems and find out if special projects are coming up." The leader then asks if any steps can improve communications. Typically, he or she will get such additional responses as "The technical documentation we have could be clearer," or "Meetings should begin on time." When it's time to turn to problem areas, the leader may begin by saying, "What about teamwork? What can we do to help everyone work together more effectively?"

This emphasis on positive findings and suggestions for improvement is one of the keys to the success of the OCA process. It makes sure that the group meetings do not degenerate into "gripe sessions" because it focuses attention on what is good, or could be good, about the unit, company, and management. Further, it prevents employees from turning the manager into a target for personal criticism about policies or practices—many of which may not even be under his or her control. In short, it encourages employees to leave the meetings with a good attitude and strong desire to make the improvements discussed.

No doubt, leaders must be highly skilled, so they can initiate and direct discussion without contributing or responding to specific comments. They should be sure that opinions and suggestions are recorded on a large, easel-mounted tablet or other easily visible device, both to keep minutes of the meetings and to make sure that discussions stay focused and all concerns are discussed.

These meetings are scheduled until all eight areas have been addressed, after which the human resources professional puts together a confidential report of meeting and survey findings for the manager. (Again, the limited scope of the questionnaire is an advantage: It reduces the amount and kind of analysis required, so that the report can be generated in two to three weeks.) No blind copies or summary reviews of this report go to higher management levels. In practice, most local managers do refer to OCA findings to support their own policy or procedural changes or justify their recommendations for changes that involve higher management, but the decision as to which and whether any findings will be shared with peers or supervisors rests entirely in the hands of the local managers.

Before any changes are planned, one more session for employees takes place—and now the manager has the option of attending. Again the leader builds a positive atmosphere, this time by asking for specific action steps based on the suggestions from the earlier meetings. For example, the leader may say, "Someone suggested that the technical documentation could be clearer. Do you have any suggestions as to *how* to make it clearer?" Such response as "Make the print bigger," or "Laminate the pages so the print won't be smudged," involve employees in developing solutions and give the manager a range of appropriate actions. Before this session ends employees are given one last chance to introduce any new areas in which changes may lead to unit improvements.

The next step of the OCA process is for the manager to develop a detailed action plan that responds to all of the employee concerns and suggestions. This can be the most difficult and complex part of the OCA process—particularly for managers who are participating for the first time. Naturally they want to take steps to solve unit problems, but their desire for action should not make them overreact. Changes should be made only when they are needed and tempered by sound business judgment. On the other hand, managers may find that although a change is warranted, they are powerless to make it. Compensation policies and rates, for example, are typically a corporate responsibility—not a local one. Certainly all employee concerns should be addressed in the manager's program, even if the only possible response is "Nothing can be done." If the hourly rate or a specific benefit is an issue, the best that the manager can do is explain how national policy is set and outline the limits of local flexibility.

To help managers develop their action plans, the human resources group prepared a guide that, in addition to outlining the entire OCA process, contains a detailed discussion of how to identify problems and the factors that contribute to them. It suggests that when formulating or considering a response to any issue, managers should ask themselves the following questions:

- Will the response solve or alleviate the problem?
- What are the long-term and short-term consequences of the response for employees?
- What are the long-term and short-term effects of the response on business objectives?
- Are there any constraints on implementing the response?
- Does the response make good business sense?

If the solution is a sound one, the guide then recommends that managers decide whether they should plan and administer the actions themselves, or whether administration should be the responsibility of local supervisors, an employee involvement team, or a higher level of management. When action plans are complete, managers generally discuss them with employees, so that employees know that their concerns have been considered and, when possible, are being resolved.

After the plan has been implemented, the last step is for the manager to develop a way to evaluate the plan. Typically, managers decide to evaluate by reviewing plans frequently—about once a month—and holding employee meetings three to four times a year. The guide suggests that during these reviews and meetings, managers ask themselves and their employees:

- Has the action plan reduced, relieved, or eliminated the employees' problem or problems?
- Has the action plan produced other problems?
- How do the employees now feel about these problems?
- Has the action plan improved employee satisfaction at the expense of key business indicators such as costs or customer satisfaction?

Concrete before-and-after measurements are also important yardsticks for determining the success of an action plan. In particular, managers look at total department output per hour, quality, and cost per unit to see how they've changed since the time that the OCA process was begun.

A COMBINATION OF ADVANTAGES

Today, the OCA process is always in use, and with good results. One employee group, for example, has seen an improvement in output despite a decrease in staffing levels, along with a large decrease in absenteeism, since it began the OCA process in 1983. Success with this type of attitude assessment, though, is not limited to the BFGoodrich Tire Group. Chances are good that this combination of quantified data, group involvement, and a positive atmosphere will improve employee relations and increase productivity in any organization.

Arthur E. Wallach is vice-president of human resources for the Worldwide BFGoodrich Tire Group in Akron, Ohio. Lauren Hite Jackson is manager, strategic planing, with the BFGoodrich Company.

21.
THE POWER OF TEAM PLAY

Sheila Rosenberg

Theory suggests that a strong sense of group involvement can overcome personal fear of failure or lack of motivation, thereby improving the goal-setting process of both the individual and the group. This is especially true for managers and executives.

Organization seeks MBA graduate to develop new business; promote, monitor and coordinate services; develop and analyze market. Initiative, maturity, creativity, and flexibility are significant requirements for this position.

Public policy consulting firm seeks MBA interested in major federal government issues. Position requires sound analysis skills and quantitative orientation. Candidate must be willing to work long, hard hours.

Highly respected institution seeks an assistant for its European offices to work in venture capital, administration at the board of directors level, and government relations. A high energy level and ability to perform in an unstructured work environment are helpful.

These advertisements are typical of those published by executive search companies across North America, and it's a rare case when such advertisements suggest that the ability to work with or lead a team of employees is a crucial job skill. Quite the contrary, most businesspeople believe that organizations run on individual achievements. Many employees and managers consider teamwork and pride in one's group to be outdated notions, and even restraints on individual effort.

Current psychological theory, however, clearly shows that groups with strong team spirit perform better than those with little. It also indicates that individuals, when placed in central positions in groups, perform better as parts of the group than they do on their own.

Such theory also suggests that a strong sense of group involvement can overcome personal fear of failure or lack of achievement motivation, thereby improving the goal-setting process of both the individual and the group. This is especially true for managers and executives.

David McClelland, a pioneer in the field of "need-for-achievement" psychology, has attempted to show that great civilizations have arisen through citizens having high aspirations for individual achievement. Other experts such as John W. Atkinson and M. T. Feather proposed in their Achievement Motivation Theory that when an individual has an opportunity to choose a goal, and to specify how hard he or she will work for it, the choice of the goal results from two conflicting tendencies: the need for achievement and the fear of failure. Until recently, psychologists have seen no need for comparable research on "need for group achievement."

FEAR OF FAILURE

Alvin F. Zander has performed many experiments which address the question, "Is the need for individual achievement more powerful to the individual than the need for group achievement?" Zander questioned whether individuals are more productive while in pursuit of their own individual goals than while in pursuit of group achievement.

Early in his experiments, Zander was able to clearly establish that groups with stronger team spirit perform better than those with less spirit. The experiments found similarities in the ways groups performed and the ways that the Achievement Motivation Theory of Atkinson and Feather predicted individuals would perform.

Atkinson and Feather learned that people with strong motives for success tend to choose goals that are challenging—neither so easy as to make success certain (since then it wouldn't be much of an achievement), nor so difficult as to make failure certain.

People with strong motives to avoid failure, on the other hand, tend to choose goals at the extremes of the difficulty continuum—tasks either too easy so they will be assured of success, or too difficult so they can say, in effect, "I made a noble effort, but I never really had a chance anyway." All decisions about goals, according to the Achievement Motivation Theory, represent a compromise between the individual's two motives and his or her evaluation of how rewarding it would be to succeed.

Groups operate similarly to individuals, Zander says. When members have a strong desire for their group to succeed, they tend to choose realistic goals and to work hard to achieve them. When they have a strong desire to avoid failure they tend to choose either very easy or very hard goals, and may not work very hard to achieve them.

Zander conducted an experiment to find out whether groups act independently of individual motives. He placed individuals with high motives to avoid failure, high motives to succeed, and intermediate tendencies in groups, where they interacted in performing tasks.

Zander focused on how the individuals with a high motive to succeed and those with a high motive to avoid failure acted when they took either the central roles in the group or peripheral roles. He found that the high achievers chose realistic but challenging goals in both positions, as expected.

The individuals with a high fear of failure also acted as expected when placed in peripheral roles. They choose goals that were either too low or too high. But when these individuals moved into central positions, they acted just like high achievers.

This demonstrated that, in appropriate circumstances, group responsibility and spirit can overcome personal motives. The group was responsible for inducing those with high motives to avoid failure to act like those with high motives for success when they occupied central roles.

Zander concluded that a sense of unity is one factor that prompts a group's wishes for success and improves its performance. He also proposed that having increased responsibility for a group's outcome is an important factor that increases team spirit and desire for success. But his most important conclusion was that when individuals who normally set goals on the extremes of the difficulty continuum—the high fear of failure group—are placed in central positions, their choice of goals improves. Indeed, they perform as "high-motive-for-success" individuals.

EXEC EXCELLENCE

These conclusions have a special meaning for executives. Among the characteristics that executives have been shown to have in common are the following:

- a high drive and desire for individual achievement;
- a positive attitude toward superiors;
- a strong sense of identification with superiors and an aloofness from subordinates; and
- a strong apprehension and fear of failure.

When executives, who have a strong fear of failure, are placed into a group, the group tends to improve the executive's decision making. The executive does not feel the need to be at either extreme of the difficulty continuum, which would be the case were he or she acting alone. The executive tends to make more realistic suggestions than when he or she is removed from the group.

The situation is the same for a mediocre employee. Place this individual in a group and the group can improve the employee because he or she does not feel the need to choose goals at the extremes of the difficulty continuum. The employee will be less concerned about failing and can take up the higher goals and efforts that the group sets for itself. Both manager and employee are now free to work more effectively and according to their own skill levels.

Organizational objectives are not achieved by isolated individuals, but by groups of people working together. Therefore, not only can individual performance be improved by creating a sense of unity in employees, but performance at all levels within an establishment will be improved if such a sense can be created. A strong fear of failure can be overcome if the manager can override his or her feelings of aloofness from subordinates. Participation in the group process itself is often the best method to address his or her fear of failure.

Zander also suggested that "working conditions that emphasize the negative consequences of failure actually reduce performance." Obviously, this sort of emphasis actually breaks down a sense of unity. The surest way, according to Zander, for a group to develop a strong fear of failure, thereby causing the group to set goals on the extremes of the difficulty continuum, is for it to have failed often in the past.

Indeed, many of Zander's experiments showed that repeated failure led group members to see themselves and others in the group as less helpful, to feel less responsible for the outcome of projects, and to say that it was less important for them to belong to the group. All of these effects tend to decrease high motives for success and to maintain a vicious cycle of failure.

Groups that set their own goals can climb out of such a cycle by setting their goals at a level they can reach. But groups that do not exercise control over their own goals do not have such an alternative.

Another of Zander's findings was that organizational structures that emphasize and reward individual achievement tend to splinter rather than unify groups. Similarly, when a group exists mainly to determine how many dollars each member will take home, as in group incentive plans, group pride may not develop at all.

Since group motives naturally develop in some circumstances and not in others, managers should seek to nourish them. The most important step is to shift control downward whenever possible, giving those who do the work more say about how much they do and how they do it. This, in effect, places each member in a more central position, transferring more responsibility for the group's success or failure onto his or her shoulders.

Figure 1
How Good Groups Work

The following are characteristics of well-functioning, creative groups, as outlined by Douglas McGregor, drawn from his observations of the management of large companies.

- The atmosphere tends to be informal, comfortable, relaxed.
- There is a lot of discussion in which virtually everyone participates, but it remains pertinent to the task of the group.
- The task or objective of the group is well understood and accepted by the members. There will have been free discussion of the objectives at some point

until it is formulated in such a way that the members of the group can commit themselves to it.
- The members listen to each other. Every idea is given a hearing. People do not appear to be afraid of being foolish by putting forth a creative thought, even if it seems extreme.
- There is disagreement. Disagreements are not suppressed or overridden by premature group action. The reasons are carefully examined, and the group seeks to resolve them rather than dominate the dissenter.
- Most decisions are reached by a kind of consensus in which it is clear that everyone is in general agreement and willing to go along. Formal voting is at a minimum. The group does not accept a simple majority as a proper basis for action.
- Criticism is frequent, frank, and relatively comfortable. There is little evidence of personal attack, either open or hidden.
- People are free in expressing their feelings as well as their ideas both on the problem and on the group's operation.
- When action is taken, clear assignments are made and accepted.
- The leader of the group does not dominate it, nor, on the contrary, does the group defer unduly to him or her. In fact, the leadership shifts from time to time, depending upon the circumstances. There is little evidence of a struggle for power as the group operates. The issue is not who controls, but how to get the job done.
- The group is conscious of its own operation.

Each group should be able to evaluate its own performance, and on the basis of its past effort and the organization's present needs, have a strong voice in setting goals. Then members will react to the results of the group's work not as another piece of interesting data, but with satisfaction, which cannot help but influence their future performance. The successful group usually chooses to progressively raise its goals, continually pursuing satisfaction. Well-functioning, creative groups have certain attributes in common, as Figure 1. outlines.

The manager's and executive's task is to release the full powers of group members, helping them to diminish their inhibitions. For most employees, this is more likely to happen if the manager is an accepting person who allows the group to attain its freedom and a social stability built on cohesion, not coercion.

Sheila Rosenberg is a consultant for special events at the Division of Continuing Studies at the University of Nebraska, Lincoln.

22.
HAS PARTICIPATIVE MANAGEMENT BEEN OVERSOLD?

Jan P. Muczyk
Bernard C. Reimann

> Despite its many enthusiastic endorsements, participative management cannot be effective in many organizational settings without a complementary dose of management direction. Management direction, however, does not preclude employee participation; in fact, both are complementary dimensions of leadership.

The virtues of participative management or democratic leadership have been extolled by many management theorists and practitioners. Yet, is participation all that it's cracked up to be? Haven't management writers overlooked the fact that many employees may not want more participation in decision making? More important, haven't they overlooked the fact that employees often need or even want some direction? We intend to show that participative management has been oversold at the expense of another key dimension of leadership: direction, or follow-up.

Take the case of Jim Clark, a former executive of a *Fortune* 100 company. When asked what he believed to be the principal difference between managing a division of a major, well-run organization and running his own small company, he answered without hesitation:

> When I was group vice-president at [the large company], I had only two kinds of managers reporting to me. One group consisted of individuals whom I would tell what to do once without ever following up, knowing full well that it would be done properly and on time. The second group consisted of individuals to whom I would issue instructions and then follow up once before being certain that my instructions were executed properly and on time. At my small company, I have neither of these two kinds of managers.

Despite his strong preference for democratic leadership, Jim Clark, found that, to get anything done in his new firm, he had to follow up repeatedly on his

157

instructions or directives as well as on decisions that had been made jointly with staff members. We, too, have found that many organizations, especially smaller ones, have few or none of the two kinds of managers who reported to Jim Clark when he worked at the *Fortune* 100 company.

Why do smaller companies tend to have more managers who need direction? By the time employees are promoted to management positions in well-run, mature organizations, they generally have the necessary self-discipline to take initiative and to execute directives satisfactorily without repeated follow-up from their supervisors. In smaller, less sophisticated organizations, however, many managers lack the necessary self-discipline to take initiative; establish goals, objectives, and priorities; and manage their time effectively. Consequently, higher-level managers in such organizations must constantly follow up on staff members to ensure that instructions are faithfully executed and objectives attained.

Even at less sophisticated large corporations, we have observed a lack of the kinds of employees, systems, or structures needed for extensive employee participation to be effective. We therefore propose that managers who adopt a participative leadership style may need to engage in frequent follow-up. However, we are not saying that democratic leadership styles are necessarily inappropriate for organizations in which employees require considerable direction. We are saying that an equally important dimension of leadership—direction—must also be considered.

PARTICIPATION VERSUS DIRECTION

To appreciate how direction both differs from and complements participation, the process of making a decision needs to be recognized as being separate from the process of executing that decision. Participation is associated with making a decision, while direction is associated with executing a decision once it has been made.

Democratic leadership is typically defined as involving employees in significant day-to-day, work-related decisions. However, involving employees in decision making is unrelated to the amount of direction that a leader provides in executing decisions. Hence a leader can be participative or democratic by consulting employees during decision making yet still be directive by following up closely on progress toward mutually established goals and coaching employees on means to achieve those goals.

This concept of directive leadership has special importance for organizations that lack the sophisticated structure or systems of large, mature institutions. If organizations have a high proportion of employees who lack self-discipline and initiative, a democratic leadership style with a high degree of permissiveness could be a dangerous combination, causing serious problems with productivity, goal achievement, and even morale.

Participation in decision making and direction (follow-up) should therefore be considered two independent dimensions of leadership that can be combined in an infinite number of ways. However, a more practical approach for discussing the relationship between these dimensions is to focus on the two extremes of each dimension to produce four different combinations (while recognizing that most combinations will actually fall somewhere between these extremes). The resulting four "generic" leadership styles (directive autocrat, permissive autocrat, directive democrat, and permissive democrat) are illustrated in Exhibit 1. These leadership styles and the kinds of situations in which each would be most effective are discussed below.

SITUATIONAL FACTORS

To be effective, a leader must induce followers to act in ways that he or she desires. Clearly, the nature of the circumstances in which leadership will be exercised will strongly influence the style that is most likely to be effective. In their article "How To Choose a Leadership Pattern,"[1] Robert Tanenbaum and Warren Schmidt identified three major situational forces that affect the exercise of leadership: the organizational situation, the nature of the workforce, and the leader's own preferred (or natural) style.

The organizational situation can vary from a total lack of structure to a clearly defined one. The more unstructured a task, the more proactive a leader must be to provide the necessary structure. Some situations require quick, timely responses, while others allow more time for deliberation and involvement of employees in making decisions.

The nature of the workforce may vary from highly independent, responsible, and capable employees to unmotivated, irresponsible, or inexperienced employees. The former may resent excessive supervision; the later may be unable to operate without constant guidance.

Since a leader may have a strong preference for a particular leadership style,

Exhibit 1 **Four Generic Styles of Leadership**		
	Extensive Employee Participation	*No Employee Participation*
Extensive Follow-up	Directive Democrat	Directive Autocrat
No Follow-up	Permissive Democrat	Permissive Autocrat

he or she may be extremely uncomfortable with any other. That is, some leaders are naturally autocratic and would find it painful to be democratic. Others may find it equally abhorrent to be directive, preferring to let employees, "do their own thing."

In addition to those three situational forces, organizational culture must be considered when evaluating the suitability of a given leadership style. For example, William G. Kagler, former president of The Kroger Co., was forced out of office by Lyle Everingham, chairman and chief executive officer of Kroger, over differences in leadership style. Apparently, Kagler's performance was not even an issue; in fact, he was given credit for making many substantial and beneficial changes during his tenure. The problem was a clash between Kroger's corporate culture and Kagler's leadership style. Whereas Everingham, a deliberate consensus builder, had succeeded in creating a "family" atmosphere at Kroger, Kagler, an action-oriented executive, tried to control decision making in the organization. His leadership simply did not fit the company's culture, irritating his staff and especially his boss.

DIRECTIVE AUTOCRAT

This type of manager makes decisions unilaterally and supervises the activities of employees very closely. A directive-autocratic leadership style would be appropriate for a task that requires quick action, with no time for extensive employee participation. It would be effective in an organization or an organizational unit of limited scope or size and with relatively unstructured tasks. The low amount of delegation coupled with extensive follow-up would overburden a leader in larger, more complex organizational units.

This leadership style is particularly appropriate when a staff consists of new, inexperienced, or under-qualified employees. It may also be required if employees have an adversarial relationship with management and must be constantly prodded to do their work. However, for this leadership style to work, a manager must be very knowledgeable about all aspects of the organizational unit's mission and be comfortable with an autocratic, controlling style.

An example of an organizational setting in which this leadership style would be appropriate is a small, entrepreneurial company operating in a dynamic, competitive environment with new or inexperienced employees. The entrepreneur (leader), who knows the business inside and out, must make quick decisions and cannot (or will not) trust employees to operate without close follow-up.

A directive autocrat may also be an appropriate leader in a large organization producing a uniform product with simple technology. For example, as long as the Coca-Cola Company remained a one-product organization, the directive autocratic leadership style of J. Paul Austin and his predecessor, Robert W. Woodruff, served the company well. Once Coca-Cola diversified into the entertainment and food service industries and decentralized geographically

(53% of operating profit comes from overseas), a permissive-democratic leadership style, exemplified by Robert C. Goizueta, became necessary.

PERMISSIVE AUTOCRAT

This type of manager still makes decisions alone but gives employees wide latitude in accomplishing their delegated tasks. Again, this leadership style would be appropriate for a situation calling for quick responses. To be effective, however, either tasks must be relatively simple and structured or employees must have good experience, ability, and initiative. Although this type of leader is autocratically inclined, he or she trusts employees to carry out their orders without constant follow-up. Sometimes the leader simply lacks the time to follow-up.

At first glance, permissiveness and autocracy do not seem to mix. After all, what self-respecting autocrat would take the risk of losing control over the activities and outputs of employees? To avoid this loss of control, permissiveness, or lack of directive leadership, requires some kind of substitute for personal direction, such as well-defined or routine tasks, technology, incentive systems, or a highly motivated and trained workforce.

One example of a situation requiring little personal direction would be a department with a highly routine task in a structured (bureaucratic) organization where employees have little interest in (or hope of) participating in higher-level decisions. Or it could be a department or a company with technically capable, trustworthy employees who have no desire to participate in management decision making. Technicians such as scientists, engineers, and programmers in a high-technology company, for instance, might be quite content to be left alone to do their work. Because of their professional training and peer influence, they may have developed a high level of self-esteem focused on doing a "professional" job. However, in either of these situations, the autocratic leader has to have the depth of expertise needed to make decisions without consulting staff members.

DIRECTIVE DEMOCRAT

This type of manager encourages employees to fully participate in decision making. However, he or she supervises employees very closely to make sure that they properly carry out their democratically assigned tasks.

This leadership style would be appropriate when employee involvement is important to the decision-making process, such as when a very complex undertaking involves many interdependent activities. In that kind of situation, a timely response is less important than a technically correct one. However, substantial direction may be needed if employees lack either experience and ability or reliability and initiative. Directive-democratic leadership would also be appropriate if a leader is predisposed to sharing decision-making authority but does not really trust the reliability of staff members.

Although direction and participation do not seem to go together, this combination may actually be the most effective in the vast majority of leadership situations, especially in smaller companies or organizational units that lack the systems to permit extensive delegation or the resources to attract, train, and keep employees capable of extended, independent action. It may also be effective in larger, bureaucratic organizations that treat employees as expendable and do not invest in the long-term development of human resources.

PERMISSIVE DEMOCRAT

In a sense, this manager is the ideal leader since he or she gives employees a high degree of participation in decision making as well as a high degree of autonomy in completing assigned tasks. This leadership style is exemplified by the popular phrase at Texas Instruments Incorporated: "Every employee a manager." It would be appropriate for any organization in which employee involvement has both informational and motivational benefits. However, it requires highly qualified employees, some effective substitute(s) for personal direction, as well as enough time to reach a consensus during decision making. In addition, a leader who is a permissive democrat must value the democratic process and have trust in employees' capabilities, judgment, and motives.

Many examples of this situation could be drawn from the list of "excellent" companies cited in books such as William G. Ouchi's *Theory Z*[2] or Thomas J. Peters and Robert H. Waterman, Jr.'s *In Search of Excellence*.[3] Unfortunately, only a few relatively successful and sophisticated companies have the combination of factors (situation, employees, and leaders) needed for this democratic and permissive style to be consistently effective.

A COMPLEMENTARY PAIR

The unbridled enthusiasm for democracy and personal autonomy that pervades the very fiber of U.S. society seems to have blinded many scholars and practitioners to the fact that few organizations can really achieve this ideal state in the workplace. Because of the caliber of employees in most organizations (especially in small to medium-size companies), the complementary leadership dimension of direction, or follow-up, is needed to ensure that organizational goals are accomplished efficiently and effectively.

We have attempted to demonstrate that direction is a dimension of leadership in its own right, associated with the execution of decisions and largely independent of participation in decision making. This viewpoint differs from the prevalent one in the literature on leadership, which either has ignored this dimension or has failed to consider it independently of participation in decision making. We have shown that the combination of the two dimensions of participation and direction can provide a typology of four generic styles of leadership and have described the situation in which each of these types might be most appropriate.

Studies of the effects of employee participation on performance have yielded conflicting results. We believe that the omission of the direction dimension of leadership may account for some of the discrepancies. Failure to pay attention to this important dimension can result in the choice of inappropriate leadership styles and lead to poor morale and lower performance by employees. In smaller, resource-poor organizations, the end result may even be insolvency.

References

1. Robert Tannenbaum and Warren Schmidt, "How to Choose a Leadership Pattern," *Harvard Business Review*, May-June 1973.
2. William G. Ouchi, *Theory Z*, Addision-Wesely Publishing Company, 1981.
3. Thomas J. Peters and Robert H. Waterman, Jr., *In Search of Excellence*, Harper & Row, 1982.

Jan P. Muczyk is a professor of management and special assistant to the provost in charge of academic planning at Cleveland State University. Bernard C. Reimann is professor of management at Cleveland State University.

23.
THEY HEAR YOU . . .
BUT THEY'RE NOT LISTENING

Robert J. Aiello

> Frequently the quality of the communication largely determines the quality of employee efforts. Good management and good communication go hand in hand. A sound communications program can yield improved internal relations and increased productivity.

The young employees of the 1980s represent significant challenges for employers. Their attitudes and aspirations are far different from those held by older employees, creating a new kind of barrier for internal communications to breach.

Today's young workers are better educated, more affluent, given to higher expectations, desirous of self-fulfillment through good performance, and more loyal to the work itself than to the employer. The demographic changes relative to income and education have long been anticipated, but the different psychological approach to work sometimes surprises those who deal with the "new employee."

The young employee maintains the attitude of an outsider rather than of the loyal, lifetime employee with familial ties to the company. Dad may have been "married" to the company—his children are more detached.

Utah University Distinguished Professor Frederick Herzberg, speaking at the 33rd Public Relations Society of America Conference, described the employees of the '80s as filled with hostility as they realize the gap between their psychological expectations and the real facts of the work world. Prof. Herzberg believes this is largely due to the inability of management to deal separately with "the two dynamics that underlie all human value systems: the need for growth through meaningful work and the need to avoid the pain of making a living."

The young worker's hostility and new work orientation have led many older managers to criticize their apparent lack of the traditional work ethic. Surveys conducted by Ketchum Public Relations and other firms, however, have shown the criticism to be misguided. The change is in the motivation behind the work ethic. Whereas salary increases and promotions may have been enough in the past, workers now demand self-fulfillment as well.

When psychological rewards are not offered, employee performance can suffer. Employees are becoming less loyal to their companies, but more dedicated to their occupational disciplines or professions. Employees express a strong need for professional growth. Witness these comments from two pursuing communications careers:

> My experience on this newspaper has been full of ups and downs. For two years I was a general assignment reporter—which I hated because I was idle some of the time, and because I had to take assignments from a city editor who didn't know what was happening. For several months I filled in as science writer, court reporter, religion editor, police, youth affairs—those were my best experiences because I was on my own.
>
> Now I've been named the new human affairs writer, a plum of a job. The beat was created a few years ago to cover the neglected part of society, so it's a tool for social change. Now I'm happy again—I feel a responsibility to help people who are alienated from the establishment.
>
> Although those two jobs produced heavy dissatisfaction, I don't not rue the experience. They were both necessary transitions to the end result of a "good" job. [One job] afforded me a working knowledge of a big organization and, I might add, valuable contacts. [One boss] was sheer hell temperamentally, but I learned so much. Without it, I wouldn't have my present job . . . A good motto is: Don't worry how, but fatten your portfolio.

WORKING BY 'ENTITLEMENT'

Management must contend with a variety of rising expectations of employees—expectations that may not always be easily fulfilled. Benefits such as a secure retirement and health coverage are often expected as a matter of social right by employees. These expectations are part of what one researcher calls the "spreading psychology of entitlement." Young workers increasingly believe they are entitled by social right to a meaningful job and all its benefits.

Employees' desire to balance their work obligations with family responsibilities is another major challenge to employers. The changing family pattern includes the replacement of the extended family with the nuclear family, more single-parent families, and more working wives and mothers. Workers who have grown up since the 1940s are more likely than their elders to see family obligations as equal to those of the job.

When expectations are not met, employees can become highly vocal about their discontent. Modern education includes being taught to question and examine. This can lead to conflicts with management on day-to-day operations. Answers based on authority alone will not be effective over the long run. "We do it this way because I say so" must be replaced with "Here are the reasons for doing this."

James O'Toole, management professor, University of California, in his book, *Making America Work* says, "The manager who cannot demonstrate . . . competence to employees can no longer expect their respect. Instead of cracking the whip over employees, today's manager must adopt the role of an expert consultant."

Such an approach represents a change from an *employer* orientation to an *employee* orientation. The spotlight is focused on individual workers rather than on those who control and supervise them. The old-style employer orientation is reflected in the six fundamental problems in management-employee communication identified by Daniel Mills, professor, Harvard School of Business Administration:

1. Management dictates to employees too much and listens too little.
2. Too little of what is communicated is understood.
3. Too much of the content of management communication is of concern to management, but not to workers.
4. Too much propaganda is communicated.
5. There is too little candor.
6. Communication bears too little relation to the possibility of change.

REORIENTING COMMUNICATION

Each of the above six problems singly can seriously disrupt the smooth operation of a company. They become overwhelming when combined. The following six alternative approaches to employee communication are offered as solutions.

1. Human values orientation. Management must become more responsive to human values. Communication must address employee needs. Workers want to understand what is going on around them, to be respected as individuals and to have a sense of the purpose and future of their own work and of the entire organization.

2. Planning. Employee communication, like any other corporate function, must be planned. It must operate 365 days to achieve continuity and credibility. It is imperative for the company to avoid the cry-wolf syndrome when communicating with employees, who will soon realize management is not really interested in honest communication. Employees will know their bosses only bother to establish contact when they think employees misunderstand their position or when they want to "sell" ideas.

3. Effective procedures for grievances. A company's grievance procedure must offer employees a direct and empathetic hearing that results in equitable solutions. Some companies have ombudsmen, but establishing a climate of genuine listening will accomplish the same results.

Industrial Marketing [February 1982] reported on a gripe session held by an industrial company for its marketing and employee communication executives. At the invitation of the corporate staff, 63 staffers spent a week at a resort, first airing their gripes and then attempting to find solutions for the problems that emerged. According to the article, William J. Connolly, Combustion Engineering Inc.'s vice president for corporate and investor relations, "wanted to be sure his corporate staff heard comments from the trenches firsthand, and that, in airing their gripes, C-E's business unit staffers would find solutions on their own. The report card is not yet in on the effects of the company's innovative approach to dealing with complaints."

4. Responsive supervisors. To the employee, the supervisor is the company. For many supervisors, effective, responsive communication is not innate, and they will need training.

If the company takes the position that it is interested in employees as individuals and in good communication with them, supervisors will be an integral part of the process. One way to accomplish this is to involve subordinates in determining performance standards. A study conducted by Richard J. Klimoski of Ohio State University and Noreen J. Hayes of H.A. Jones Co., Dayton, Ohio, reported in *International Management* [November 1981], discovered that when subordinates are involved in determining performance standards, employees exert more effort and performance at higher levels. The study also identified as effective leadership traits explicitness in giving instructions, support for efforts to perform effectively and consistency toward subordinates.

5. Active listening. Despite the increasing complexity of the corporate structure, management must not lose touch with the rank and file, but must develop the skill of "active" listening. In the most formal cases, this may mean an employee attitude survey, but informal contacts also must be planned. (The additional visibility will be valuable.)

6. Management involvement. Management must pay considerable attention to the direction, quality and content of all communications with employees. Management involvement has always been a key to successful communication programs, and this is as critical with employee communication as with any other communication the corporation undertakes.

While these six guidelines will not solve all the employee problems management will face, they 'n respond to the demands of young employees for more and better communication. Frequently the quality of the communication largely determines the quality of employees' efforts. Good management and good communication go hand in hand. A sound communication program can yield improved internal relations and improved productivity.

Robert J. Aiello is senior vice president, associate director, and group manager, Ketchum Public Relations, Pittsburgh, Pennsylvania.

24.
SUCCESSFUL EMPLOYEE RELATIONS

John P. Bucalo, Jr.

> This system clearly recognizes that management must maintain its rightful prerogative to run the business and direct the work force. This is *participative* management, not *permissive* management. Confident and competent management will embrace such a system and use it to achieve good business results. A lesser management might view it as a threat to its authority.

The old saying that "management gets what it deserves" is never more true than in a situation where a union successfully organizes the employees in an organization. After the union has arrived on the scene, management realizes all too late the many mistakes it made that could have prevented unionization. Therefore, the purpose of this article is to outline the details of an overall employee relations system that can help prevent unionization. This system will be covered from a pragmatic viewpoint, rather than a conceptional one.

Figure 1. provides an overview of the employee relations system, which is comprised of three parts: 1) the core programs of the system, around which all other programs revolve and interrelate; 2) the primary programs which, along with the core programs, are the most important ones in the system and should be implemented concurrently with the core programs; and 3) the secondary programs, which can be implemented after the core and primary programs are in place.

TYPICAL CAUSES OF UNIONIZATION

To thoroughly and effectively establish a good employee relations system one must understand the typical causes that tend to encourage employees to seek out a union. Understanding these causes is critical to the development and success of the system, since it should be designed to counteract these typical causes (assuming they are present within your organization) and any other causes that might be present. Most or all of the following typical causes tend to be present in organizations that are susceptible to unionization:

Figure 1

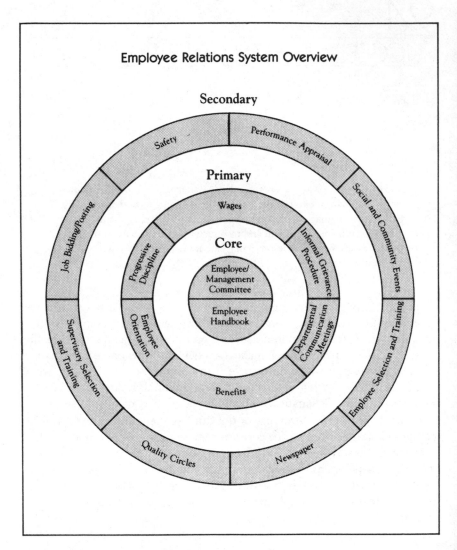

Employee Relations System Overview

- Management's attitude toward employees is such that they tend to treat them as though they didn't exist or without any modicum of respect. This manifests itself in making decisions and developing plans that affect employees without asking for or even considering their input.
- Failure to recognize the seniority of employees in wages, benefits and policy matters.
- Poor lines of communication with employees—both formal and informal.
- Unfair or inconsistent discipline, which strongly suggests that

management will not protect the rights of employees from being im-
properly disciplined, especially for the capricious discharge of employees
for little or no just cause without following progressive disciplinary
principles.

- Favoritism granted to certain employees who might support management
  beliefs on certain issues at the expense of all other employees. This
  manifests itself primarily in overtime offerings, promotional offerings,
  shift preference, lack of appropriate discipline, etc.
- There is no effective means for employees to have their complaints or
  disagreements reviewed by management.
- A facility with many unsafe or unhealthy job hazards.
- Failure to minimize the opportunity for layoffs by "leveling" production
  schedules, thereby fostering job insecurity.
- Inadequately training employees in their job duties.
- High turnover, which provides a union with a larger number of junior
  employees who will tend to vote more readily for unionization.
- Where promotions are not filled from within or where the use of
  "qualifications only" is the sole basis for promotion, thereby excluding
  consideration of seniority.
- Failure to listen to and resolve problems developed by dissatisfied
  employees, even when such problems are bona fide.
- Leaving employees "in the dark" concerning company profits, products,
  operating goals, new equipment, etc., which reinforces the thought that
  they are not a member of the "team" and that they aren't important.

A sound employee relations system should respond to these causes and any
other causes that might be present in the organization.

Before proceeding, it should be stressed that all of the above reasons usually
manifest themselves through the first-line supervisors who have the most
frequent contact with the employees. This underscores two major points: First,
the extremely important role of the first-line supervisor; and second, the critical responsibility of management to recognize that importance by ensuring that
they are well trained to carry out that role.

CORE PROGRAMS

The presence of a joint employee/management committee and a thorough
employee handbook is the heart of the employee relations system.

Employee/management committee. The purpose of this joint committee is to
establish a formal and informal means of communication between employees
and management. This allows management to consider the input of employee
ideas and suggestions for improving operations before major decisions,
programs or policies are implemented. However, this committee should not act

in any way, shape or form as the bargaining agent for the employees. Instead, management is providing the means to acquire employee input, to listen to and consider that input carefully, and to respond with quick and efficient management action—whether or not such action agrees or disagrees with the input. And, once the decision is made, it is communicated in the most effective means possible . . . preferably in writing. Therefore, management is considering the input of all its employees in the decision-making, policy-making, problem-solving, planning and general operations of the organization *without* absolving itself of the responsibility or accountability for the final decision. This is participative management at its most fundamental and effective level.

The subjects discussed by this committee should be proactive as well as reactive. As a rule of thumb, the committee should spend approximately 50 percent of its time discussing upcoming plans and programs, such as changes to plant policies, production schedules and their effect on overtime, revising existing programs on performance appraisal, benefits, computerization of manual programs, and any future plans that affect the organization (proactive), while the other 50 percent of the time is spent responding to employee concerns and complaints (reactive). This percentage breakdown facilitates a meeting agenda that is usually distributed equally between items that management wants to discuss and those that the employees want to discuss.

On the proactive matters, management is usually advising the employees of the plans and programs that they have already developed. Employee committee members can then ask questions concerning the plans and programs and make any comments they feel are appropriate. For example, management can develop a new wage structure plan and explain how it works to help assure employee understanding. Therefore, the employees, having their input into the decision-making and planning process, will be more supportive of management's decisions and actions because: 1) they've had their input into the process; 2) they know the eventual decision that was made; 3) they know the rationale for the decision; and 4) they know when it will be implemented.

Such participation allows the committee members to feel important and part of the "team." Part of the employee's responsibility as a committee member requires "passing the word" concerning such management actions and decisions to other employees—a responsibility they can share jointly with first-line supervisors.

The committee membership should consist of more employees than management personnel; preferably a two-to-one ratio. The majority of the employee members should be a cross-section of senior employees at the higher job grade levels, while representing all shifts, major departments and age groups. A few junior employees should act as members too. Even a few pro-union or management antagonists should be included in the membership so that management is better able to hear their concerns—responding to the legitimate ones while letting the majority of the committee members turn down their illegitimate ones. This allows management to effectively take advantage of their good ideas while "neutralizing" their leadership role.

The senior employees will be able to speak on behalf of all employees. However, on important subjects affecting policy, fringe benefits preferences, new program introduction and so on, management should have the employee committee members actually survey all other employees to acquire their input. A simple written form can be used to tally the votes that would be published in the meeting minutes. On important subjects, a survey assures management that it is receiving a statistically accurate accounting of what the majority of employees feel (assuming that approximately two-thirds of the forms are returned), rather than relying solely upon the input of the employee committee members.

A major concern confronting management is the operation of the committee since some of its activities could be in violation of the National Labor Relations Act. Section 8 (a)(2) of the Act states that it is an unfair labor practice for an employer to dominate or interfere with the formation or administration of any labor organization or contribute financial or other support to it. This section of the Act was established to prevent "company unions" that employers would implement to circumvent the intent of the Act. Case law clearly indicates that most employee/management committee activities would classify it as a labor organization under the definition provided in Section 2(5). Therefore, one must assure that management does not "dominate or interfere" with the committee so as to make it in violation of the Act. Management can be assured that any competent union organizer will carefully investigate the activities of the committee before considering how to implement a formal organizing effort.

Although case law indicates that there is no clear distinction between lawful and unlawful employer assistance and support, these are some guidelines which can be used in the operations of the committee:

1. The committee should either be initiated by employees or jointly by employees and management
2. Committee membership should be voluntary
3. Committee members should be rotated at regular intervals, e.g., six months
4. The stated purpose of the committee should be in writing and should indicate the following:
   • Means of accessing employee suggestions and ideas for improving operations—on both existing and future plans, programs and policies
   • Means of facilitating better communications between management and employees
   • It is *not* designed as a labor organization for the purpose of collective bargaining

5. The committee should not discuss, refer or imply any antiunion animosity

Figure 2
Seniority

Background—One measure of a company's strength is the number of years its employees have remained in its employ. We are very proud of the continuing service record being established by our senior employees. Accordingly, we strive to reward seniority because, generally, our senior employees are our most productive employees. Seniority is defined as an employee's length of continuous service with the company from the most recent date of hire.

We reward seniority—This company believes that employees should be recognized and rewarded for their continual service. Therefore, we use seniority as a basis for:

- Seniority-oriented wage structure
- Automatic wage progression
- 50 percent of wage/merit increase
- Job promotions for Job Grades 1-4 are based primarily on seniority, while promotions for Job Grades 5 and above are based on qualifications and seniority
- Pension benefits and vesting
- Overtime offerings
- Increased life insurance
- Shift preference
- Protection from involuntary layoff
- Scheduling and amount of vacation
- Service awards
- Annual Christmas gifts.

6. Employee committee members should not view the committee as even remotely resembling a labor organization in the ordinary sense of the term

7. Committee membership, responsibilities, agendas and minutes should be jointly prepared and approved by employees and management, or employee prepared and approved

8. The subject matter and ideas in the meetings should come from both management and employees

9. Do not discuss employee desires for wages or wage increases, individual grievances, rates of pay, hours of employment or conditions of work—however, the company's wage structure, method of determining and allocating wage increases, discipline policy, the rationale for the hours of employment and so on can be explained to help ensure employee understanding

10. Management should take all valid ideas and suggestions under consideration while avoiding to agree or disagree in the meeting to help alleviate any impression of the committee acting as the bargaining agent for the employees

11. Though it is not critical, meeting off the company's premises and off the company's time is helpful

12. The committee is *not* formed in an effort to thwart a union's outside organizing attempt.

    Because the distinction between unlawful management assistance and support and lawful management interaction with its employees is not particularly clear from a legal viewpoint, it is recommended that one seek the counsel of a labor attorney when implementing such a committee as part of your employee relations system.

Employee-Management Relations

Management clearly recognizes the importance of sound two-way communications between itself and its employees. Open and honest communications can uncover good employee ideas and suggestions for improved operations, as well as problems. In either, we *strongly encourage* you to bring these matters to management's attention to achieve a quick and effective response. To facilitate communications between you and your supervisor, management has established many communication vehicles which are outlined below. These vehicles are covered in detail in other parts of this handbook.

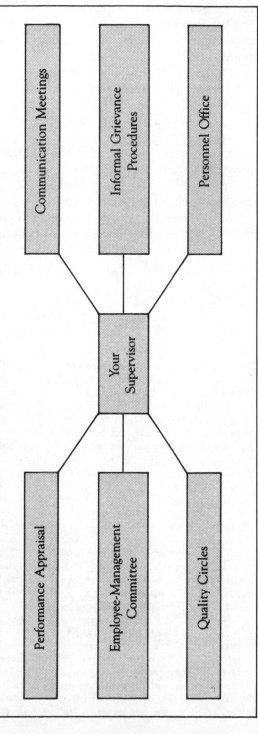

Employee handbook. The employee handbook is the employee's policy manual and "labor contract" rolled into one. It sets out the rules and policies within which employees and management must operate. The handbook should be written in nonlegal terminology and in such a way as to subtly, yet effectively, publicize to employees: 1) how management responds to the needs and concerns of its employees without the intervention of an outside "third party"; and 2) how it recognizes important items such as seniority, employee-management relations, competitive wages, etc. Figures 2, 3 and 4 illustrate how this can be accomplished.

It also should be understood that an effective handbook is constantly in the process of being revised, because policies and decisions are being changed day to day. Therefore, it is important to keep the handbook up to date. An out-of-date handbook or one that is used infrequently sends a "loud and clear" signal to all employees. First-line supervision must know the handbook very well so that they can respond to employee questions quickly and efficiently.

One final point: In the preface of the handbook be sure to indicate that although the handbook is establishing the general policies, rules and

Figure 4
Wage Policy

Background—Every job in this company has been studied and evaluated. We evaluate each job, and place it into a job grade to ensure that the pay is appropriate for the level of difficulty, experience and skills required to perform the work. Each year we compare our rates of pay with other companies in the area to ensure that our wages are better than the community average for comparable jobs.

Wage policy—We seek to provide a balance between "pay for seniority" and "pay for performance". The company "pays for seniority" by rewarding your seniority in many ways. First, we provide 60-day automatic wage increases for jobs in the first five job grades and 60- and 120-day automatic wage increases in the last six job grades. Second, because the vast majority of employees in the higher paying job grades have been promoted into these jobs, greater seniority generally means higher pay. Third, our wage structure generally allows the employees in the

higher-paying job grades to increase their pay at a faster rate than employees in the lower-paying job grades. Last, 50 percent of any wage/merit increase is awarded based on your seniority.

The company "pays for performance" by rewarding individual work accomplishments. This recognizes that all employees in a given job do not always work as hard or perform equally. Those employees who perform better will receive a larger wage/merit increase than those who do not.

Performance appraisal program—Your work will be appraised after 60 days of work, after one year and annually thereafter. If you are promoted into a new job, you will be appraised every year thereafter. You will be appraised on the quantity and quality of your work, safety, discipline and your attendance and tardiness record. This appraisal will result in an overall performance rating that covers the other 50 percent of your wage/merit increase.

regulations of the company, it does not form the basis of a binding employment contract with individual employees . . . whether written or implied. This will help the company defend its position in any potential employment-at-will matters, because attorneys representing such employees are relying on employee handbooks to argue that contractual rights exist for their clients.

PRIMARY PROGRAMS

Wages. A well-established wage structure and method for issuing wage and/or merit increase is fundamental to any employee relations system. The wage structure should be established based on a fair and equitable system of job evaluation that can be easily understood by all employees. Communicate to non-supervisor and supervisory employees the criteria used to establish the differences in job grades without divulging how the evaluation was developed. Job evaluation is especially needed in organizations where there are numerous concerns over the appropriateness of job grades for particular jobs.

In most nonunion companies, management has preferred to have a wage policy based solely on performance without any consideration of seniority. Yet, incorporating seniority in your wage policy is a sound way to counteract one of the union organizer's strongest arguments in an organizing drive. I suggest a wage policy that recognizes both performance and seniority. It involves both the wage structure and wage/merit increases.

A simple analysis of employee performance ratings by job grade level and years of service with the company usually tends to show that the more senior employees have higher performance ratings than junior employees. Accordingly, the wage structure itself is the first step in rewarding seniority in your wage policy. Figure 5. shows a structure in which the percentage of change between midpoints of each ascending job grade continually increases as you move upward in the structure, thereby rewarding seniority. The structure can also provide a relatively large "skill break" increase between entry level and semiskilled jobs, and semiskilled and skilled jobs. This type of wage structure can be developed easily without any management resistance, while rewarding seniority and providing employees with a better financial reason for seeking a promotion.

It is not uncommon for most wage structures to have little or no logic, but simply to have evolved over a period of time. As surveys are completed and the average straight-time hourly rates are calculated, Personnel usually recommends that the ranges of each grade be increased by the difference between the survey average and their present straight-time hourly rate. However, maintaining competitiveness on both a job/job grade and overall structure basis can still be achieved while building a structure similar to that in Figure 5. If it is properly communicated, a seniority-oriented Wage Structure will go far in convincing employees that a management "rewards seniority."

Figure 5
Seniority-Oriented Wage Structure

Job Grade	80% Entry Rate	85% 60 Day Rate	90% 120 Day Rate	100% Midpoint	Midpoint-to-Midpoint % Change	120% Maximum Rate
1	4.44	4.72	—	5.55	3.4	6.66
2	4.59	4.88	—	5.74	4.4	6.89
3	4.79	5.09	—	5.99	5.0	7.19
4	5.03	5.35	—	6.29	8.1	7.55
5	5.44	5.78	—	6.80	8.8	8.16
6	5.92	6.29	6.66	7.40	8.8	8.88
7	6.44	6.84	7.25	8.05	11.2	9.66
8	7.16	7.60	8.06	8.95	11.2	10.74
9	7.96	8.46	8.96	9.95	11.9	11.94
10	8.90	9.46	10.02	11.13	12.6	13.36
11	10.02	10.65	11.28	12.53		15.04

Note: Major "skill breaks" exist between Job Grades 4 and 5, and between 7 and 8.

The second part of the wage policy deals with the wage/merit increase itself. Management normally prefers to issue these solely on the basis of performance. This author believes that wage/merit increases should be awarded based on a balance between "pay for performance," which can be substantiated through a performance appraisal program, and "pay for seniority." Let's assume that the total amount of dollars available for wage/merit increases amounts to $.60/hour/employee. Using a 50 percent/50 percent balance, you could allocate increase as depicted in Figure 6.

The chart can give more emphasis to performance (75 percent/25 percent) in organizations where union organizing is not imminent and many positive employee relations programs are in effect. Also, the use of incentive or gainsharing plans should be considered in addition to the wage structure.

This wage policy can reward seniority (thereby thwarting one of the union's strong points) and performance while maintaining external wage competitiveness. One must keep in mind that failure to keep an organization competitive with other organizations in the geographic locale or industry, as appropriate, is tantamount to disaster. This is especially true if the other organizations with better wages and benefits are unionized under a labor contract. A union organizer would love such a situation in an organizing attempt, and trying to beat that union would be next to impossible.

Benefits. Fringe benefits, like wages, should be competitive with other organizations within the geographic locale and the industry. Additionally, they can reward seniority for items such as scheduling vacations, length of vacations, shift preferences, job promotions, pension benefits and vesting, life insurance, layoff procedures, service awards and so on.

As previously mentioned, the employee committee members cannot engage in bargaining of any type, However, employees can be surveyed concerning their preference for improvements in their benefits, as long as the amounts and cost of such increases are not part of the survey. For example, employees can be asked to prioritize their preferences for an improvement in medical insurance,

Figure 6
Wage/Merit Increases

$.30 – Seniority		$.30 – Merit	
Yrs. of Service	**Amount**	**Performance**	**Amount**
25 plus	$.40		
20-25	.35	Outstanding	$.50
15-20	.30	Excellent	.40
10-15	.25	Very good	.30
5-10	.20	Average	.20
0-5	.15	Marginal	.00

life insurance or sickness and accident disability, as long as it is stated that management is only taking their preferences into consideration. When management arrives at its decision, it will consider the employee's preferences along with the cost and competitiveness aspect of any benefit improvement.

Progressive discipline procedure. From the union organizer's viewpoint, generally there is no more important issue with management than discipline, which also has a tendency to be an extremely emotional issue with employees. This is evidenced by the fact that two-thirds of all arbitration cases in the U.S. involve discharge. In addition to non-competitive wages or benefits, job security and a failure to properly recognize seniority, a union organizer loves to hear about cases of unfair and unjust discipline. Therefore, the achievement of a fair and equitable progressive discipline procedure with proper union steward assistance is one of the major promises that a union organizer always gives employees during an organizing drive. To thwart this effort, management should follow a system of progressive discipline that is clearly stated and published for all employees to see. In addition, all employee rules of conduct and offenses subject to immediate discharge should be stated in writing to avoid misunderstandings.

Disciplinary action should be based upon the particular circumstances surrounding the individual violation, along with the employee's general record of performance. A four-step procedure—verbal warning, reprimand, suspension without pay and discharge—is more than adequate. It should be included in the employee handbook and acknowledged for all employees with forms that employees are required to read and sign. If it is fairly and consistently applied with proper documentation, this type of procedure is one of management's greatest arguments in responding to an organizing drive, because it assures employees that the discipline will always be fair and equitable.

A progressive discipline procedure operates on the important assumption that effective supervisory counseling with the employee is taking place at each step in the procedure. This counseling tries to eliminate or correct the situation or problem that gave rise to the discipline in the first place. If the supervisors are not making a sincere effort to help the employee, the procedure will not have the desired effect.

The procedure also assumes that management will not discipline an employee inappropriately or capriciously if the individual has been pro-union or pro-management. Inappropriate discipline of such employees may be just what the union organizer needs to help fuel the organizing effort. More importantly, however, it convinces the employees that they need a union to protect them against such inappropriate management actions. As implied earlier, dissatisfied or antagonistic employees generally have some valid reasons for their anti-management feelings and excellent ideas and suggestions about how to improve certain aspects of operations. Management might better serve its own interests by getting these employees onto the committee, taking advantage of their good ideas while giving them the appropriate acknowledgment, and helping to "neutralize" their apparent bad effect on other employees.

Informal grievance procedure. Like its labor contract counterpart, this three-step procedure is required so that employee complaints can be quickly and judiciously resolved by management. Management can resolve complaints quickly and efficiently if each step utilizes no more than three working days to be completed. Obviously, the procedures should be utilized without any fear of reprisal from management.

As part of any employee relations system, management should *strongly encourage* employees to utilize the procedure. Also, senior employees should be allowed to accompany a junior or shy employee who might need moral support and verbal assistance to explain a problem. Management should publicize the results of any third-step hearing, which probably will show that about 50 percent of the complaints reaching that level will have the initial supervisory decision reversed. This is good news to management, not bad news.

At the third step, management should not fall into the trap of wanting to "support" the first-level supervisor's initial decision, even though their actions or decisions were questionable or blantantly wrong. It should be recognized and pointed out to the supervisor involved that the supervisory action which precipitated the complaint is generally only one of hundreds of other supervisory decisions, most of which are correct. Therefore, the supervisor should *not* feel or be unjustly penalized for a justifiable employee complaint that might be reversed by management at the third step.

Employee orientation. Often, new employees are rushed into the organization with little or no orientation despite the fact that new employees are most receptive to listening to management's story before they get started on the job. In addition to reviewing the wages, fringe, benefits and safety aspects of the job, an employee orientation program should highlight and reinforce the progressive management attitude toward its employees. In doing so, it should highlight its progressive personnel policies, the use of the informal grievance procedure, the communications meetings, the employee/management committee activities, the rewards for seniority and performance in wage and benefits and any other policies or programs that demonstrate the fact that management is concerned and wants to receive the input of employees in its decision-making, problem-solving and planing process.

An orientation program as described above can be accomplished in about two hours, and will *subtly* point out that a third party (union) is not needed for an employee to express input to management—whether that be of a positive or negative nature. I do not endorse a blatant, anti-union "blitz"—in either written or verbal form—in this program or in the overall employee relations system.

Departmental communication meetings. These meetings are generally 60 to 90 minutes long. The plant manager meets with the employees of each department on company time to discuss the short- and long-range plans for the plant, including new products, new customers, new computer systems or equipment. These meetings also can include a review of any major organization accomplishments (product schedule attainment, quality level attainment, good safety record, etc.) that have occurred in the recent past. The employees can ask questions at the meeting or send them to the personnel managers in advance.

These meetings should never be scheduled regularly, such as every month. Rather, they should be scheduled when there is sufficient information to impart to the employees. This generally occurs every two to four months. Detailed meeting minutes should be taken of the questions and answers, and should be posted on the bulletin board for all employees to view. Such open and direct means of communication and the subject matter of the meetings simply highlight management's belief that employees are, in fact, an important part of the team.

Management should always keep in mind that all employees want to hear the word directly from the boss. In most organizations, these meetings can be accomplished in one day's work. Just walking through the facility and saying hello to employees is *not* the same as having one of these meetings and discussing the organizations's problems, plans and accomplishments. These meetings are 100 times more effective because they make the employee feel important—that their thoughts and ideas are worthy enough to be heard by management.

The two core and six primary programs should be top priority of the personnel manager when implementing an employee relations system. These programs are the primary means to respond to and help resolve the most sensitive and emotional issues that can contribute to a successful union organizing effort.

SECONDARY PROGRAMS

Safety. Ironically, this subject is always of great interest and concern to employees, and of little interest and concern to management. If loss of life or serious bodily harm is inherent in the facility or if safety is an issue with employees, then safety should be considered a core program. Lacking that, it should be considered a secondary one. Employees can provide valuable input concerning the adequacy of the plant safety rules and procedures, along with equipment and job safety rules. If employee input is requested, plant and equipment safety rules can be greatly expanded in a specific way to highlight potential safety and health hazards more clearly. Also, employees should work along with the safety engineer or personnel manger to complete job safety analyses of the jobs which have the highest risk of loss of life or major injury.

Clearly, employee participation on safety committees and inspection teams, for both the plant and the office, can yield extremely worthwhile results. To provide proper direction to the committee, each year the personnel managers should compile and analyze safety statistics for the past two or three years. These statistics should include the frequency, severity and incident ratios, along with the number of accidents by month, by department, by time of day, by shift, by years of service of the employee and by type of injury. Such data should be used by the committee so that it concentrates its efforts on items that cause poor safety.

Job bidding/posting. This program, like safety, might be considered a core program if job advancement is a major issue. Because most organizations have such a procedure, I consider it to be a secondary program.

Lower-level jobs in most plans are generally unskilled or semi-skilled ones which require only rudimentary job skills. In such situations, jobs can be awarded on the basis on seniority, assuming that an employee has had at least a satisfactory performance and disciplinary record. This allows the organization to continue its efforts to reward seniority whenever possible. The higher-skilled jobs clearly must be awarded on the basis of qualifications, such as quantity and quality of work, safety, discipline, technical know-how, experience, attendance, tardiness and overall ability. Seniority can be considered in these higher-skilled jobs as either one of the qualifications or when qualifications are equal.

Because the employee who is selected for promotion is usually questioned by many other employees, the personnel mangers should carefully monitor all promotions where qualifications are the primary criteria. This can be accomplished by utilizing a selection matrix that compares all job applicants against each qualification, one by one. The use of such a matrix helps ensure a fair selection, thereby precluding favoritism by an inexperienced supervisor.

One must keep in mind that favoritism has its most damaging effects in the areas of promotions and discipline. Even if management knows that there are no employees who meet the qualifications for a job, the job opening should be posted while allowing management the right to interview only those employees who meet the required qualifications.

This procedure should be monitored closely by the personnel manager, who should track the percent of jobs filled internally for each job grade level. Such information can be easily communicated to employees to substantiate your "promotion from within" policy.

It is equally important to tell those employees who applied but were not selected why they were not chosen—if they inquire. The use of the selection matrix will help provide the specific reasons in most cases. Provide the employee with the specific reasoning, not generalizations such as "she was more qualified" or "you were not qualified." Also, tell the employee what training and/or experience must be acquired to compete more effectively for the job in the future. When management fails to explain why a particular employee was not chosen, it undermines management's rationale for selecting the successful employee.

Supervisory selection and training. Clearly, individuals who are selected for supervisory positions should have both the technical and interpersonal skills to perform the work. Selecting supervisors with only one skill or the other is tantamount to disaster. Accordingly, a thorough evaluation of the individual's communication and interpersonal skills is critical. When evaluating an individual's work experience, an interviewer should seek to uncover the individual's attitude concerning employees—seeking to find someone who has worked effectively with people to achieve sound business results. Selection is the key! Training is useless if you have selected the wrong supervisor.

Supervisors must be properly trained. Rather than training them exclusively in human relations or behavioral science concepts, I suggest the following pragmatic subject matter:

• All aspects of the employee relations system, emphasizing the typical causes of unionization (do not cover the labor law aspects unless a union organizing effort is imminent)
• How unionization severely restricts management's ability to run the business and the supervisor's ability to operate the department
• An employee handbook review, including a discussion of wages, benefits, discipline and other key policies
• How to conduct a performance appraisal discussion with an employee
• How to counsel employees and issue progressive discipline effectively
• How to communicate and listen effectively.

Assuming that the supervisors have common sense and reasonable interpersonal skills, training them on this subject matter will have a far more beneficial effect toward improved employee-management relations and maintaining your union-free status.

Performance appraisal. Because management desires to provide merit increases to its employees, a fair and objective performance appraisal is needed to help ensure that first-line supervisors have an objective basis for awarding such increases. An annual appraisal will suffice. A simplistic form is sufficient in a plant environment, as long as it quantitatively measures items such as job knowledge, quantity of work, safety, discipline, attendance and tardiness. Avoid using non-quantitative measures, which generally include personality traits such as work attitude, aggressiveness, initiative, judgment, cooperativeness and ability to work with others. Most supervisors tend to be biased in their favor, and the many ratings which are questioned by employees turn into situations where neither the supervisor nor the hourly employee win; the organization and the company lose. In office environments, a management-by-objectives form provides the best opportunity for a fair evaluation.

Supervisors should keep records to justify their ratings on the quantitative measures. They should be encouraged to keep a file on each employee. The overall performance rating on the form should relate directly to the amount of their merit increase, as noted in the wages section. Supervisors also should be trained to conduct performance appraisal discussions with employees that highlight the reasons for the rating on each measure.

Quality circles. Any type of program which allows employees to make suggestions concerning the improvement of their work or the department's work should be encouraged. Generally, suggestion programs have been unsuccessful in gaining employee enthusiasm and management support. Conversely, many quality circle programs have been successful when they have had active management support and the projects undertaken were meaningful ones that were tied to cost savings. Such programs provide a formal means for employees to express their work-related suggestions and ideas in a group setting. When such groups have their management review to evaluate their work-related recommendations, only sound employee relations and improved business results are forthcoming.

Newspapers. This important communications vehicle should not be limited to employee birthdays, service awards or conveying management's plans and direction for the business. It also should be used as a means of reiterating the key policies in the employee handbook. Primarily, it should cover all the successful programs that management is implementing on behalf of the employees. It can also highlight individual departments, their functions and relationship to the overall success of the business. The frequency of the newspaper is not as important as the quality of its content. A well-written quarterly newspaper is far more advantageous than a poorly-written monthly one.

Employee selection and training. The first-line supervisor should take an active role in the selection process by interviewing the top two or three outside applicants recommended by the personnel department for any job openings that are filled from outside the company. Applicants should be screened by their geographic location. The more widely dispersed employees are, the more difficult it is for a union organizer to solicit employee interest and survey them on particular issues. Additionally, the personal recommendations of prospective employees by current pro-company employees should be given weight when considering new applicants.

Properly matching the employee's background to the technical job qualifications is important so that the employee is not over qualified or under qualified to perform the work. Such an employee can quickly become a dissatisfied and disgruntled employee, and suddenly have the time to be overly critical of various management decisions.

Once the employee is selected, appropriate on-the-job training is very important. The training should be conducted by senior employees who are technically knowledgeable and are good trainers at the same time. These senior employees should be trained to be trainers, or should have natural training skills. Additonally, the job safety analysis for the job should be thoroughly covered.

Social and community events. Events such as employee picnics, company-sponsored athletic teams, various clubs and activities, credit unions, etc., are important aspects of acquiring a team effort between management and employees. These events also should be extended to participation in community affairs such as the YMCA/YWCA, United Way, Chamber of Commerce and so on. It is critical that these events are properly and visibly supported by management personnel from all organization levels.

It is much better to have a few well-supported events than it is to have many events that have little or no support. When management personnel attend such events, employees have the opportunity to discuss job-related and other subjects in a casual environment. Employees can get their questions answered directly from management and observe that management employees are human beings, just like they are, with similar needs, wants, concerns and problems.

ATTITUDE SURVEYS UNNECESSARY

Some personnel practitioners might question why I do not include the use of attitude surveys in the system. First of all, such survey data are not needed to understand or respond to the most typical causes of unionization. Secondly, my experience has shown that such surveys do not prove an accurate measure of predicting whether employees will seek out a union or not. Dissatisfied or disgruntled employees who are seeking unionization will not tell management in the survey any information that will "tip their hand." Therefore, an overall employee relations system is an organization's best defense against unionization. Besides, the opinion of first-line management concerning these matters usually tends to be more accurate than the survey data.

COMMUNICATION

Simply stating that communication is the key to any employee relations effort is a gross over-simplification of this complex matter. "Communications" does not simply mean that managers should walk through the facility periodically and have informal conversations with employees. Nor does it mean that all you need is the traditional communication vehicles such as bulletin boards, letters, newspapers, social and community events, orientation programs and communication meetings. Effective communication should primarily concentrate on *what* is said to employees and *how often* it is said, while utilizing all the communication vehicles that are available to you.

To be effective, management should use the same key words and phrases to communicate key thoughts and ideas to employees—in a somewhat repetitious manner—utilizing all available communication vehicles such as the employee handbook; employee/management committee meetings and meeting minutes; the communication meetings and meeting minutes; the newspaper; the orientation program; all types of daily supervisory conversations with employees; quality circles; safety meetings and meeting minutes; performance appraisal discussion; and employee training. If management wants to consistently communicate the same key words and phrases to employees, the next question is: "What are some of those key words and phrases?" To answer this question you have to ask yourself a question: "What do you want your employees to remember about your management policies?" This author would suggest some of the following key phrases:

- Seniority is highly regarded. We reward seniority in our wage structure, merit increases, benefits and work rules.
- We pay based on a balance between "pay for seniority" and "pay for performance."
- We "promote from within" utilizing seniority at the lower job grades and seniority and qualifications at the higher job grades.
- We don't talk about safety: we do it.
- Management and employees work together as a team to achieve good business results that are beneficial to both.
- We have a progressive discipline procedure that is applied fairly and consistently to all.
- Management strongly encourages employees to speak up about their problems to their supervisor. If needed, utilize the informal grievance procedure.

One word of caution: Don't utter such phrases unless you are implementing the programs to back them up.

SUMMARY

An employee relations system which is geared to respond to the typical causes of unionization (as well as your unique ones) can help you maintain your union-free status and help prevent a union from organizing your employees. When implementing the system, there must be a visible management attitude that the employees are valuable and intelligent people, and their input into the planning, decision-making and problem-solving processes is needed and desired on all matters.

This system still clearly recognizes that management must maintain its rightful prerogative to run the business and direct the work force. This is *participative* management, not *permissive* management. Confident and competent management will embrace such a system and use it to achieve good business results in both the near- and long-term. A lesser management might view it as a threat to its authority. In the end, this system is merely good employee relations.

John P. Bucalo, Jr., is vice president of personnel and productivity improvement for Nichols-Homeshield in Aurora, Illinois.

25.
WHY "TALKING IT OUT" ALMOST NEVER WORKS OUT

Losana E. Boyd

> "Talking it out" means you are not dealing with problems until after they have occurred. That is an inefficient practice that successful managers avoid. Do not assume that employees automatically understand what you expect of them and do not leave it to their intuition or imagination. Tell them.

The best way to communicate with your employees is to chat informally with them, and the only way to solve personnel problems is to talk things out. Right? Wrong.

Managers of small companies in particular think they can rely on informal lines of communication and skip the formal processes that large corporations use. They may even pride themselves on that informality.

"We talk to each other around here." says the president of a New York advertising agency. "If someone has a problem, we talk it out until it is solved."

But talking it out means you are not dealing with problems until after they have occurred. That is an inefficient practice that successful business people avoid when devising marketing strategies, developing product lines or doing just about anything else. Informal communications can even create problems. Consider:

- If you shy away from written job descriptions, employees are left to develop their own understanding of their functions within the company. An employee may perceive his job to be something other than what you think it is.
- If you rely on word of mouth exclusively, inconsistent versions of the same story tend to crop up, and the rumor mill starts to turn.
- If you do not tell employees what is going on, they cannot properly direct their best efforts. "We tend to go after a piece of business whatever it is," says an account executive at a New York film production company.

"There is no interaction until we are already into a project. People are constantly running in 47 different directions." Forces are scattered, and projects often have little or nothing to do with employees' areas of expertise. Consequently, those projects show little profit.

The first step in avoiding such problems is to develop a written description of your business and give it to all employees. It is obvious to you and your top managers what your business is about. Now make sure all your employees understand as well.

A written description reinforces to everyone the importance of the work your company does. The more they learn about your business, the more accurately they can direct their performance toward meeting company goals. And if you want them to get excited about your business, tell them how you feel about it. Your enthusiasm will be contagious.

An excellent place for a description of the company and your business philosophy is the employee handbook—strangely, almost never found at small companies. I advise the heads of these companies that if they employ more than two people, they should consider a handbook.

You can use a newsletter to announce promotions, performance bonuses and rewards for good suggestions. Such a newsletter sends messages about the importance of individual contributions.

Supervisors are another important channel for communicating with employees—a two-way channel that can feed messages back to you. The next step is to give employees the information they need about where they fit into the organization.

In a small company it is not always clear what a job involves. Many times a job is a combination of duties that previous incumbents performed plus any extra skills the new person brings. After a series of turnovers, a job can evolve into something management never intended.

Naturally, positions overlap in a small company. Flexibility is a common trait among small business employees, and most enjoy doing a variety of tasks. But the situation can get out of hand. Turf protection may become an issue as the company grows. Accountability for key projects may get shuffled around, and other management headaches can appear.

So describe each job. The descriptions do not have to box people in; they can incorporate flexibility.

Ask each employee to distill onto one page the following information:

• The tasks he or she performs.
• The amount of time spent on each task.
• The skills needed to perform those tasks.

You and your management team should go over the summaries carefully. Any differences between what you consider important and what your employees actually do will emerge. Those differences can then be resolved to meet company goals.

Perhaps you employ an accountant who is responsibile for processing orders as well as keeping the books. Your accountant may spend more time on the books because his or her bookkeeping training and skills are strong. But the order processing is critical. By describing and weighting the two areas of responsibility—say, 70 percent of the accountant's time should be devoted to order processing—you can let the accountant know the priorities. Leave that employee in the dark, and your frustration will mount until he or she quits or is fired.

Rapid turnover is a way of life for some small businesses, and in low-skill positions perhaps the speed of the revolving door is no real problem. But to companies that need skilled help, from clerks on up, rapid turnover is nothing but a drain on profits.

Turnover confronts you with the expense of recruiting and training new people. How many weeks go by before the new hire is anything more than a financial liability? And if turnover results from having to fire people because management did not do its job, the company also incurs the expense of unemployment compensation, the cost of which escalates as the layoff record worsens.

The owner of wholesale food business recently complained that three key managers had left after less than a year. "I guess they just don't understand what this business is all about," he said.

What my client did not understand was his role in their departures. When turnover is a sign of lack of communication, the new hire probably will not last any longer than his predecessor.

Employees appreciate some degree of structure. They need to know where they fit into the organization. Do not assume they automatically understand what you expect of them. And do not leave it to their intuition or imagination. Tell them.

Once your employees understand the nature of your business and their roles in meeting your company's objectives, take the final step: Identify and communicate standards of performance for each job.

Performance standards are specific, concrete and measurable indicators of an employee's work. They are based on two elements: the job description and the company goals. Setting them offers the small company a consistent way of appraising each worker's contribution to the business.

They mean less guesswork in the management of people, fewer general impressions and more concrete observations about each employee's work. Management can measure the employee's performance against his clearly defined responsibilities.

To set performance standards, ask each supervisor to sit down with each employee and agree on the activities the employee will perform during the next quarter. These standards should be written and, if necessary, reviewed by top management.

If it is part of someone's job to process orders, then a standard of performance might be to handle 90 percent of all orders within one week and the rest by the following week.

At review time the supervisor and employee can discuss how well this standard was met.

To preserve the flexibility that most businesses prize, the performance standards themselves should be reviewed. When a new computer system is introduced, the supervisor and the employee might agree that 90 percent of orders can be processed in only three days. Since the computer will free more of the employee's time, the employee and the supervisor can determine together what other tasks he or she will assume. The important thing is that everyone knows the changes in the game plan.

Best results come from informal reviews conducted several times a year, not an annual appraisal. The object is to encourage rather than dictate high-quality performance.

Clear communication enhances managers' ability to develop their employees for the benefit of the company. The chief executive officer who succeeds is not the one who says, "Give me the right people and I'll work wonders," but rather the one who asks, "How can I make the most of the people I have?"

Losana E. Boyd heads Management Communication Services, a consulting firm in New Providence, N.J.

Part IV
WORK DESIGN AND EMPLOYEE SATISFACTION

26.
COMPUTERS, CORPORATE CULTURE AND CHANGE

Jane C. Linder

In an era in which computers are affecting virtually every part of a company's operation, it might have been predicted that computerization would also affect the cultures that guide those operations. In fact, many managers now look to human resource information systems (HRIS) to *help* them influence corporate culture.

When starting in a new job, it's always within days and often within hours that a new co-worker says, "Around here, this is how we do things."

This sort of informal communication is more formally known as corporate culture. Culture is generally defined as a subtle and complex set of unwritten rules and matter-of-fact prejudices; a value system.

Establishing that value system involves nearly every aspect of the firm's operations, controls and reward mechanisms. This should be no surprise since culture touches every part of an organization. Its subtlety, however, does not diminish its importance as an area of management responsibility.

In an era in which computers are affecting virtually every part of a company's operation, it might have been predicted that computerization would also affect the culture that guides those operations.

Whether predicted or not, that influence is now readily apparent in many organizations. In fact, many managers now look to human resource information systems (HRIS) to *help* them influence culture.

Information systems, planned with a human resource perspective, are tools that have great potential. HRIS can have a major, predictable impact on a company's culture. Some examples will illustrate.

Executive management of a large subsidiary of a Fortune 100 consumer goods firm authorized, with parent company approval, two personal computers for one of its large plants.

Located almost 900 miles from headquarters, the plant manager put the computers to work automating manual procedures and gaining control over operations. Previously, only central systems support had been available, and not much of that.

Corporate management experienced some unexpected results. The plant manager began lobbying aggressively for funds for additional innovative projects to improve his plant operation.

In fact, on their visits to the plant, senior management thought they saw many more computers than they had formally approved. This bottom-up entrepreneurship was an attitude that headquarters executives thought they had extinguished years earlier when the subsidiary was acquired.

In XYZ Corp., a diversified industrial goods firm, the corporate controller had led the way to automating financial information, from general ledger through sophisticated consolidation with modeling capabilities.

He insisted, however, that only senior financial people have access to "his" data bases. In addition, he used the information to embarrass line managers with widely distributed reports about deficiencies in their operations.

Some retaliated by commissioning bandit financial systems and stonewalling the closing cycle. Hours were spent haggling over which set of numbers was correct. Although the senior staff had once operated as a team, new hires were now told to "look out for number one."

As these examples illustrate, computerization can affect behavior. Used consistently over the long-term, in coordination with other mechanisms, this effect will influence culture.

Human resources managers can use the impact to strengthen or to change culture, to build a set of shared values that will support a firm's strategy.

MANAGEMENT SHOULD TAKE THE INITIATIVE IN CULTURE CONTROL

Senior executives often ask the HRIS department to establish the strategic direction for computerization without themselves understanding the ramifications. Human resources executives are rarely involved in developing HRIS plans for the entire company.

If these managers misjudge the importance of their involvement in this area, they may wake up one day to find their culture disheveled and a long, if not impractical, rebuilding process before them.

There is a method by which executive management and human resources management can avoid a potentially negative cultural impact of computerization projects.

It involves determining cultural characteristics that are consistent with the company's strategic objectives, then appropriately selecting and positioning systems to help achieve them.

To use HRIS as a tool to influence culture, there are four steps that should be followed: 1) identify cultural objectives that are consistent with the company strategy; 2) determine the types of systems that will support these objectives; 3) identify the proper organizational power structure for those systems; and 4) formulate a migration strategy for moving toward a culture-consistent systems environment. The model is better understood when it is considered in detail.

Identify the desired corporate culture. First, define the cultural characteristics the company wants to encourage. This step is critical because the culture's content—shared values, beliefs, implicit motivators —is a powerful, positive force in implementing company programs.

It is difficult to find a clear framework for describing culture. Therefore, for purposes of this article, I have amalgamated several authors' work into five dimensions of culture. These represent preferred behaviors: What is appropriate and "smart" behavior within the organization and what is not.

These dimensions are clearly over-simplifications of complex cultural patterns. Furthermore, for the most part they address a company's internal relationships. I will rely on them, however, because they are useful in understanding the information systems. The five dimensions include:

Entrepreneur vs. conservative. Conservative companies are typically formal, deliberate organizations averse to risk. The people in them adhere to procedures—they are more concerned with how something is done than what is actually achieved.

Entrepreneurial firms tend to be exactly the opposite. They are informal, aggressive, and impulsive, and encourage taking risks. Above all, they value results.

An outsider might view Westinghouse as conservative, Wang Laboratories as entrepreneurial. Xerox used to be considered entrepreneurial but now might be seen as conservative. Most would agree that AT&T is trying to change from conservative to entrepreneurial.

Clear lines of authority and responsibility vs. ambiguous ones. Companies with clear lines of authority place decision-making in the hands of a specific person. They align authority with responsibility and reward people for "stopping the buck."

Firms with ambiguous authority need to build support for ideas and action plans before they proceed. They lean toward matrix management structures in which authority and responsibility are often shared or out of balance.

The military is an example of an organization with clear lines of authority. Texas Instruments's pre-1983 matrix management structure—since changed—institutionalized ambiguity.

Familial vs. individualistic. Familial companies value teamwork. People build strong relationships across organizational units and strata. Senior people nurture and cultivate their subordinates to assume their responsibilities when they move up in the company. Individualistic firms place great importance on com-

Individualistic firms place great importance on competition. They are populated with stars who close big sales or produce hit shows.

Japanese firms epitomize the familial culture. The stereotype of the large law office is individualistic.

Led vs. managed. When a company is led, it has clear, long-term goals to pursue. It has a vision of the future, it is creative, and it cares about the big picture.

A firm that is managed has financial objectives, often shorter in term. Its statement of values depends on the problem at hand, yet it is a hotbed of the latest analytical techniques.

Lee Iacocca's Chrysler, despite its attention to financial matters, is led. IBM and Hewlett-Packard are led. Colgate-Palmolive's ill-conceived shopping spree of the '70s reflects the fact that it was managed.

Ethical vs. amoral. Ethical companies distinguish between right and wrong. They value honesty and fair play. An ethical firm would never bribe foreign officials, even if it were the accepted way of doing business.

Amoral cultures are Machiavellian. Success is good, regardless of how it is achieved.

In Search of Excellence and similar books provide a set of value judgments about these dimensions. Peters and Waterman advise companies to aspire to an ethical, familial culture with entrepreneurship, clear lines of authority, and leadership. Information systems can be used as a means to promote these objectives. They can help reach the overall goal of establishing a set of shared values that guide employees to strategically valuable behavior.

Determine what kind of system supports the desired culture. Our culture determines how we prefer to process information.

Entrepreneurs, for example, compile and analyze market information to find new niches. They use cost statistics to identify opportunities for savings that preserve service.

Conservative companies use the same information to make sure operations are under control. In a familial culture, we want to share what we know. Individualism breeds privacy. Leaders want to see the big picture; managers want to get into the numbers.

Most HRIS professionals have been aware that company culture affects their success in building systems. However, the reverse is also true. By building certain kinds of information systems, managers can help influence culture.

This phenomenon is readily apparent with the personal computer. PCs are often justified on the basis of labor savings. Once installed, however, the user begins to learn.

This has been noted repeatedly in the HRIS literature, and it is critical. Just having the machine available inspires the owner to devise new ways to use it.

The system influences his or her behavior—how this microcosm of business is conducted. With time and encouragement, the behavior is internalized and copied by others, and culture changes.

Of course HRIS influences, alone, will not build culture. A computer system cannot create ethics or leadership where none exist. The essence of culture, though, is that it is shared throughout an organization. If chosen properly, systems can reinforce other culture-building activities and make major progress in disseminating new behavior patterns.

How does one decide what kinds of systems to choose? There are several adjectives that can be used to describe a firm's systems. They may be: 1) tightly or loosely coupled; 2) proceduralized or *ad hoc*: or 3) batch or interactive.

These attributes are independent of the business functions performed. Instead, they describe the interaction between user and system. How much judgment is required to use the system? How strict are its rules? How much feedback does it give? How hard is it to master?

Identify the proper organizational power structure for systems. The generic systems characteristics have a cultural bias. They do not, however, represent the whole picture.

A system's "power structure" determines to what extent it is accepted into the fabric of the company and has a significant influence on behavior.

An information system interacts with the political environment of a company to confer or deny status, improve or hinder the user's ability to make decisions, and change organizational dependencies.

A system's power structure is determined by the organization that controls the system, its information value to those who control it, and its strategic importance to the company.

Culture is influenced by who controls the system—who sets the pace of decisions, who pays the bills, and even who has physical possession of the hardware.

The individual who directs a system's evolution is the one who determines what business needs are met and how they are addressed. As a result, he or she has great influence over how business is conducted.

The individual's style and values can be codified in the system. Furthermore, the more stature that person has in the organization, the greater the impact of this power. When the responsibility for directing system evolution is shared, the power is spread among the owners.

As businesspeople are well aware, computing increases the power of selected people in the organization by giving them access to information that no one else has. Personal computers and query systems can have particularly potent information value.

A computer-literate manager has the ability to analyze more alternatives than his or her peers. This advantage translates into politically useful credibility and stature.

Executives can influence culture by identifying the individuals with values that are strategically important, then assigning them to champion heroic systems.

What are heroic systems? They are systems that give the company a competitive edge. For American Hospital Supply, the ASAP direct order entry system is heroic. Deere's new robotics system also qualifies as heroic.

The system's competitive value translates directly into cultural power for the owner.

The inability of one large company to address a strategic business issue illustrates the potential impact of systems heroism.

In this firm, the manufacturing, distribution, and marketing organizations worked from three separate sales forecasts. Inventory was out of control, and last minute production schedule changes were the rule. In their cost-competitive, mature marketplace, this was a strategic issue for them.

The single sales forecast problem had been identified three years earlier and each year since by various consultants and task groups.

As the associated staff reports indicated, a successful systems implementation would have required that lines of authority be clarified and operating responsibility be delegated to marketing managers.

In fact, the project could not get started because senior management would not name a champion. Given their conservative, centralist, ambiguous-line-of-authority values, the project would have been counter-cultural, and the leader a powerful hero.

They preferred a tenuous competitive position to this kind of cultural gaffe.

In general, to encourage a particular culture, management should identify a system that is strategically important to the company, then assign a culture-consistent champion to drive the implementation, own the resulting system, and have primary access to its information.

CULTURAL DIRECTION IS INFLUENCED BY SYSTEM DESIGN

How does management translate its cultural direction into information systems? These are recommendations for each aspect of culture in the paradigm.

Entrepreneurial vs. conservative. To encourage conservativism in a company, systems should be procedural, batch systems. Traditional transaction processing systems are good examples.

They require fixed inputs and outputs, and rely on strict organizational procedures for their care and feeding. They focus users' attention on error-free data entry because any mistake adds an entire day to the transaction cycle.

A conservative attitude thrives when these systems are static and difficult to change. To the extent new systems reflect current company practice, the speed and degree of organizational change are managed within acceptable limits.

Putting conservative systems in a firm will slow its decision-making pace. Before goods can be shipped to a new customer, the record must be added to the data base. In batch systems, this can take days.

Before a new line of business can be introduced, the central systems must be modified to handle it. The more inflexible they are, the more difficult, time-consuming, and expensive this process becomes.

One large company has been postponing a much-needed product line profitability analysis because it is unwilling to untangle its eight old, inter-woven cost systems.

The optimal control structure for conservatism is the steering committee. Systems and computer resources should be shared across diverse groups and businesses.

No single group can drive the system to meet its own business requirements quickly, but this is consistent with a careful, methodical approach.

The monthly meeting, normal for steering committees, builds lead time into addressing issues and taking action. To enhance this effect, individuals with conservative attitudes should be chosen to participate in HRIS planning, development, and implementation.

Many firms accomplish this by positioning most HRIS responsibilities under a conservative finance or administration organization.

Implementing *ad hoc* systems—query systems that answer today's question today—encourages entrepreneurship. When these systems are interactive and easy to modify they foster a change-oriented attitude in the users.

The associated business practices can be quite different from current activities. In other words, the system can be a vehicle for implementing organizational change. The risks and rewards of pioneering, and the system's invitation to learn, excite management toward active innovation.

Placing computing power in the hands of innovators builds entrepreneurship. With their direction, the resulting systems represent an ac-tion-oriented style.

Clear lines of authority and responsibility vs. ambiguous ones. Distributed systems foster clear lines of authority. (These are systems that are dedicated to a particular function or business, rather than being shared throughout a com-pany.)

The manager of an area has control over what operations are automated and how business is conducted. The information that the distributed system must pass to central systems begins to delineate his or her supervisor's aegis.

In other words, the supervisor defines some performance and control measures for his or her subordinates by stipulating what information they must pass along.

Ambiguity in authority and responsibility is fostered by systems that are tightly tied together and "unowned," shared systems. These are systems that cut across organizational lines, but have no single champion to focus decision making.

In a multi-plant environment, consider the impact of requiring all plant managers to use a centralized MRP (Material Resource Planning) system that is shared by three diverse lines of business.

Further, give headquarters product managers, materials management, production planning, and distribution equal access to detailed data in the system.

This approach, with the most detailed reports directed to central and senior management, supports ambiguous lines of authority. No one knows who actually owns the inventory.

Familial vs. individualistic. Broad access to corporate information supports a familial culture. Relatively unrestricted data bases and widely available query tools pave the way for users to explore the rich interrelationships between functions and businesses. "Owned," shared systems also support cooperation. The sharing invites conflict resolution, and the owner enforces it. Implicit in ownership, though, is the latitude to disagree. Thus, owned shared systems may diverge.

Another systems factor in increasing familial cooperation is technology standardization. When the personal computers, the data bases, and the spreadsheet packages are compatible, users can easily share information and ways of looking at it.

Local area networks, becoming a reality for many companies today, will intensify this cooperative effect.

To encourage individualism, each system should be under the control of an owner who allocates the resources, sets the priorities, and pays for the hardware.

These can be private, stand-alone systems that deliver information value to the owner. Even corporate systems can be structured for an individualistic culture: access to the data can be restricted to the owner and his or her allies.

Privacy makes the distinction between owned systems that encourage individualism and owned systems that establish clear lines of authority. With the latter, information access is not restricted to the system owner.

Led vs. managed. Today's computer systems cannot create leadership. They can, however, disseminate it through the use of organized data structures.

The key success factors for a firm and an industry can drive the overall contents and arrangement of the corporate information bases. (This is what corporate data modeling is all about.) Computer systems can deliver strategically selected information to decision-makers at all levels.

Developing a corporate vision is as much an intuitive process as an analytical one. Systems that deal in concepts and pictures, although in their infancy today, will soon become accepted business tools.

The value of graphics in communicating complex material quickly and in identifying major trends is already apparent. Picture-oriented systems hold great potential for promoting strategic leadership.

Information requirements in managed companies change frequently because there is no substantive long-term direction.

As a result, flat, detailed data bases must be maintained to enable any question to be answered. (Managed firms are often concerned with their HRIS spending as a percent of sales. The irony is that their short-term, financial objectives dictate expensive, detailed, central information sources.)

Ethical vs. amoral. Ethics start with people. Computer systems can spread the word—influencing high standards of behavior with internal checks and balances.

This form of "policing" is much more palatable than audits and supervisory reviews. The more traditional approaches establish an atmosphere of defensiveness; people are seen as basically untrustworthy.

Computer controls are automatic, quiet, de-politicized inspections. In addition, ethical behavior is more easily internalized when violators are always caught.

Will the absence of computer controls encourage amorality? This sounds a little silly, but in fact it sends a clear message.

In one large, high-tech firm, there was no automated (or manual) system to insure that what was shipped was also billed. There was no way to identify what capital equipment each department owned. In that company, it was common practice for company property to find its way into employee's homes.

Salespeople often "loaned" company products to favored customers. It is interesting to note that senior management looked to a tighter set of computer controls for the solutions to this problem.

MIGRATION PLANS DEPEND ON WHETHER THE OBJECTIVE IS CHANGE OR STRENGTHENING

At this point, human resources managers have helped corporate executives articulate their strategic and cultural objectives, then identify the types of systems and power structures that will support their direction.

The fourth step of the method is to prepare a migration plan.

To manage culture through systems, executive, human resources, and HRIS management should evaluate their existing systems portfolio and planned system implementations to determine to what extent they encourage the chosen culture.

A migration plan can the be formulated for cultural strengthening or cultural change.

A detailed systems and organizational review identifies the cultural status of the systems portfolio. First, the major systems must be ranked in order of importance to the company.

Starting with the most important (existing and proposed) systems, each should be evaluated for cultural consistency, both in terms of generic characteristics and power structure.

Packages should be included in this review, as they may provide the required functionality. They may also subvert the desired culture.

The paradigm of culture I have used here obviously simplifies a very complex concept. The menu approach explicitly disregards the need for balance in the cultural fabric.

Even a company that is led cannot be 100 percent leaders. Many have noted the importance of constructive competition in a cooperative environment.

Formulating an HRIS migration plan, then, is not just the straightforward application of a formula. Although a company's most important systems should be culture-consistent, the system's (and culture's) architects must make sure appropriate counterpoints exist.

I recommend working toward cultural objectives with strategically important systems, and using supporting systems to provide balance.

An entrepreneurial company, for example, might concentrate *ad hoc* systems in marketing and manufacturing, yet make solid, but flexible, transaction processing engines in finance.

The migration plan itself depends on whether the company's effort is toward cultural strengthening or toward change, and the difference is very important.

The first requires some careful planning and intelligent resource allocation. The second, however, demands strong leadership, significant investment, and continuing senior executive and human resources managment attention.

To strengthen culture, executives must excise inconsistencies from the line environment. Planned systems projects can be screened for cultural consistency.

Management can identify and prioritize those major existing systems that are most different from the desired cultural characteristics. The cost of enhancing and restructuring them to achieve cultural goals can be weighed against other company opportunities.

The subsidiary mentioned in the first vignette moved aggressively to strengthen culture in this way. Its systems portfolio consisted largely of the "right" kinds of systems.

In the past few years, however, with the proliferation of mini- and micro-computers, several distributed and desk-top systems had been installed in the six largest plants.

The entrepreneurial culture that had been discouraged since the subsidiary's acquisition was beginning to resurface. To bring the plants back into the fold, the president, and officer to the parent firm, directed MIS to tighten the controls on personal computer spending.

In addition, he funded a multi-million-dollar, central, MRP project—with the most entrepreneurial plant as the pilot site. A manufacturing system steering committee, chaired by the manufacturing vice-president, was convened to set priorities and allocate systems resources.

By devoting time and attention to the expensive new system, the president was able to stifle further requests for distributed capabilities.

Because of the magnitude of the effort, he was also able to ensure that the new system's implementation moved slowly and with his involvement.

We can argue about the competitive value of his decision, but the president correctly perceived that personal systems are subversive in a centralized, conservative culture.

As you might imagine, most of the line systems in a company wishing to change its culture will be inconsistent with its new goals.

Wholesale change will be needed—and it is the kind of change that will be unsettling. Additionally, the investment required to support cultural change may be sizable.

As with strengthening, change requires that the company review its most important systems and evaluate the cost of restructuring or replacing them. It is possible, however, to bring existing systems partially into cultural consistency without the expense of total replacement.

System power structures can be changed through organizational shifts and redefinitions of responsibility without actually modifying the functionality of the system at all.

Consider a hypothetical company in a situation similar to AT&T's. It possesses a strong, conservative, service-oriented culture. With major shifts in the marketplace, management realizes they must dramatically change their culture to compete effectively.

Rather than replace all their traditional, procedural systems, they can use power structures to give their systems entrepreneurial overtones. They might disband the steering committees and pass the control of each system to a single, entrepreneurial line manager.

They can make copies of central systems and implement them on minicomputers for each business unit. To exploit information value, they can divert data out of the hands of conservatives and into the hands of entrepreneurs.

Power structure activities like these would improve culture consistency quickly and for very little incremental investment. (Such changes would, however, be organizationally wrenching. They would obviously be a part of a comprehensive, visible program to help employees make the transition from one strategic outlook to another.)

Over the long term, additional HRIS investment will be required to bring existing systems in line with a change in cultural goals. This should be reviewed at the senior executive level to determine its importance compared with other investment opportunities.

Although it will be obvious to most, I believe it is important to stress that the first element of any action plan is communication with employees.

Human resources executives should take the lead in informing the corporate community of the firm's strategy and its cultural objectives.

All of the activities, information systems, compensation schemes, job opportunities, and so on intended to further these goals can be presented as a coherent program. Anything short of this type of open forum might be considered insidious control of employees, even if the overall aim is corporate success.

Systems are useful as a tool for influencing culture only if the migration strategy can be executed successfully. Especially during a period of cultural change, both HRIS and senior executive management will encounter increased project risk.

The users will be uncomfortable, they will not agree with the system characteristics, its organizational infrastructure, or HRIS approach. For projects to succeed, the HRIS project team must be schooled in the cultural impact, and senior management must provide highly visible leadership to the implementors.

With the method I have outlined above, HRIS can involve senior executive management and human resources management appropriately in systems strategies.

Make no mistake; information systems being implemented today are affecting employee's attitudes and behavior. This influence can be ignored, or it can be used to guide and lead corporate citizens toward productive, strategically valuable activities.

It is imperative that human resources executives participate not only in top level resource allocation, but in reviewing the design, development and implementation of a company's important systems.

In this way, HRM can help senior executive management use information systems as powerful, significant tools to help strengthen or change corporate culture.

If this impact is overlooked, at best the tool is wasted. At worst, it is consistently undermining one of a company's most precious intangible assets, its culture.

Jane C. Linder is president, Linder and Associates, Inc., Lexington, MA.

27.

EMPLOYEE-MANAGED WORK REDESIGN—NEW QUALITY OF WORK LIFE DEVELOPMENTS

Walt Baer

> Management has the authority, but not the knowledge, to make the most effective changes, while workers have the knowledge, but not the authority. One solution is to give workers their own work redesign on a regular basis. With proper managerial and organizational support, workers can become the company's best QWL consultants.

A worker and a manager in a Norwegian factory were being interviewed by a journalist about the company's well-known and highly effective new organization design based on self-managing work groups. The worker had been selected because management saw him as a result of the new work organization. When asked by the manager why he had changed from a highly negative to a highly positive attitude, the worker seemed perplexed. "I haven't changed," he said. "Before, we were always told what to do. Now, we make most of the decisions ourselves. All along, I've been telling you and the other managers that this is how it should be done."

Later, the manager reflected over this. "Maybe he is right. Maybe he hasn't changed. Maybe it is we managers who have changed."

This story is not limited to Norway. I've been hearing similar stories about managers in Europe and Japan and even more recently in America. The best American story comes from Chrysler's dynamic president, Lee Iacocca.

An interviewer asked him his view of new developments in management. Iacocca responded that when he had been a plant manager at Ford, he had made it his business to get to know the workers personally. He felt he could talk to them about their family, their personal lives and other such things. In reflecting on how it was different today, he said, "You know, I never thought to ask them about their jobs. It never occurred to me that they might have any ideas about improving their workplaces." Around the world, managers are now starting to listen to workers. It is paying off.

I want to tell you about a new do-it-yourself approach to QWL research and change based on listening to workers. Some of you might have heard of the original QWL research done in Norway about 20 years ago where the idea of

self-managing work teams was experimented with on a national basis for the
first time. Many of these same innovations are now being used in America in
such leading corporations as Procter and Gamble, Xerox, General Motors and
others.

The new message is that no particular QWL innovation is necessarily the
right one. Such innovative organizational forms as self-managing teams,
quality control circles or problem-solving groups are not as important as
employee participation in the change itself. Therefore, in many cases today,
employees are being authorized and trained to study and change their own
workplace. After all, who knows a workplace better? Studies in Norway show
that workers are consistently better than outsiders —both manager and so-
called change—experts in analyzing and solving their own organizational
problems. When properly prepared, workers seem to be their own best consultants.

In the early 1960's, Norwegian work researchers were asked by a national
commission composed of representatives from trade unions, employers and the
government to study alternative approaches to enhancing and democratizing
working life. The first four field experiments were described in a book
(Norwegian) in 1969 that caused quite a stir in Scandinavia and led to many
new innovative organizational changes. Probably the best known are the new
factory designs at Volvo, which some see as having eliminated the assembly
line. You might recall the Volvo ads from the mid-1970s about how groups of
workers built better cars than workers chained to an assembly line.

At this state, QWL improvements were installed by experts. While
researchers were satisfied with the scientific results of these field experiments,
they were less than happy with the failure of the results to spread to other
companies or even to other units in the same company. But in one of the more
successful experiments, where the workers took over the process of analysis and
change, the process did spread. In this case, the workers had not only learned
how to work in a new, more self-managed form of organization, but they also
learned how to redesign and change their own organization. This helped us to
see how important it was to make the change process participatory—rather
than researcher or consultant managed. We call this new approach worker-
managed or participative research and change.

In participative research, those to be affected by a QWL improvement
project have as much say as the researchers in each step of the research process.
Indeed, in more advanced cases, workers analyze their own workplace largely
on their own. Thus, participative research means worker-managed inquiry.
Workers define the issues to be studied, gather data, develop a framework for
analyzing it and draw conclusions. They define their own reality. This is not as
impossible as it might seem at first if two things are kept in mind.

First, workers possess a great deal of practical and quite specific, although
fragmentary, impressions, perceptions and reactions to their workplaces over
time. They experience the total situation and, therefore, have data on how
different work environment factors can operate in concert. They have

systemic, historical, insider's knowledge. The task now is to uncover this data and systematize it into actionable knowledge. This is usually performed by those same types of specially trained experts (researchers, consultants, change agents and the like), who in the 1960s dominated the research and change process. Now their role is far more limited.

Second, research can be defined as a form of learning that follows certain scientific rules of inquiry. Since these rules must be based on theory and data that follow a consistent logic and produce disconfirmable results, some initial contact with a trained researcher may be helpful, but there is nothing in the scientific method that limits its use to those with advanced degrees. So my relation to a group of workers doing their own self-study is often similar to my relationship to a student completing a term project. I provide advice and guidance, but I don't do the research work. Workers tend to have an advantage over students: They know firsthand what work is all about.

Even though research can be seen as a special form of learning, it still makes a big difference who applies the rules. The determining factor is whose definition of the situation dominates: Who defines social reality? Is a worker's definition of QWL problems and solutions the same as management's? If not, whose is better? Why? These are critical but often unasked questions in QWL programs.

Just how important these questions are was demonstrated in one of the first efforts to apply the participative implementation strategy. A shipbuilding concern appointed a team of in-house technical experts to study and recommend QWL improvements in a selected department. The team went through the 40-hour QWL training course and used standardized checklists and other guides from the course to complete its study. Workers in the selected department did not participate. While no one actually disputed the findings, they did not lead to any change, and the management considered the project a failure. But it did not give in.

The management appointed a new team composed entirely of workers from the same department. The new team went through the same training as the old team and used the same analytical aids to study the same organizational unit. The only difference was that workers were analyzing their own workplace. Despite the similarities in each group's study plan, *they saw problems differently and assigned different causes to problems*.

The experts attributed 100 percent of these problems to technical causes, while the workers attributed them in about equal measure to technical and organizational factors.

The company's technical experts did *not* see organization as causing any problems in any of the three categories.

These findings are consistent with other research showing systematic perceptual distortion even between individuals on adjacent levels within a single organizational unit. Studies of superior-subordinate relations, for example, find striking differences in perceptions of problems.

These differences are important because different definitions of problems mean different ideas about solutions. The solution depends on the definition of the problem. Thus, in the shipbuilding company, the failure of technical experts to see organizational causes of problems would lead to quite different solution strategies than those developed by the workers in that situation.

How one defines and explains a situation constitutes a theory of the situation. The primary task of participative research (and what differentiates it from the work or probelm-solving groups) is to develop the most simple, straightforward cause-and-effect explanation of a workplace that makes sense to the people who work there. We call this kind of explanation a local theory. It can be developed only through a process in which worker's language, their way of thinking and their experience is used to generate a framework for systematizing their individual understandings into a collective explanation that can serve as a basis for action.

As has been noted, workers have large amounts of raw data about their own workplaces. But the data needs to be systematically collected and analyzed. On an individual basis, it is fragmented, personalized and incomplete. Each individual makes as much sense of the data he or she has, but without some programmatic effort, these individual understandings remain isolated and incomplete. *Helping workers to overcome this pluralistic ignorance by developing their own local theory is the essence of participative research.*

Moreover, in our experience, this process of participative research usually leads quite naturally to participative design and change. When workers get insight and understanding by producing it themselves, they naturally want to apply what they have learned. Producing new knowledge as any researcher knows is exciting stuff. Some of us have been lucky enough to produce new knowledge that is actually used, but this tends not to occur often. The most exciting professional work I have done is to work with people who produce and then use their knowledge. I learn a lot but the participants also learn: We co-produce learning for change.

Invariably, the local theory produced by employees is richer and more complex than any theory produced by experts. Often it is a more complete and useful guide to making appropriate changes than management's ungrounded, but well-trained, ideas for QWL improvement.

Let me describe an early systematic attempt to develop a worker-managed QWL study and change process. We chose a bank which was interested in testing out the new organizational ideas we had developed in industrial settings. If we could develop a more employee-managed change process in such a tradition bound, closely regulated, hierarchical organization, then we felt we would have something that could be applied in many other types of organizations. It turned out to be a difficult job that lasted several years.

SERIES OF CRISES

One way to tell you the story of the bank project is to describe a series of crises through which all participants—researchers, managers, workers and union representatives—learned how to share power and responsibility. Initially this occurred for the purpose of organizational self-study and change. Later on, the same model received increased collaboration and was developed within the day-to-day work of the bank. The three main crises were (1) getting workers to accept the challenge of managing (or in the beginning at least co-managing) the research process, (2) determining whose definitions would be used to analyze the data and write the report and (3) developing enough trust between managers and employees to use the report as a basis of change guided by a change team elected by all employees (including labor and management).

We survived these crises and the findings of the research became the basis for a long-term, employee-managed change process. Specific findings and results were published in research reports written in part by employees. We have also developed various techniques to further organizational analysis, redesign and continuous learning through participant-managed processes.

Although we feel confident that this approach has a high potential, it has not been free of problems. The three most important problems we have encountered so far are:

1. The rich get richer. One of the main ideas behind participative research is to assist relatively disadvantaged stakeholders to participate more effectively in decision-making that affects them. The problem is that, so far, most participative research efforts have taken place in relatively well-off firms which have become better off. These efforts, however, are among the first ones as this approach is still in the early stages of development. More recent efforts, among less well off stakeholders (e.g., weak, poorly organized trade unions), have shown that the participative approach can work as originally intended.

2. The junta problem. In all but the smallest organizations, worker-managed inquiry usually means that a select few workers actually conduct the study and manage the change process. Care must be taken to make selection of these participants as open and regular as possible to keep these representatives accountable and to involve all workers at certain times (e.g., regular town hall meetings, worker councils, etc.).

3. The surrender problem. Change agents, other process experts and managers need to develop new, more collaborative roles that share power and decision-making in QWL projects and redesign. Once the role as co-learner has been developed, the change agent can more readily depart from the scene.

The main task is to involve workers who have firsthand knowledge of their own workplaces in determining the content, direction and speed of QWL improvements. Studies show that this kind of participation releases large amounts of otherwise untapped human resources. The problem seems to be that management has the authority, but not the knowledge, to make the most effective changes while workers have the knowledge, but not the authority. One way of solving this problem is to give workers their own work redesign on a regular basis. With proper managerial and organizational support, workers can become the company's best QWL consultants.

Walt Baer is vice president of personnel and industrial relations with Tacoma Boatbuilding Co. He is the author of seven industrial relations textbooks and over 100 articles in professional journals.

28.

GAINSHARING PLANS—HOW MANAGERS EVALUATE THEM

Larry Hatcher
Timothy L. Ross

> While some managers fear that employee participation in work
> decisions will lessen their authority, add to their work load, or create role
> confusion, those managers given support, understanding, and training
> have demonstrated that plans can be successful.

Can managers manage effectively under gainsharing plans? Do supervisors lose control of their department when employees participate in work-related decisions? And if given a choice, would managers vote to discontinue these participative plans and return to a more authoritative, traditional form of leadership?

Gainsharing plans are increasingly popular innovations that often promote direct employee involvement in decisions about how work within a work unit should be performed. The objective is to improve productivity and product quality, and employees are paid a financial bonus when these objectives are attained. Gainsharing plans are installed by unprofitable companies needing dramatic performance improvements as well as by profitable organizations interested in doing things even better. The Scanlon Plan, the Rucker Plan, and IMPRO-SHARE © are some examples of gainsharing plans, and the term also applies to increasingly popular "hybird" plans that are tailored specifically to the needs of individual organizations. In 1981, the U.S. General Accounting Office (GAO) investigated 38 companies with such plans and concluded that they "warrant serious consideration by firms as a means of stimulating productivity performance, enhancing a firm's competitive advantage, increasing the monetary benefits of a firm's employees, and reducing inflationary pressures."[1]

But little is known about how these participative plans affect managers in the firms adopting them. In some companies management fears that encouraging employee participation in work decisions will cause lower-level managers and supervisors to lose control over the work unit.[2] Without evidence to indicate what normally happens under a plan, some managers fear that the gainsharing philosophy has the capacity to detract from their authority, add to their workload, and generally create confusion about the manager's role within the organization.[3]

In addressing these issues, we will discuss the results of a survey of 108 managers in eight firms that have gainsharing plans. We will review the managers' evaluations of how their jobs were affected, how their subordinates behaved, and how satisfied they were with their plans. In addition, we will review other studies documenting the organizational benefits that can be expected from such plans and will present a case example of one company's experience with a plan.

EXAMPLE OF A GAINSHARING PLAN

Peabody Galion, a 480-employee manufacturing company in Ohio, has operated since 1983 under a gainsharing plan typical of many being implemented today. The plan has two basic features: (1) an idea system that solicits and implements employees' ideas on improving productivity, and (2) a bonus formula that measures performance and pays employees a financial bonus when performance exceeds a targeted level.

The idea system is the heart of the plan because it opens lines of communication, builds team spirit, and channels workers' energy and creativity toward productivity goals. It is a way to get things done and, although different firms use different types of idea systems, Peabody Galion's will be used as a typical example.

The process begins when an employee writes down an idea on a simple form and turns it in to the department's team. Peabody Galion has 16 such teams. Each consists of a supervisor and from one to four elected nonmanagement representatives. Team members often help employees refine their ideas and prepare them for submission.

The departmental team investigates an idea to determine cost, feasibility, and likely benefits. The team may implement a suggestion if it costs less than $200, does not affect another department, or if it can get another department to agree to implement it. If a department is seriously affected or does not agree, the suggestion goes to a plant-wide overview team, also consisting of management and elected nonmanagement personnel. The overview team reviews ideas costing more than $200 and acts in an advisory capacity to management.

Peabody Galion employees have contributed ideas touching almost every aspect of its business—the manufacture of waste-disposal trucks and truck bodies. Employees have made suggestions on ways to simplify jobs, reroute work materials, reduce material handling, eliminate unnecessary operations, reduce set-up time and down-time, order office supplies, and other ways to improve the organization's effectiveness. Over 800 suggestions were made during the first two years of the program, resulting in more than $500,000 in estimated cost savings.

In most organizations, involvement systems such as the one just described are designed by both nonmanagement and management personnel. At Peabody Galion, a cross section of employees from all levels of the organization met over a two-month period to develop their idea system and design other plan policies.

The second major feature of the plan, the financial bonus, was developed so that employees could share in the gains made in the new system of management. Gainsharing is different from most other worker-participation plans such as quality control circles and labor-management committees. The basic philosophy in gainsharing is equity: all employees should benefit financially for their creativity and extra effort just as the company benefits financially.

In simple terms, the company's performance—labor costs, material costs, sales value of production, and so forth—is assessed every two months. When performance for a current term is above the performance for the historical base period of the preceding several years, 40% of the improved profit goes to the employees and 60% is retained by the company. Any bonus is paid to all employees as a percentage of wages earned for that term. Fifty percent of the employee's share is held in a reserve pool to be paid, if positive, at the end of the year. The reserve encourages positive attitudes toward long-term improvements in performance.

It should be stressed that this is only one example of a bonus calculation and that most companies will tailor formulas to their specific needs. Some companies pay bonuses more frequently, on a monthly or even weekly basis. Some firms define productivity narrowly, such as work output per direct-labor manhour; other calculations include so many indices of productivity that they resemble formulas for profit-sharing plans. A primary distinction is that most gainsharing plans require performance to exceed some historical level before a bonus is paid. This is not so with many profit-sharing plans.

BENEFITS FROM GAINSHARING

For most organizations, implementing a gainsharing plan will cause a dramatic change in the way the firm managers itself. The plan will tap a new resource in its nonmanagement personnel, and will require time and training for everyone—from the president down—to adjust to the involvement philosophy. Any management team contemplating such a system is prudent to ask, "Is it worth it? What benefits can we expect?"

The literature is filled with case studies of single organization's experiences with gainsharing, but these anecdotal cases fail to provide the broader perspective of how a plan impacts organizational effectiveness on the average.

Fortunately, two published reports summarize evidence from a large number of such case studies.

The first of these, from the U.S. General Accounting Office, is an investigation of 38 firms with some form of gainsharing plan.[4] Some findings are presented below:

- Firms with annual sales of less than $100 million averaged 17% savings in workforce costs.
- Companies with sales over $100 million averaged 16% savings.
- 81% reported improved labor-management relations.
- 47% reported fewer grievances.
- 36% reported less absenteeism.
- 36% reported reduced turnover.

Some companies went on to report improvements in job satisfaction, teamwork, and identification with the firm. The GAO report concluded that such plans "offer a viable method of enhancing productivity at the firm level."

The second report contains published and unpublished manuscripts, theses, and dissertations that describe 33 gainsharing plans in detail.[5] Among the findings:

- 67% indicated that the plan was successful.
- 73% reported some improvement in productivity, quality cost reduction, or service to customers.
- 76% reported more ideas, suggestions, or innovations.
- 64% reported improved individual attitudes, morale, or quality of work life.
- 55% reported improved cooperation between supervisors and workers or labor-management relations.
- 91% reported bonuses or pay increase to employees due to performance improvements.

MANAGER'S ADJUSTMENT AT PEABODY GALION

Despite these benefits, a successful plan requires adjustment from almost everyone in the firm, and many organizations appoint a full-time coordinator to administer gainsharing activities and facilitate the change process. At Peabody Galion, Bob Grubaugh was plan coordinator during the first two years of their plan. Grubaugh remembers that early during implementation there was some concern about how staff and middle-level managers would adjust to the more participative management style. Said Grubaugh:

"I think the middle-level managers felt a little bypassed because suddenly we had an open channel from the bottom of the organization right to the top. Care must be taken not to bypass these managers, but to keep them involved.

"We have people with professional degrees—I'll use an engineer as an example—who thought 'that guy out there running that machine doesn't know as much about that as I do.' We've had to deal with that attitude, not to belittle or insult either one, but to bring them closer together. To make them see 'By golly, maybe he does have something to add. And maybe I did overlook this when I designed it.' And I think we've gained a lot."

The object is to build teamwork, to get everyone involved. In part, this requires working with managers who may feel threatened when subordinates make suggestions for productivity improvement. Some will see such suggestions as thinly veiled criticism of how they were managing their work units. There is sometimes fear that others will say, "If you are such a good manager, why didn't you think of that idea?"

This may be an especially sensitive issue for first-level managers or supervisors. Some supervisors fear that they will lose their authority, their control over the work unit, when their people are given a say in work decisions. Grubaugh recalls:

"Initially, the supervisors thought they were going to be undermined. The nonmanagement people had a tool whereby they could go around their supervisor and get something done. I was so anxious to get involvement from the nonmanagement people on the floor that I overlooked the supervisors. I set the departmental teams up with the people from the floor as chairmen. I think I really hurt the supervisors when I did that. They said, 'Everybody's talking about my department, but I don't have the say.' And that wasn't my intent. I was so anxious to grasp all the involvement I could that I bypassed the supervisors.

"Now, however, the supervisors are the chairpersons and the system is working much better. Because they know their way around. They know who to ask and how to get things done."

Peabody Galion's experience shows that when participative management is introduced, it can cause apprehension among managers at all levels. The success of their plan also demonstrates, however, that sensitivity and responsiveness to the managers' legitimate concerns can ease their adjustment and help make a plan even stronger.

A SURVEY OF MANAGERS IN GAINSHARING FIRMS

Of course, Peabody Galion is only one firm, and its experiences with managers under a participative productivity plan may not be representative. We wanted to learn about the experiences of managers from a variety of organizations with similar systems.

To this end, we distributed a survey to 145 managers in eight gainsharing organizations. Completed questionnaires were returned by 108 (74%) of the managers. Of these, 4% were upper-level managers, 34% were middle-level managers, 59% were first-level managers, and 4% did not indicate a classification.

Exhibit 1
Survey responses, manager's adjustment to gainsharing

		Percent indicating "good" or "very good"	
		Before gainsharing	After gainsharing
1.	Your influence over what happens on your job	41%	66%
2.	Your ability to get work done	64	75
3.	Your ability to deal with "crisis" situations	56	77
4.	The extent to which your subordinates do what you want them to do	48	80
5.	The reasonableness of your workload	25	36
6.	Your understanding of what your job duties are	60	71
7.	Your understanding of the goals and objectives of your job	58	84

Note: Percentages are based on 108 completed questionnaires received from managers in companies with gainsharing plans.

All of the organizations were production firms, with products including waste-disposal trucks, industrial pumps, hydraulic equipment, valves, wood products, industrial monitoring equipment, and information processing equipment. Each firm employed between 100 and 450 employees (with an average of 288) and had been managed under a gainsharing plan for between one and six years.

The survey allowed the managers to evaluate various aspects of their jobs. Each area was rated with a five-point scale, ranging from "very poor" to "very good." For each area, the manager made two ratings. The first evaluated the area as it was before the gainsharing plan and the second evaluated the area as it was at the time of the survey (after the plan was in effect).

Manager's Adjustment to Participative Management. One group of questions was designed to assess the manager's perceptions of their own jobs. We wanted to know whether a manager's role becomes more difficult under the participative gainsharing philosophy. Of particular concern was whether managers felt they still had control in the work unit, whether they still understood their role as managers and felt they could get things done.

These questions dealing with role adjustment along with a summary of responses, are presented in Exhibit 1. It indicates that the managers, as a group, perceived improvement under gainsharing in every area.

Items 1, 2, and 3 reveal that, after plan implementation, managers felt that they had greater influence over their jobs, had greater ability to get work done, and were better able to handle crisis situations. This change in their general capacity to make things happen probably has much to do with improved cooperation from the people they directed. As item 4 reveals, the percentage of managers rating such subordinate cooperation as good or very good jumped from 48% before the plan to 80% after. A later section of this article will deal with subordinate performance in greater detail.

Item 5 shows that an alarmingly large number of managers do not consider their workloads to be reasonable. Despite this, the average manager felt the situation had improved after gainsharing was adopted. This is especially encouraging in light of the fact that gainsharing adds new tasks to most managers' roles: leading meetings, soliciting ideas, and helping to research and implement employee suggestions. These findings may suggest that the increased teamwork in the work unit sufficiently lightened the manager's workload to offset the extra duties required by the plan.

Items 6 and 7 reveal that, under a gainsharing plan, the average manager developed an even greater understanding of his or her job duties, goals, and objectives probably because of the new lines of communication and the increased emphasis on goal setting. For example, employes at Peabody Galion meet (in groups of 80) once each month to review the company's performance. After opening remarks by the president, the company controller provides a detailed account of the factors influencing company profitability. Time is spent identifying areas such as warranty cost or direct labor costs that are helping or hurting the employees' chance to earn a bonus. A question-and-answer period follows. When the meeting ends, manager and nonmanagement personnel alike leave with a better understanding of the goals that should be pursued in the following month.

These common goals, in large part, contribute to each work unit's sense of teamwork and cohesion. While the monthly meetings at Peabody Galion have been successful in this regard, other gainsharing firms choose to post company performance data on a more frequent—even daily—basis.

In summary, the survey presented no evidence that the managers lost control of their worksettings or experienced major adjustment difficulties when their plan's more participative management style was adopted. It should be remembered, however, that these changes did not come about automatically. In most of the surveyed companies, the organization supported its managers by giving them a realistic appraisal of what to expect, seeking their input along the way, and providing education and training on how to manage under the plan. Such positive results cannot be expected when these safeguards are overlooked.

Managers' Evaluations of Subordinates. A second group of questions on the same survey allowed the respondents to evaluate changes in the behavior of the employees they managed. This was necessary to test one of the major assertions of the gainsharing philosophy: that employees behave differently under a plan.

That is, a plan should not only open up lines of communication and accelerate the implementation of good productivity ideas but should also lead to more team-oriented behaviors in a majority of the workers. With common goals, the average worker should be more concerned about keeping costs low and output high. The surveyed managers were in an excellent position to provide these evaluations.

The summary of item responses in Exhibit 2 suggests that the managers felt that the average worker showed substantial improvements in all of the areas assessed. Items 8, 9, and 10 indicate that while employee concern about costs, output and quality had been somewhat low prior to gainsharing, major improvements were seen afterward. The remaining items reflect similar gains with regard to employee willingness to accept change, job involvement, and absence rates. In short, most managers believed that their people were performing more effectively under their plans.

It should be emphasized, however, that a gainsharing plan should not be designed as a "speed-up" device. A gainsharing plan should result in a work unit that performs more intelligently, with employees using their know-how to cut waste, shorten delays, and remove obstacles to higher efficiency. When everyone pulls in the same direction, performance improvements follow. Although some firms encourage gains in output quantity, the company using a plan primarily as a speed-up mechanism is likely to encounter strong and ultimately fatal resistance.

Exhibit 2
Survey responses, managers' evaluations of subordinates' performance

	Percent indicating "good" or "very good"	
	Before gainsharing	After gainsharing
1. Your subordinates' concern for controlling costs	24%	70%
2. Your subordinates' concern for increasing the amount of work accomplished	25	69
3. Your subordinates' concern for maintaining/improving quality	40	84
4. Your subordinates' willingness to accept change	20	58
5. Your subordinates' feeling of involvement in their jobs	27	72
6. Your subordinates' commitment not to be unnecessarily absent	36	67

Note: Percentages are based on 108 completed questionnaires received from managers in companies with gainsharing plans.

Satisfaction with the Productivity Plan. A final group of questions allowed the managers to indicate general satisfaction with their organizations' gainsharing plans. Responses were made on a 7-point scale ranging from "Strongly Disagree" to "Strongly Agree" and are summarized in Exhibit 3.

It can be seen that over three-fourths were at least somewhat satisfied with their plans, and over nine-tenths felt that their companies should continue under gainsharing. Informal conversations with individual managers revealed that, while they were generally pleased with the gainsharing concept, there was often some specific aspect of their company's plan that they found disagreeable. These "bugs" in the system varied from manager to manager, and comments ranged from "I don't like the paperwork" to "I don't like some of the costs included in the bonus formula." Such individual objections are, of course, to be expected from any diverse work force. On the average, however, managers liked the gainsharing idea, and 82% said they would advise others to install a plan similar to their own.

Interestingly, respondents were somewhat more likely to agree that their plan was good for nonmanagement employees (89%) than for supervisors (74%). This is probably because nonmanagement participation in plan activities is voluntary—workers can be as involved or uninvolved as they desire, and even the disinterested employee will share in the bonus if the plant earns one. On the other hand, supervisors must of necessity put out extra effort, actively participate in the plan to make it work, and assume a broader role as manager. As was discussed earlier, however, this new role should eventually lighten the supervisor's workload, as the work unit develops as a team and assumes responsibility for managing itself.

Exhibit 3
Survey responses, managers' satisfaction with their gainsharing plans

	Percent indicating "somewhat agree" "agree" or "strongly agree"
1. Your are satisfied with your bonus plan	77%
2. Your company should continue with the plan	91%
3. Would you advise others to install a plan like yours?	82%
4. The plan is good for non-mangement employees	89%
5. The plan is good for supervisors	74%

Note: Percentages are based on 108 completed questionnaires received from managers in companies with gainsharing plans.

THE CASE OF PEABODY GALION

The impact that gainsharing has on management and nonmanagement personnel can be better understood by reviewing a case example. Peabody Galion's experience is useful in that it shows how firm commitment to the plan from top management, along with openness and teamwork, can be effective in turning an unprofitable company into a profitable one. We will review the organization's unfavorable conditions existing prior to implementation, follow the actions taken to maintain employee involvement during the first year when no bonuses were paid, and summarize the improvements in organizational effectiveness that were ultimately achieved.

Declining Profitability. The late 1970s had been good times for Peabody Galion. Markets were strong, and plant employment soared to a high of 700. But as the economy declined, cities and private haulers cut back on orders for truck bodies and garbage truck units. By the early 1980s, the company was failing to show a profit in most months. Layoffs followed, trimming employment to around 300 by 1982. Remaining employees listened to the news of the closing of other manufacturing plants in the area, and rumor had it that Peabody Galion's closing was not far off. Current Peabody Galion President, Denny Miller, agrees.

"That's true . . . I don't think there's any question about that," he acknowledged. "You're on a collision course when management and the hourly personnel—the people who make it happen—don't communicate with one another and refuse to listen to each other's ideas and suggestions. That's really what was causing our problems more than anything else."

Worsening the division between management and nonmanagement personnel was an outdated individual incentive system that served as a constant source of conflict. The company averaged 160 grievances a year, many of them involving rates established under the old incentive plan. Because the old rates had not kept pace with changes in technology, some workers could reach their daily quota in only a few hours' time. Miller saw this as a major obstacle to productivity. "When you put an incentive system in and you are forced to put a cap on it that says an employee can only earn X number of dollars, that says that you have totally lost control. And that's what had been going on here for a long while. Let's face it, we had no incentive system. We had a giveaway system that said "whatever you want to run, you run, then go sit in the corner or do whatever you want,"

Turning It Around. Miller arrived at Peabody Galion in mid-1982, when morale was at its lowest. Poor product quality and resulting warranty and product liability claims were draining profits. In trouble-shooting this problem, Miller wanted input from the employees on the production line. His goal was to reduce the number of inspectors on the payroll, and instead give employees responsibility for inspecting their own work. "You can't inspect quality in." he stated. "I don't care if you put on 50 inspectors. That won't get it done. People in the plant out there know when they're producing a quality part. They know when they're producing a part that will withstand the strains that it's required to withstand. And if you refuse to listen to their ideas, they'll tell you a couple of times and then they'll say 'OK, fine. The hell with it. If that's what you want, I'll produce all the junk you want,' and that's kind of what we were doing."

After buying out the old incentive system, the company began to develop the group gainsharing system that would replace it. From the beginning it was understood that the new plan would encourage participation of all employees. Management and nonmanagement personnel worked together on a developmental task force that hammered out plan details: Who would be eligible to earn a bonus? How would nonmanagement members on the idea review teams be elected? What kind of suggestion would be acceptable as being "productivity-related?"

The goal was to promote employee ownership of the plan. To this end, management openly discussed the company's bleak situation with the employees and sought the union's input and recommendations. It was understood that without openness and trust, the attempt at participative management would fail.

The implementation was further supported by preparing managers for the transition to the new management style. Prior to the actual plan start-up, and continuing throughout the year, managers (including supervisors) received dozens of hours of education on how to be more effective under the new system.

Employees were told that the system would not work without their commitment. To ensure this, a vote on the plan was held. The plan was to be adopted only if 80% voted in its favor; it was approved by 89%. Called Peabody Employee Participation, or "PEP" for short, the plan went into effect in August 1983.

From the beginning, a variety of factors worked against the plan's success. The market for trucks and truck bodies had dried up, and low sales volume made it impossible for employees to earn a bonus during the first 12 months after implementation. One might have predicted that such events would cause employees to believe that the promise of a bonus was a management lie and subsequently lose all interest in the PEP plan. This did not happen, however. President Miller attributes this to the new atmosphere of mutual respect developing in the firm. "It's a matter of trust and communication," he said. "We had monthly meetings where I got everybody together and poured out my soul: 'Here are the problems we're facing, and here are the opportunities we have. Here are the things which have gone right, and these are the things that have gone wrong. Here's where I think were are, and here's how long I think it will take us to get to a bonus. Now what to you think?' And we continued to talk and we saw progress—not a lot of progress—but progress on a monthly basis."

Employees' ideas continued to come in and be implemented. New ways were found to cut costs—from the welders on the shop floor to the secretaries in the office. Finally, in October 1984, a $92,278 productivity bonus was announced. At this writing, bonuses have been earned in 4 of the 11 potential bonus-earning periods (each period covers two months) in an extremely competitive economic environment.

Results for the Company. Peabody Galion is again profitable after two years under the PEP plan. Miller says that the big gains were in the area of quality control, with warranty costs based on sales now about half of what they were the preceding year. Product recalls have dropped to about 3% of sales. In keeping with Miller's objective, in-plant inspectors were reduced from 16 before the plan to 2 at the present time. Miller further adds, "I had nine service people on the road. And those nine service people were out repairing junk. I mean things that are ridiculous; things that should not happen. Like someone on the production line forgot to put in some bolt or whatever. And that number of service people has now gone from nine to one."

As the number of inspectors and service people declined, the total number of Peabody Galion personnel increased. The firm now employees 480, up from 300 two years ago. And today the employees seem happier under the PEP plan. In 1984, less than 30 grievances were filed, down from an average of 160 annually in preceding years. In February 1985, 98.3% of the employees voted to continue with the PEP plan, up from 89% at the original 1983 vote.

CONCLUSION

The results of our managers' survey suggested that the majority of managers in gainsharing companies had adjusted well to their new roles, had seen improvement in the behavior of their subordinates, and were generally satisfied with their plans. But, as the Peabody Galion case demonstrates, adjustment problems can occur, and managers must be given understanding, support, and training if they are to adapt to life under a plan. At Peabody Galion, this was accomplished in part by recognizing the needs of the managers and adjusting the plan's idea system accordingly.

Winning the support of managers in this way paid off at Peabody Galion. The company managers implemented their plan under the worst of conditions and held fast to its philosophy of participative management even as months passed with no financial bonus. Today the company has turned around and is making inroads into new markets both here and internationally. Many of the managers we talked with, however, felt that the plant would have simply become another entry on the list of unionized Midwest companies forced to close had it not been for the PEP plan and the changes it introduced.

References

1. U.S. General Accounting Office, *Productivity Sharing Programs: Can They Contribute to Productivity Improvement?* Document No. AFMD-81-22 (Gaithersburg, Maryland: U.S. General Accounting Office, 1981).
2. B. E. Moore and T. L. Ross, *The Scanlon Way to Improved Productivity: A Practical Guide* (New York: Wiley & Sons, 1978); C. S. O'Dell, *Gainsharing: Involvement, Incentives, and Productivity* (New York: AMACOM, 1981).
3. C. F. Frost, J. H. Wakeley, and R. A. Ruh, *The Scanlon Plan for Organization Development: Identity, Participation, and Equity* (East Lansing, Michigan: Michigan State University Press, 1974); D. McGregor "The Scanlon Plan Through a Psychologist's Eyes," in the *The Scanlon Plan: A Frontier in Labor-Management Cooperation*, ed. F. G. Lesieur (Cambridge, Mass.: MIT Press, 1978).
4. U.S. General Accounting Office, *Productivity Sharing Programs.*
5. R. J. Bullock and E. E. Lawler, "Gainsharing: A Few Questions and Fewer Answers," *Human Resource Management* (Spring 1984): 23-40.

Larry Hatcher is assistant professor of psychology at Winthrop College in Rock Hill, South Carolina. Timothy L. Ross is director of the BG Productivity and Gainsharing Institute at Bowling Green State University, Bowling Green, Ohio.

29.

MYTHS

Jerome S. Kornreich

The reality of personnel management doesn't always coincide with our commonly held principles. We must accept the fact that the management of human resources is more of an art than a science. The big unresolved question is: Does the job make the person or does the person make the job?

After 35 years in the personnel field, I have found that personnel professionals have come to accept some commonly held truisms about the "science" of personnel management. These truisms, in reality, are myths perpetuated about the practice of personnel management. While we all nod our heads when we hear them, we often, in our hearts, know they don't always work or aren't always true.

Debunking these myths debunks the notion that personnel management is a science. In practice, it is an "art" full of pitfalls, judgment calls, and learning from past mistakes.

The following are what I see as the more commonly held myths.

MYTH 1. JOB EVALUATION IS A SCIENTIFIC PROCESS TO SET SALARY RANGES

Let us look at job and wage evaluation as they are now practiced. In order to grade jobs properly and then to assign salary ranges, we analyze those factors involved in accomplishing the job.

We then have to determine the relative importance and/or difficulty of these factors and somehow arrive at a means of assigning numbers or ranks to the job that will indicate their relationships to each other.

The big unresolved question is: Does the job make the person or does the person make the job?

We all know of employees who fail to perform some of the required duties, yet are considered superior performers. Is this because they performed some duties or assumed some responsibilities not included in their job descriptions. Or does it mean that some of the items in their job descriptions should be omitted? Are we describing the wrong job, or did the job itself change?

Assuming that we could validate the duties and responsibilities of a job, the next step in job evaluation would be to assign weights to the different factors involved in carrying out those specific functions.

Very little research has been done to validate the independence of the factors selected for job evaluation. Even less research has been done on the validity of weights or rankings assigned to the chosen factors.

There are tough questions to be answered, such as how many degrees should be assigned to each factor, how can objective measures be devised to determine the correct level, how comparable are the factors in arriving at a total number of points, etc.

Who hasn't experienced the difficulty of the subjectivity involved in determining how many degrees to assign to a factor? All of us have witnessed supervisory manipulation of job descriptions to back a higher labor grade so that a pay increase could be justified and granted.

Is contribution to profit part of a job description? It is certainly a factor that affects job evaluation. If a job is rated very high in complexity or difficulty but makes little direct contribution to profit, should it be assigned a high labor grade?

If the labor market is nonexistent for janitors and you are forced to hire "sanitary engineers" at a higher labor rate, does that mean the job evaluation of a janitor should be set higher than, for example, a secretary?

The theory of job evaluation is clear-cut, but valid application of the theory is a difficult if not impossible task.

The tremendous problems yet to be faced in the current debate over comparable worth only reemphasize the difficulties involved in trying to practice scientifically valid job evaluations.

MYTH 2. WAGE AND SALARY EVALUATION IS A VALID PROCESS FOR DETERMINING WAGE RATES

Assuming that we somehow succeed in determining a valid labor grade for each job, then wage and salary evaluation calls for assigning pay rates and pay ranges for each grade. These pay ranges must reflect the job difficulty and/or industry pay scales and salary differences by geographical area.

The mathematical calculation of ranges spreads, overlaps, percentiles, averages, etc., is a fascinating process, but the validity of the results is questionable.

Years ago, the director of research of a major labor union addressed a gathering of business executives on the subject of wage evaluation.

"Gentlemen," he said, "wage evaluation is a great tool and has a lot of advantages.

But when it comes to how much you will pay for a job, you will have to pay what you have to pay." His words continue to ring true.

The customary approach to setting pay levels is to use survey data of some sort. The inadequacies of wage surveys are well known. They include the problems of defining comparable jobs, the differences caused by size or location of company, and the errors created by combining data from different industries.

Assuming we have access to a valid survey, the usual approach to assigning wage scales is to make a comparison of benchmark jobs.

The importance of job definition now becomes obvious. How do we know for certain that our benchmark job is the same as the job in another company? And even if we are reasonably certain of comparability of jobs, how accurate are the figures we obtain for comparison?

Have you ever suspected that data from a competitor are fudged a bit to conceal the real pay scales in an effort to keep competitive levels down? It certainly is not unusual to discover a company offering pay levels in excess of their reported pay scales.

Wage and salary surveys are by nature inflationary. The moment data are released, the data become obsolete.

The companies that are well below the average are forced to take corrective action and raise their pay scales. The result is a rise in weighted averages that is not reported until the following year. At that time, the inflationary cycle starts all over again.

Wage and salary scales are also affected by tradition, and this factor cannot be handled by the usual approaches to job or wage evaluation.

Why is it that marketing jobs pay more than engineering or production jobs? Why do staff positions earn less than line positions? I feel that these differences are based more on tradition and belief than on fact.

MYTH 3. PERFORMANCE APPRAISALS ARE ACCURATE AND CAN BE USED TO DETERMINE FAIR COMPENSATION

No one questions the importance of feedback to employees, or their need to know how they are doing. However, the use of performance evaluations to accomplish this is a failure in most cases.

Much has already been written on the importance of reviewing observable and measurable performance without relying on a discussion of attitudes or personality factors. Still attitudes and personality factors frequently permeate performance reviews.

Even appearance has an effect on how we evaluate performance. Why is it that obese employees tend to be rated lower than others? Why is it that tall, attractive employees tend to be rated higher?

When numbers are assigned to performance ratings, the problems escalate. How many degrees of response should there be in rating a factor from low to high?

Can supervisors really differentiate between a "3" or a "4" rating? Should ratings be forced into a normal distribution curve, or should we assume a distribution skewed to the right because of selectivity in hiring and retention of employees?

I believe supervisors can accurately pick out the extremes: those employees who should be discharged or the outstanding star employees. However, most employees fall into a vague middle area, and minute distinctions of performance are not valid.

(There is some justification to the union argument that all employees performing a given job should receive the same pay, and therefore, promotions should be based on seniority, not merit.)

Even if we could assign valid numbers to performance ratings, should each factor have the same weight? Are the factors under review independent of each other or are they different measures of the same thing? How many factors should be used?

Factor analyses made on performance ratings usually show that two factors—productivity and quality—account for most of the variability in ratings.

In addition, how do we handle the beginner's review versus that of the experienced employee? Do we rate the beginner on how well he or she is doing as a beginner? Or do we rate the employee on how well he or she is doing in terms of job performance?

With all these areas of confusion, is it any wonder that supervisors first decide on the pay raise and then figure out what kind of rating they must give to justify it?

In the final analysis, the identification of competencies possessed by individual employees boils down to a matter of judgment.

Even if we analyze in terms of "good" and "bad" performers, who can say whether the performance would not be better if the job were held by a different employee?

Despite the attempt to rely on objective performance measures, these measures are often influenced by wishful thinking—such as profit and loss—or measures in themselves that are subject to debate.

MYTH 4. MANAGEMENT BY OBJECTIVES IS INDISPENSABLE FOR SUCCESSFUL MANAGEMENT

According to the Management by Objectives (MBO) gospel, the path to productivity and improved morale depends on: setting and communicating mutually acceptable goals; agreeing on how progress will be measured (standards of performance); measuring and communicating degrees of achievement of these goals; and planning achievement of these goals in the next go-around.

Usually goals are set for six-month periods or 12-month periods. Occasionally, three-month periods are used.

The MBO process sounds simple, but it rarely is. The goals set six months earlier quickly can become obsolete by changing conditions. The supervisor may find at the end of the review period, she really wanted other goals than those agreed upon.

Even if the goals are unchanged, failure to obtain them may not be the fault of the employee. Product mix, delays in deliveries, changes in organization and a myriad of other factors may make it impossible to achieve well-intentioned goals.

A worse situation exists when the well-intentioned goals do not relate to the critical, more important facets of the job. The conscientious employee can knock himself out chasing goals that do not really count.

Setting critical goals is not an easy task. Not all types of jobs render themselves easily to MBO. However, it is probably true that if a job can't be measured, it doesn't exist.

They may prove to be of benefit to the individual employee, but that is not always the case.

Since it would be foolish for a company to offer a program that is of no benefit, why should such a program not be offered on company time and be considered a cost of doing business?

Finally, who has not experienced the company that gives lip service to the importance of employees, yet in practice belies these statements?

The annual report may stress the importance of employee contributions. Yet, the company may offer the lowest pay scale possible.

The president may talk of fair and equitable treatment for all employees, but allow favoritism to run rampant.

Or they may talk about productivity and then order across-the-board layoffs to improve the bottom line.

STILL SEEKING BETTER WAYS

Fads come and go in the personnel field. The human resources field has made progress, but is has been painfully slow. The anticipated panaceas have turned out *not* to be the final solutions.

We are still seeking better ways to solve wage and salary problems. Inflation and salary compression have added new problems to the old.

Despite books, manuals and training programs, we are still searching for better ways to conduct successful performance evaluations.

Although selection and development techniques have become more sophisticated and perhaps more accurate, there remains much room for improvement.

No matter what areas of human resource activity we survey, new and (assumed) better ideas and techniques are constantly being promoted.

Should we, in the face of all this uncertainty, give up on trying to make a science out of human resources? Definitely not.

We all should continue to try to develop the science of human resources. However, it would be foolish to expect the development of even a reasonably acceptable science of human resources in the foreseeable future.

Until that golden age arrives, we must accept the fact that the practice of human resources is much more of an art than a science. We must seek out the gifted practitioners of this art and do our best to emulate their successes.

Jerome S. Kornreich is Corporate Staff Specialist (Human Resources), M/A-Com, Inc., Burlington, MA.

30.

MANAGING HUMAN ASSETS— IT'S TIME FOR NEW THINKING

Michael Beer
Bert A. Spector

Today's managers must understand their employees and develop new relationships with them. Managing human assets means viewing the men and women of the corporation as important "social capital." At the center of the new relationship is a continual effort to give employees more influence over their work and their work environment.

The American manager has begun to look at the management of "human assets" (resources) with new concern. Buffeted by recession, deregulation of some industries, and international competition in others, business executives are searching for ways to improve productivity and quality. They have seen that these goals cannot be achieved without dramatic change in the *relationship* between management and employees and, where a union exists, between union and management.

When the American executive looks at Japan, our chief competitor, he or she sees a different, yet successful management model. Within the context of the society and culture, the Japanese have found ways to involve employees and develop a collaborative relationship between management and employees, as well as management and unions. Dramatic advantages in quality and cost over American companies are the result.

It has become quite clear to many large American enterprises (General Motors, Cummins Engine, Ford Motor, Bethlehem Steel, Honeywell Corp., People Express, and Goodyear Tire and Rubber, to name a few) that they must manage their human assets quite differently if they are to compete in today's market.

Enormous time and effort go into ensuring that financial assets are employed most effectively. The most current ideas available are used to plan the strategic direction of the company, and the latest technology particularly new information technology in the office is being purchased to improve productivity. Yet many of these efforts to improve effectiveness fall short because the employee who must implement the effort is not sufficiently concerned, committed, or competent to do the most effective job.

Problems facing today's corporations include adversarial union-management relations, low employee motivation and trust, excessive layers of management, emphasis on top-down management, restrictive work practices, and employee resistance to innovation. At the same time there are corporations—not just Japanese, but also American—that have invested in developing effective practices for managing human assets.

The dramatic improvements in productivity, quality, and employee commitment and development experienced by these companies require the attention of all managers. What these improvements suggest is that the best return on investment may come from innovations in human resource management.

The corporation's survival in the marketplace is not the only force that has led to greater emphasis on human resource management. Just as competitive pressures have raised questions about how companies can encourage employees to feel more obligated to contribute to the enterprise, so there has been an increasing concern in American society about employee rights. A more highly educated work force has challenged management to find ways of increasing employee involvement, responsibility, and participation.

The traditional authority relationship between manager and subordinate is less acceptable to these employees, just as it is costly in terms of underutilization and lowered commitment. Adding impetus to these concerns has been the entry of women and minorities into the work force. Their special concern with equitable treatment and utilization has led to an examination of management practices affecting all employees.

Concern about employee rights is evidenced in several societal trends, such as legislation governing fair employment not only for women and minorities but also for other employee groups. The increase in the number of legal suits about the right of corporations to hire and fire employees makes it clear managers must be concerned about employee rights.

WAKING UP

A new relationship between management and employees is emerging. The old relationship was firmly rooted in management prerogative and authority. In return for accepting authority and control of management, employees were well paid. In the case of the automobile worker, pay for doing a narrow assembly-line job under the direction of autocratic supervisors became so high that the automobile companies lost their competitive advantage. Workers were being paid off for being used in a very demeaning way: they were being paid for foregoing any hope of development and advancement.

In some of the more innovative corporations, the new emerging relationship is based on a different exchange. That exchange provides employees with equitable pay consistent with competitive wages, but it also provides the chance for challenging work, involvement in decisions, influence on policies affecting them, and opportunities for personal growth.

In return, the corporation obtains higher levels of commitment, a flexibile work force, good union-management relations where a union exists, and a work force motivated to learn and problem solve. Employees may be more stressed because they are involved, but they are also more satisfied because they are able to develop new competencies if they so choose.

The old human resources model treated employees as a cost to be contained and had as its goal the containment of conflict. The objective was to hire people, assign them to a job, and prevent problems from arising. The new human resource model treats employees as a human asset, an investment. While management continues to be concerned about cost and conflict, it places greater importance on enhancing commitment and competence. These add value to the assets of the company as much as building a new plant or investing in new office technology would add.

The new relationship is particularly important for managers of white-collar office workers who must face the new information technology. That technology, if not carefully managed in a way consistent with the human assets perspective, may create the same problems in the office that many "smokestack" companies have experienced during the last 50 years.

Therefore it is of paramount importance that managers of office personnel learn to develop the new relationships, to manage in accordance with the new model. New technology creates unusual opportunities to enhance employee involvement and to redesign jobs so they are broader and more challenging. By involving employees in the introduction of technology, managers improve the utilization of that technology and at the same time signal a new relationship.

A NEW FRAMEWORK

A "four-policy framework," developed at the Harvard Business School, Boston, provides a means by which managers can diagnose their own human resource management practices, just as the framework provides a guide for rethinking the human resource management task (see Figure 1.). At the center of the triangle is the core policy of *employee influence*. Each manager must decide how much influence he or she is willing to give employees over the affairs of the company, division, department, or office. That decision will obviously be influenced by the manager's own values and style, as well as the culture of the larger organization.

Innovative companies are moving to increase employee influence by several means. Employee task forces or committees are being formed to study various problems and recommend new approaches. Common subjects include new technology, vacation policies, communication, and career development. Periodic attitude surveys, preferably managed by an employee task force, are another means of upward influence. An open-door policy that encourages employees to seek out higher levels of management to redress grievances, or employee committees that offer formal hearings, have been adopted by some companies.

Finally, we see a more frequent use of team building, an off-site meeting where employees are encouraged to raise department problems as well as concerns about their manager's style.

Human resources flow is the movement of people in, through, and out of the organization. That flow must be managed to provide a mix of employees that will be able to accomplish today's task, as well as develop employees for tommorow's requirements. Moreover, decisions about hiring, promotion, and termination must be perceived to be fair.

Many companies are increasing the amount of information and influence

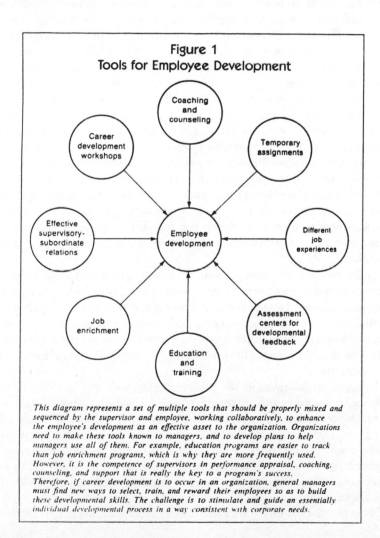

Figure 1
Tools for Employee Development

This diagram represents a set of multiple tools that should be properly mixed and sequenced by the supervisor and employee, working collaboratively, to enhance the employee's development as an effective asset to the organization. Organizations need to make these tools known to managers, and to develop plans to help managers use all of them. For example, education programs are easier to track than job enrichment programs, which is why they are more frequently used. However, it is the competence of supervisors in performance appraisal, coaching, counseling, and support that is really the key to a program's success.
Therefore, if career development is to occur in an organization, general managers must find new ways to select, train, and reward their employees so as to build these developmental skills. The challenge is to stimulate and guide an essentially individual developmental process in a way consistent with corporate needs.

employees are given in these decisions. Existing employees are asked to participate in hiring decisions, using their knowledge of the task and the social environment to select employees that "fit." Open job-posting systems are also giving employees more control over their careers. Finally, education, job rotation, and broader involvement in decisions are all aimed at developing broader employee competence, making the work force more flexible and promotable.

Reward systems must be designed and administered to attract and motivate employees. Traditionally, compensation has been the primary reward managers have offered. The new relationship requires managers to manage employees and arrange work so that psychic rewards of challenge, responsibility, recognition, and influence over one's destiny are offered through the work itself and through the participative style of management.

What, then, is the role of compensation in the new relationship? Equitable compensation continues to be important in attracting and keeping people, but somewhat less emphasis is given to the bonus and individual incentive as a means of stimulating motivation. Results are rarely within the sole control of employees; they must work as a team to accomplish organizational purpose. Individual incentives may actually reduce teamwork. Moreover, individual performance, except in routine work, is difficult to measure, raising questions about the merit and bonus award.

More emphasis on involvement as a motivator is warranted, and pay should be administered equitably, making a minimum of discriminations necessary to recognize unusually good and poor performance. More emphasis should be placed on organization-wide gains sharing plans, reinforcing the concept of teamwork. Finally, employee participation in pay design and administration is an effective means of enhancing feelings of equity. Some innovative companies use peer evaluations to decide pay and promotion decisions. At a minimum, employees can become involved in reviewing pay administration policies.

A *work system* is the arrangement of technology, information, tasks, and supervision that creates the work experience. In traditional settings, that work experience does not provide employees with much control over the whole job. Routine and narrow tasks comprising only a small part of the total task are assigned, with employees receiving little information about the organization's goals, how their department fits into the whole organization, or the end results of their efforts.

Managers get information about cost, quality, delivery, or other relevant performance measures and use these to direct employees. Companies attempting to develop a new relationship with employees try to provide "whole jobs," giving employees responsibility for planning and controlling their work. Where a whole job cannot be accomplished by one person, employees are organized into teams with total responsibility for the task. The supervisor's role then changes from directing employees to enabling teams to accomplish their work themselves.

Obviously, the design of office technology has a great impact on the nature of work in the office. It is for this reason that the new relationship requires considerable influence by employees on the design of that technology, well before vendors have been selected and while there is still room to influence the type of work system that will emerge.

Managing human assets means viewing the men and women of the corporation, and the relationship between management and these employees as important "social capital." At the center of the new relationship is a continual effort to find means for giving employees more influence over work and their work environment.

The results for companies moving in this direction will be greater productivity, improved quality, and increased employee satisfaction. Ultimately, the survival of American corporations in world markets may depend on how well today's managers are able to understand and develop this new relationship.

Michael Beer is a professor at Harvard Graduate School of Business Administration. Bert A. Spector is assistant professor of Human Resources Group, Northeastern University College of Business Administration. Michael Beer and Bert Spector co-authored Managing Human Assets *published by The Free Press.*

31.

OFFICE AUTOMATION'S IMPACT ON PERSONNEL

Zane Quible
Jane N. Hammer

People often feel substandard when equipment is introduced into the office environment. Human resource management takes on a new perspective as managers adjust to employee fears. Involvement and understanding are key.

Office automation is frequently associated with rapidly changing equipment. While the term "automation" implies using equipment rather than people, a decline in the number of personnel is not now apparent. As office equipment changes, people's jobs are also changing—but jobs are still there.

People have traditionally resisted change. With the advent of robots in factories in the Orient, factory workers in the U.S. expressed concern about the stability of their jobs. As automation—or at least the term—entered the office, people began to fear being replaced just as they feared the electric typewriter when it entered the office scene.

The introduction of any type of change creates problems for those associated with that change. The people who use the new equipment have problems and thus create problems for supervisors who must also adjust to change. Human resource management takes on a new perspective as managers adjust to employees trying to cope with their own fears. These changes create challenges for human resource managers of any organization contemplating the implementation of automation.

OFFICE PERSONNEL

The impact of automation of office personnel will be significant. The equipment which these employees use in their jobs will enable them to perform their duties with more sophistication, greater ease and higher efficiency.

The traditional typewriter will disappear from the desks of many office personnel. The functions for which the typewriter has been used for decades will be performed on more sophisticated equipment. Although these new desktop devices vary considerably in their capabilities, those used in automated office systems have two fundamental characteristics: They are electronically linked to other devices; and they facilitate electronic storage of material.

Linking devices electronically increases the overall sophistication and efficiency of automated office systems. The linking of devices is accomplished through electronic networks. In most instances, devices linked to another are more functional; thus linking increases the efficiency with which employees are able to perform their jobs.

Storing material electronically makes it available for later use, which is also advantageous from an efficiency standpoint. When an author wishes to make changes in the first draft of a document, only the changes have to be entered since the material has been stored electronically from the time that it was first entered. If a letter is to be sent to a number of individuals, the letter only has to be typed one time. The names and addresses of the recipients are merged with the letter, and the equipment automatically prepares an original for each recipient.

Word processing is a common function of office personnel in organizations that have installed automated office systems. The equipment these employees use for word processing is quite diverse. Some of the equipment is capable of performing only word processing functions. Other devices are capable of performing as word processors and as terminals for performing data processing functions. Personal computers loaded with the appropriate software can also be used for word processing.

Attaching the devices used to perform word processing functions to a network increases their functionality. Interconnected devices can send documents to each other (in electronic format), as well as communicate with a computer. The devices can be used for maintaining one's electronic calendar as well and for sending electronic messages and mail to other individuals inside and outside the organization. The number of ways in which office personnel will use the equipment in automated office systems will continue to expand as new equipment is developed.

A day in the life of an office employee. The following describes a typical day in the life of Pat, a fairly high-level office employee who works for an organization that has implemented an automated office system. Upon arriving at the office each morning, Pat accesses the electronic message file to see if any messages have been received during the night. This task is easily accomplished by using the terminal keyboard to enter the appropriate accessing codes into the system. Almost instantly, the messages appear on the terminal screen. (When desired, messages also can be permanently filed in electronic storage.)

Pat notices a message from one of the managers. This manager, who is presently out of town, asked Pat to schedule a meeting of a committee. The meeting is not to last more than two hours, and is to be scheduled either next

Wednesday or Thursday. Pat asks the computer to provide a list of two-hour blocks of time on these two days during which all committee members are available. Four different blocks appear on the list, and Pat selects the 10:00 to 12:00 block of time on Wednesday. Pat then directs the computer to place this meeting on each of the member's electronic calendars and also asks that they be notified (by electronic message) of the meeting as soon as possible.

Shortly thereafter, Pat uses the terminal keyboard to view a screen display of the day's activity schedule. Pat examines the schedule to determine which activities have to be completed by day's end. Pat, like most individuals, prefers to put a reminder notice in the schedule a few days before a major project is due.

Pat also has some word processing responsibilities. The more sophisticated word processing installations found in automated office systems enable word originators (executives) to record their dictation 24 hours a day. Pat notices that some dictation to be "keyboarded" was stored during the night. The originator has asked that the first draft be returned so that editing can be performed. The edited copy will be returned to Pat, who keyboards the changes, and another draft is prepared for the originator to review. When authorized for release, a final draft of the letter is prepared.

The originator specifies that the final draft of the letter should be transmitted electronically to the recipient. Accordingly, Pat performs the steps necessary to facilitate the transmission through a network. The recipient receives the letter on a terminal screen. After reading the letter, the recipient uses the terminal to file the letter in electronic storage. (The letter could also have been sent by mail or by facsimile process.)

Originators, including some for whom Pat works, are using their desk-top devices to compose their work. In some instances, office employees check their work and make any corrections needed in spelling, punctuation and grammar. Other originators have office employees keyboard the original draft from dictation or handwritten material. Once the material is keyboarded, the originators use the terminals on their desk tops to keyboard changes in the material resulting from the editing process. Some originators, especially those who have excellent mechanical composition skills, are finding that it is easier for them to compose a document on a keyboard than it is to dictate or handwrite the material. Pat typically spends part of each day refining material keyboarded by the originators.

Pat, who also has responsibilities for maintaining the department's budget, uses the terminal to update figures and to request copies of the new budget. In addition, Pat often uses the terminal to prepare graphics for reports prepared by the originators.

One of the managers for whom Pat works is preparing a speech for delivery to a national management association convention. The manager has asked Pat to access several videotext subscriber services to determine if any information is contained in these electronic files that might be helpful in writing the speech. A hard copy of the desired information can be easily obtained. The manager also asks Pat to make his airline and hotel reservations for the convention. Pat uses her disk-top terminal to make the desired reservations.

Because Pat had to leave work early for a doctor appointment, all work was not completed. Pat also knows that tomorrow is going to be a hectic day, especially since today's backlog has to be carried over. Since Pat has a personal computer at home that is compatible with the organization's system, the backlog is completed at home and subsequently transmitted to the organization over standard telephone lines. A modem is used in the transmission process.

Problems encountered by office personnel. The installation of an automated office system is not universally accepted by all office personnel in all organizations. In some organizations, the installation of a system is met with considerable resistance. An awareness of the reasons that office personnel resist the installation of an automated office system is quite helpful in dealing with their lack of acceptance.

Office employees are likely to resist the installation of office automation for two basic reasons: 1) they fear being replaced by the new sophisticated, more efficient equipment; and 2) they experience anxiety when confronted with having to learn to use new sophisticated, technical equipment.

Involving employees in designing and installing the system will help allay their fears and anxieties. The following types of involvement are possible: Participating in the process of planning for the new system, having early hands-on experience using the equipment and receiving extensive information about the reasons for installing such a system, its benefits, how the system works and how it will affect them.

It is also important to assure office employees that the installation of an automated office system will not cause them to be terminated. Rather, it will enable those whose jobs become more automated to work more productively and efficiently. The attrition rate of office personnel in most organizations is sufficient to accommodate any temporary employee surpluses.

To a large extent, office employees' acceptance of automated systems is affected by the amount of orientation, indoctrination and training they receive. The more familiar employees are with a system, the more they will support its use. Employees who are poorly trained will find the equipment difficult to use, which will affect their attitudes and their productivity.

MANAGERS

Managers will be affected just as much as office personnel by office automation—and in some cases, even more so. The way they carry out various job duties will change drastically, primarily because of the availability of new equipment. Managers will be making greater use of the executive work station, an electronic device placed on their desk top. The electronic equipment which executives will use is similar in many ways to the equipment that office personnel will use. It will be more sophisticated in order to handle a few different functions, especially in areas such as data base management and inter-office communications.

Executive work stations support a variety of different functions, including word processing, data processing, electronic messaging, electronic mail, graphics preparation, scheduling and calendaring. The functional capability of the equipment is continually increasing as new technology is developed.

The two characteristics of the equipment used by office personnel will also be found in the equipment used by managers. These characteristics include the electronic storage capability and the electronic linkage of devices.

A day in the life of a manager. An effective way to illustrate how office automation will affect managers is to describe a day in the life of a manager. Although the various automated office systems will affect manager's jobs differently, the following description is fairly typical.

Before leaving home for work, Leslie uses a personal home computer to access an electronic message file at the office as well as the day's schedule. Leslie discovers a message from a superior. Leslie is asked to provide additional documentation to support a request for two new employee positions in the department. On the train to work, Leslie is able to keyboard a response on a briefcase-size computer. After Leslie arrives at work, the message is entered through a modem into the organization's system and subsequently sent as an electronic message to the superior.

Leslie looks at the day's schedule and notices that a committee meeting is to be held that afternoon. Several subjects need to be discussed under "new business" at the meeting. To help Leslie remember key points about these subjects, several thoughts are keyboarded and printed on the small printer attached to the briefcase-size computer.

Leslie is also reminded to prepare some background material for use by the members of a committee that meets next week. Upon arriving at the office, Leslie uses the desk-top terminal to compose this information and then asks the secretary to review the work for spelling, punctuation and grammatical accuracy. Leslie also asks the secretary to transmit the material to each member after the work is corrected. After making a few changes, the secretary depresses a few keys on the terminal's keyboard and the system electronically transmits the information to each recipient.

Leslie then dictates a memo that is to be sent to various individuals in several branch offices. After it has been keyboarded by the secretary and approved for release, the system automatically dials the telephone number of each recipient and the memo is sent in electronic format to each individual. Each recipient is asked to respond to a certain item in the memo. Several do so by electronic message. When Leslie returns from lunch, a light is blinking on the work station that indicates the receipt of a message since the last time the electronic message file was "emptied". These messages are received on the terminal screen.

Another blinking light on the work station indicates the receipt of electronic mail. Accessing the electronic mail file reveals the names of the individuals from whom letters have been received as well as the time each letter was received. To read the letters, Leslie simply depresses several keys on the keyboard and each letter is displayed—one by one—on the screen. The decision is made to keyboard an immediate reply to one individual. As soon as the reply is composed, Leslie directs the system to send it to the recipient. Since the recipient's phone number is already stored in the system, the letter can be transmitted without additional human effort.

Leslie remembers to call her insurance agent about homeowner's insurance. The keyboard is used to access the name/address/phone number file. When the agent's number is located, Leslie depresses a button on the keyboard which directs the system to dial the phone number. The agent's line is busy, so the system continues to dial the number every 30 seconds or so until the call goes through. The speakerphone on Leslie's desk frees Leslie from having to hold the telephone handset during the time the system automatically continues to redial the agent's number.

The telephone not only allows Leslie freedom from dialing frequently called numbers and freedom to do other things during a phone conversation, but it also allows Leslie to determine whether or not talking with the phoned person is necessary. If Leslie determines that leaving a message for the agent is adequate, electronic voice messaging provides a store-and-forward capability that enables Leslie and the agent freedom from the phone while still allowing them to send and receive massages. No longer does the caller have to play "telephone tag" with the recipient. All Leslie needs to do is to leave a message which is recorded on the agent's telephone. When the agent returns to the office, a light signaling the presence of a message allows the agent to listen and respond to the message. Leslie can continue with the tasks for the day knowing that the situation has been handled.

Employees in the organization in which Leslie works recently received their midyear bonuses. Leslie wants to invest about half of the bonus in the stock market. When a particular stock reaches a certain price, Leslie plans to buy. Leslie uses the terminal to access a stock market videotext subscriber service that will give the current stock prices. The organization subscribes to a number of other videotext services as well. Leslie is a frequent user of several of these when collecting data for use in research-oriented projects.

Before Leslie leaves the office at the end of the work day, the schedule is accessed to see what activities will be necessary during each of the next several days. Leslie notices the absence of any face-to-face appointments scheduled the day after tomorrow, and there are no other activities on the schedule that would require Leslie to be physically in the office.

The organization allows employees, once they reach a certain managerial level, to "telecommute." Leslie calls the superior to get permission to telecommute the day after tomorrow. After getting the necessary permission, Leslie notifies the system that there are to be no face-to-face appointments that day.

Leslie is working on the year-end report and feels that the uninterrupted time which is available by working at home will be especially conducive to getting the report finished. Any electronically stored data or information which is needed to work on the report will be accessible through Leslie's home computer. Once Leslie has finished editing the report, the text can be sent over telephone lines to the organization. The 20 paper copies of the report which are needed can be printed and ready to distribute to the appropriate individuals when she arrives at work the next morning.

Problems encountered by managers. Some of the problems encountered by managers are similar to the problems encountered by office personnel. Most common among these are the fears and anxieties experienced by managers when having to adjust to new ways of doing their work. Because older managers matured before the computer era, they are likely to experience more anxiety when an automated office system is installed than are younger managers.

Managers who help plan and design the system often find it a complex task. They have to make sure that the system is capable of doing what the employees want, is cost effective, and can be expanded and/or modified as the need arises. In some organizations, the planning and designing process is so complex that consultants have to be used.

Another problem experienced by managers is keeping up to date with new developments in automated office systems. Unless they keep abreast of these developments and implement those which are desirable and justifiable, the new system could become dated quite quickly.

Top management support of the installation of an automated office system is also crucial. In some instances, the lack of top management support is a stumbling block. Although top management may endorse the idea, it is not always willing to provide support at the level needed to get the system installed.

One of the more deep-rooted concerns of top management is likely to be the security of the organization's data base. The electronic storage of most of the organization's information and data will create a huge data base. Management's concern will focus on securing it and making it inaccessible to unauthorized individuals.

SUGGESTIONS FOR THE TRAINER

Working with managers as well as with office personnel in adapting the office automation presents many challenges. One must consider age, previous exposure to electronic devices and status in the organization.

Age and previous exposure are often closely related. The younger people are, the greater is the chance of their having encountered electronic devices before. Rather than surprising employees by presenting them with an electronic device, they should be prepared psychologically to ensure their acceptance and use of equipment.

Understanding that people do fear electronic devices, identifying that fear and allaying it are crucial to the automation of the office. Employee participation in the equipment selection process is a key to acceptance. Explaining the need for the equipment and how that equipment will make their jobs easier is crucial to the acceptance of automation. People often feel that they are substandard when equipment is brought into the office environment.

Employees who have some input in the choice of equipment will be more likely to use that equipment than if the decision is made without consulting them. While management may be able to dictate the general type of equipment to be installed, employees can give vital information about and provide a fresh perspective on what will make their jobs easier. Identification of a need can be added as well; the quality circle concept can work in the office as well as on the assembly line.

Status is one key to executive use of equipment. The status of an electronic work station is much greater than the status awarded to typewriters. Typewriters were—and still are—viewed as the tool of a subordinate. Consequently, many executives want nothing to do with them. Fortunately, the keyboard associated with the executive work stations has no image problem to overcome. Approaching the equipment from the standpoint of ease of use as well as from the standpoint of increased productivity can help give the equipment—and consequently the user—increased status in the executive's eyes. One-to-one relationships in instructing individuals how to get the equipment to do the things necessary to make the executive's life easier are crucial.

Involvement and understanding are necessary for a trainer working with the implementation of office automation. Whether working with a manager or with office personnel, the human resource manager must consider the impact of automation on *people*.

Zane Quible is a professor of office management and coordinator of graduate programs in business education at Oklahoma State University in Stillwater. Jane N. Hammer is an assistant professor of administrative services and business education at Oklahoma State University.

Part V
CAREER PATHING: DEVELOPMENT, PROMOTION, AND PLATEAUS

32.
WHO GETS THE PROMOTION?

Roderick Wilkinson

The higher you are on the corporate ladder, the harder it can be to
select the *right* person for a promotion. To ensure your decisions are fair
and objective, try this 15-point checklist.

A first-line supervisor usually has far more experience than the company
president in promoting the right people. He has to do it often; there are more
people and more changes taking place at the supervisors's level than up there in
Mahogany Row.

I have worked with some senior management people who have never
promoted *anyone* in years. They "inherited" most of their subordinates. Others
were promoted by a presidential committee somewhere.

These are exceptional cases. Whether they like it or not, most top-rank
executives sooner or later will be confronted with the promotion problem—
personally. Recommendations from experts are all very well, but in the end the
executive has to live with the person he chooses. You might think that the
selection rituals which take place farther down the pyramid have no relevance
to the selection of people for high-ranking jobs, but it is precisely in those
upper echelons that some form of guidance is usually needed most.

What kind of guidance? A fast-action, do-it-yourself judgment kit? A book
of some kind that supplies every answer to every question about selection
people? A computer?

Let's face it, no device will enable a manager to select the best man or
woman for promotion *every* time. This is one reason why management will
never be replaced by anything except management. All we have to assist us in
the selection of people for promotion are: A complete description of the job to
be filled, names of the people who should be considered, their history folders or
work records, the verbal opinions (substantiated by fact) of other managers

who know the candidates, interviews with all or a selection of them, and a scoring device or some other means of analyzing comparative data.

POLICY

Most companies have something to say about promotion. They say it either in written policy statements or they say it every day in the way they handle promotions. A company's personnel philosophy emerges when it decides to train and promote people from within, or to engage them every time from the outside—or to do a little of both.

Is it too much to ask a senior manager to understand his company's high-sounding policy on promotion-from-within so that he can apply it himself with ease and competence? What does he do about jealousy? Having promoted someone to a higher-graded job, how can he justify it to other people who consider themselves better qualified—or to colleagues who protest about a lack of fairness? How can he sharpen his own judgment so that he is confident that he has promoted the right person?

Perhaps he needs something that, at least, will assure him that he conscientiously considered everything he should consider. Something like the self-quiz checklist below.

1. Do I know the exact job that is to be filled?
2. Have I examined the job description, and do I agree that it is accurate?
3. Do I know the classification or the grading of the job and the salary it pays?
4. Do I know the most desirable age group for candidates for the job?
5. Have I checked carefully to see if there is a potential candidate within my own business circle in the organization?
6. Does the outstanding candidate have the appropriate educational background?
7. Has he previous experience in this type of work—or work closely related to it?
8. Have I checked his history folder?
9. Are there any adverse remarks or "warning signals" in his record?
10. Have I checked to see whether he is medically fit for the job?
11. Is it truly a *promotion* for him?
12. Can I write down the three principal requirements of the job and truthfully say that the candidate fulfills these with high marks?
13. If there are *two* candidates, have I given marks to each of them so that the successful one's qualifications can be clearly shown?
14. If both have equal qualifications, do I know who has the most service with the company?
15. If there are *no* suitable candidates in the departments or company units

with which I am familiar, have I considered a wider search within the organization—perhaps at a distant plant or in a sister company?

If these questions can be answered properly, and if the decision is based on the answer, it will be difficult for anyone to contest an executive's judgment and sense of fair play. And, chances are, the person who gets the promotion will succeed in the job.

Roderick Wilkinson is a Glasgow, Scotland-based business consultant, writer, and lecturer who spent 22 years as an employee-relations executive with a U. S.-based multinational company.

33.
TRAINING STARTS WITH TOP-DOWN ACCEPTANCE

Carol Tomme Thiel

> Don't underestimate the power of good example. Employees are very adept at reading their boss's true feelings. Managers' open-minded acceptance of new technologies can influence their worker's attitudes and help ease the transition to use of automated systems.

Only 10 percent of the 10 million executives in the US today are said to be computer literate. Yet most of them have staffs who will be expected to learn to use computer-based office systems over the next decade.

If employee attitudes filter down from the top, it's no wonder so many workers are having problems accepting office automation. Seeing managers balk at the thought of learning to use a terminal or a personal computer only reinforces worker's misgivings about learning new ways of performing their own jobs.

"Resistance is based on the frame of reference of the people being affected." says Gloria Gery, president of Gery Assoc., West Hartford, CT. If they see resistance in the boss, while being told, "This is good for you," they're getting conflicting signals.

In addition to mixed signals, workers who must learn to use the new systems may have irrational fears about what's expected of them, says Gery. They might fear they'll lose their status, or their co-workers, or that their job definition might change for the worse. Sadly, some of their fears may be grounded in reality.

Consider the following examples:

- A secretary with a new word-processing system might start getting sloppier texts from the boss. This same boss might feel more inclined to make minor changes each time a new draft is printed. No longer can this secretary intimidate the boss with a glare or hopeless expression and the words, "not again."

- An administrative assistant may have looked forward to distributing mail as an opportunity to get up from the desk and say hello to co-workers. With the introduction of company-wide electronic mail, the excuse for getting away from the desk is gone, along with the daily social interaction.
- A clerical worker who supported one or two bosses and felt some degree of loyalty to them might now be expected to support 5, 10, or 20 different people. It will be difficult to spread loyalty that thin.
- A manager who's been in a "comfort zone" for years might be expected to learn to work at a terminal in order to request reports that used to be sent out automatically. How will the manager feel if a younger, lower-level staff member is assigned as the manager's computer instructor? If the manager is slow to learn the system, will he or she try to live without the information in the reports?
- What about managers who are so enamored by the word processor they elbow the secretary away from the machine while they compose letters, memos and reports that used to be part of the secretary's job? How will the secretary feel about using the system for little more than keying in changes and corrections?

As clerical, secretarial, administrative, and even managerial jobs evolve with the aid of new technology, the aim should be to take away the junk work, not add to it or give it all to the person at the bottom, says Gery.

"A lot of workers' perceptions are that management is thinking, 'Boy, can we get a lot of work out of them now. And we can use the system to spy on them,'" says Gery. So the emphasis in the newly automated office sometimes changes from "getting the job done" to protecting yourself.

TRAINING STRATEGY

Is there some way companies can develop a training strategy that avoids negative reactions ranging from employee ego-bruising to employee alienation?

"It is important to diagnose your organization before you decide how you will train people to use new office technologies," says Gery. Take a serious look at how people do their jobs now. Then consider how their daily activities will be changed by new automated equipment.

"Involve the group in making the decision," says Gery. You've got to give people options in terms of the kinds of products and systems they'll be expected to use. Reassure them that new technologies won't eliminate the parts of their jobs that were good before, she emphasizes.

"The worker knows the job best," says David J. Cirillo, Human Resources Group, Wang Laboratories, Lowell, MA. Getting the workers involved in the selection and implementation of automated equipment lets them "become more committed and feel less threatened," he says.

But don't raise their hopes unrealistically about what the equipment can do or how easy it will be to use, warns Cirillo.

BUYING IN

Perhaps the most important element of getting people to accept and to learn to use new technologies is convincing them that it's worth the effort, says Gery. "If you introduce something new and don't give them reason to buy in, they won't," she declares.

Gery says a prime example of resistance to something new was the US' reaction to the metric system. "In Canada, they took away Fahrenheit and inches. There was motivation to learn the new way, she says. But in the US, the attitude was, "Why do I need to remember Celsius?"

Unless there's an obvious payoff, even if it's mere survival, it's going to be hard to convince people to take the change seriously.

Managers might be getting in the way of users' acceptance, suggests Gery. "Management wants instant gratification from installation of new equipment, but won't allow time for people to get used to it," she points out. "Just because people have gone through the workshop doesn't mean they learned the system. It's the same as three days of management classes not equalling two years of Columbia Business School."

Gery stresses that *training is not an event*. And managers have to plan for the learning, adaptation and acceptance of new technologies if they hope to see these technologies embraced by users.

When it comes to training, there is no "one-size-fits-all." But according to Gery, a number of dos and don'ts should guide you.

1. Don't neglect the persons or groups who are willing to try what's new. Take advantage of their enthusiasm to spread the word.
2. Don't spend a lot of time concentrating on resisters, especially those who've been in a company a long time. Aim to motivate a critical mass and most of the others will be carried along by the tide of acceptance.
3. Protect egos. Make sure different peer levels are not mixed in the same training classes. Choose trainers in the image of the training audience. Executives should be taught by executive trainers, clerical staff by clerical trainers, engineers by engineers.
4. Don't let technical experts design the training program by themselves. They don't realize how technical they really are, and probably can't remember what it was like before they learned what they know now.
5. Make sure users see the payoff. Any training workshop should teach the system in terms of real-world functions that employees use in their day-to-day tasks.

6. Don't try to teach an application product before users understand the application. (What good is VisiCalc to me if I don't understand what a spreadsheet is?)
7. If you're using prepackaged instructions, take time to evaluate it in terms of your own organization's needs. If something is missing, provide supplementary training in that area.
8. Once you've installed new equipment, don't rely on old performance in terms of the new system, but not until users have had a chance to become comfortable with it.

Office automation (OA) isn't going to go away, no matter how many people resist. But the way it is introduced can make a difference in how soon users of the systems will become productive. If your organization hasn't yet installed OA equipment but plans to, start a needs analysis right away, suggests Gery.

Wang's Cirillo states, "Successful use of OA is dependent on human factors." Don't forget to talk to the people who are going to use the systems and find out from them what they need to do their jobs better.

And don't underestimate the power of good example. Employees are very adept at reading their bosses' true feelings. Managers' open-minded acceptance of new technologies can influence their workers' attitudes and help ease the transition to use of automated systems.

Carol Tomme Thiel is a senior editor with Infosystems.

34.
REACTIONS TO THE CAREER PLATEAU

Janet P. Near

Plateaued managers may be disenchanted and less productive. But survey results indicate that such problems may not be as widespread as "common sense" would dictate. Not only is there life after the plateau, there is also growth, if parties involved work toward this goal.

One major incentive offered to managers by American firms is the opportunity for advancement. Although rapid advancement may be less important to managers in other cultures (Japan, for instance), the cessation of advancement—the career plateau—is a significant event for most American managers.

In many cases the cause of the plateau is not personal but organizational: older managers block upward channels, slow growth prevents the opening of new channels, or management policies such as promotion from outside limit access to higher-level positions. The organization acts as a funnel, limiting promotions of managers who might otherwise be qualified to move up the ladder.

Few firms notify a manager when the career plateau has been reached, because it is assumed that this will reduce the individual's level of motivation. Of course, most managers recognize their plateau eventually. How do they react at that point? Are they in fact bitter, demotivated, and withdrawn?

REACTIONS TO THE PLATEAU

Based on interviews with 200 managers from various firms, half of whom reported themselves to be plateaued, it appears that managers adapt reasonably well to the plateau.

Interviewed as part of a national study of employment,[1] these managers represented various types of functions from a diverse group of firms. Asked when they expected to receive their next promotion, ninety-eight of the managers responded "twenty years from now" or "never"; this group was classified as plateaued managers. The group classified as nonplateaued managers included those who said they would be promoted within the next one to ten years. It undoubtedly included a few plateaued managers; however, of this group, very few (four) believed promotion would not occur for five to ten years, so including them in the category of nonplateaued managers should not have affected the results greatly.

Plateaued managers did not differ much from nonplateaued managers in terms of background. The percentage of plateaued managers who are married (93 percent) is not significantly higher than the number of nonplateaued managers who are married (84 percent). Most plateaued managers were men (77 percent), as were most nonplateaued managers (86 percent). Most plateaued managers were white (98 percent), as were most nonplateaued managers (95 percent). Plateaued managers averaged about the same number of children (2.5) in their families as nonplateaued managers.

When asked why they were plateaued, well over half of the ninety-eight managers reported that higher level positions were unavailable (see Table 1). One-fifth of this group claimed to be happy where they were. Few of the plateaued managers saw themselves as unqualified in any way for future promotions, not intellectually, technically, physically, or due to age. Nearly 10 percent were dissatisfied with the plateau, calling themselves "disenchanted," or were planning to leave the firm.

Only 12 percent of these plateaued managers felt there were significant problems in the handling of promotions. When asked what criteria should be excluded from consideration in promotion decisions, 7 percent said seniority should not be a criteria for promotion. Plateaued managers did not favor the exclusion of other common criteria, including ability, favoritism, or politics (see Table 2). In fact, when asked what changes they would like to see made in

Table 1
Reactions to the Plateau

Why manager is plateaued:

Happy where he/she is	21%
Not intellectually qualified	0%
Not technically qualified	4%
Not physically qualified	0%
Doesn't intend to stay	5%
Has highest position available	64%
Disenchanted	4%
Doesn't want higher position	5%
Too old	1%

Note: Figures in Table 1 do not add to 100 percent due to rounding error.

Table 2.
Desired Changes in Handling of Promotions

Plateaued managers would like to see:

More opportunities for promotion	7%
More emphasis on seniority	0%
More emphasis on ability	18%
Better processes of evaluation	3%
Promotion from within	7%
More emphasis on tenure	0%

the handling of promotions, nearly one-fifth of the plateaued managers wanted more emphasis on ability. A surprisingly small group favored changes in organizational policies, including greater opportunities for promotion and promotion from within the firm.

In spite of these favorable reactions to advancement criteria, 80 percent of the plateaued managers felt it was overly difficult to get their job assignment changed. Apparently their discontent was due to the lack of new job duties and less to the lack of advancement available to them. This implies that managers would find the plateau less onerous if lateral transfer or job rotation of some sort were offered to them.

DIFFERENCES BETWEEN PLATEAUED
AND NONPLATEAUED MANAGERS

If plateaued managers are not negative about their experience, how precisely do they differ from nonplateaued managers?

Plateaued managers differ widely from nonplateaued managers in two respects: they are older and less likely to have attended college. Of managers who are plateaued, only 35 percent are under 40 years old, as opposed to 68 percent of all nonplateaued managers. Over half of all plateaued managers (53 percent) have not attended college, compared with 36 percent of nonplateaued managers.

On the job, plateaued managers are slightly less satisfied than their nonplateaued counterparts (see Table 3).

Plateaued managers describe jobs in ways similar to those used by their nonplateaued counterparts. In rating the difficulty, challenge, time pressures, and benefits associated with their jobs, they agree substantially with the nonplateaued managers. This may be interpreted to mean that the types of jobs held by plateaued and nonplateaued managers do not differ, at least as perceived by the job incumbents themselves. (We cannot determine whether a nonplateaued manager comparing both jobs would agree.)

Plateaued managers are as likely as nonplateaued managers to rate favorably

Table 3
Percent of Managers "Highly Satisfied"

Percent	With job	With life
100		
90		
80		
70		
60		
50		
40		
30		
20		
10		
0		

≡ Non-plateaued

▬ Plateaued

their relations with co-workers; however, they are much more likely to rate negatively relations with supervisors. Only 43 percent of all plateaued managers give their supervisors favorable ratings, compared to 73 percent of all nonplateaued managers.

Plateaued managers have worked for the firm for a longer period of time, an average tenure of nine years as opposed to six years for nonplateaued managers, as has been found in other studies. Yet contrary to Veiga's findings,[2] plateaued managers in this sample earn significantly less, with an average salary of $11,332 versus $12,654 for nonplateaued managers (in 1970 dollars).

The career plateau also affects performance. Most plateaued managers work fewer hours per week, although a small minority work more hours than do nonplateaued managers (Table 4). Plateaued managers are absent more frequently but are late about as often as nonplateaued managers (Table 5). When asked how they see themselves at work, virtually equal numbers of plateaued and nonplateaued managers felt that they were highly successful, knowledgeable about the job, and motivated to do their best on the job.

Off the job, plateaued managers' satisfaction with life in general is nearly as high as that of their nonplateaued counterparts (Table 3). Plateaued managers are less likely to describe their health as excellent, either currently or five years ago (Table 6); this may be due, however, to the fact that as a group they are older than nonplateaued managers.

Table 4
Percentage of Managers Who Work:

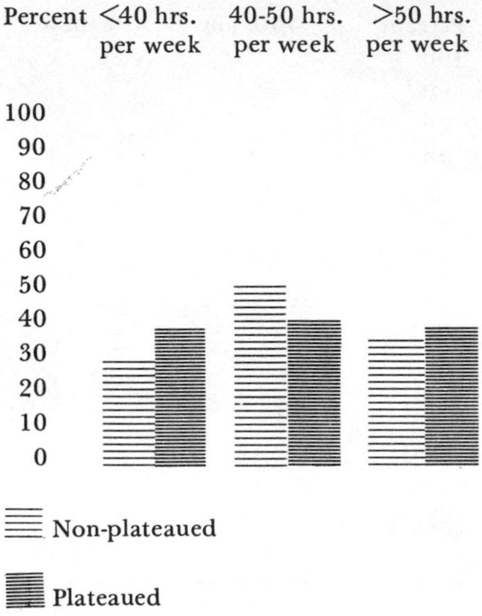

Table 5
Percent of Managers Absent or Late in Last Two Weeks

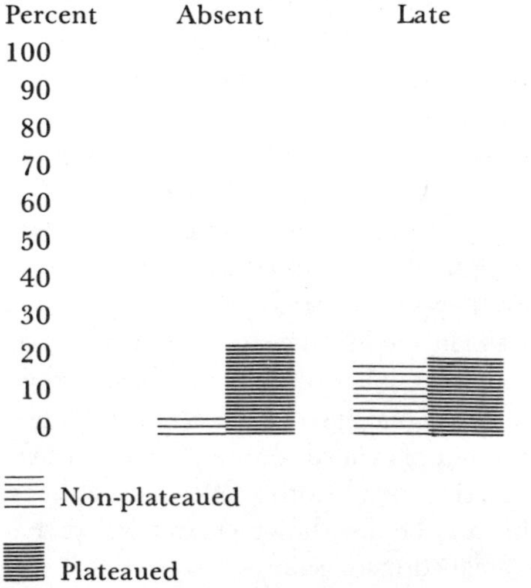

Table 6
Percent of Managers Whose Health Is "Extremely Good"

Percent	Currently	5 Years ago
100		
90		
80		
70		
60		
50		
40		
30		
20		
10		
0		

☰ Non-plateaued

▰ Plateaued

THE PLATEAUED MANAGER:
MUCH ADO ABOUT NOTHING?

On the basis of figures presented here, about half of all managers are plateaued and most of these could be called "solid citizens"[3]; they are managers who are unlikely to receive future promotions but have maintained acceptable levels of performance.[4] Since their promotions slow in rate several years before they reach a plateau,[5] these managers may adjust to the idea of being plateaued long before they are. Yet other managers believe the career plateau constitutes a serious problem.[6]

Plateaued managers, at least those who recognize their plateau, apparently do not agree. Although the vast majority would like to change jobs, few are clamoring to change management levels. Many would welcome the opportunity to do so, should a higher level position become available, but most accept the fact that it probably will not. Their performance on the job does not suffer greatly as a result, although they are significantly more likely to be absent and somewhat more likely to work fewer hours per week. Their attitudes toward the job and life in general are about as favorable as those of nonplateaued managers, although the plateaued managers' health may be somewhat poorer. The plateaued managers also report poorer relations with their supervisors.

The point is that plateaued managers are widely assumed to be disenchanted and discontented. Indeed, some plateaued managers probably are. As the

results here indicate, most managers cope with and adapt to the career plateau
without too much difficulty.

COPING WITH THE PLATEAU

A study of managers who received demotions provides clues as to how the
plateaued manager adapts.[7] Both the organization and the individual manager
collude to help the manager make this adjustment.

The firm, on the one hand, does not clearly inform individuals who have
plateaued. In fact, the indications that a manager has reached a plateau may be
very ambiguous. The manager may still receive bonuses or be asked to attend
executive training programs. The manager may even receive geographic transfers which may be interpreted as promotions. Since the criteria for promotion
decisions are vague, no one can be too sure exactly when the plateau has been
reached. This may explain why the managers in this study were not very critical
of the criteria used for promotion decisions; perhaps the lack of criticism is due
to uncertainty as to the nature of the promotion criteria used.

The manager also avoids facing up to the true implications of the plateau. As
Goldner notes, the manager may emphasize the negative features of a promotion: longer hours, increased pressure, greater responsibility. This disavowal of
interest in promotion may become a self-fulfilling prophecy, actually preventing the manager from receiving further promotions. When the plateau is
reached, the manager has a convenient rationalization: the individual is happy
with the current position. Whether such managers truly prefer to plateau
(voluntary plateauees) or simply want to withdraw from the game before they
lose (anticipatory plateauees) cannot be determined. As this study indicates, a
large percentage of plateaued managers claim to be very happy with their
current position.

Managers may also compensate for the disappointment of the plateau by
putting their energies into activities outside the job. Such activities may
provide a needed outlet for the manager, and may even improve job
performance (for example, the sales manager whose golf game wins
customers). These activities may be quite successful as compensation:
plateaued managers in this study reported levels of overall life satisfaction comparable to those among nonplateaued managers. The off-the-job activities in
which plateaued managers indulge may have helped them to maintain these
relatively high levels of life satisfaction.

Finally, plateaued managers might hide their embarrassment over the
plateau from their peers by moving to a new job in the firm. Goldner found that
demoted managers preferred to leave their current position. If plateaued
managers feel similarly, this may account for their apparent desire to change
jobs, reflected in the complaint that such job changes are overly difficult to
obtain.

The manager faced with a plateau thus has several options: to prepare for the
plateau before it arrives by finding other sources of satisfaction, by becoming

involved in activities outside the job once plateaued, and by requesting transfers to new positions, as needed, so that the job will retain challenge and variety. The manager dealing with a plateaued subordinate must decide how to inform the plateauee and how to provide opportunities for further growth, both on and off the job. The results presented here imply that the plateauee frequently blames the supervisor for the situation. Transferring the plateauee to a new position may avoid this conflict and help the plateauee to save face with peers. If transfer is not feasible, the supervisor should consider other ways to add challenge and variety to the job. Ironically, the supervisor may be put in the position of persuading the plateauee that there are other things in life besides the job; helping the plateauee identify off-the-job activities may provide compensation for dissatisfactions felt on the job. Finally, the supervisor should recognize the plateau as part of the overall context; the plateauee is older, more apt to suffer health problems, more likely to put in fewer hours and to be absent. This change may reflect the plateauee's motivation or reduced capability, or both. The supervisor wishing to resolve the problem needs to be aware first of its source, whether motivation or capability, before taking any other steps.

Coping with the plateau requires the joint effort of both the plateauee and his or her supervisor. Not only is there life after the plateau, there is also growth, if the parties involved work towards this goal.

References

1. The data used in this study were made available by the ISR Social Science Archive. These data, taken from the Quality of Employment Study, were originally collected by Robert P. Quinn, Thomas W. Mangione, and Stanley R. Seashore of the Survey Research Center, Institute for Social Research, the University of Michigan. Neither the original collectors of the data nor the Archive bears any responsibility for the analyses or interpretations presented here.
2. J. F. Veiga, "Do Managers on the Move Get Anywhere?" *Harvard Business Review*, March-April 1981: 20-35.
3. J. P. Near, "The Career Plateau: Causes and Effects," *Business Horizons*, September-October 1980: 53-57.
4. T. P. Ference, J. A. F. Stoner, and E. K. Warren, "Managing the Career Plateau," *Academy of Management Review*, April 1977: 602-612.
5. J. F. Veiga, "Plateaued Versus Non-plateaued Managers: Career Patterns, Attitudes, and Path Potential," *Academy of Management Journal*, March 1981: 566-578.
6. Near.
7. F. H. Goldner, "Demotion in Industrial Management," *American Sociological Review*, May 1965: 714-724.

Janet P. Near is an Associate Professor of Management at Indiana University.

35.
HIRING FOR EXCELLENCE

Lester L. Tobias

> Organizational policy emphasizes "managing" for excellence rather
> than "selecting" for excellence. Seldom do companies treat human
> acquisitions with anywhere near the care with which they treat capital
> acquisitions. There are too many misconceptions, biases, and excuses
> that get in the way of the hiring process.

Given all the current emphasis on achieving excellence, I find it curious that
most of the references center on "managing" for excellence rather than on
"selecting" for excellence. Truly excellent organizations start with excellent
people, and no amount of managing is going to magically transform a "settled
for" organization into an excellent one.

Why is selecting for excellence given short shrift? There are a number of
forces and misconceptions that operate to tip the scales against it.

Managers are under intense pressure to fill positions to meet short-term
needs and quotas, to beat a hiring freeze, or just to prove to their boss that they
are action-oriented. Sometimes they succumb to fatigue or lose faith in finding
the best candidate, so they settle for the "best of the lot."

Many managers do not understand employee-turnover costs, particularly in-
sofar as it is often near impossible to assign numbers to intangible costs and
because it is hard to see sales not made or projects not completed as "real" costs.

HIRING PITFALLS

Seldom do companies treat human acquisitions with anywhere near the care
with which they treat capital acquisitions. There are too many
misconceptions, biases, and excuses that get in the way of the hiring process.
Here are some that will get a manager in trouble:

- Hiring expediently under the pressure of time. That's the "buy now and pay later" approach.
- • Hiring on the basis of product knowledge rather than ability. I once consulted with a meat wholesaler whose entire sales force was made up of butchers.
- Resorting to hiring the "best of the batch" out of desperation.
- Using the "don't some of us have to be Indians and not chiefs" argument to talk yourself out of your high standards. That may be the case, but there are excellent Indians as well as mediocre ones.
  •Hiring the castoffs of admired companies and, conversely, hiring the superstars of mediocre companies. Neither is a guarantee of anything.
- Naively assuming that a track record is a guarantee of future performance.
- Explaining away inconsistencies in a person's presentation or record. Remember that if you give someone the benefit of the doubt, you may have to accept the cost of that doubt.
- Hiring with the hope that the person will change.
- Hiring only for a specific position and ignoring promotability.
- Hiring anyone solely on the objective facts while ignoring your personal feelings or gut reactions.
- Going only on first impressions and then finding justification in what follows.
- Hiring an underachiever on the assumption that the manager's energy and success will be contagious.
- Assuming that a job candidate's persistent followup indicates real motivation. Maybe so, but not necessarily the kind needed for the job.

REASSURE YOUR MANAGERS

What can be done to ensure that, throughout the organization, managers are hiring for excellence? Managers must be encouraged to maintain high hiring standards with tangible reassurances that hiring delays will be tolerated in order to find the best people.

Performance reviews of managers should explicitly address "qualitative" as well as "quantitative" issues such as turnover improvements among subordinates on a long-term basis.

It is essential to continually stress that each person hired shall be viewed as a company acquisition and not just as a vehicle for helping a particular manager achieve goals.

Lester L. Tobias is a partner in the Westborough, Mass., office of Nordli, Wilson Associates, management consulting psychologists, and president of Psychological Services International, Westborough, Mass., and New Haven, Conn.

36.
WHOSE CAREER IS LIKELY TO PLATEAU?

John W. Slocum, Jr.
William L. Cron
Linda C. Yows

More people are reaching plateaus earlier in their careers than did their predecessors—and far earlier than their own expectations. It is important, therefore, for organizations and individuals to prepare for this phenomenon, particularly when the signs of an impending plateau are observed.

Sooner or later almost everyone's career reaches a plateau, and these days it's more likely to be sooner than later. How do individuals and organizations know that a plateau is approaching, and in what situations is plateauing most likely to occur?

Entry-level employees have no place to go but up on the corporate hierarchy. But what happens to individuals who are well into a career when they realize that they are going nowhere at all? These people are *plateaued* and their problem is just beginning to be recognized.

The reasons that people reach plateaus are complex, but the problem of plateauing is inevitable for most people. Plateauing refers to the slowing down and the inevitable end of promotions. Plateauing can occur for two reasons: personal and organizational.

Personal plateauing occurs when employees decide not to pursue further advancement in the corporation. Although they may have the ability, they have lost their desire to play the tournament mobility game.

Organizational plateauing occurs when people *want* to advance but don't. Either the company has no openings, or management believes that the person lacks the executive skills to be promoted.

As people climb the corporate pyramid, the number of positions decreases dramatically and the opportunities to continue to move upward decrease accordingly. This means that plateauing must happen to almost everyone. It is normal, and it has little to do with failure or success.

Unfortunately, most people regard promotions as the only reward that really counts. Increased responsibilities, status symbols, and other material rewards that go hand in hand with promotions carry the message, "I am a winner." When promotions stop, many managers feel like failures.

The problems for today's managers is that promotions stop long before retirement. In contrast to managers ten years ago, today's managers are plateaued for longer periods of time. Therefore, the psychological adjustment period is longer, and very few companies have prepared their employees for career plateaus.

The purpose of this article is to aid individuals and organizations in identifying the signals of plateauing and the situations in which plateauing is most likely to occur. Salespeople in a large chemical- agriculture company were surveyed and data were analyzed to see:

- Why plateaued and nonplateaued people change jobs;
- How long they stay in each job;
- The moves made by plateaued people as compared to nonplateaued people; and
- The characteristics of their territorial assignments.

THE HISTORICAL PERSPECTIVE

The problem started with the baby boom between 1946 and 1960. Many people born during this period are trying to get top jobs in companies at a time that companies are trimming their managerial ranks.

Because many fathers of baby boomers enjoyed a smooth ride to the top, their children's expectations were raised. Their fathers entered the job market when most companies needed every manager they could recruit. From the late 1940s, the U.S. experienced an extraordinary period of economic expansion. The number of corporations increased by 56 percent.[1] A major problem was trying to hire people to fill management spots. Because of the low birthrate during World War II, competition for the top corporate positions was not so keen as it is today. Compared to today, few managers went to college. As a result, those who did and performed well attained top management positions in their companies.

These high expectations led the baby boomers to spend more time being educated. They put off their job searches until they had completed their education. According to the U.S. Office of Education, the number of college students receiving bachelor's degrees since the 1960s has increased by 91 percent.

During the 1970s, many young people thought that the MBA degree was their union card to the top corporate jobs. In 1960 graduate schools of business awarded only 4,500 MBA degrees. By 1986, these same schools awarded more than 71,000 degrees.[2]

The largest population of educated and qualified people in U. S. history is now competing for a limited number of managerial positions. An estimated 55 million or so baby boomers are now between the ages of 25 and 39. In earlier times it was almost always white men who climbed the corporate ladder. The ladder is becoming increasingly coed and color-blind, further exacerbating the problem of too many people for too few spots. Armed with their MBAs and high expectations, these people are now facing culture shock. They are not moving through the corporate ranks as fast as they want, and they are not receiving the material rewards that they thought they would receive. In the future, unless the plateauing problem is understood, more employees will be disappointed and frustrated.

All of these factors point toward more people reaching plateaus earlier in their careers than did their predecessors—and far earlier than their own expectations. It is important, therefore, for organizations and individuals to prepare to cope with the phenomenon successfully, particularly when the signs of an impending plateau are observed.

WHY PEOPLE PLATEAU: RESEARCH TO DATE

Researchers have suggested several causes for career plateauing. Some of these reasons are related to job function, personal characteristics, and the strategy and corporate culture of the firm.

Job Function. Plateauing does not necessarily connote negative performance. One model classifies plateaued persons as either *solid citizens* or *deadwood*.[3]

Solid citizens are high performers who are satisfied with their positions.

Deadwood employees produce work of poor quality and generally do not have positive feelings about their jobs.

The same model distinguishes between two kinds of nonplateaued persons:

Comers, those with promotion possibilities who are not yet high performers because they are still high on the learning curve; and

Stars, employees who are high performers and anticipate continued promotion.

Many low performers (deadwood) have expressed the opinion that promotions are based on personality, education, and reputation within the company, instead of on professional ability or the quality of job performance. This attitude suggests that people with low visibility to senior management are more likely to become deadwood than those in jobs that give them high visibility.

Most high performers perceive their jobs as challenging, satisfying, clearly defined, and important to the company. Self-perception can be one reason for plateauing. Solid citizens sometimes see themselves as indispensable to the company. Therefore, they choose to stay in their positions instead of moving to new positions.

Personal characteristics. Plateaued people sometimes list personal decisions as causes for plateauing.[4] Continuing promotion usually brings greater responsibilities to an employee and therefore is more demanding. An employee may decide not to pursue upward career mobility in order to reduce job-related stress. Someone with a family may feel the necessity of declining a promotion that would require relocation. Because dual-career families are more common today than in the past, the need to consider a spouse's career and priorities can limit the personal sacrifices made in regard to transfers and decreased personal time.

Age is sometimes a factor in plateauing. Traditionally, older employees are more likely to plateau than younger ones. As people get closer to retirement and the conclusion of their careers, they may feel less need for promotions as symbols of success. Employers may also be less willing to promote persons who will have a shorter future in a position than those with whom a long-term relationship can be built. The idea that learning slows with age could also deter managers from promoting older persons; they may believe that a younger person could sooner assimilate the necessary information.

Janet Near has identified several common assumptions about plateaued employees, who are assumed to have:

• Lower job performance;
• Lower motivation and satisfaction;
• Lower aspirations;
• Bad attitude and behavior in nonwork factors; and
• Lower rating of their own jobs.[5]

In terms of lower job performance, she found that plateaued employees had higher absenteeism that nonplateaued employees. The theory that plateaued employees have lower motivation and satisfaction was not supported by her data. Plateaued employees were neither less motivated nor less satisfied than their nonplateaued peers. Near's studies also did not support the popular notion that plateaued persons have poorer attitudes and work behaviors than nonplateaued persons. Plateaued persons did, however, report slightly poorer health than their nonplateaued colleagues. Plateaued employees rated their jobs as less challenging and rewarding than did their nonplateaued peers. They also reported much lower career aspirations than nonplateaued employees. These lower aspirations may explain some of the reasons for personal plateauing, as opposed to organizational plateauing.

Business strategy and corporate culture. The research of Slocum, Cron, Hansen, and Rawlings indicated a relationship between the business strategy of the firm and the incidence of plateaued employees.[6] Employees in a firm with a *defender* strategy had proportionately more plateaued employees than those in the analyzer firm. A defender is a firm in a mature industry with an established product line and little growth potential. It competes by staying in its niche and improving its production efficiency.

Plateaued employees in either firm showed higher satisfaction with immediate supervisors and the work itself than did nonplateaued employees. Stars and solid citizens considered professional success more important than did the deadwood. Nonplateaued employees showed a job history with shorter average tenure in each position than did plateaued employees. Nonplateaued employees were also more likely than plateaued employees to be willing to leave the company or take a geographic transfer if such a move involved promotion.

IN SEARCH OF PLATEAUS

Why do people in various stages of plateauing move between jobs? What is the job tenure of plateaued and nonplateaued employees? Do these two groups of employees come from similar or different functional areas?

To answer these questions, data were gathered from the sales force of a large chemical-agriculture company. The firm competes primarily in a mature industry. During the past five years, the industry experienced a 2.5 percent growth rate. With a 15 percent market share, this is a dominant firm. The company is slowly adding some new products in high-growth segments of its market. Marketing expenditures are relatively high for new products. Annual sales for the company exceed $130 million.

The company employs a sale force of 299. A total of 187—62 percent of the sales force—returned completed surveys. Participants were surveyed on a variety of personal and professional issues. In order to avoid biases, supervisors were also surveyed about each employee's promotional possibilities and actual sales performance.

The sales position in the company is an entry-level one that may be filled by either an experienced or an inexperienced salesperson. Because the sales force is the most important element of the promotional mix, interpersonal customer relationships are highly valued. For this reason, it is not unusual for sales people to stay in their initial territories for extended periods. Compensation is such that extended field experience need not limit financial success. Promotions from sales positions are generally into management positions in the same divisions. As people progress through the hierarchy, fewer management positions exist.

Clarification of what is meant by a "plateaued" salesperson was a primary concern. Although no hard and fast criteria define when a person is plateaued, job change, not age, is regarded as the salient variable. Therefore, we decided to consider as plateaued people who had not been promoted or had a lateral job change in five years or more. The time factors involved in the most recent move and probability of future moves were confirmed by assessing promotion possibilities with the sales managers. Following these criteria, we classified 141 people as nonplateaued and 46 people as plateaued. Then we segmented these major categories by sales performance.[7] *Stars* (N = 83) were nonplateaued people in the upper half of their sales performance distribution. *Comers* (N = 58) were nonplateaued people whose sales were in the lower half of the company's performance distribution. *Solid citizens* (N = 8) were plateaued persons whose sales were in the upper half of the performance distribution, whereas *deadwood* (N = 38) were plateaued people whose sales were in the lower half of the sales distribution.

JOB TENURE

Those surveyed gave a complete chronology of all full-time jobs held. In addition to giving position and company, they listed the month and year in which they started each job and the month and year in which the job ended.

The job tenure varied between *stars* and *comers* within the nonplateaued employees and between *deadwood* and *solid citizens* with the plateaued category. The *deadwood* stayed in their first position only about 21 months and their second position only about 30 months. This suggests that, earlier in their careers, these people moved rather frequently but now had reached career plateaus. In comparison, *solid citizens* averaged 36 and 54 months in their first and second positions respectively. Earlier in their careers, these people appear to move more slowly, but they are currently more productive than the deadwood. Job changes for both deadwood and solid citizens slowed in the third position to 55 months and 45 months respectively. The pattern of previous job tenures for *comers* and *stars* is different from that of plateaued employees. Their tenure on each subsequent job is shorter. *Stars* spent an average of 30, 39, and 31 months on their first, second and third jobs. By comparison, *comers* spent an average of 47, 32, and 31 months. Not that employees in both groups spent a considerable amount of time in one of their previous three positions. This suggests that each of these categories of mobile people spent some time developing their interpersonal and sales skills and management contacts in a particular position, which enabled them to continue progressing in their careers.

REASONS FOR JOB CHANGES

In giving a history of job changes, each employee was asked what situation or triggering event led to each job change. Forty-two reasons were categorized into seven major issues:

- Family problems;
- Financial problems;

- Reorganization in the company;
- New opportunity in another job;
- Company bankruptcy or a strike;
- Going into business for oneself or changing industries; and
- Personal (health, retirement) issues.

For each job change, the person's reason was put into one of these seven categories.

As Table 1 shows, plateaued and nonplateaued salespeople give significantly different reasons for job changes. The two most common reasons cited by nonplateaued employees for changing positions are financial and a new opportunity. Both of these reasons indicate that employees consciously choose to manage their careers. In fact, both suggest motivations of success and advancement.

Plateaued employees, however, cite with equal frequency a change in company policy or a company reorganization, a new opportunity, and personal reasons. A reorganization is something over which the employees have no control. Attributing a move to company and personal reasons (health, early retirement) may indicate that plateaued persons who are not performing well cite external events when attempting to justify their movement to others. Socially acceptable reasons for mediocre performance are poor health, too much stress, or company policies. Once the employee internalizes this belief, a form of self-fulling prophecy unfolds.

FUNCTIONAL AREAS

Salespeople were asked to indicate the functional areas in which they were assigned on each job. They could check one of three categories: sales, production, or general management.

Table 1
Reasons for Movement to Present Position

Reason	Nonplateaued	Plateaued
New opportunity	18%	22%
Reorganization	13%	22%
Financial reason	21%	13%
Personal reason	8%	22%
Family issues	14%	11%
Company reason	16%	7%
Career change	10%	4%

Note: Figures may not total 100% because of rounding. A chi-square test indicated that there are significant differences between the reasons that nonplateaued and plateaued people change jobs ($X^2 = 12.96$, $p < .04$).

As Table 2 indicates, we found no statistically significant differences in the functional areas from which plateaued and nonplateaued employees moved, though nonplateaued employees were more likely to have been in a sales function (52.5 percent) in their previous positions. In both categories there is a concentration of people moving from general management to sales. These data may be skewed because the survey deals exclusively with salespeople.

SALES TERRITORY ASSIGNMENTS

Employees and their immediate supervisors each classified the territory assignments according to the BCG matrix. Product market growth and market share were evaluated in each territory. A determination was made of the percentage of sales within the territory or products/services that were growing at a rate of 10 percent or more. The salespersons were also asked:

- The percentage of products/services growing at more than 10 percent of sales in which they held first or second market share within their territory; and
- The percentage of low-growth products (less than 10 percent growth) in which they held a first or second market share within their territory.

Each territory was classified as one of the four BCG types—star, problem child, cash cow, or dog—according to the dominant characteristics of its sales. A *star territory* was one with most of its sales in product lines with the dominant market share in the territory and high growth rates. A *problem child territory* had a majority of its sales in high-growth products with low market shares. *Cash cow territories* had most of their sales in low growth-dominant products. *Dog territories* were those characterized by sales in low-growth, low-share products.

To check on the validity of the territory characteristics, the sales manager of each salesperson was asked to respond to the same set of territory characteristic questions. The correlation between the responses of the salespersons and their managers was positive and significant.[8]

Studies have indicated that different types of territories are related to the

Table 2
Job Change by Function for Last Move

Function	Nonplateaued	Plateaued
Sales	52.5%	37.1%
General	30.3%	25.9%
Production management	17.2%	37.0%

Note: A chi-square test indicated no significant differences between nonplateaued and plateaued people.

Table 3
Territory Assignment and Plateauing

Territory Characteristics	Nonplateaued	Plateaued
High-share, high-growth (star)	14%	5%
High-share, low-growth (cash cow)	12%	14%
Low-share, high-growth (problem child)	20%	5%
Low-share, low-growth (dog)	54%	76%

Note: A chi-square test indicated a significant difference between nonplateaued and plateaued people by territorial assignment ($X^2 = 12.96$, p $< .04$).

performance of individual sales persons and that management does not always properly evaluate sales performance in light of the characteristics of the assigned territories.[9] As Table 3 indicates, the plateaued employees are more likely to have been assigned to dog territories than any other territory type.

Nonplateaued persons were more likely to be assigned to cash cow territories than plateaued persons. Although this may suggest that plateaued persons are given the less attractive territories, there may be some question as to whether the person was assigned a dog territory or if the area became a dog territory because of the person assigned to it.

Although it is difficult to pinpoint cause and effect, the assignment of newcomers to a cash cow or dog territory most certainly increases their chances of plateauing early in their careers.

AN EMERGING PROFILE

What profiles emerge from our study of the plateaued employee? Plateaued employees have had long tenure in their present positions but relatively short tenure in their careers. Rapid early movement, particularly among the deadwood, has slowed considerably in their more recent job positions. Seventy-six percent of the plateaued people were assigned to areas with low sales growth and market share. With little mobility and unattractive assignments, these people are not likely to find challenging and rewarding career opportunities in the organization. The high probability of a performance decline among solid citizens in these conditions should be of considerable concern to top management.

For the nonplateaued persons, it appears that early assignment that enabled them to learn interpersonal and management skills eventually paid off. These people paid their dues by learning the needed skills before moving ahead in the organization. When they moved, it was usually for financial advantage and for company reasons that involved increased responsibility and sales authority. Their assignments into problem-children sales territories enables them to effectively utilize the skills that they learned earlier in their careers.

WHAT CAN MANAGERS DO?

According to Bardwich and our research, managers can do a great deal to help employees cope with the plateauing process.[10]

First, they should *make the facts about plateauing known*. Plateauing is a normal phase of one's working career. If this information is available, it will challenge the traditional belief that plateaued persons are failures. Early in their careers people can set more realistic expectations about promotions.

Second, for the solid citizens, *try to eliminate content plateauing*, which occurs when someone performs the same set of activities over a period of years and little learning takes place. When a content plateau is reached, an employee, though proficient, becomes bored with the routine of the job. IBM, Monsanto, Brooklyn Union Gas, and other companies have plans that prevent content plateauing by moving people laterally. For example, at Brooklyn Union Gas, employees who are content-plateaued are given opportunities to move into other jobs at the same organizational level with no extra compensation or perquisites. This company employs a version of the Hay Compensation System, which assigns a certain range of points to each job classification. Employees who elect to move laterally retain their Hay points and salary. For example, to avoid content plateauing, an employee moved from principal engineer to director of credit collection. Although some people who are content-plateaued remain productive and satisfied knowing that they have mastered their work, others need challenges and want to achieve other satisfactions from their work. Managers might think about jobs as collections of responsibilities that can be distributed to several qualified people. This exchange can take place at the same grade level or even between levels, if status and other reward differentials are not too great.

Third, managers can *use rewards other than promotion and money to motivate* the solid citizen. Almost anything can be a reward if it is something that people value. For example, many rewards—putting a person's picture in the company newspaper or permitting the person to attend an executive development program—are readily available in most companies and cost the company little. These may be of tremendous emotional support to the solid citizen.

Employees need to learn the value of career success through increased job responsibilities rather than moves up the corporate ladder. As promotions become increasingly scarce, managers must reward differently those who are plateaued and performing well and those who are plateaued and performing poorly.

Fourth, *give honest feedback*. Because, for human and political reasons, managers seldom give negative appraisals, performance appraisals are typically positive. However, managers owe their employees honest assessments of their strengths and liabilities and opportunities to correct their weaknesses. A common symptom of plateaued workaholics is increasing the amount of time they work and the effort they put forth because they do not know what else to do. Unfortunately, this additional energy is usually not rewarded by the organization in terms of money or promotion. As long as plateaued employees are frantically busy, they seldom have time to think about their situation. This pace increases their vulnerability to stress, job burn-out, or depression because, in the long term, they do not achieve success.

Fifth, managers should *pay special attention to the characteristics of the territory when hiring newcomers* to their sales force. If the goal of the company is to maintain its market share in a market that is not very attractive, then hiring a plateaued person might be more effective than hiring a nonplateaued performer.

Nonplateaued performers want challenging assignments that increase their chances of promotion and their visibility to senior management. A low-share but high-potential territory would afford them the opportunity to demonstrate their sales acumen. However, a low-share and low-growth assignment (dog) probably would deny them the opportunity to display their sales talents to senior management. Because senior management does not want that territory to grow, the likelihood of their receiving recognition and other material reward from senior management is low, even if they should succeed in working wonders.

AREAS FOR FURTHER STUDY

Do different types of plateaued persons need different management? This question deserves additional study. Solid citizens and deadwood probably need to be managed entirely differently. Solid citizens need reinforcement of the positive attitudes that make them productive. If these solid performers are plateaued by choice, including them in projects and committees that can benefit from their experience may enhance their jobs, allowing them to stay productive and happy in their present positions for even longer periods of time. Deadwood, on the other hand, might need other managing—career counseling, job enhancement, or even lateral transfers. To ignore them will only cause further deterioration in work quality and personal esteem.

Another area worth examining is the type of positions most likely to have plateaued persons. It is possible that staff positions produce plateaued persons for different reasons than line positions. It may be that the personal characteristics and career paths of plateauing employees differ significantly by the type of position held. Managing needs probably will also vary with staff or line positions. Although no studies have been done specifically along this line, because line positions offer greater competition and a more glorified reward system than do staff positions, the effects and treatment of plateauing may well differ. Deadwood in a line position may feel unable to complete effectively, but a solid citizen with the recognition and rewards of a line position may continue working indefinitely.

Just because there is less recognition and less exposure to upper management, staff positions may be inherently more subject to plateauing than are line positions.

The results of this study indicate that plateauing is related to a specific profile of previous job movements and reasons for changing jobs. Plateaued people spend progressively longer periods of time in each job prior to their present position. They are also less likely to move for reasons of personal and financial growth. External events beyond their immediate control are likely to be given as the reason for their moving. Their present assignment may also facilitate plateauing. Plateaued people were more likely to be assigned to low growth and market share territories than were nonplateaued people.

We are cautious in generalizing these results, however, because the sample consisted entirely of salespeople and mostly of men. People in staff positions and many women are likely to have different job histories.

References

1. See T. Vogel, "Business Fails to Fulfill Dreams of Baby Boomers," *The Dallas Morning News*, December 10, 1985, Section D.
2. See J. Bardwich, *The Plateauing Trap: How to Avoid It in Your Career*. New York: AMACOM, 1986, pp. 22-25.
3. T. P. Ference, J. A. F. Stoner, and E. K. Warren, "Managing the Career Plateau," *Academy of Management Review*, October 1977: 602-612.
4. See two articles by Janet P. Near: "The Career Plateau: Causes and Effects," *Business Horizons*, October 1980: 53-57, and "Reactions to the Career Plateau," *Business Horizons*, July-August 1984: 75-79.
5. Janet P. Near, "A Discriminate Analysis of Plateaued Versus Nonplateaued Managers," *Journal of Vocational Behavior*, April 1985: 177-88.
6. John W. Slocum, Jr., William Cron, R. Hansen, and S. Rawlings, "Business Strategy and the Management of Plateaued Employees," *Academy of Management Journal*, March 1985: 133-54.
7. In this we followed the methodology outlined in Slocum et al. (note 6).
8. See William Cron and John W. Slocum, Jr., "The influence of Career Stages on Salespeople's Job Attitudes, Work Perceptions, and Performance," *Journal of Marketing Research* 23 (May 1986): 119-30.
9. Adrian Ryans and Charles Weinberg, "Territory Sales Response," *Journal of Marketing Research*, November 1979: 453-65; John Mowen, Janet Keith, Stephen Brown, and Donald Jackson, "Utilizing Effort and Task Difficulty Information in Evaluating Salespeople," *Journal of Marketing Research*, May 1985: 185-91.
10. See Bardwich (note 2). For additional reading in this area, see E. K. Warren, T. P. Ference, and J. A. Stoner, "The Case of the Plateaued Performer," *Harvard Business Review*, January-February 1975: 146-48; J. F.

Veiga, "Plateaued Versus Nonplateaued Managers: Career Patterns, Attitudes, and Path Potential," *Academy of Management Journal*, September 1981: 566-78; M. Evans and E. Gilbert, "Plateaued Managers: Their Need Gratifications and Their Effort-Performance Expectations," *Journal of Management Studies*, January 1985: 99-108; and J. Carnazza, A. Korman, T. P. Ference, and J. A. F. Stoner, "Plateaued and Nonplateaued Managers: Factors in Job Performance," *Journal of Management*, Spring 1981: 7-72.

John W. Slocum, Jr., holds the O. Paul Corley Professorship in Organizational Behavior at the Edwin L. Cox School of Business, Southern Methodist University, Dallas. William L. Cron is an assistant professor of marketing at the Cox School. Linda C. Yows is vice-president of credit administration for the Allied Bank of Dallas.

37.
SIX STEPS TO HIRING SUCCESS

Sam Skeegan

The hiring process is based on comparison and compromise. There is no such thing as the perfect person for a given job, but rather, the best person *available* for the position. Proper planning and prompt decision making are critical. Here are six steps you should follow to ensure success in your recruiting.

Whether you're hiring the first employee or the hundredth in your management career, be it a secretary or a manager, it may seem like a venture into the unknown.

This is where proper planning and prompt decision making can really make a difference for you. This article outlines the six steps you should follow to make a successful hire.

1) PLANNING

Table 1 shows the proper planning steps for any hire. Give careful thought to the reason you're hiring someone and to what you hope that person will accomplish. Then write a complete, *realistic* job description. Make sure that you differentiate between your absolute minimum job requirement and the assets you'd like your employee to have, but are not absolutely essential. Also, set the desired hiring and starting dates. If you need somebody immediately, you may have to hire a temporary person for the short term rather than make a rushed decision on a full-time employee.

Another consideration is to persuade your company to commit financial resources. Determine the salary range for this position, and whether this allows you any flexibility in your offer (which includes early review, raise schedules, and bonus eligibility). Fringe benefits will be important to many candidates, so be prepared to explain them fully. Highlight any unique fringe benefit you may

Table 1
Planning Your Hire

Write a realistic job description.

- Clarify your absolute minimum requirements.
- Identify your preferred, but not mandatory, requirements.

Identify your financial resources.

- What are your salary restrictions?
- What is your recruiting budget?
- Realistically, when does the position have to be filled?
- What necessary benefits can the position offer in the near future?

Honestly evaluate what you have to sell.

- Why would someone want to work for your company?
- What is attractive about the position?
- What are your own strengths and weaknesses?

offer, such as tuition reimbursement, day-care, trips to conferences, or profit sharing.

You should also know what you're allowed to spend in recruiting for this position. Your budget could include advertising expenses, interview costs, personnel-agency fees, and even relocation allowances. All of these factors could affect your ability to attract qualified candidates.

Once you know the type of person you want, and how much you can spend, it's a good idea to write everything down and put it aside for a couple of days. Then, take a fresh look to be sure that the job description, salary range and time schedule still seem realistic. During this period, it would help to sit in on an interview that someone else in the company is conducting, to more clearly see the assets you want in an employee.

You should also take time at this point to honestly evaluate your key marketing assets. How are you going to sell the candidate you want on the position and your company? Why should someone want the job? Likewise, why should this person want to work for you? Assess your strengths and weaknesses in terms of personality, preferences and technical abilities.

There is no such thing as a perfect person for any job. Look for the best person available for the position open. Hiring is based on comparisons.

Therefore, know what you're looking for in a candidate in terms of the job to fill, and the objectives of your staff and the entire organization. Determine your hiring goals quickly, and make them known. Before you bring in the first candidate, have your interviewing and hiring procedure clearly delineated, including identification of the final decision maker.

2) ATTRACTING

The quality of your candidate pool depends on where, how and when you're looking. If you're doing this yourself, you will have to advertise in your local newspaper as well as national newspapers.

Advertising, unfortunately, can be ineffective or a complete waste of money if not done well. You must know the marketplace of talent. Describe the job in terms job hunters understand, and explain your requirements clearly and comprehensively. Be both sufficiently general to attract responses from a wide group, and sufficiently detailed to attract a group that's appropriate to your needs.

Ads—properly prepared and in the right places—can help in attracting candidates, but they are no substitute for a total recruiting and screening program. If you have a personnel department, seek their help in identifying candidates for your positions.

3) SELECTING

If you devise a measurement scale for the various job components (Table 2) and decide on the importance of characteristics you're looking for in a candidate, you can make a good decision. Quantify each function and results as specifically as possible, so you don't end up with vague needs such as "to manage people" or "good typing."

When developing your selection criteria, remember that the position exists under specific working conditions, not in a theoretical model. Try to consider real-world situations, such as office politics and real as opposed to imagined authority.

4) INTERVIEWING

Plan the interview process well in advance, and make sure you know the answers to the following questions:

- Who will see the candidates?
- When will the first round of interviews be conducted?
- How many interviews will be conducted with each candidate?
- What interview questions will you ask each candidate? (Table 3)

The following are several points to keep in mind during the interview.

- It's a two-way street. A well-run interview reflects good working relationships on your staff, and shows respect to the candidate.
- Surroundings are important. You need to put people at ease, so that they willingly reveal goals, qualifications, and interests.

Table 2
Sample Interview Grading Sheet

Grading
A = above average
B = satisfactory
C = less than satisfactory

Candidate _____ Date _____

Characteristics	Grading	Rank in Importance (1-10)
Management skills	_____	_____
Personality	_____	_____
Education	_____	_____
Ability to work independently	_____	_____
Ability to produce immediately	_____	_____
People-supervisory experience	_____	_____
Profit-and-loss experience	_____	_____
Experience with similar organizations	_____	_____
Potential for growth	_____	_____
Technical background	_____	_____

Interviewed by _____

- Keep the conversation open-ended for the same reason. Do not ask a string of questions that simply call for yes or no answers.
- Be prepared to offer ample information about your organization.
- Use a standard form for recording the results of each interview. Do it after—not during—the interview.

Do not take notes while the candidate is with you, because it will block the flow of information. Standard forms will help you keep track of the candidate's traits and skills.

5) CHECKING

The final step in screening is checking references. This should be done over the phone and not in writing; people don't tend to commit themselves in writing. Even on the phone, people usually say only good things about an

Table 3
Sample Interview Questions

1. How many people have you directly supervised? Where?

2. How many department heads have you supervised?

   What were their titles and functions?

3. What types of programs have you developed?

   Briefly describe them

4. How would you describe your motivation techniques?

5. What kind of a boss (employee) do people describe you as?

6. What do you consider your greatest management success?

7. Describe how your boss would think of you as a communicator?

8. What do you like most about your present job?

9. What are your career goals now and for the next five years?

10. Have you read the job description?

Do you have questions about the job or the company?

applicant, so it's necessary to ask probing questions. A run-of-the-mill reference check nets nothing. It may produce dates and little else.

You should talk to a person within the candidates's prior company, someone who knows the applicant's on-the-job performance. Find out basic qualifications during the reference check.

If your company has a severe problem in credit management for example, determine if the applicant has had experience in developing credit programs from scratch, or was primarily involved in maintaining programs someone else had created. Find out how well the applicant handles credit checks. Does he or she work well under pressure? Has the credit program been better or worse since this individual has been involved? These are the specific kinds of inside questions that someone in the applicant's department can answer.

This telephone check should bring the pool of applications down to the top two, with possibly another two in reserve. Then decide to whom you will make the offer, and what exactly it will include.

6) CLOSING

Now, you have to land him or her. You have to make an offer stick before another organization does. Make your decision quickly. Remember that the pool of available talents is always in flux, and your candidate will not be a candidate for long. Make your decision as quickly as possible after the inter-view, and let the person know.

Treat the candidate in a thoroughly professional manner, from the selection process onward, and be responsive to his or her needs.

Above all, make a fair and competitive offer. Do not try to buy cheap at the last minute. You'll lose your candidate, and, at the same time, your entire in-vestment in the search process. You can block competitive offers by confirming your offer in writing, and setting a reporting day soon after the date of hire.

Following these six steps will help you choose the right employee for your organization in a fair and professional manner.

Sam Skeegan is president of Roth Young Personnel Services of Detroit, Inc., Detroit, Michigan.

38.
HELP YOUR SUBORDINATES GROW

Larry W. Sanders

Companies traditionally have followed a "manufacturing" approach to developing their managers. In this approach individuals are appraised, rotated, promoted, and trained within a framework that allows them little input into their career development. The "growing" approach is an alternative.

Managers want positive results from their investments in subordinate development. Unfortunately, attendance at workshops, seminars and other learning experiences frequently seem to have little effect on subordinate behavior back on the job. Studies indicate that many training dollars are wasted—that no positive behavior change occurs as a result of training activities.

The cause of this lack of results can often be traced to a flawed philosophy of management development. Douglas McGregor addresses this problem in *The Human Side of Enterprise.*[1] He pointed out that companies traditionally have followed a "manufacturing" approach to developing their managers. In this approach individuals are appraised, rotated, promoted, and trained within a framework that allows them little input into their career development. It assumes that since most people want to get ahead, they will benefit from the activities and programs that are selected for them.

In actual practice, this assumption seldom is sound. McGregor recommended an alternative method of management development—one he identified as an agricultural or "growing" approach. Comparing the two approaches to a specific developmental activity reveals significant differences in their methods and results.

THE MANUFACTURING APPROACH

Using the manufacturing approach to send a subordinate to a developmental seminar:

1) The manager selects the seminar based on his or her perceived needs for the subordinate.
2) The subordinate is notified.
3) The subordinate attends the seminar.
4) The manager expects that improved performance will be forthcoming.

These steps represent a severe form of the manufacturing approach but, as many seminar leaders can attest, it is a common one. When asked, "Why are you attending this seminar?" a familiar response is, "My boss sent me."

The manufacturing approach assumes that the learner wants to improve, knows what is needed to improve, and can identify material that will be useful back on the job. Finally, it assumes that the individual will apply what has been learned. The closer these assumptions are to being correct, the better the process works.

UNNEEDED PROBLEMS

Experience has shown that the manufacturing approach does work but there are too many assumptions in the system for it to work well or reliably. Thus, training dollars are wasted. In addition to the loss of dollars, this approach often creates unneeded problems for the organization.

Individuals who are simply selected and sent for training are likely to be unsure of what their selection means. Are they being told indirectly that their work is unsatisfactory in some manner? Are they being rewarded for good work with a trip and a few days on an expense account? Or is it simply their turn to go to school? They may never know.

When their behavior on the job doesn't change after the training, the manager may assume that the subordinate lacks the motivation to apply what was presented or that the training program was ineffective.

THE AGRICULTURAL APPROACH

The agricultural approach follows the steps required to produce an agricultural crop: preparation, planting, and continued cultivation. For the subordinate, preparation involves creating a desire to improve and a readiness to learn. The planting is the training experience, and continued cultivation is the follow-up activities and follow-up support that insures improved performance.

Ideally, preparation to receive training will begin long before the seminar is attended. As part of a coaching or appraisal process, areas where improvement would be beneficial should have been identified. If this hasn't been done, the seminar provides an excellent opportunity to discuss the value of improved performance. The manager, in a positive and enthusiastic manner, should discuss and seek agreement on how the seminar will help meet performance improvement objectives.

The manager should be prepared to discuss areas where performance is not up to standards or where improved performance could pay valuable dividends. It is important that the discussion remain enthusiastic and growth-oriented, with a strong flavor of positive expectation.

IDEA ALERT

The manager should encourage the subordinate to be especially alert during the seminar for ideas and information. The subordinate should be asked:

- to make a list of all ideas that possibly could be used back on the job
- to evaluate the list and develop a brief statement on ideas he or she plans to implement
- to talk with fellow participants and take notes on sound practices used by their organizations
- to be prepared to discuss the lists and plans with the manager immediately upon return from the seminar

To complete the preparation, the manager should ask the subordinate to prepare a mini-version or review of the seminar and present it to appropriate organizational members along with ideas for implementation.

At this point, the agricultural approach has accomplished several important objectives. The subordinate:

- knows why he or she is attending the seminar
- is aware of specific developmental needs
- knows he or she should share seminar content with colleagues
- is aware of the manager's enthusiasm about the seminar and expectation of positive results

In the agricultural approach, the brilliance of the training activity is not critical. The training must be sound but the need to maintain attention and stimulate participation is markedly reduced. The attendee's attention, retention, and involvement will be at peak level. New ideas and concepts will fall on fertile soil. The attendee's perception and mental processes will be entirely different from the attendee who was simply sent without preparation.

CONTINUED CONTINUATION

Follow-up action by the manager is critical once the subordinate returns from training. The returning interview should be held as quickly as possible—certainly within the first day back on the job—with sufficient time allowed for thorough review and discussion. The manager's role during this interview should be enthusiastic, supportive, and non-critical.

Ideas for implementation can be considered at a general level, with future sessions scheduled to work out details. Dates for the training mini-session should be set. The important thing is to maintain momentum and keep the subordinate's interest and motivation high. As ideas are implemented, the manger will need to cultivate the new behaviors by being particularly attentive and providing continuing encouragement. This cultivation should include:

- a few minutes each day to ask, "How's it coming?" in a friendly, supportive manner and to discuss concerns or complications
- early identification of positive results from the new behaviors and reporting them enthusiastically to the subordinate
- when appropriate, working with the subordinate to develop a formal report to upper management on efforts and results
- continuing these activities until the new ideas and behaviors have become permanent.

POSITIVE CHANGES

The probability of positive behavior change is markedly increased by the agricultural approach to subordinate development. It requires the manager to establish a coaching relationship characterized by constructive, candid communication about important developmental needs. The manager using this approach makes behavior change on the job occur by actively expecting change and by providing encouragement and support.

The subordinate's commitment to change is reinforced as information and ideas from the seminar are shared with others in the organization. Slipping back into old behavior patterns becomes considerably less likely.

References

1. McGregor, Douglas. *The Human Side of Enterprise* (New York: McGraw-Hill Book Company, Inc. 1960).

Larry W. Sanders is supervisor of training and development, PPG Industries, Inc., Wichita Falls, Texas.

39.
COPING WITH THE CAREER PLATEAU

James F. Kelly, Jr.

> The facts are obvious to both parties, yet there is a prevailing lack of candor by both the employee and the employer regarding the career plateau. Most plateaued managers in this survey seem to have accepted the reality of the plateau. Candor does involve risk, but the consequences of ignoring this widespread reality are greater by far.

In his monumental study of adult male life cycles, *The Seasons of a Man's Life*, Daniel Levinson states that "for every executive at about [age] 40 who gains the prize and the affirmation he has been seeking, there are perhaps 20 who get little or nothing." This failure, Levinson says, results partly from incompetence and partly from organizational power struggles, but mainly from the pyramidal structure of management.[11]

While his statistical odds for executive success may appear, at 20 to 1, a bit long, his characterization of the 97.5 percent who didn't gain the "prize" as failures seems downright uncharitable. Nevertheless, in the business and professional world as we know it, we must reluctantly concede that most of us will inevitably reach our own career plateaus: That point where it becomes painfully evident that further job advancement is blocked for any or all of a variety of reasons including those cited by Levinson.

Does this really denote a high failure rate among American executives, or rather is our American corporate system guilty of failure to provide a higher probability of achieving executive success? Perhaps we need to redefine the term *executive success*. Why does the term *career plateau* seem to carry with it such a stigma of failure? What can be done on an individual and organizational basis to cope with this condition?

This article will examine these and other questions associated with what is commonly called the career plateau. I am primarily concerned with managers and executives, but most of the observations apply equally to other employees in organizations including scientists, engineers and educators.

THE PROBLEM

The intensely competitive nature of contemporary American organizational hierarchies results in a high degree of value being placed upon career success measured primarily by promotion, greater responsibilities, higher wages and visible perquisites of rank. Failure to gain a desired or expected promotion or, worse, to become regarded as unpromotable, subjects one to speculation on the part of peers and subordinates regarding the cause, and sometimes with regard to residual authority.

The military services provide a good illustration of this syndrome. In the armed forces, annual eligibility lists for promotion to each rank are published. Names of selectees are contained in selection lists, which are disseminated widely. Those who "fail selection" are, by omission, revealed to all and are, in fact, commonly referred to as "passed over." Either label, "failed of selection" or "passed over," certainly carries connotations of failure.

In civilian organizational hierarchies, the process is generally far more subtle but perhaps no less painful. Supervisors tend to be less than candid in discussing the plateaued status of employees out of concern that motivation and productivity might suffer. Thus, the plateaued individual is rarely among the first to know.

Because of the negative connotation associated with the career plateau and the potentially negative effect upon productivity, it behooves American employers and individuals as well to come to some common understanding regarding the significance of reaching this terminal level of career development and to formulate some strategies for dealing jointly with it. This undertaking must, moreover, assume a new degree of urgency because of the changing nature of the American work force. For the remainder of this century, the growth of the middle-aged-to-older segment of the work force will be its salient characteristic.[14] Escalated retirement costs and federal laws protecting older workers from discriminatory treatment because of age make it mandatory that we retain older workers and keep them productive.

This aging of the work force is being accompanied by equally profound changes in the values that these older adults bring to the workplace. R. J. Erickson cites attitude surveys reported in the *Harvard Business Review* which reveal that traditional concerns for pay and working conditions are being replaced by greater concern for esteem-related factors such as recognition, respect and promotion.[2]

An increasing rate of technological change, moreover, may be accelerating the climb to the career plateau. For example, "the half-life" of a graduate engineer's usable technical knowledge is now estimated at between five to seven years. Today's 35-year-olds are retraining for jobs that did not even exist 10 years ago, and it is predicted that those joining the work force today will face major career redirections every 10 years or so.[16]

But as Levinson has alleged, "an executive today knows that he must reach a certain level or rank by age 40.[11] Otherwise he will be unable to advance further. He will be trapped, given a lateral promotion that represents failure, or be demoted to make room for the younger men now moving up." With increased career mobility now in evidence everywhere, however, the need to reach "a certain level" by age 40 would seem somewhat over-ambitious for most executives for whom change and mobility is fast becoming the rule rather than the exception.

While it is the pyramidal structure of American management which is generally blamed for the densely populated career plateau, I take issue with the notion that an individual's career prospects automatically decline as that individual climbs the pyramid. Certain indicators such as recent promotion patterns, turnover, growth or reorganization in various departments may provide early clues for assessing career prospects at sequential promotion gateways. In other words, choice and timing of job, department or career track changes may be more important than vertical progress up the pyramid.

Others have described various strategies to avoid certain risky promotions which may represent deadend situations, carry high risk of failure, become candidates for disestablishment or might otherwise result in career blockage. George L. Mild describes strategies for recognizing and skillfully avoiding "promotions" which, if accepted, would result in earlier arrival at a plateau.[13] Redefining the corporate pyramid as a *squat pear*, he describes how executives, reaching the bulge in the pear, can opt for certain survival strategies such as job broadening and artfully backing away from certain promotions and career paths that lead toward executive congestion.

LIFE CYCLES AND CAREER STAGES

Thanks to the highly-popularized books of Roger Gould and Daniel Levinson, there is an emerging awareness of the various stages of adult male development. In the corporate world, the principal focus seems to be upon the middle adult stage. There seems to be a popular misconception to the effect that some significant mid-life crisis will inevitably affect job performance or career development during this period. It is almost as if some manifestation of bizarre behavior is to be expected. Although it is likely that most workers pass through this period without any mid-life crisis affecting their careers, it is also evident that many new awarenesses surface during the middle adult stage that are related to one's career. Those might include feelings of job entrapment, stagnation and a sense that a dream or career goal will probably not be achieved. The disappointment and perhaps even bitterness can negatively affect attitude and job performance. If the effects are obvious enough and are not read accurately by an understanding employer, they can influence that employer's perception of the individual's potential and promotability. In this manner, perfectly normal midcareer fears that one may be approaching a career plateau can become a self-fulfilling prophecy.

The widely held notion that mid-life crisis is a universal experience commonly leading to career crisis or job change is disputed by Barbara S. Lawrence.[19] And career change, when it occurs, does not always imply a personal crisis.

Researchers persist, though, in linking career stages to life cycles. Gill, Coppard and Lowther superimpose a career cycle over the adult development stages of Levinson, Super and Erickson.[4] In this composite model, the development phase *Getting into the Adult World* corresponds to the career stage *Exploration*. *Settling Down* and *Becoming One's Own Person* corresponds to the career stage *Trial Establishment*. There follow at about age 45, three alternate career stages: *Growth*, *Stagnation*, and *Maintenance*, the latter term describing what we are calling the career plateau.

Douglas T. Hall describes the period from the forties until retirement a *maintenance period*: A period for preserving what has been achieved and not a time for breaking new ground. This is somewhat at odds with the picture of the ambitious careerist in their midforties, a period described by Super as one of *generativity*. It seems rather difficult to be generative without breaking new ground.

While life cycle changes and transitions can affect career development in highly direct and visible ways, attempts to portray career and life cycles as closely linked appear somewhat contrived. Careers may, in fact, have cycles of their own that are entirely independent of adult life cycles. Ference, Stoner and Warner have outlined four stages of career development (learner, star, solid citizen and deadwood) that are independent of life cycles development and permit movement in alternate directions between the stages.[13] E. H. Schein describes seven basic career stages, ranging from *aspiration/recruitment to commitment to retirement*, which are represented as linked to life cycle stages. In his model, an expected peaking or leveling of performance occurs as a substage of the third phase. The implication is that there is, indeed, life beyond the career plateau; in this, case, four stages: *Subsequent assignment and substages, granting of tenure, focus on retirement* and *commitment to retirement*.[19]

Douglas Hall has summarized many popular career stage paradigms, some linked to life cycles and some described independently of them.[6] All seem useful in characterizing the composite anatomies of typical careers and the reader is free to choose a favorite. For our purposes, it is sufficient to acknowledge that there are various distinct stages in most careers and that the ability to recognize the characteristics of the stages, whatever their labels, is useful to the career plateau.

Transition to the career plateau may be gradual and unremarkable, particularly if not accompanied by some midlife crisis. But it can be far from smooth if one is undergoing a turbulent life cycle transition and particularly if a marked change in family relationships is taking place simultaneously. Such events can precipitate a new and vivid awareness of age, physical change and limitations and other symptoms of mortality. A person experiencing such feelings may come to a rather abrupt realization that certain career goals now seem unattainable.

A growing sense of despair or obsolescence may subsequently set in. This may be more pronounced among scientists, engineers and technicians who may perceive themselves as less attractive resources in a job market that prizes state-of-the art skills. Ensuing feelings of job entrapment may compete with conflicting concerns for job security. Discernible symptoms may be a lessened willingness to take chances. To the employer, however, this can come across as a loss of ambition or motivation.

Although their skills may be less perishable than those of scientists, engineers and technicians, managers, sensing the career plateau, can exhibit detectable symptoms including aversion to new and untried responsibilities and a new drive to achieve some intermediate but secure niche that they can fill by virtue of some unique, if minor, skill, knowledge or temperament. Other signs may include new interest in training, acquiring new skills, pursuing new civic, social or professional associations or becoming involved in clubs, company-sponsored activities or union affairs in an effort to enhance value to the employer and to achieve some measure of indispensability.

Manifesting what Stuart Klein and Kenneth Rose refer to as "the seven-year itch," many employees tend to complain at about that point in their careers that opportunities for career growth are not what they had hoped for.[8] They are typically, critical of low executive turnover, lack of expansion and executive congestion at various promotion choke points. Frustration is a common result.

As noted earlier, life-cycle events can exacerbate these symptoms substantially. Ill health and physical changes remind us of our mortality and can cause greatly heightened awareness of advancing age. An employee preoccupied with such thoughts is likely to display sensitivity to any perceived references to age or declining abilities, however subtle or good-natured. Sincere offers of assistance may be interpreted as an insinuation of diminished capacity. Such persons might attempt a new and strenuous exercise routine, sport or hobby, perhaps over-compensating in an attempt to act younger then they feel.

Modifications to family routines and circumstances such as the "empty nest syndrome," reduced contact with children or grandchildren, marital strife or the death of friends can cause symptoms at work that are similar to those caused by job anxiety.

COMPANY ATTITUDES AND PRIORITIES

Corporate management, for the most part, treats plateaued employees with something akin to benevolent neglect. Reporting on an analysis based upon interviews with 200 mangers from various firms, Janet Near observed that few firms notify managers when their career plateaus have been reached because of the common assumption that motivation and productivity would decline.[15] Yet most plateaued managers in the survey seemed to have accepted the reality of the plateau reasonably well.

But large organizations can employ subtle ways of removing from the mainstream employees whose contributions are no longer regarded as essential but who are considered immune from firing. Some companies actually establish "graveyard divisions" staffed by unpromotables.[1]

Corporations may, in fact, make frequent reference to these unpromotables as the "deadwood" in the organization. These thoughtless, demeaning and utterly unnecessary labels are resented by plateaued employees who may still be productive and even vital to the organization. On the other side are the promotables who are, in the words of Edward Roseman, the "corporate elite."[18] They are the upwardly bound, "beautiful people" who get tender, loving care and management grooming. At a career stage where training or career redirection might have the greatest possible impact and value, corporate management may prejudge an employee as nonprofitable and then deny the training, choosing to devote constrained training budget dollars to those judged promotable. It is, of course, a familiar pattern of the rich growing wealthier and the poor becoming even less prosperous. Management, by its very attitudes and priorities, can prejudge or confirm promotability and non-promotability, institutionalizing those classifications and creating reality.

EMPLOYEE ATTITUDES AND VALUES

There is a noteworthy lack of candor on the part both of employer and employee regarding the career plateau and the status and future of the plateaued employees. There are several reasons, but the primary reason for management's reluctance to address this issue with the employee is concern that motivation and production will be diminished. On the employee's part, embarrassment and fear of loss of prestige are primary reasons for avoiding open discussion on the subject. Contributing to these reactions is the strong connotation of failure attached to the plateau.

Many employees at all levels simply withdraw themselves from competition altogether rather than risk loss of face, defeat or having to acknowledge that they have been passed over. Many go to some length to disavow interest in further promotion or responsibility, stating that they wish to avoid the stress, long hours and time away from family in an attempt to camouflage the fear of rejection or to avoid disappointment over failure to be promoted.

Clearly, some employees are sincere about wishing to avoid these things. Many do seek additional leisure time to pursue hobbies and interests or to find time to participate in professional organizations, service clubs, church activities, higher education, writing or other activities they have put off for years.

Still others, upon sensing their plateaued status, seek other careers. Candidates for second careers tend to be in their forties. In fact, peak mobility is said to exist in the 35-40 age bracket despite historical age-related barriers to employment, recent legislation notwithstanding.[20]

The inevitable realization that one has become unpromotable can be devastating at one extreme or accepted with some measure of relief at the other. In *Transformations*, Roger Gould expresses the view that people pursue careers with enthusiasm because they accept the "mythology of work," namely that one can become invincible with money, power and status.[5] The higher the rank the "bigger" and less vulnerable we become. In the forties, he continues, one realizes that promotions do not necessarily make one invulnerable (to sickness, defeat, disappointment, failure, etc.). As work subsequently loses some of the illusionary protective powers we have conferred upon it, additional interests and values can begin to surface and we tend to fear career failure much less. Gould would undoubtedly predict a more graceful acceptance of the plateau once one has experienced this transformation.

Donald Wolf and David Koll appear to echo this view, describing an emergence of the "self" having been previously suppressed by career concern.[21] Again, this sharp reversal of values, say these writers, customarily occurs during the early forties of the male life cycle, coinciding with the midlife transition. In women, however, they note a delay in the emergence of "self" over career since family demands typically have suppressed earlier career concerns. Thus, the career tends to remain dominant for women through their forties.

STRATEGIES

As noted previously, some researchers link career phases with life cycle events, others deal with career phases independently of them. In formulating strategies for coping with career plateau, it is helpful if both management and the individual are able to recognize the characteristics and manifestations of both, whether they are related or not. Managers and supervisors must learn to become more perceptive in recognizing these characteristics and be willing to discuss them, discreetly but candidly, with the employer. Training films dealing with this area would be useful in coping with the natural reluctance to discuss this topic. To be sure, there are risks in such personal discussions where feelings of failure may cause resentment or defensiveness, but the risk in ignoring this widespread reality is greater by far.

There must be a clearer realization on management's part that plateaued workers comprise a large and growing segment of the work force. They are, moreover, a vital segment. Management cannot afford to alienate them or to cause apathy and loss of productivity among this group, which is so indispensable to the day-to-day operations of America's businesses. Moreover, workers over 40, who comprise the bulk of the plateaued population, are a protected group under federal regulations and may not be denied employment opportunities because of age. It is essential, therefore, that management find ways of keeping them motivated and productive.

First and foremost, organizations must cease entertaining the myth that middle-adulthood is necessarily a time for abnormal behavior. Nor does every employee in midcareer undergo a midlife crisis. Such is the exception rather than the rule. And if an employee is experiencing one, it doesn't necessarily follow that bizarre behavior at work will be a consequence.

But should it occur, it needs to be discussed frankly and remedies sought which are mutually satisfactory. If an employee has, in the view of management, reached a maximum level of occupational growth, that perfectly normal situation needs to be discussed in a sympathetic and understanding manner. The employee's views, concerns and desires should be heard and considered. Management should initiate this discussion early enough so that options can be considered.

If retraining or career redirection for a middle-aged, plateaued manager is a feasible option, programs should be oriented less toward technical duties or rigidly structured procedures and more toward duties requiring judgment, reconciliation of opposing interests and application of experience. Training and coaching younger members of the organization may at this stage, be particularly appropriate.[12] The experience of plateaued managers may also find productive outlets in technical writing and policy formulation activities and in consulting roles. Changing values, decreased appetite for competition and a lessened concern with promotion and status may combine to produce a more detached and objective outlook, facilitating the critical analysis that is so essential in an internal consulting role.

It is critically important to provide enough career challenge to prevent stagnation. This requires either job enrichment or some form of job rotation. Such rotation may be lateral or even downward. But value changes in older workers may cause them to place greater emphasis upon job security and risk avoidance. They may, therefore, resist the prospect of new duties or responsibilities, even if labeled "job enrichment," if they perceive substantial risk of failure. They may, on the other hand, be receptive to downward job rotation if some means can be found to legitimize or destigmatize such a move.[7]

The military services defer career stagnation to some extent by frequent, regular rotation, normally at the two- or three-year point. While the pros and cons of such frequent rotation are debatable, it is clear that boredom and stagnation are not outcomes of such a rotation policy. Corporations could profit by being somewhat more aggressive in rotating duties and job settings, even to the extent of manager exchange programs.

Many technical workers, scientists, engineers and teachers, encountering what R. A. Payne refers to as the *mid-career block* seek to become managers or administrators in order to progress further. It is, in my view, one of the tragedies of our time that many excellent scientists, teachers, and engineers become mediocre managers and administrators in order to obtain a promotion. Corporations and institutions should make every realistic effort to prevent this waste of creative talent by providing dual career paths, where possible, that provide recognition and upward mobility without having to abandon the classroom or laboratory. Loss of management ability and productivity through career stagnation is serious enough but loss of creativity from whatever cause is a calamity, the effects of which will be magnified not just throughout the economy but throughout society.

Research on aging and the concomitant loss of cognitive abilities suggest that "older" people tend to become more scrupulous in the use of decision criteria.[20] They are less likely to use bridging mechanisms to link concepts and are, in general, less willing than younger managers to commit themselves without a high probability of certainty. While admittedly a detriment in some critical aspects of leadership and management, it can also be a strong attribute in consulting, research, long-range planning, security, arbitration and other roles where certainty, accuracy, reason and judgment are more important factors than speed, innovation and creativity. Imaginative and progressive organizations will find productive uses for these often untapped talents and characteristics residing in some plateaued workers.

A diminished drive to be competitive and to avoid stress-producing activity may also be accompanied by a new sense of cooperativeness. No longer consumed with a desire to get ahead, they may enjoy new respect, credibility and confidence among their peers and juniors. Again, resourceful and perceptive organizations can utilize these traits and abilities in mentoring, employee relations, ombudsmen and labor relations.

Individuals who sense that they have reached or are about to reach their own career plateau should consider first of all that they have plenty of company. The brass ring wouldn't be worth reaching for if everyone succeeded in grabbing it. Nor does it denote failure, per se.

Sooner or later every career peaks and few, upon retiring, can say with honesty that they attained every position, responsibility or title to which they aspired. So be it. It is a perfectly natural process, not to be confused with failure. The latter term, when used in a career context, should be reserved for the consequences of substandard performance or lack of effort.

This career stage, for that is what it is, is a superb time for reflecting upon the things which truly matter in life. Viewed in retrospect, work is only one of those things.

Freed from the constant and consuming competition for promotion and incessant drive to acquire more authority, one is better able to recognize and nourish other interests that can enrich life and even prolong it. As pressure and stress subside, moreover, work may even take a new meaning. A much better balance between work, family, community and personal development can result.

American managers, and particularly males, seem inclined to be particularly territorial in their passion to acquire authority over resources, particularly human resources. This drive can dominate their thinking and actions, distorting their creativity and value. Authority, promotion and responsibility are not the only legitimate goals of working nor are they the most important. There is a certain nobility in just working. Americans of every social level need to be reminded more often that there is nothing wrong with working to earn a living.

Working to achieve self-fulfillment is neat but it is a luxury attainable by only a small fraction of the earth's population and it is not, by any means, a constitutional right. Self-fulfillment may just have to come from activities outside the workplace.

Melvin L. Kohn states it well when he says, "What matters about work . . . is not any of its attendant rewards or social experiences, but the work itself."[9]

References

1. Andrew J. DuBrin, *Winning at Office Politics*. New York: Van Nostrand, Reinhold, 1978.
2. R. J. Erickson, "The changing workplace and work force," *Training and Development Journal*, 34, 1980, pp. 62-65.
3. T. P. Ference, J. A. F. Stoner and E. K. Warres, "Managing the career plateau," *Academy of Management Review*, 2, 1977, p. 603.
4. Steven Joel Gill, Larry C. Coppard and Malcolm A. Lowther, "Mid-life career development theory and research: Implications for work and education," *Aging and Work*, 6, 1983, pp. 15-29.
5. Roger L. Gould, *Transformations*. New York: Simon & Schuster, 1978.
6. Douglas T. Hall, *Careers in Organizations*. Santa Monica, CA: Goodyear Publishing Co., Inc., 1976.
7. Timothy J. Keaveny, "Developing and maintaining human resources," *Training and Development Journal*, 37 (7), 1983, pp. 65-68.
8. Stuart M. Klein and Kenneth W. Rose, "Formal policies and procedures can forestall unionization," *Personnel Journal*, 61, 1982, pp. 275-281.
9. Melvin L. Kohn, "Job complexity and adult personality," in Neil J. Smelser & Erik H. Erickson (Eds.) *Themes of Work and Love in Adulthood*. Cambridge, MA: Harvard University Press, 1980.
10. Barbara S. Lawrence, "The myth of the mid-life crisis," *Sloan Management Review*, Summer 1980, pp. 36-49.
11. Daniel J. Levinson with Charlotte N. Darrow, Edward B. Klein, Maria H. Levinson and Braxton McKee, *The Success of a Man's Life*. New York: Ballantine Books, 1978.
12. Harry Levinson, "On Being a middle-aged manager," *Harvard Business Review*, July-August 1969.
13. George L. Mild, *The Squat Pear Principle: Why Managers Rise and Fall*. Chicago: Contemporary Book, Inc., 1982.
14. Malcolm H. Morrison, "Retirement and human resource planning for the aging work force," *Personnel Administrator*, 29 (6), 1984, pp. 151-159.
15. Janet P. Near, "Reactions to the career plateau," *Business Horizons*, 27 (4), 1984, pp. 75-79.
16. William R. Nehr and Leopold Hauser, III, "How computers can help adults overcome the fear of learning," *Training*, 19, (2), 1982, pp. 48-50.

17. R. A. Payne, "Mid-career block," *Personnel Journal*, 4, 1984, pp. 38-48.
18. Edward Roseman, *Confronting Non-promotability*. New York: AMACOM, 1977.
19. E. H. Schein, *Career Dynamics: Matching Individual and Organizational Careers*. Reading, MA: Addison-Wesley, 1978.
20. Jeffrey Sonnenfeld, "Dealing with the aging work force," *Harvard Business Review*, November-December 1978.
21. Donald M. Wolfe and David A. Kolb, "Beyond specialization: The quest for integration in mid-career," in Brooklyn Derr (Ed.) *Work, Family and the Career*. New York: Praeger, 1980, pp. 239-279.

James F. Kelly is assistant vice president and training and development manager of Great American First Savings Bank in San Diego, California.

40.

MENTOR PROGRAMS: MAKING THE RIGHT MOVES

Michael G. Zey

Mentor relationships develop informally in every corporation, but companies that actively develop such relationships help more than just the participants. Mentor programs improve cooperation between junior and senior managers, assure help to those minorities most in need and, most importantly, develop untapped potential.

What do AT&T, Johnson and Johnson, Merrill Lynch, Federal Express, the Internal Revenue and the US Army have in common? All have abandoned the hope that mentoring relationships would develop by themselves and have implemented policies to actively develop mentor programs.

It has become increasingly apparent that it isn't only the specific participants who gain something from mentoring efforts.

These programs fulfill a variety of corporate needs: they foster the growth of relationships between junior and senior managers, they become a major component of the management/professional training function, and they ensure the extension of mentoring to groups that have had the most difficult time finding seniors to serve as sponsors, namely women and minorities. To that extent, formal mentor programs help corporations meet their affirmative action mandate.

But perhaps the greatest contribution the mentoring process can make is developing the protege into a full-fledged manager or professional. This informal training often occurs in subtle ways: the mentor teaches the junior both technical and people skills, instructs him or her in the ways of the corporate culture, and acclimates the protege to the values and expectations of the corporation.

Also, the mentor familiarizes the students with the resources necessary to become a better manager, and can often make those resources available.

CONSIDER MENTOR PROGRAMS FROM EVERY ANGLE BEFORE IMPLEMENTING ONE

When developing a mentor program, the implementing department (e.g., human resources) must outline the program goals, criteria for participation, and methods of mentor/protégé interaction.

A document of regulations and by-laws that make these goals and procedures explicit should be drawn up and distributed to all participants at the start of the program.

Goals should always be clarified. One large pharmaceutical company established its formal mentoring program as a mechanism for seniors to communicate the corporate culture and values to the younger manager.

Other programs are designed with the idea that the senior manager, the mentor, will get involved with training the junior person in either specific aspects of job performance or in more general managerial skills, including the vast array of people management skills.

The goals of the program should be specific. Ask yourself: What is it we expect after six months or a year of mentoring? By the time the protégé completes the program, should he or she merely know how to do his or her own job better or should the participant be totally familiar with the workings of the entire organization?

In short, decide if the concept of training is interpreted narrowly or broadly. In addition to program goals, five other factors should be considered before implementing a program:

1) *Who should participate?* The question of who should participate in this formal program is also crucial. Many programs choose the mentor strictly from middle management, and usually from the same division and specialty as the protégé.

If the goal of the program is narrowly defined as job training, that is probably the best course to follow. On the other hand, if the intention of the training is more to "communicate the corporate culture," then a senior manager with a broader knowledge of the organization's values and practices (e.g., dress code or informal expectations) might be a better mentor.

Corporations vary widely in their selection criteria for the protégé. Some require that all incoming junior managers automatically enter the program. Most companies allow incoming junior managers to decide for themselves if they want to participate.

In such cases, the personnel department communicates information about the program to the new comer in much the same way it distributes information about benefits and regulations.

2) *Matching the mentor and protégé.* Some formal programs limit the autonomy of participants to choose a specific mentor or protégé. Although

limits expedite an often tedious and protracted process, many corporations find it advantageous to allow greater participant control.

For example, the federal government program allows the junior person to choose from a pool of mentors. The junior manager in effect interviews the various senior managers to determine who could most effectively serve as a coach or teacher.

3) Length and timing of the program. Although the federal government's program runs for two years, most programs run for only six months.

The length of a formal program is the product of its goals. The six month program should be sufficient to accomplish such training goals as acclimating the junior to the corporate culture and teaching him or her management skills.

The majority of companies recognize that informal mentor relationships might develop that transcend the time limits of the formal system. In many cases, mentors and protégés are encouraged to pursue the relationship beyond the official program period.

A related dimension of the program is timing. Many companies feel that programs should be organized in such a way that an entire cohort of junior managers start and finish at the same time.

This method has several advantages over the random entrance of new individual participants. The program can be more easily managed by human resources personnel if it has a set beginning and end. The program, and its results, can also be evaluated more easily if all mentor relationships begin at the same time. Finally, orientation and debriefing of participants can be faster and more uniform if the cohort technique is used.

4) Mode and frequency of interaction. Programs vary in terms of the amount of interaction between mentor and protégé. A minimum contact between the protégé and mentor, such as twice a month, is commonly established. They are then allowed to meet informally as often as they like.

Without a set minimum of interaction, relationships often unravel and cease being helpful. Protégés at the major investment bank's program complained that they felt as if they did not have a mentor, mainly because there was no stipulated meeting schedule.

In addition to specifying the frequency of contact, the formal by-laws of the program should indicate the preferred location of this contact. The senior manager's office is an optimum location since it affords the protégé the opportunity to watch the mentor work, meet his colleagues, and get a feel for the worklife of the upper manager.

5) Mentor responsibilities. Once a program goal is stated, such as "improving management training" or "introducing the junior manager to the corporate culture" specify exactly how the mentor should go about meeting the goals.

Some companies regard a well-trained manager as one who is familiar with resources, departments, and corporate practices. In such cases, perhaps the mentor should be required to introduce the protégé to the heads of various departments during the formal program period.

Alternatively, the student should be allowed to walk through an entire project for the six month program period in a combined worker/observer role.

One company defines management training as an "assimilation of new managers into the company and into an understanding of its culture and management styles."

Consequently, the mentor is specifically exhorted in the program by-laws to discuss the particulars of corporate culture, including the importance placed on company-sponsored functions, such as parties and picnics. He or she explains to the junior manager the diverse preferences and management styles in use within the company, and shares the organization's written codes and value systems.

A TYPICAL PROGRAM MIGHT INCLUDE SEVEN STAGES

In developing a formal mentoring program, there are seven distinct stages to consider:

1) Development. The first stage of any formal mentoring program should be the program development period in which goals, criteria of participation, and mechanisms of interaction are specifically spelled out.

A document should be drawn up by the implementing department and various management groups.

2) Notification. The implementing department should issue a memo notifying the target audience of the existence of the formal mentoring program, the benefits to the company, and length of program.

This should be an invitation that is distributed to the predetermined eligible groups, such as all successful middle and senior managers and all incoming junior employees.

3) Selection. All interested candidates should be interviewed individually, apprised of the specifics of the program, and evaluated according to set criteria. One company seeks only those who are solid performers and enjoy respect throughout the organization.

4) Orientation. All the senior and junior participants chosen should then attend an orientation meeting. This meeting will not only facilitate communicating information about the by-laws and expectations of the program, but will also serve as a vehicle to begin to break the ice between the two groups.

5) Pairing. Some mechanism for matching the protégé with the right mentor have already been discussed, and many programs allow for independent selection of a partner.

But if the overseeing department assumes responsibility for partner pairing, it will be able to make these decisions based on the information gathered during the selection stage interview.

6) Implementation. The participants now begin the actual mentoring, meeting at set times and places.

7) Evaluation. The bottom line concern in evaluating a program is the extent to which it has met its goals, e.g., management training and development. Evaluation takes place in several ways. For instance, the mentor group and the protégé group can each meet *en masse* with the program formulators to give post-program feedback, and provide suggestions for improving the program for the next group.

Since the mentors may serve as a constant pool for each subsequent group, their suggestions for changes and improvements should receive particular attention.

This stage should also be used to debrief participants and to encourage seniors to remain in the program as mentors. Of course, evaluation can be an ongoing activity throughout the program.

PROGRAM SUCCESS DEPENDS ON MORE THAN SPECIFICS

Simply having clearly defined goals and methods is not enough to guarantee program success. As in most things, the human variable will play an important part in shaping a mentor effort.

The better you anticipate potential conflicts and pitfalls, the smoother and more effective your program will be. Based on the experiences of existing programs, consider these seven suggestions:

1) Communicate the program goals to all participants. Some programs suffer because participants have not been told what the programs are actually set up to accomplish.

This often leads to confusion and false expectations. Some protégés think that completing this program is an automatic means to a higher position, whereas the program might have been formulated merely to sharpen the junior's skills or familiarize him with the organization's structure.

Written explanation, plus verbal communication of program goals during the initial interview and orientation, can prevent later misunderstandings.

2) Enlist the cooperation of the entire organization. If the peers, managers, and supervisors uninvolved with the program do not understand the rationale for its existence, they may be less inclined to cooperate with it.

The rationale, goals, and mechanics of mentoring must be explained early on to the entire organization through official materials, group discussion, and organization-wide meetings.

Be clear about the benefits of the program to the organization, solicit suggestions about the operation of the program, and ask employees what problems they foresee.

A centralized method for recording and responding to non-participants' complaints about the program must be established.

3) Make the selection process as autonomous as possible. When mentors and protégés are allowed autonomy in choosing a program partner, the program is more successful.

4) Be sure that mentors are committed to the project. The selection of mentors for the program must be as careful as choosing the students. Programs that coerce senior managers into participating, however subtly, are bound to fail.

One way to increase senior executive commitment is by informing them of the job and career benefits that accrue to seniors who play the mentor role.

5) Permit withdrawal from the program. If either party feels that the mentor relationship is not working, he or she must be permitted to withdraw from it. However, there should be a closed review of the rationale behind the withdrawal from the formal program.

This will provide those overseeing the program with feedback that can enable them to modify the program if necessary. At the very least, a structured exit interview should be required.

Also, if the dissatisfaction arises early in the program, i.e., in the first few weeks, the participants should have the option to change partners instead of having to abandon the program.

6) Continually evaluate the program. Although structured evaluation is the final phase of the formal mentor program, some form of assessment should be incorporated as an ongoing activity. It should involve the following:

- The mentors and protégés should be interviewed at set points to get general and specific feedback regarding satisfaction and dissatisfaction.
- A quantitatively based organization-wide survey should be made at regular intervals. The questionnaire used need not be long or complicated, but it should be comprehensive enough to monitor the attitudes of both participants and nonparticipants toward the program.
- Suggestions for change and improvement should always be solicited.

- Channels should always be available for anonymous and confidential airing of grievances.

7) Give the program a long-term test period. A half-hearted attempt at developing and operating a formal mentoring program is doomed. The program must be given enough time to prove itself as a management training tool.

Remember that these programs, no matter how rigidly formal, evolve over time. The government program was originally conceived of as a way for a senior to train a protégé and show him or her the ropes.

Over time the mentor's activities expanded to include the opportunity for the protégé to attend high level meetings not ordinarily attended by juniors, facilitate his travel and mobility, and even place the protégé into a supervisory position.

If new mentor activities prove beneficial, they should be noted and formally included in revised by-laws governing the next group's training.

In closing, it must be emphasized that formal mentoring programs have already begun to benefit some corporations, and in the future will have an expanded role as a management/professional training tool.

But mentoring must be coherently conceived and uniformly administered. The hope is that research findings on mentoring will be used to improve the effectiveness of the current mentoring programs and to serve as a foundation for mentoring programs yet to come.

Micheal G. Zey is a sociologist and a management consultant specializing in organizational development and formal mentoring programs. He is the author of The Mentor Connection *published by Dow Jones-Irwin.*

41.

ANY DEVELOPMENT PROGRAM CAN WORK

W. Wary Buchanan
Frank Hoy
Bobby C. Vaught

> Employee development is a necessary process, but one that few
> managers believe really works. Every program offers something of value; it
> is management's responsibility to communicate that value to program
> participants.

Employee development is a major American industry. Consider the millions
of dollars that larger industries in every sector of the economy are pouring into
the effort to tap the untapped potential of human resources.

It is also an industry in danger. For every company or manager convinced of
the value of employee development there is a skeptic, one who is unsure of its
real value.

Such skepticism is not entirely unfounded. However valuable employee
development might be, its results are rarely tangible. In an era of frantic pursuit
of bottom-line profit, intangibility can be fatal.

But the industry can be saved relatively easily; all it really takes is the effort
to place development programs in perspective. Management must consider the
legitimate problems of employee development and deal with those problems
directly.

Every development program is different, of course, but there are some
strategies that any company can incorporate.

RESISTANCE IS USUALLY BASED ON EXPERIENCE

Any confrontation of the problems must obviously begin with definitions of
those problems. Many of the obstacles to success are nothing more than
management doubt. That doubt is manifested in a variety of ways. The typical
objections include:

- Time off the job in development programs is nonproductive, and thus incurs hidden costs.
- Development programs are mostly designed to motivate employees and have only a short-term impact.
- The content of programs is seldom directly applicable to the job currently being performed since development, as opposed to training, is by definition long-term.
- Development programs are difficult to evaluate, leading to faddish or entertaining content.
- Employees seldom change old work habits after attending programs.
- Employees resent having their work pile up while attending programs.
- Employees perceive programs as an attempt by top management to give them only a sense of organizational development, and therefore to keep them pacified.
- Money spent on development can be better invested elsewhere, especially in new equipment or machinery.
- Concepts taught in development programs are inappropriate for the unique environment of the specific organization and only cause disruptions when employees attempt to apply them.

Numerous other obstacles to development could he cited. The point to be made, however, is that there is likely to be resistance to formal employee development programs within an organization.

This resistance is often based on the previous experience of employees and their immediate supervisors with the less-than-successful results of many programs.

Managers often evaluate a program using a superficial measure, such as the level of enjoyment experienced in attending the program, instead of on such measures as changes in behavior or improvement in work accomplished. They usually suggest a process of management development centered on recurring organizational problems.

Programs are often labeled unsuccessful because managers do not see improvements in the performance of participants or their work groups. There are several possible causes of this apparent lack of improvement.

First, co-workers, whether peers, subordinates or supervisors, were not prepared for possible changes in the behavior of participants. Thus, they felt uncomfortable with any observable changes that were inconsistent with their previous perceptions, and they overtly or covertly punished the participant until he or she reverted to earlier behavior patterns.

Second, the participants were unable to match the program's content with their on-the-job needs; therefore, they concluded that the program provided nothing for immediate application.

Third, the program was carelessly selected or poorly designed, therefore, the participants simply received nothing of practical value.

Finally employee development needs were not accurately determined; thus, program objectives and evaluation procedures were difficult to establish.

To overcome these obstacles an integrated approach must be used that will address the causes outlined above.

Such an approach will eliminate many of the root causes of management's dissatisfaction with development programs, such as ambiguous goals, incomplete program development and design, inattention to models of behavioral change, and emphasis on the inappropriate unit of analysis.

EVERY DEVELOPMENT PROGRAM OFFERS SOMETHING OF VALUE

This technique for improving the results of development programs focuses attention on achieving results by taking an integrated approach to implementing the program.

The model places minimal emphasis on the actual selection and design of the program. It operates on the premise that virtually any development program offers something of value to participants. The burden of the organization is to ensure that participants glean what is useful from the program and apply those concepts to their work.

Ultimately, all employee development is organization development (OD). What would be the purpose of improving long-term employee performance if not to achieve a synergy of those improvements for increased effectiveness of the total system?

Since these issues can be addressed through careful planning by involved organizational members, an approach is needed that brings together input from the personnel department, top management, supervisors, individual learners, and, when appropriate, external parties (such as instructors or evaluators).

A model of employee development should include:

- A system that highlights individual objectives (and deficiencies) as related to the organization's performance objectives
- A behavioral awareness that the primary responsibility for change and self-development rests with each individual learner
- An evaluation procedure, designed and implemented by the users and personnel, based on observable performance gain
- A social and economic support system that recognizes that commitment of the organization to long-run productivity.

Awareness stage. The model begins and ends with each individual employee. The employee prepares a written statement of the major objectives of his or her position and then evaluates each one, using as criteria the skills necessary to accomplish them.

Such a self-audit places the responsibility for development on the individual employee, who is, after all, in the best position to honestly assess current performance and personal objectives.

Once the self-audit is complete, the supervisor meets with the prospective participant to discuss the organization's role in employee development. Strengths and deficiencies are noted in the employee's current performance.

Program objectives are then written depicting specific outcome-oriented measures that will be used to evaluate the program. Thus, much of the program's success will depend on the degree of cooperation and joint goal-setting between the supervisor and the subordinate.

Decision stage. After program objectives have been developed, personnel staff are asked for assistance in either developing or selecting a program aimed at meeting these performance-based measures.

At this point, top management's input will also be necessary in terms of overall organizational objectives, policies and resources. Larger organizations, with somewhat homogenous needs involving many employees, may decide to design a custom program.

This decision will largely depend on the available facilities, time and manpower. Given limited experience in the area under consideration, some companies may decide to obtain the talents of outside development specialists, such as universities or consultants.

Implementation stage. Once the program has been developed or selected, its objective statement becomes crucial, especially when the program is external. The instructor and students should periodically return to the objective statement to ensure that the program content is consistent with the statement.

Although the program cannot be tailor-made for each individual learner, a certain amount of congruence is necessary for the employee to obtain the knowledge and/or skills needed for job improvement.

Also, in order for the employee to be motivated to change job behavior, the program should meet both personal and job objectives.

Evaluation stage. At the end of each program session, the participants should complete an attitudinal evaluation. This feedback is important to the development unit since it could lead to changes in style or presentation during other sessions of the program. The program should also be evaluated immediately upon return to the workplace and three to six months later.

In addition, the participants and his or her supervisor should discuss the implementation of any new skills learned, relating them to the objectives developed during the self-audit (awareness stage).

At this point, the supervisor's role is one to support and counsel, i.e., remove barriers, suggest alternatives, and delegate responsibilities. The supervisor should point out the rewards, both extrinsic and intrinsic, that can accrue to the performance-oriented employee. However, the supervisor should also make the participant aware of the undesirable consequences of change.

The entire process seeks to enhance improved performance by assessing personal and company objectives and estimating the likelihood of obtaining them. The complete evaluation process can be repeated as often as necessary at three to six month intervals.

Support stage. The organization must be prepared to support the improved performance through recognition, money, advancement, and other visible rewards.

The type and amount of the reward will vary from company to company and from employee to employee. If necessary, the organization is in a better position to redesign jobs, systems and procedures that may be barriers to the employee's productivity.

The peer group, as well as the participant, must be prepared for the changes occurring in the participant's behavior. Generally, employees resist change: they grow accustomed to the routine.

A change in a peer's, supervisor's or subordinate's behavior suddenly makes decisions more difficult because group norms may have been violated and the participant's actions are not as predictable as before.

Support is critical to the success or failure of the entire process. The organization, and its members, must be prepared for more adaptability, more creativity, more independence, and in general less predictability from the participant.

The system must socially, as well as economically, support the employee's quest for better long-run productivity.

Feedback. It is always necessary to provide some feedback. Each stage is not independent of the others. It is often necessary to change company policies, rules, methods, and job descriptions. Development programs may be rescheduled, revised, or discontinued.

Individual learners may be promoted, transferred, or terminated. This can create new vacancies and new manpower requirements. In addition, successful development programs may mean increased funds for future programs or a change in hiring policies and/or pay policies.

THE PROGRAM IS BOTH GENERAL AND SPECIFIC

As attractive as models are in helping to visualize a concept, they are often too abstract to apply to specific situations. This model is applicable to a broad spectrum of organizational environments, but it is sufficiently specific to be useful with little or no modifications.

An actual case concerning a trade association that applied the model in an attempt to insure a successful outcome for a specific employee development program will help illustrate this point.

Awareness stage. A statewide association of home health care agencies had, as one of its organizational goals, the education of members. In particular, the association was responsible for collecting and disseminating information helpful to the member agencies for the improvement of professional and administrative activities.

The association, consisting of 43 geographically dispersed agencies, both profit and non-profit organizations, provided health care service throughout one state.

The notion of offering a supervisory development program to its membership was raised at association meetings for at least two years before a decision was finally reached.

Representatives of the various agencies were unable to agree on the nature of a specific program because of differences among organizations in such aspects as size, number of units, purpose, affiliation and legal status. There was, nevertheless, a feeling that a development program was needed. Employees in the agencies were, after all, predominantly trained in the medical professions, with little formal managerial education.

Finally, representatives questioned the agency personnel to ascertain their personal goals, needs and preferences. A handful of the larger agencies arranged for professional consultants to prepare job descriptions for their employees.

Ultimately, the association board made the commitment to offer a supervisory development program at three locations across the state; however, member agencies still had to make a decision whether or not to participate.

Therefore, each agency had to examine its own objectives to determine if the proposed program would satisfy its needs; the decision at the association level triggered awareness at the agency level. The awareness, in turn, required agency managers to examine their employees as organizational resources.

The units were offered once a month at three locations over a four month period. Each unit was taught in one six-hour day.

Within the agencies, two decisions were required of administrators: whether to involve their respective agencies in the program, and, if so, whom to send.

Most agencies chose to register employees in the program. Those that did not cited distance from program location as the primary factor influencing their decision.

Selection of participants was almost invariably made unilaterally by agency administrators. The justification was, generally, that the agencies would gain more from developing the supervisors that the administrators chose than if they were to rely on self-selection.

Implementation stage. The final content development of the program rested in the hands of university continuing education personnel. Also, the university was responsible for providing instructors—three faculty members and an outside consultant.

One instructor was assigned to each curriculum/unit and this instructor taught at each of the three seminar sites during a one week period. All sites were located at facilities of the university system.

Instructors were provided with basic outlines of course content. The outlines had been modified from the university's traditional supervisory development program and permitted the instructors considerable flexibility in enriching their presentations.

Instructors were encouraged to tailor the presentations to the audiences.

Evaluation stage. As the model requires, the evaluation process was initiated during the program. Representatives of the university system at each location administered questionnaires to participants at the conclusion of each curriculum unit.

The questionnaire was a standard form normally used in university continuing education programs, soliciting impressions of the value of seminar content and the effectiveness of the instructor's presentation.

Top management had to evaluate each potential participant in terms of his or her personal characteristics and ambitions in the context of the organization's objectives.

This evaluation process was facilitated by a statement outlining perceived training needs that was included on the program's registration form. Therefore, the prospective participants audited their own job habits to identify areas in which development was needed.

Decision stage. The association board, in reaching a decision to sponsor a supervisory development program, chose to contract with the state university system for program delivery.

The association itself had no formal personnel function, nor did the majority of the members have full-time personnel staffs; internal expertise was simply not available. After considering financial resources and assessing industry practices, the association board sought a proposal for a development program from the university's continuing education office.

The board worked closely with university personnel to tailor the university's standard supervisory development program to the needs of the agencies and to arrange the mechanics of the program delivery.

The completed registration form that served as a self-audit instrument provided input into the design of the program.

The form also contained three essential items of information that were used during the evaluation stage:

1) brief description of present job;
2) expectations of personal benefits to be received from training; and
3) expectations of specific job-related benefits to be received.

Subsequently, university personnel met with the education committee of the association to develop a curriculum outlining approximately 24 hours of supervisory level training.

The curriculum was divided into four distinct units: 1) organizing for effective performance; 2) getting the most from your staff; 3) your managerial style and your subordinates; and 4) special problems of the supervisor.

Responses were fed back to both the university's continuing education staff and to the association administrators. This feedback permitted modification of future seminars.

For example, some women felt that the first instructor addressed them in a condescending manner. This was reported to subsequent instructors to ensure that a professional manner would be maintained.

In the middle of the series, a seminar was held for the administrators of all participating agencies. The administrators received a review of the objectives of the program, a summary of past units, and a preview of forthcoming units.

This was an opportunity for the administrators to report their impressions of the initial results of the program on their personnel and to receive reinforcement encouraging the changes the program was designed to engender.

At the completion of the program an evaluation instrument was sent to all participants. This was a questionnaire derived from the participant's original self-audits contained within the applications.

This two-page instrument was approved at an earlier stage by both association and university personnel. Forty-five percent of the mailed questionnaires were returned to the university.

In addition to questions about the quality of the seminars, participants were asked if they had (or were planning to) put into practice anything they had learned. If so, they were asked to specify what they were or would be doing differently.

Several key questions on the evaluation were compared with the three essential items on the application form (self-audit). For example, one respondent indicated that a reason for attending was to increase effectiveness and productivity.

In the post-evaluation, the same person said that time management ideas had been implemented and that she was better organized. Overall, 78% of the respondents said they had implemented or planned to put into practice a new idea learned at the program.

As part of the session with agency administrators, which was held in the middle of the program, instructions were provided for a program evaluation to occur approximately six months after the program was completed.

The university and the association agreed to a final evaluation to be conducted by a university office separate from the continuing education division. This was to ensure an evaluation by a party with no vested interest in the success of the program. This evaluation involved a phone interview with each of the respondent's supervisors. A total of 40 supervisors were interviewed. Responding to questions relative to observed changes in subordinates who attended the program, seven supervisors had observed at least one change and 16 had observed more than one change.

Only nine reported no changes. Most of the questions called for open-ended responses. The questions were, however, directive, requesting information regarding supervisors' observations of specific behaviors expected from material covered in the program and from respondents' self-audits.

Support stage. The interviews also verified that organizational support was provided by the supervisors for behavioral changes by participants. Of course, one purpose of the telephone calls was to reinforce supervisory behavior of looking for changes and encouraging them.

Support varied from agency to agency and from supervisor to supervisor. Some participants received intrinsic rewards, such as increased self-confidence. Some were even promoted.

The support for changes was further reflected by feedback that generated a new awareness. The association met several months after the conclusion of the program and, upon its own initiative, voted overwhelmingly to offer another program the following year.

The content of the program was to be based on the feedback received from the various evaluations of the previous program.

In short, the association proved that a comprehensive, integrated model was effective in getting positive and observable results from an employee development program.

Typical complaints associated with development programs, such as wastes of time and money, were overcome by committing employees, at the time of their selection to the program, to apply the concepts learned during the program on the job.

Complaints were also eliminated by using evaluations to modify the program in-progress and to reinforce employees beliefs in the development effort. Finally, complaints were avoided by supporting both employees and their immediate supervisors in post-program attitude and behavior changes.

Many managers criticize development programs as poor investments of organization resources. They resent the time employees spend off the job and consider such activities to be unproductive.

Organizations must, however, invest just as heavily in employee maintenance as in machinery if increases in productivity are sought. This model provides a framework that management can use to improve the results of development programs.

W. Wray Buchanan is professor of marketing at Kennesaw College. Frank Hoy is associate professor of management at the University of Georgia and Director of the Small Business Development Center of Georgia. Bobby C. Vaught is associate professor at the Southwest Missouri State University.

Part VI: BEHAVIOR, CONFLICT, AND DISCIPLINE

42.
YOUR ATTITUDE IS YOUR ALTITUDE

Ethel C. Sherman

No two people are alike. The best worker is not always the best supervisor; the best supervisor may not be the most effective on a production job. Each has strengths and weaknesses depending on the nature of the job. The elements of failure in one situation may be the elements of success in another.

Bill Rich, a supervisor for Globe Manufacturing Co., learned from experience that treating all employees fairly does not mean treating all alike. He gave careful instructions to Joe and Helen on how a new operation should be handled, with significantly different results. Joe listened carefully, then asked additional questions to make certain he fully understood. Helen said nothing but Bill later heard her say to another employee, "That guy acts as if we are stupid. He goes into detail about every little thing. Doesn't he think we can figure out anything for ourselves?" The difference in the responses has nothing to do with either sex or ability. It relates to basic attitudes. Attitude-wise, Joe is a "blue liner" and Helen a "red liner." Before we explain what we mean by "red line" and "blue line," let us consider another illustration.

The emphasis on seniority and the effort to reward a good employee proved to be a mistake for the Atlas Co. Sue Hampton, the best operator in the department, had been with the company for 12 years. George Stone was considered because he asked for the job, but Sue was promoted to supervisor because she had seniority. Sue failed as a supervisor because she became frustrated with the many decisions she had to make and the variety of activities for which she was responsible. The uncertainty made her excessively nervous and her efficiency decreased. The company gained a poor supervisor and lost a good worker. In this case Sue, who wants to have structure and organization in her work, is a blue liner. George, who seeks variety, challenge and independence, is a red liner.

No two people are exactly alike. The best worker is not always the best su-

319

pervisor; the best supervisor may not be the most effective on a production job. Each has strengths and deterrents depending upon the nature of the job.

Why do we act the way we do? It is important to understand ourselves and our actions. Attitudes govern our approach to life and to the job. They control the way we organize our work, use creativity and imagination, communicate with and relate to people, handle problem situations and assume responsibility. Many years of research has shown that the most strongly held attitudes have to do with the degree of freedom or of control which the individual seeks. Some people want a situation where they are free to respond to their inner feelings and sensitivities, as did Helen in the first situation and George in the second. Others want structure and certainty as did Joe and Sue.

These attitudes are neither good nor bad, but is has been clearly shown that *the elements of failure in one situation may be the elements of success in another.* In industry as in all business, different jobs call for different basic attitudes. One job requires strict conformity and high tolerance as needed for repetitive tasks, while another calls for adaptability and enjoyment of variety and challenge in solving frequent problems that disrupt production. The detail conscious, methodical, disciplined, habitual and unimaginative person is referred to as a blue liner. In relationship to people, this individual is agreeable, cooperative, cautious and sensitive to criticism.

The red liner, in contrast, is independent, innovative, eager for new experiences and may be impatient and undisciplined. This person like being the center of attention, is gregarious and may be argumentative. The individual usually likes the leadership role and is highly competitive.

Note that there are highly desirable attitudes in each of these groups and some less desirable. Which is better depends entirely upon the needs of the particular job. Most of us have some of each of these attitudes, but one usually dominates. If all attitudes are so close together the person may be indecisive and have difficulty getting into action.

They are named red and blue to differentiate between attitudes which show preference for adventure, freedom and independent values vs. those which show security, comfort and control needs.

IT DEPENDS ON THE JOB

Which makes the better supervisor? It depends on the job. One work situation is highly structured and repetitive. For this job, the blue line supervisor maintains the status quo and is probably best. On the same job, the red line supervisor is likely to become bored and restless. On a job that is full of problems and requires frequent change, the red line supervisor is happier and better able to deal with the situation without excessive stress. Management's problem is one of fitting the person to the job.

It is important to understand why we act the way we do, but equally important to understand others. The experienced supervisor may set the climate in a particular department, but employees vary and one of the goals of the supervisor should be to better understand the workers as individuals as a way of knowing what is needed to motivate and challenge them.

The basic concept expressed here was developed by Mrs. Jessie Runner, a sociologist, and further validated in the factory situation by her son, Dr. Kenyon Runner, a psychologist. The Runner Studies of Attitude Patterns has been used by the writer in her work as an industrial psychologist for the past 20 years. It has been constantly used for screening and training in many work situations. Most of all, it is a tool for self-understanding and a way of looking at people. While a complete analysis requires that the person answer 150 questions which are then scored and an evaluation written by the consultant, some valid indications are found in the sample questions. Transfer your attention to those questions and answer them according to your own feelings. There are no right or wrong answers. Any answer is correct to the extent that it is an accurate reflection of your own feelings.

INTERPRETING ANSWERS

Before interpreting your answers, there are some significant points that should be emphasized.

a. Being red line or blue line is neither "good" nor "bad." Each attitude has positive and negative implications.
b. Our society and most businesses need both of these attitudes. The important thing is to recognize them in ourselves and others.
c. It is not uncommon for one attitude to dominate in the basic attitudes and the other in the people attitudes.
d. Basic attitudes remain reasonably stable throughout life. Certain attitudes concerned with people may change temporarily because of conflicting or frustrating experiences.
e. There are no sex or racial differences. Attitudes apply equally to men and women and to all races.

A LOOK AT YOURSELF

Circle Y for "Yes" and N for "No" . . . whichever best describes your *feelings*. There are no right or wrong answers.

1. On a job, is it important to you to feel free to develop your own ideas?   Y   N
2. In general, do you like to have your supervisor decide what methods you should use in doing your work?   Y   N

3. Do you like best to work in spurts rather than follow a planned program?   Y   N
4. Do you especially like work that is carried out according to well-established procedures?   Y   N
5. Do you feel that your best work is the result of inspiration rather than careful planning?   Y   N
6. Are you quite particular about getting the details of a project worked out ahead of time?   Y   N
7. Is it more important to you that an idea "feels right" than that it be logically supported?   Y   N
8. Do you give careful attention to preparing yourself for emergencies?   Y   N
9. When you have made up your mind to do something are you likely to be quite stubborn about it?   Y   N
10. Are you careful to observe the rules of proper social behavior at all times?   Y   N
11. In informal groups, do you seek the leadership role?   Y   N
12. Unless you have warm friends available to you, are you likely to feel very lonely?   Y   N
13. Are you alert to opportunities to win favorable comparison over other people?   Y   N
14. Are you sometimes bothered by the feeling that others may be disappointed in you?   Y   N
15. Do you enjoy trying to persuade others to do what you want them to do?   Y   N
16. If someone offends you, do you usually shut your mouth and say nothing?   Y   N
17. Do you prefer to be head of a project rather than work under someone?   Y   N
18. Do you have a tendency to do whatever people ask of you whether you want to or not?   Y   N
19. Would you like to have the responsibility for decisions which importantly affect the lives of many other people?   Y   N
20. Are you likely to worry when someone you respect criticizes what you have done?   Y   N

INSTRUCTIONS FOR SCORING

Count the number of Y scores on each row of the first 10 questions. If there are more Ys on the even numbers, you are a blue liner in your basic attitudes.

The high blue liner wants approval and acceptance from others. This person likes plans but may be dependent on others to provide them. He or she can be expected to be dutiful, loyal, rigid and have preference for a definite program of work. If there are more Ys in the odd numbers, you are a red liner. You want to go your own way. You are fun loving and resourceful, willing to take risks and may not always follow-through. You resist social pressure and like to experiment.

To score your people attitudes, count the number of Ys in each column on questions 11 through 20. If there are more Ys on the even-numbered questions, you are sympathetic and polite, want to be liked and fear rejection. You seek reassurance, support and encouragement. You tend to be cautious and wary but are genial and agreeable. You are blue line. If there are more Ys on the odd-numbered questions, you like the leadership role, are self-confident, expressive, expansive and competitive. You want recognition and like being the center of attention.

In spite of its brevity, it is hoped that this questionnaire will help you to take a look at yourself as well as the people with whom you work. Think about yourself and those around you. In so doing, you will recognize individual differences and the way they influence your performance on the job. You will see how your attitudes can become your altitudes.

43.
MANAGING CONFLICT

Leonard Greenhalgh

Conflict is not an objective, tangible phenomenon; rather, it exists in the minds of the people who are party to it. Only its manifestations, such as brooding, arguing, or fighting, are objectively real. To manage conflict, therefore, one needs to empathize, that is, to understand the situation as it is seen by the key actors involved. An important element of conflict management is persuasion.

Managers or change agents spend a substantial proportion of their time and energy dealing with conflict situations. Such efforts are necessary because any type of change in an organization tends to generate conflict. More specifically, conflict arises because change disrupts the existing balance of resources and power, thereby straining relations between the people involved. Since adversarial relations may impede the process of making adaptive changes in the organization, higher-level managers may have to intervene in order to implement important strategies. Their effectiveness in managing the conflict depends on how well they understand the underlying dynamics of the conflict—which may be very different from its expression—and whether they can identify the crucial tactical points for intervention.

CONFLICT MANAGEMENT

Conflict is managed when it does not substantially interfere with the ongoing functional (as opposed to personal) relationships between the parties involved. For instance, two executives may agree to disagree on a number of issues and yet be jointly committed to the course of action they have settled on. There may even be some residual hard feelings—perhaps it is too much to expect to manage feelings in addition to relationships—but as long as any resentment is at a fairly low level and does not substantially interfere with other aspects of their professional relationships, the conflict could be considered to have been managed successfully.

Conflict is not an objective, tangible phenomenon; rather, it exists in the minds of the people who are party to it. Only its manifestations, such as brooding, arguing, or fighting, are objectively real. To manage conflict, therefore, one needs to empathize, that is, to understand the situation as it is seen by the key actors involved. An important element of conflict management is persuasion, which may well involve getting participants to rethink their current views so their perspective on the situation will facilitate reconciliation rather than divisiveness.

Influencing key actors' conceptions of the conflict situation can be a powerful lever in making conflicts manageable. This approach can be used by a third party intervening in the conflict or, even more usefully, by the participants themselves. But using this perceptual lever alone will not always be sufficient. The context in which the conflict occurs, the history of the relationship between the parties, and the time available will have to be taken into account if such an approach is to be tailored to the situation. Furthermore, the conflict may prove to be simply unmanageable: one or both parties may wish to prolong the conflict or they may have reached emotional states that make constructive interaction impossible; or, perhaps the conflict is "the tip of iceberg" and resolving it would have no significant impact on a deeply rooted antagonistic relationship.

Table 1. presents seven perceptual dimensions that form a useful diagnostic model that shows what to look for in a conflict situation and pinpoints the dimensions needing high-priority attention. The model can thus be used to illuminate a way to make the conflict more manageable. The point here is that conflict becomes more negotiable between parties when a minimum number of dimensions are perceived to be at the "difficult-to- resolve" pole and a maximum number to be at the "easy-to-resolve" pole. The objective is to shift a viewpoint from the difficult-to-resolve pole to the easy-to-resolve one. At times, antagonists will deliberately resist "being more reasonable" because they see tactical advantages in taking a hard line. Nevertheless, there are strong benefits for trying to shift perspectives; these benefits should become apparent as we consider each of the dimensions in the model.

ISSUES IN QUESTION

People view issues on a continuum from being a matter of principle to a question of division. For example, one organization needed to change its channel of distribution. The company had sold door-to-door since its founding, but the labor market was drying up and the sales force was becoming increasingly understaffed. Two factions of executives sprung up: the supporters were open to the needed change; the resistersargued that management made a commitment to the remaining sales force and, as a matter of principle, could not violate the current sales representatives' right to be the exclusive channel of distribution.

Table 1
Conflict Diagnostic Model

Viewpoint Continuum

Dimension	Difficult to Resolve	Easy to Resolve
Issue in Question	Matter of Principle	Divisible Issue
Size of Stakes	Large	Small
Interdependence of the Parties	Zero Sum	Positive Sum
Continuity of Interaction	Single Transaction	Long-term Relationship
Structure of the Parties	Amorphous or Fractionalized, with Weak Leadership	Cohesive, with Strong Leadership
Involvement of Third Parties	No Neutral Third Party Available	Trusted, Powerful, Prestigious, and Neutral
Perceived Progress of the Conflict	Unbalanced: One Party Feeling the More Harmed	Parties Having Done Equal Harm to Each Other

Raising principles makes conflict difficult to resolve because by definition one cannot come to a reasonable compromise; one either upholds a prinicple or sacrifices one's integrity. For some issues, particularly those involving ethical imperatives, such a dichotomous view may be justified. Often, however, matters of principle are raised for the purpose of solidifying a bargaining stance. Yet, this tactic may work *against* the party using it since it tends to invite an impasse. Once matters of principle are raised, the parties try to argue convincingly that the other's point of view is wrong. At best, this approach wastes time and saps the energy of the parties involved. A useful intervention at this point may be to have the parties acknowledge that they *understand* each other's view but still believe in their own, equally legitimate point of view. This acknowledgment alone often makes the parties more ready to move ahead from arguing to problem solving.

At the other extreme are divisible issues where neither side has to give in completely; the outcome may more or less favor both parties. In the door-to-door selling example, a more constructive discussion would have ensued had the parties been able to focus on the *economic* commitment the company had to its sales force, rather than on the *moral* commitment. As it was, the factions remained deadlocked until the company had suffered irrevocable losses in market share, which served no one's interests. Divisible issues in this case might have involved how much of the product would be sold through alternative channels of distribution, the extent of exclusive territory, or how much income protection the company was willing to offer its sales force.

SIZE OF STAKES

The greater the perceived value of what may be lost, the harder it is to manage conflict. This point is illustrated when managers fight against acquisition attempts. If managers think their jobs are in jeopardy, they subjectively perceive the stakes as being high and are likely to fight tooth and nail against the acquisition. Contracts providing for continued economic security, so-called golden parachutes, reduce the size of the stakes for those potentially affected. Putting aside the question of whether such contracts are justifiable when viewed from other perspectives, they do tend to make acquisition conflicts more manageable.

In many cases the perceived size of the stakes can be reduced by persuasion rather than by taking concrete action. People tend to become emotionally involved in conflicts and as a result magnify the importance of what is really at stake. Their "egos" get caught up in the winning/losing aspect of the conflict, and subjective values become inflated.

A good antidote is to postpone the settlement until the parties become less emotional. During the cooling-off period they can reevaluate the issues at stake, thereby restoring some objectivity to their assessments. If time does not permit a cooling off, an attempt to reassess the demands and reduce the other party's expectations may be possible: "There's no way we can give you 100 percent of what you want, so let's be realistic about what you can live with." This approach is really an attempt to induce an attitude change. In effect, the person is being persuaded to entertain the thought, "If I can get by with less than 100 percent of what I was asking for, then what is at stake must not be of paramount importance to me."

A special case of the high-stakes/low-stakes question is the issue of precedents. If a particular settlement sets a precedent, the stakes are seen as being higher because future conflicts will tend to be settled in terms of the current settlement. In other words, giving ground in the immediate situation is seen as giving ground for all time. This problem surfaces in settling grievances. Thus, an effective way to manage such a conflict is to emphasize the uniqueness of the situation to downplay possible precedents that could be set. Similarly, the perceived consequences of organizational changes for individuals can often be softened by explicitly downplaying the future consequences: employees are sometimes assured that the change is being made "on an experimental basis" and will later on be reevaluated. The effect is to reduce the perceived risk in accepting the proposed change.

INTERDEPENDENCE OF THE PARTIES

The parties to a conflict can view themselves on a continuum from having "zero-sum" to "positive-sum" interdependence. Zero-sum interdependence is the perception that if one party gains in an interaction, it is at the expense of the other party. In the positive-sum case, both parties come out ahead by means of a settlement. A zero-sum relationship makes conflict difficult to resolve because it focuses attention narrowly on personal gain rather than on mutual gain through collaboration or problem solving.

Consider the example of conflict over the allocation of limited budget funds among sales and production when a new product line is introduced. The sales group fights for a large allocation to promote the product in order to build market share. The production group fights for a large allocation to provide the plant and equipment necessary to turn out high volume at high-quality levels. The funds available have a fixed ceiling, so that a gain for sales appears to be a loss for production and vice versa. From a zero-sum perspective, it makes sense to fight for the marginal dollar rather than agree on a compromise.

A positive-sum view of the same situation removes some of the urgency to win a larger share of the spoils at the outset. Attention is more usefully focused on how one party's allocation in fact helps the other. Early promotion allocations to achieve high sales volume, if successful, lead to high production volume. This, in turn, generates revenues that can be invested in the desired improvements to plant and equipment. Similarly, initial allocations to improve plant and equipment can make a high-quality product readily available to the sales group, and the demand for a high-quality product will foster sales.

The potential for mutual benefit is often overlooked in the scramble for scarce resources. However, if both parties can be persuaded to consider how they can both benefit from a situation, they are more likely to approach the conflict over scare resources with more cooperative predispositions. The focus shifts from whether one party is getting a fair share of the available resources to what is the optimum initial allocation that will jointly serve the mutual long-run interests of both sales and production.

CONTINUITY OF INTERACTION

The continuity-of-interaction dimension concerns the time horizon over which the parties see themselves dealing with each other. If they visualize a long-term interaction—a *continuous* relationship—the present transaction takes on minor significance, and the conflict within that transaction tends to be easy to resolve. If, on the other hand, the transaction is viewed as a one-shot deal—an *episodic* relationship—the parties will have little incentive to accommodate each other, and the conflict will be difficult to resolve.

This difference in perspective is seen by contrasting how lawyers and managers approach a contract dispute. Lawyers are trained to perceive the situation as a single episode: the parties go to court, and the lawyers make the best possible case for their party in an attempt to achieve the best possible outcome. This is a "no-holds-barred" interaction in which the past and future interaction between the parties tends to be viewed as irrelevant. Thus the conflict between the parties is not really resolved; rather, an outcome *is* imposed by the judge.

In contrast, managers are likely to be more accommodating when the discussion of a contract is viewed as one interaction within a long-term relationship that has both a history and a future. In such a situation, a manager is unlikely to resort to no-holds-barred tactics because he or she will have to face the other party again regarding future deals.

Furthermore, a continuous relationship permits the bankrolling of favors: "We helped you out on that last problem; it's your turn to work with us on this one."

Here, it is easy, and even cordial, to remind the other party that a continuous relationship exists. This tactic works well because episodic situations are rare in real-world business transactions. For instance, people with substantial business experiences know that a transaction is usually not completed when a contract is signed. No contract can be comprehensive enough to provide unambiguously for all possible contingencies. Thus trust and goodwill remain important long after the contract is signed. The street-fighting tactics that may seem advantageous in the context of an episodic orientation are likely to be very costly to the person who must later seek accommodation with the bruised and resentful other party.

STRUCTURE OF THE PARTIES

Conflict is easier to resolve when a party has a strong leader who can unify his or her constituency to accept and implement the agreement. If the leadership is weak, rebellious subgroups who may mot feel obliged to go along with the overall agreement that has been reached are likely to rise up, thereby making conflict difficult to resolve.

For example, people who deal with unions know that a strong leadership tends to be better than a weak one, especially when organizational change needs to be accomplished. A strongly led union may drive a hard bargain, but once an agreement is reached the deal is honored by union members. If a weakly led union is involved, the agreement may be undermined by actions within the union, which may not like some of the details. The result may well be chronic resistance to change or even wildcat strikes. To bring peace among such factions, management may have to make further concessions that may be costly. To avoid this, managers may find themselves in a paradoxical position of needing to boost the power of union leaders.

Similar actions may be warranted when there is no union. Groups of employees often band together as informal coalitions to protect their interests in times of change. Instead of fighting or alienating a group, managers who wish to bring about change may benefit from considering ways to formalize the coalition, such as by appointing its opinion leader to a task force or steering committee. This tactic may be equivalent to cooptation, yet there is likely to be a net benefit to both the coalition and management. The coalition benefits because it is given a formal channel in which the opinion leader's viewpoint is expressed; management benefits because the spokesperson presents the conflict in a manageable form, which is much better than passive resistance or subtle sabotage.

INVOLVEMENT OF THIRD PARTIES

People tend to become emotionally involved in conflicts. Such involvement can have several effects: perceptions may become distorted, nonrational thought processes and arguments may arise, and unreasonable stances, impaired communication, and personal attacks may result. These effects make the conflict difficult to resolve.

The presence of a third party, even if the third party is not actively involved in the dialogue, can constrain such effects. People usually feel obliged to appear reasonable and responsible because they care more about how the neutral party is evaluating them than by how the opponent is. The more prestigious, powerful, trusted, and neutral the third party, the greater is the desire to exercise emotional restraint.

While managers often have to mediate conflicts among lower-level employees, they are rarely seen as being neutral. Therefore, consultants and change agents often end up serving a mediator role, either by design or default. This role can take several forms, ranging from an umpire supervising communication to a messenger between parties for whom face-to-face communication has become too strained. Mediation essentially involves keeping the parties interacting in a reasonable and constructive manner. Typically, however, most managers are reluctant to enlist an outsider who is a professional mediator or arbitrator, for it is very hard for them to admit openly that they are entangled in a serious conflict, much less one they cannot handle themselves.

When managers remain involved in settling disputes, they usually take a stronger role than mediators: they become arbitrators rather than mediators. As arbitrators, they arrive at a conflict-resolving judgment after hearing each party's case. In most business conflicts, mediation is preferable because the parties are helped to come to an agreement in which they have some psychological investment. Arbitration tends to be more of a judicial process in which the parties make the best possible case to support their position: this tends to further polarize rather than reconcile differences.

Managers can benefit from a third-party presence, however, without involving dispute-resolution professionals per se. For example, they can introduce a consultant into the situation, with an *explicit* mission that is not conflict intervention. The mere presence of this neutral witness will likely constrain the disputants' use of destructive tactics.

Alternatively, if the managers find that they themselves are party to a conflict, they can make the conflict more public and produce the same constraining effect that a third party would. They also can arrange for the presence of relatively uninvolved individuals during interactions; even having a secretary keep minutes of such interactions encourages rational behavior. If the content of the discussion cannot be disclosed to lower-level employees, a higher-level manager can be invited to sit in on the discussion, thereby discouraging dysfunctional personal attacks and unreasonable stances. To the extent that managers can be trusted to be evenhanded, a third-party approach can facilitate conflict management. Encouraging accommodation usually is preferable to imposing a solution that may only produce resentment of one of the parties.

PROGRESS OF THE CONFLICT

It is difficult to manage conflict when the parties are not ready to achieve a reconciliation. Thus it is important to know whether the parties believe that the conflict is escalating. The following example illustrates this point.

During a product strategy meeting, a marketing vice-president carelessly implied that the R&D group tended to over-design products. The remark was intended to be a humorous stereotyping of the R&D function, but it was interpreted by the R&D vice-president as an attempt to pass on to his group the blame for an uncompetitive product. Later in the morning, the R&D vice-president took advantage of an opportunity to point out that the marketing vice-president lacked the technical expertise to understand a design limitation. The marketing vice-president perceived this rejoinder as ridicule and therefore as an act of hostility. The R&D vice-president, who believed he had evened the score, was quite surprised to be denounced subsequently by the marketing vice-president, who in turn thought he was evening the score for the uncalled-for barb. These events soon led to a memo war, backbiting, and then to pressure on various employees to take sides.

The important point here is that from the first rejoinder neither party wished to escalate the conflict; each wished merely to even the score. Nonetheless, conflict resolution would have been very difficult to accomplish during this escalation phase because people do not like to disengage when they think they still "owe one" to the other party. Since an even score is subjectively defined, however, the parties need to be convinced that the overall score is approximately equal and that everyone has already suffered enough.

DEVELOPING CONFLICT MANAGEMENT SKILLS

Strategic decision making usually is portrayed as a unilateral process. Decision makers have some vision of where the organization needs to be headed, and they decide on the nature and timing of specific actions to achieve tangible

goals. This portrayal, however, does not take into account the conflict inherent in the decision-making process; most strategic decisions are negotiated
solutions to conflicts among people whose interests are affected by such
decisions. Even in the uncommon case of a unilateral decision, the decision
maker has to deal with the conflict that arises when he or she moves to *implement* the decision.

In the presence of conflict at the decision-making or decision-implementing
stage, managers must focus on generating an *agreement* rather than a decision.
A decision without agreement makes the strategic direction difficult to implement. By contrast, an agreement on a strategic direction doesn't require an
explicit decision. In this context, conflict management is the process of
removing cognitive barriers to agreement. Note that agreement does not imply
that the conflict has "gone away." The people involved still have interests that
are somewhat incompatible. Agreement implies that these people have become committed to a course of action that serves some of their interests.

People make agreements that are less than ideal from the standpoint of serving their interests when they lack the *power* to force others to fully comply with
their wishes. On the other hand, if a manager has total power over those whose
interests are affected by the outcome of a strategic decision, the manager may
not care whether or not others agree, because total power implies total compliance. There are few situations in real life in which mangers have influence
that even approaches total power, however, and power solutions are at best
unstable since most people react negatively to powerlessness per se. Thus it
makes more sense to seek agreements than to seek power. Furthermore, because conflict management involves weakening or removing barriers to
agreements, managers must be able to diagnose successfully such barriers. The
model summarized in Table 1 identifies the primary cognitive barriers to an
agreement can be easily honed by making a pastime of conflict diagnosis. The
model helps to focus attention on specific aspects of the situation that may pose
obstacles to successful conflict management. This pastime transforms accounts
of conflicts—from sources ranging from a spouse's response to "how was your
day?" to the evening news—into a challenge in which the objective is to try to
pinpoint the obstacles to agreement and to predict the success of proposed
interventions.

Focusing on the underlying dynamics of the conflict makes it more likely
that conflict management will tend toward resolution rather than the more
familiar response of suppression. Although the conflict itself—that is, the
source—will remain alive, at best, its expression will be postponed until some
later occasion; at worst, it will take a less obvious and usually less manageable
form.

Knowledge of and practice in using the model is only a starting point for
managers and change agents. Their development as professionals requires that
conflict management become an integral part of their uses of power. Power is a
most basic facet of organizational life, yet inevitably it generates conflict be-

cause it constricts the autonomy of those who respond to it. Anticipating precisely how the use of power will create a conflict relationship provides an enormous advantage in the ability to achieve the desired levels of control with minimal dysfunctional side effects.

Leonard Greenhalgh is Associate Professor at the Amos Tuck School of Business Administration, Dartmouth College.

44.
THE WHEN, WHY & HOW OF DISCIPLINE

Dan Cameron

> Discipline may be the least favorite responsibility of management.
> These guidelines can help standardize the process and make it easier on
> everyone involved. In the disciplinary situation, managers are doing what
> they normally do: solving problems.

Employee discipline is a thorny and unpleasant managerial task for most
supervisors. Even the potential disciplinary cases cause apprehension.

To alleviate some of the managerial fears and problems surrounding disciplinary procedures, this article gives some practical guidelines for handling disciplinary action. A union environment is assumed, but the process applies to
all organizations, union and non-union alike.

The area of discipline is, by its nature, dynamic, and there are no final
answers. However, the following approach is of value to those who are
formulating disciplinary policies and procedures.

WHEN SHOULD A MANAGER DISCIPLINE?

The key to knowing when to discipline lies in determining the kind of
problem employee performance discipline can remedy. Disciplinary action is
taken for misconduct that the employee has the capacity and ability to correct.

For instance, misconduct is when:

- The employee knows, or could reasonably be expected to know, what is
  required on the job.
- The employee is capable of carrying out what is required.
- The employee chose to perform in a manner other than required.

As a guideline, the employer—recognizing that there are "grey" areas—can use the following question:

Is this an instance where the employee *can't* perform or *won't* perform?

If the employee *can't* perform, discipline is not appropriate.

Employees usually can't perform due to incompetence, incapacity, personal problems, or other factors that have an adverse affect on job performance.

In these instances, a non-disciplinary approach, such as counseling, training, transfers, medical referral or demotion are appropriate supportive measures. (Failure to resolve these problems can lead to a non-disciplinary dismissal.)

If, on the other hand, the employee *won't* perform, then disciplinary action is called for.

COUNSELING: THE STEP PRIOR TO DISCIPLINE

In many circumstances, merely pointing out the violation of a work rule or behavior adversely affecting performance is enough to prompt an employee to correct the situation.

In other instances, unacceptable behavior may continue to develop into a pattern of misconduct. If this happens, formal counseling can be used:

- Meet with the employee in private.
- Point out the work rule violation or errant behavior that is occurring.
- Hear the employee's explanations.
- Outline the behavior that is required and why.
- Set a future date for a performance review.

Such counseling and related documentation should not have disciplinary overtones or references to future disciplinary action. The sole purpose of this counseling step is to establish a base line for performance.

The counseling session should be summarized in writing with a copy to the employee. This documentation needs to restrict itself to specifying job requirement and is not considered a disciplinary written reprimand at arbitration. Instead, it is the specific delineation of the on-the-job performance required of the employee.

WHEN ACTUAL DISCIPLINARY ACTION IS NEEDED

Inevitably, managers are faced with the question of what to do when misconduct actually occurs.

Practice has shown that the following eight-step process is effective.

Determine what occurred. Gather the facts that indicate misconduct. In some situations, the supervisor may witness the act. More commonly, the offense is reported and must be investigated. The objective is to verify the alleged incident of misconduct.

Seek advice on the case. Once a disciplinary offense has been determined, the manager should consult with labor relations authorities on how to proceed. Normally, no disciplinary sanction should be applied until consultation has occurred.

Discipline is a specialized area and expert advice is required during all phases. Although management is required to act promptly to avoid the appearance of condoning the offense, it is sufficient to inform the employee that disciplinary action may be taken and that an investigation of the matter is underway.

Conduct the discipline hearing. This hearing is management's opportunity to explain the alleged misconduct. It is the employee's opportunity to respond to the evidence of misconduct. The disciplinary hearing is a key step in the investigation of the case.

Once management has presented and clarified its evidence, the responsibility shifts to the employee. The employee's (or union's) explanation—or lack of—should be recorded.

Investigate the employee's explanation. Attempt to verify the employee's defense. This investigation may involve questioning supervisors, fellow employees or private citizens.

Documentation related to the offense, such as work schedules, overtime claims, and sick leave applications, should also be retained.

Consider mitigating forces. Consider those factors that might indicate no disciplinary action, or a lesser disciplinary sanction, be taken.

Common mitigating considerations, as borne out in arbitration decisions, include length of service, previous work record, awareness of rules violated, impact of conduct on operations, handling of the offense, and so forth.

Record the results of the investigation. As the case proceeds, all steps should be thoroughly documented.

At the beginning, the employee misconduct and disciplinary action may be forefront in the supervisor's mind, but within the passage of time the manager could forget critical evidence.

At arbitration, the burden is on management to prove that discipline was warranted. Therefore, the importance of accurate and complete information cannot be overemphasized.

Give management's decision. In meeting with the employee (probably with the union steward present), the supervisor should cover the following points:

- What occurred and when.
- The employee's explanation.
- The results of the investigation.
- The disciplinary decision.
- Requirements for future conduct with an explanation of why.
- The consequences of further misconduct.

These points should be summarized in writing with a copy to the employee.

In this setting, the role of the union is to act as a witness. If the employee or union disputes management's decision, they should be informed that grievance action is the appropriate recourse.

Management must remain calm throughout. If the employee or union representative becomes abusive, the meeting should be adjourned to a later time. Management must make clear that the matter can only be dealt with fairly in a rational environment.

CONDUCT THE DISCIPLINE REVIEW

The supervisor should meet with the employee at some date after the disciplinary meeting to review work performance.

At that time, she should acknowledge the employee's progress in achieving the correct behavior. Such a review can serve as an incentive to improved performance.

THE PURPOSE OF DISCIPLINARY SANCTIONS

The purpose of disciplinary sanctions is to give the employee a clear warning on required behavior and the consequences of continued misconduct.

Disciplinary sanctions are symbolic, serving as milestones to indicate the degree of seriousness with which management views the offense and to indicate where the employee stands on the discipline continuum.

The objective of disciplinary sanctions is correction, with a clear warning on what is required and the consequences of non-compliance.

Where such a progressive system is used, arbitrators will evaluate the sanction against arbitral norms to determine the fairness of the disciplinary system.

Disciplinary sanctions normally applied are written reprimand, suspension (not more than 10 days), and discharge. Occasionally, oral reprimands are part of the disciplinary process. However, given their oral nature, they are not particularly good evidence in an arbitration case.

Sanctions should be applied in progressive fashion: the initial disciplinary response is appropriate to the misconduct; further misconduct results in stronger sanctions.

The selection of a specific sanction in a given instance—where not specified in the collective bargaining agreement—can be difficult.

However, the organization can draw up in advance a list of disciplinary responses for specific misconduct. Arbitration practices can serve as a guide for appropriate responses.

The key consideration in formulating this list is the impact of a specific misconduct on the operations of the organization. The disciplinary response for a particular misconduct may vary from organization to organization, or from work unit to work unit within the same organization.

THE ROLE OF UNIONS

Most managers are apprehensive about the union role in a disciplinary situation. Normally, this hesitancy is based on an uncertainty about the union's actions.

It should be remembered that the objective of the union is to ensure that discipline if fully warranted, and that all factors are taken into account.

The interaction with the union normally occurs during the discipline hearing. Management will first set out the evidence warranting disciplinary action.

The union may challenge this evidence by asking for clarification or further information. Once the union's initial fact finding is finished, the onus then shifts to the union to advance evidence indicating why discipline is not warranted or that the proposed penalty is too severe. Management may in turn, question this evidence.

The investigative responsibilities of the union are similar to the activities undertaken by management. The union may advance information that is valuable in reaching a disciplinary decision. The efforts of the union may add credibility to the process used by the organization.

THE APPROPRIATE ATTITUDE

One of the common problems in disciplinary action is that very little direction is given to managers or supervisors about approach and attitude.

This is generally left to the individual manager's discretion, and two common approaches occur:

Parent to child: the manager assumes the role of the punishing parent, and the employee takes on the role of the child—a traditional view of discipline. Most managers find this role uncomfortable, and most employees find it humiliating.

Supervisors as judge: the supervisor assumes the role of prosecutor and judge imposing sentence, and the employee is the accused. The role of executioner is one that few supervisors relish, since they must continue to interact with the disciplined employee.

Neither approach is truly effective in correcting behavior.

The appropriate attitude is based on management's primary concern in the situation: effective performance.

The appropriate management attitude is based on the following:

The discipline problem is the employee's to solve. Management needs to remember that it cannot "make" an employee perform effectively. Only the employee can make this happen.

The employee must understand that, as a result of his or her misconduct, he is on a road that leads to discharge. However, the employee, by his own choice, can change this route at any time.

Further, when the disciplinary policy has been clearly enunciated, any employee who violates the policy knows he or she runs the risk of a disciplinary response.

The employee makes those choices and assumes the risk. The employee's options are to resolve the problem or risk future employment.

The interaction is one adult to another with the options clearly outlined to the employee. Based on the above assumptions that the problem is the employee's, the supervisor has a clear view of where the responsibility lies.

The focus is on the behavior required for effective job performance, not on the employee personally.

The interaction must make clear that discipline is not employee specific. Any employee, in similar circumstances, would be treated in a similar manner. The supervisor indicates he or she is simply enforcing the rules for all employees.

The supervisor must view the disciplinary situation as a normal operating problem.

Manager and supervisors are primarily involved in operations management and problem solving. In the disciplinary situation, they are doing what they normally do: solving problems.

PREVENTION IS THE KEY TO REDUCING DISCIPLINARY ACTION

Disciplinary action commonly occurs when employees violate the organization's work rules. The following are some guidelines on the formulation, dissemination and enforcement of work rules that may prevent violations before they happen.

Formulation of the work rules. Are the proposed work rules clear and reasonable? Is the connection between the rule and its contribution to effective operation seen? Is employee behavior explicitly clear?

Will the rule be perceived by employees as fair and equitable? Employee belief that rules are reasonable is critical to their acceptance.

Are the work rules consistent with the collective bargaining agreement with the union?

Are the work rules regularly reviewed in the face of changing operations to ensure they remain valid?

Dissemination of the work rules. Employees and unions should be informed of work rules orally and by posting them in a given and central location.

Do not assume employees will learn rules simply by word of mouth.

Posted rules should remain accessible at a given location and are considered the basic law of the shop.

All new employees should be briefed on plant rules.

Enforcement of work rules. Enforce all rules promptly, consistently and without discrimination. When this is not done, disciplinary action may be prejudiced at the grievance arbitration stage.

Where an employee has been disciplined, review and acknowledge progress in writing. Such acknowledgments are an incentive to improvement.

It is accepted that not all work rules can be posted nor all forms of conduct anticipated. However, the posted rules should make clear that any misconduct—which detrimentally affects the work performance of the employees or other employees—may result in disciplinary action.

Dan Cameron, is Labor Relations Advisor, Public Service Commission, Government of Saskatchewan, Regina, Saskatchewan, Canada.

45.

PROPER HANDLING OF SUBORDINATE PROBLEMS

Alan Farrant

> You will find all on-the-job problems easier to resolve if you catch them early. Too many supervisors seem to think such problems will solve themselves—or even disappear, but they will more likely only increase in complexity.

An unliked responsibility for a supervisor is taking care of subordinate on-the-job faults and problems. They are often difficult to correct, but it is part of your responsibility as a supervisor to make a concentrated effort to solve them. First be sure you fully understand what the fault or problem actually is. Do not rely on someone else telling you about it.

Frequently, your first talk with a subordinate having a problem can provide an opening for discussion——but be prepared for a defensive attitude—even to the point of refusal to admit the problem exists. Unfortunately, that is a common response. The one in trouble is mobilizing all possible strength to protect him/herself against your claims. Usually the guilty one knows of the wrong, but is afraid of it being officially confirmed. Some people become very angry and say you are picking on them. Many will deny the problem altogether. Others will tell you it is all in your imagination. It rarely is!

Do not take this negative attitude on their part personally, which may cause you to have hurt feelings. The subordinate is frightened and is attempting to gain control. He is trying to eliminate his own hurt feelings. Have written documentation of the items you claim are serious: complaints from customers, days missed from work, short hours, drinking on the job, complaints from fellow workers. If you do not have a written list, the details are apt to be forgotten in a tense situation. Do not let the subordinate have a chance to get the upper hand by drawing you away from the facts. You, in turn, should concentrate on the subject matter exclusively.

CATCH PROBLEMS EARLY

You will find all of these problems easier to resolve if you "catch 'em early." Too many supervisors take the wrong attitude, they think such problems will solve themselves—or even disappear without being solved. Only a minute percentage will have this result. From experience, you will learn the quicker you take needed action, the easier it will be for you and an offending subordinate. Not only easier, but time will be saved and there will be less resentment by the guilty party.

Explain that you have to talk about this because that is part of your job as a supervisor, but you also want to be cooperative yourself. But be sure and state you are not going to actually be personally involved.

Instead of "beating around the bush," come right out and say what is wrong. Then stop. Let the other person say something. Try your level best not to get into an argument—especially an angry one. Let others yell, you remain calm. By you doing so, it will help the other person calm down and talk sensibly.

If the problem is one brought about by "at home" conditions, you will be expected to listen to a long list of complaints and reasons for the trouble. Without being rude, attempt to stop the listing of what "my husband said," and "my wife is always." Quickly explain you cannot become involved in personal troubles—you want only to make conditions on the job as they need to be.

Also you will be told, "Well, now, you just ask Joe and he'll agree with what I'm saying." Perhaps he would. But so what? You have the job of straightening out an on-the-job condition. It does not matter what other employees' opinions may be. All you and the person in trouble need to get settled is the "wrong" that exists between that person and the job.

To get yourself some assistance, it is a good idea to talk to fellow supervisors about like conditions. Possibly they have experienced the same—or almost the same—cases. What did they do? How did they initiate the start? What reactions did they have? What were the results? Were these results lasting?

When talking it over, be cooperative and answer their questions regarding your present problem. Should you have a supervisor over you, then take advantage of this by asking for some assistance. Not only will you get some answers, you will create some approval—everyone likes to be asked for advice.

In many instances, others from your group will be aware of your involvement with the problem employee. Some will resent the extra attention you are devoting to this person. They will be jealous, wanting you to spend just as much time with them. A few may mention this to you, while others talk about it with friends within the group. To those mentioning it to you, tell them it is part of your job as a supervisor to attempt the elimination of problems which affect the job—and you are not showing partiality. As for the "behind your back" talk, ignore it.

Chances are, you have experienced the same conditions with subordinate in the past. Even though each case is at least slightly different, you can rely on your former experiences to help in current ones. But when talking to the present offender, never mention another employee by name. To do so is unfair to the other. It will only give some ammunition to the present one, by having arguments presented about what happened to that person.

ASK FOR HELP

You may be fortunate and have this offender ask for help—yours or others. Be fully prepared for this possibility. Decide in advance what you are willing to do and not do. Be able to suggest counseling sources. Have in mind how much time away from work you will allow for the subordinate to get this needed help. Many conditions require no time—they should be adjusted and corrected as the "work and employee perform the required task."

If the one involved happens to be a personal friend, your job is more difficult. But you must ignore the friendship aspect—this is work. Part of your own work responsibility is getting satisfactory results from each member of your group.

The other extreme is dealing with someone with whom you never did get along very well. About all you can do is realize you have a job to do and do it.

At the end of your first discussion, know at least roughly what you must decide. Obviously, a correction must be made. Speak up and state what the terms and conditions are, that you want put into effect. State the fact you will check up on these rules to learn if they are being followed. Don't be "touchy" about it, but do express yourself in a stern and serious manner.

If there is a specific time period decided upon, be sure and set goals to be met within this period. Emphasize the importance of reaching the goal, on time. Not to set a limit, for an offense requiring one, encourages the condition to drift along just as it has been in the past. Depending on the things you have found wrong, the time might be from two to five weeks.

YOU TALK

Talk to the one needing to make changes in a private place or at least where no one else can hear the discussion. Often the problem to be talked about is something in connection with the family. Perhaps there is marital trouble, drinking away from the job, financial woes. The reasons are endless.

If the subordinate's performance improves and stays acceptable after your first talk, you have solved the problem. But if performance does not get better or takes a downward slide again, you need to be prepared to take further action.

Supply a written reprimand. The written reprimand should remind the subordinates of your first talk and outline the goals you initially established. Show that not enough, or any, improvement has come about. In this written message, let the person involved know the next unfavorable step will be placing this person on probation for a specified amount of time.

Should the written reprimand not get the necessary results, put this employee on an unpaid suspension of 3 to 15 days. Include a suggestion the employee use this time off to get help in settling the problem.

If immediately following the suspension there is not a noticeable improvement, you have no choice but to fire the offender.

Firing a subordinate is rarely easy for a supervisor. But you know of the effort you made to bring about satisfactory improvement, so don't let firing get you down. Most likely, the actual notice of termination will be handled by the front office—but the same reasoning applies to you.

From friends of the person fired, you may get some verbal objections. Other complaints may reach you by the grapevine. What do you do about such remarks? As little as possible! When made directly, give a short explanation: "Well, I gave John Doe plenty of opportunity to get squared away." Then change the subject. Fortunately, such resentment quickly vanishes.

Then you are ready for the next problem of this type. And you are almost sure to get it!

46.
NEGOTIATING: MASTER THE POSSIBILITIES

James F. Rand

The average manager spends as much as 20% of his or her time resolving conflicts, usually through negotiating. Moreover, conflict can affect the other 80% of his or her time. These basic guidelines can make any manager a better negotiator and more effective leader.

The push—and pull—is coming from everywhere. Human resources executives have been placed in the unpleasant position of having to please the government, employers, employees and consumers. Every group wants something, and they want it in an environment of changing laws, developing technology and shifting demographics.

The reality, therefore, is that the need to balance numerous (and often conflicting) demands requires human resources executives to spend a lot of time engaging in an activity they have little formal training in: negotiating. Without effective negotiating skills, professionals can be frustrated at every turn; with them, they can become the effective leaders they must be.

NEGOTIATION INTEGRATES LEADERSHIP STEPS

The link between effective leadership and negotiation is direct and crucial. Negotiation helps integrate the three phases of sound leadership strategy: preparation, action and follow-up. Understanding that connection, of course, first requires understanding the three phases of leadership itself.

In the preparation phase, leaders analyze the situation and establish specific goals and strategies to achieve expected results. Some of the key questions answered in this phase include:

- What is the situation in terms of such resources as people, time, capital, space and equipment?

- What are the organization's philosophies, strategies, structure, climate, leadership style, technology and so forth?
- What are the environmental pressures, including political, economic, labor, competitive, legal, social and cultural considerations?
- What are the specific issues of the situation and what are the specific facts and circumstances surrounding those issues?
- What are the objectives in terms of profitability, productivity, and organizational and individual development?
- What are the strategic and tactical action plans to achieve those objectives?

In the action phase, leaders are primarily concerned with transforming goals into a reality that balances organizational, community, and individual interests. Some of the key questions leaders must ask in this phase include:

- How have the specific goals and strategies been communicated to all people involved?
- What coalitions should be developed to facilitate the decision-making process and implementation?
- Who should be involved in specific action teams and what development is necessary?
- What type of individual recognition is appropriate to establish an environment in which individuals can be self-motivated?

During the follow-up phase, leaders determine whether the expected goals have been achieved and whether organizational, community and individual interests have remained balanced during the process. Some of the key questions that should be answered are:

- What specific administrative procedures are required to ensure that the action is appropriate?
- What are the feedback mechanisms?
- What training is required?
- How do the formal and informal reward systems contribute to the desired results?

NEGOTIATION MUST BE CAREFUL AND METHODIC

Although the three phases of effective leadership are logical and reasoned, negotiating is often the antithesis. Probably no statement better summarizes the American negotiating style than, "shoot first, ask questions later."[1]

This impetuous mentality may be traced to several sources. As a people, we share a frontier history largely defined by a high regard for fiercely independent leaders. More recently, training in our business and law schools has contributed to a collective adversarial negotiating stance.

The problems are obvious because negotiation is, by definition, characterized by interdependence that involves decision making, problem solving, setting objectives and planning for action. The negotiation process is not an end in itself, but a vehicle to help individuals and organizations resolve their issues in a fair, efficient and mutually acceptable manner.

Preparation. Leaders who do not understand and aggressively pursue a negotiation strategy are likely to be trapped in a quagmire of irrelevant detail and to strive for agreement when, in many instances, agreement is not the best resolution for a particular issue.[2]

Leaders should obtain the following information before the dialogue phase of negotiations:

- Identify such resources as people, time, capital, space and equipment.
- Review such organizational factors as philosophy, goals, strategy, climate, management style and technology.
- Identify apparent problems, symptoms and issues by defining what *is* happening versus what *should* be happening. Identify the reasons for the differences between what is happening and what should be happening.
- Research all pertinent facts and circumstances of the specific issues.
- Identify all pertinent contractual or legal provisions or precedents that might affect the negotiations.
- Summarize and evaluate positions of all parties.

The next aspect of the preparation phase includes key decisions concerning who should be part of the negotiation team, including a spokesperson, the people present at the discussions, and people and resources required for caucus and consultation.

Arriving at a decision involves awareness of assumptions. Decisions made during negotiations are based on both facts and assumptions. Leaders must be able to defend their assumptions and modify their negotiating decisions when new facts becomes available.

For example, a corporate attorney may recommend discharging an employee who allegedly initiated a fight. If the facts indicate provocation, however, a modified decision may be in order.

After you have identified alternatives, evaluate them and select the one most appropriate to resolve the particular issues. The next step is to establish objectives and strategies.

The objectives for a negotiation session should be relevant to higher organization objectives, results oriented, measurable and time-bound. They should identify both economic and non-economic results. The objectives should also include an alternative to a negotiated settlement in the event the parties are unable to reach agreement.

Establishing a strategic direction is the last step of the preparation phase of negotiations. The strategy should include directions regarding information, economics, time, and the environment.

In summary, the key questions of the preparation phase include the following:[3]

- Have you defined and analyzed the situation in terms of resources, organization and environment?
- What are the issues?
- How do time constraints impact the negotiations?
- What are the interests, motives and concerns of each party?
- Do the parties have alternatives to the negotiated agreement?
- Who should make the first offer?
- What should the first offer be?
- Has a reasonable pattern of consessions been defined?
- Can negotiations be done in stages?
- Who should negotiate?

Dialogue. The issues of greatest importance to the other side should have been identified during the preparation phase. There will be conflict (defined in this instance as an issue or issues about which two parties have different viewpoints) between what one side wants to happen and what the other parties want to take place.

People will have strong feelings about the issues being discussed. The major challenges is to focus the discussion on the issues and not the personalities involved.

How can face-to-face negotiations be managed successfully? The essential principles are:

Recognize that negotiation starts the moment participants first meet. Even the exchange of greetings is a form of negotiation. Decide in advance how to handle the pleasantries.

The first meeting should focus on a mutual understanding of each party's needs without taking major positions. The discussion should define the goals each party wants to meet through the communication.

When trying to interest a distributor in taking on a new product for nationwide sales, for example, make sure the meeting room has an informal and comfortable atmosphere. Help the distributor with travel plans to establish a cooperative climate before your first meeting.

Show your product and talk about its features. Answer questions about the marketability and predicted success of the product. Steer conversation away from such critical issues as price and terms, which can be discussed later.

Identify both positions and interests.[4] Interests drive positions. For example, a party may be demanding a $200,000 settlement in lieu of a suit for wrongful termination. It would be wise to determine why the party is interested in that particular amount.

The response may be house payments, bills, living expenses, career counseling, résumé printing, job search assistance, or other specific reasons. The company may be able to provide these services and thus reduce the actual dollar amount settlement, which could be in the best interest of both parties.

Take up the less controversial issues first, which promotes an open attitude of acceptance when critical issues are tackled. If you can make concessions on small issues early in the discussion, the other side is likely to make concessions later. In communicating your offer, follow these points:

- Make it simple, emphasize major points and be specific about what you want.
- Make it attractive by stressing mutual interests and creating a favorable picture of what will result from making a deal.
- Use illustrations, charts, product models, slides, video, symbols, design, and colors to emphasize your points.
- Offer the other party an opportunity to ask questions about each point. Rather than saying, "Do you have any questions?," say "What further information can I provide you?," which sounds less threatening.
- Summarize your proposals in a list of key points that you can present to the other party for review. Have those key points on paper so the other party can read them. This provides for greater impact and data retention.
- If you're negotiating as part of a team, don't be reluctant to meet with those on your team if you want to talk about the counter proposal. Walk away from the table so you can talk about your team's strategy privately.
- Make sure you clearly understand the proposals advanced by the other side. It is vital that you ask questions to clarify key points. If you are part of a team negotiation, appoint one person who focuses only on keeping track of the issues.

The dialogue phase also includes documentation of the negotiation session. The documentation may be written as a joint effort between the parties or may be written by one party and reviewed by the other. Careful analysis of the writing and documentating methodology is essential.

In summary, some questions to consider during the dialogue phase of negotiations include:[5]

- Are the parties problem solving?
- Have you separated the people from the problem?
- Have you focused on interests rather than positions?
- Are both parties inventing options for mutual gain?
- What objective criteria have been considered?

Whatever action is taken in the administration of the negotiated agreement, precedents may well be established.

Such methods of conflict resolution as arbitration, conciliation, mediation, and fact finding are being adapted and applied in novel ways. Moreover, interests in alternatives to litigation have resulted in an explosion of research and legislative endorsement, that has been labeled ADR (Alternative Dispute Resolution).

Court administrators and legislators alike have shown interest in many forms of ADR as methods of relieving the burdens on our judicial system and as a means of providing affordable and accessible justice to a greater number of people.

These questions should be considered during the administration phase of negotiation:

- Are both parties using an issue resolution method?
- Will resolution create a precedent for future proceedings?
- What conflict resolution methods are appropriate? Options include conciliation, mediation, fact finding and arbitration.
- Is legal action a viable alternative to resolving the dispute?

Disputes, as every personnel executive knows, are inevitable. But the dispute may be resolved fairly, and the precarious balance of corporate politics kept intact, if all those involved follow the logical, distinct steps of preparation, dialogue and administration.

If mastered, the process can be one of the most effective tools a leader can have to transform the goals of an organization or an individual into a reality.

References

1. Graham, John L. and Herberger, Roy A., Jr., "Negotiators Abroad—Don't Shoot from the Hip," Harvard Business Review. July-August 1983.
2. Fisher, Ury, Getting to Yes. Boston: Houghton Mifflin Company, 1981.
3. Raiffa, Howard, The Art and Science of Negotiation. Cambridge, MA: Belknap Press, 1982.
4. Fisher, Ury, Houghton, op. cit.
5. Ibid.

James F. Rand has represented Kimberly Clark Corporation and U and I Incorporated as a labor relations officer, and taught labor and employee relations courses as an adjunct professor in the University of Utah's Graduate School of Business.

47.
IS EMPLOYEE DISCIPLINE OBSOLETE?

Richard Discenza
Howard L. Smith

> Few organizations escape the need to discipline employees. Yet discipline is a topic that is more often avoided than pursued. At best, discipline guidelines are vaguely integrated with the other factors of behavior and climate. Discipline, an essential activity in the management process, deserves more attention.

Theory Z, quality circles, searches for excellence, participate management, organization culture and organization development are a few of the more popular topics in personnel administration. These management strategies are generally concerned with creating a supportive organization climate in which employees can attain optimum productivity. The belief that positive human relations are essential to effective personnel administration has been accepted for decades. It has helped organizations reach new milestones in producing goods and services. Despite this history of success, however, there is a continuing suspicion that prevailing behavioral management concepts are too one-sided. Managers invariably encounter situations in which they feel that positive approaches may be counterproductive.

Few organizations escape the need to discipline or punish employees. Yet discipline is a topic that is more often avoided than pursued. As a result, managers may not be adequately prepared to administer discipline. This is unfortunate because it is impossible to utilize a wide variety of methods when disciplining employees. Employee probations, temporary layoffs, demotions, discharges and wage maintenance are typical examples. Even though there is a wide variety of methods, the success of disciplinary action is still contingent on skillful implementation. Disciplining employees can promote better organizational performance, or it can precipitate organizational crisis.

Disciplinary issues often form the largest category of grievance cases reaching arbitration. This may indicate that, as a skill area, effective discipline is neglected by managers. Surprisingly, in view of the potential impact on human resources in organizations, discipline continues to be largely ignored as an area of management development in favor of motivation issues. Given these trends, it is appropriate to question whether employee discipline is reaching obsolescence.

DISCIPLINE AND PERFORMANCE

Employee discipline had been neglected by practicing managers for a wide variety of reasons. Foremost is that discipline simply has yet to receive the systematic analysis it deserves. This condition may have come about because:

- Managers are sometimes hesitant to enforce their authority
- Organizational policies and rules are often not clearly defined
- Recent collective bargaining contracts and managerial education emphasize positive motivation as opposed to punitive action.

Nonetheless, discipline is an essential activity in the management process, and it is a subject deserving more attention. Before exploring the improvements that can be made in disciplining employees, it is helpful to consider the factors underlying employee discipline.

As seen in Figure 1, typical factors influencing employee performance include individual dimensions (e.g., abilities, perceptions, motives, goals, needs and values), the motivational and compensation climate, leadership style, group dimensions (e.g., status, norms, cohesiveness and communication) and organization structure (including the macro element of control and planning). These factors constrain employee performance. Performance, in turn, influences organizational and individual goals.

Productive employee performance, by definition, contributes to goals and generally requires no reprimands or discipline. Non-productive employee performance results from unsatisfied organization and individual goals. Most managers implement disciplinary action at this point, usually as an afterthought in management practice. Although policies and rules may have been clearly formulated, these policy statements remain meaningless unless they are continually reinforced by positive (motivating) and negative (disciplining) actions.

Managers are generally adept at addressing the motivational issues when supporting organizational norms and individual performance. However, when it comes to the disciplinary dimension, they often lack knowledge, experience and implementation skills. At best, discipline guidelines are vaguely integrated with the other factors (i.e., individual dimensions, motivational and compensation climate, leadership, group dimensions and organization structure) influencing employee performance. Usually the application of discipline is sporadically undertaken when non-productive performance occurs. In cases of a blatant violation or the threat of union intervention, supervisors will dis-

Figure 1
Influences on Employee Performance

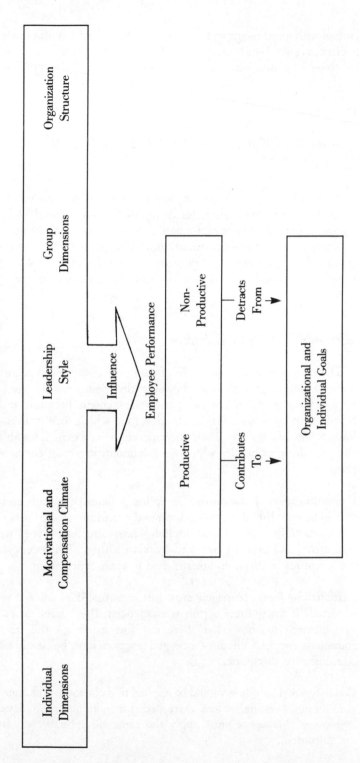

cipline with forethought and decisiveness, but seldom in other cases. Rarely is a link created between a violation and broader organizational processes—focusing on the violation is indicative of this problem.

ORGANIZATION AND BEHAVIOR ASPECTS OF DISCIPLINE

A broader approach to employee discipline is needed in personnel administration which includes discipline as an integral element in the management of employee performance. In attaining more effective discipline, two major dimensions—organization and behavior (motivation)—appear to be essential for discipline programs. These dimensions are comprised of policies often used by managers in forming a discipline program.

ORGANIZING PRINCIPLES

The importance and usefulness of employee discipline is acknowledged by many management authorities; however, the treatments are often set forth in very general terms. A review of the management literature indicates that several principles are consistently identified which form the organizational basis of a good employee discipline program. (See Figure 2 for an overview of the organizing principles which set a foundation for an effective discipline program.)

Communication of standards. Discipline policies, standards and procedures should be established in written form and communicated to personnel. Communication in this context includes providing employees with written statements and oral explanations for clarification. Employees should know what rewards or penalties are attached to each expectation.

Establishing facts. Managers must gather factual data when a violation has occurred. If disciplinary action is challenged, the burden of proof is upon management to show that there was just cause for the treatment. All statements, actions, circumstances and reactions must be clearly established in administering discipline.

Consistency. Discipline should be applied in a consistent manner. Where inconsistency prevails, a loss of respect for standards will develop among employees. Managers must apply the same disciplinary action in similar circumstances.

Figure 2.
Organizational Basis of Discipline

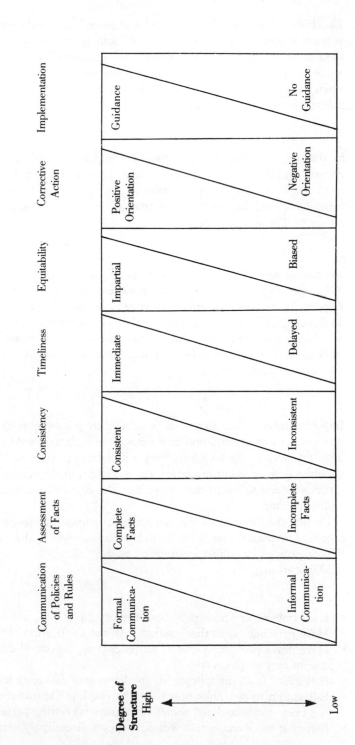

Timeliness. It is generally recognized that discipline should be applied as soon as possible after a violation has occurred. Sufficient time should be allotted to adequately ascertain that a violation was committed and to appropriately assign responsibility. The exception to this principle is found in situations where tempers are highly volatile. Implementing discipline should be more deliberate under these conditions.

Equitability. Disciplinary action should be impartially applied in proportion to the standard that has been violated. Managers must refrain from inequitable treatment of employees if a successful discipline program is to be established. Inequitable discipline applications may adversely affect production and job satisfaction of all employees.

Positive action. Discipline should be corrective and positive in orientation. When possible, it should provide employees with a second (or additional) opportunity to achieve normal performance before full penalties are imposed. In this manner, managers and personnel may examine the basis of the violation in order to prevent further, and possibly more critical, problems. It may be discovered that the nature of the policy, task or work flow is responsible for causing violations.

Implementation. The extent to which each principle is thoroughly implemented in an organization may range from high to low depending on the foresight given to the administration of a discipline program. Other relevant variables (e.g., number of employees, unionization, leadership skills among supervisors and so forth) may also affect the organization underlying a discipline program.

Despite the integrity of the preceding principles for organizing discipline programs, managers may fail to include each principle in their own program. Several reasons cause this apparent oversight. Managers may:

- Lack training or knowledge about the principles
- Have personal values that conflict with the application of the principles
- Have developed "group-think" attitudes (i.e., no one else is disciplining employees)
- Feel guilty (i.e., disciplining an employee may damage a friendship)
- Fall victim to rationalization (i.e., the employee knows that a violation has been committed and therefore requires no further action)
- Fear that top management will not support disciplinary action.

These excuses arise because discipline has remained a skeleton in many managers' closets.

BEHAVIORAL PRINCIPLES

Management behavior as a punitive or motivating force is a second discipline dimension that, like structure, is more implicitly than explicitly addressed by managers in discipline programs. Three factors can be identified that contribute positively to managers' discipline behavior.

First, managers' disciplinary actions should motivate personnel to conform to established policies, rules and standards. When management action is punitive instead of motivational, personnel are punished without consideration of long-run behavioral consequences. Second, after a discipline violation has occurred, personnel should be counseled by reviewing proper standards of behavior in order to prevent future discipline violations. In contrast to counseling, some managers treat the violation in a formal manner with little emphasis on violation of a formal policy/rule. Third, managers should attempt to construct a discipline climate which reflects the organization's interest in the employee as an individual. When these three factors are combined, they form the behavior dimension of personnel discipline illustrated in Figure 3.

A vast number of contradictory disciplinary approaches exist, leaving many managers bewildered as to which one can be relied on as a guide for implementing the behavioral side of discipline. As a result, a consistent approach to discipline behavior may never be set. Thus, discipline may become an even more difficult and unpleasant part of any manager's job. Few probably enjoy taking disciplinary action when an employee has broken a rule. However, discipline must be maintained so that the organization's policies and procedures are carried out in a proper and effective manner. The main question is to attain a firm yet supportive behavioral approach.

The form of discipline that most employees receive during their careers generally falls under the category of training and coaching. This is usually received from immediate supervisors and other close administrative personnel. The supervisor acts as a regulator and takes corrective action when employee outputs do not conform to standards. In maintaining this supportive behavioral climate, it is important that managers provide frequent feedback on job performance. The feedback should consist not only of pointing out areas of weakness and lower-than expected output, but it should especially highlight recognition for good performance. (As Figure 3 suggests, a positive climate can then be built because discipline is then motivational and employee oriented.)

When managers provide frequent feedback on job performance and acknowledge exceptional performance, discipline will seldom develop into a significant problem. Behavior is supportive in nature. It consists of building and maintaining an employee's sense of importance, dignity and personal worth. This helps reinforce commitment to the organization and to its goals.

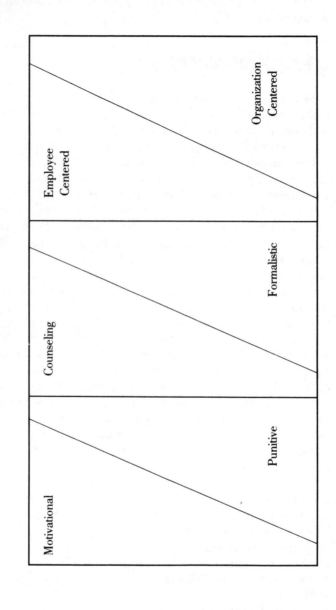

Figure 3
Behavioral Basis of Discipline

Figure 4.
Integrating Discipline Structure and Behavior

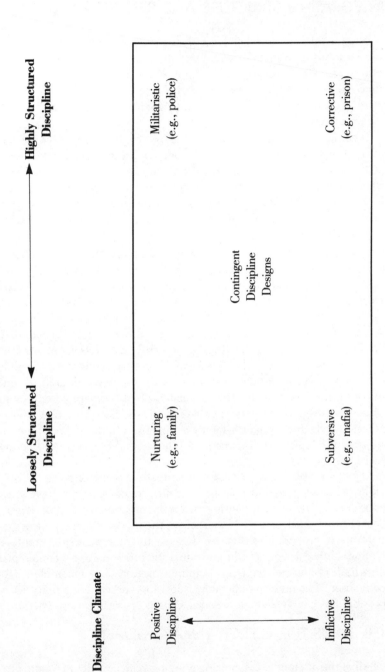

INTEGRATING STRUCTURE AND BEHAVIOR

The organization and behavior of discipline can be combined to identify various forms of discipline possible in an organization. These configurations can vary from a nurturing environment where the individual is advised in an affectionate manner to a purely corrective climate which involves formal treatment of the discipline violation. Figure 1 implies that the orientation can vary within a given dimension.

Together the disciplinary organizing principles and behavioral methods present a matrix of management action for nonproductive employee performance, as shown in Figure 4. The four main discipline responses surface when management combines the behavior and organization dimensions: Loosely organized—motivational discipline; loosely organized—punitive discipline; highly organized—motivational discipline; and highly organized—punitive discipline.

The model depicting the integration of discipline structure and behavior is useful for personnel administrators to consider for several reasons. First, the model explicitly indicates that there is no single best way to discipline. Organizations will implement different discipline models depending on the nature of their goals. Thus as an organization, a family is usually concerned about child growth within a loving atmosphere. Discipline standards are eventually formulated during the life of a child but are seldom written down (i.e., loosely organized). Parents focus on positively motivating children to behave well even under the most severe violations of the discipline standards. In contrast, a prison usually has formulated a highly organized set of standards whose violation is met with punitive methods. The goal of a prison is to punish, while the goal of a family is to raise children. Each organization requires a unique discipline model in view of the goals that are germane to each.

Figure 4 is also useful because it accentuates a realm of possibilities for disciplining employees that personnel administrators may not have previously considered. Discipline is contingent on the organizational situation and the goals in that organization. Nonetheless, the model visually portrays the importance of bringing together two dimensions when managing employee discipline. Unless personnel administrators and other managers contemplate the organization and behavior of disciplinary actions, an incomplete model is being used. The result, predictably, is less appropriate disciplinary action and possibly less effective employee, department or organizational performance.

THE BASIS FOR EFFECTIVE MANAGEMENT

All of the disciplinary organizing principles can contribute toward attaining a well-developed program in which employees obtain clear, concise explanations of discipline policies and rules. This organizational dimension, however, is not sufficient for achieving management effectiveness in disciplinary issues. Managers must also address their (and others') behavior while implementing the discipline program. Thus, organization *and* behavior are both very important dimensions in achieving an effective discipline program that satisfies the needs and requirements of managers as well as employees.

It also appears that organizational discipline is a many-faceted concept that deserves more refinement and exploration within organizations. Discipline has at least two dimensions—and perhaps more. Managers should concentrate on defining these dimensions practically. In addition, they should consider the relationship of both dimensions with other personnel management topics such as motivation and leadership. The discipline area must be combined with these more well-established management concepts if further progress in productivity is to be achieved. Personnel administration strategies which do not at least implicitly integrate discipline issues should be revised.

PROGNOSIS FOR THE FUTURE

Is the theory and practice of employee discipline obsolete? The answer to this question is certainly "no." However, the theory and application of discipline in an organization can be considerably extended in the future. In guiding renewed efforts in this area, several new directions for discipline can be identified.

First, motivation theories and management practice should be revised to clearly underscore the interaction with discipline. Emphasis must be placed on integrating motivation and discipline. Once this synthesis is achieved, further analysis should be made of the impact of both motivation and discipline on job satisfaction. Managers and researchers have focused excessively on incremental aspects of motivation.

Second, investigation should ascertain whether the size of the organization, its environment, structure and other contextual variables require inclusion in operational discipline models. For example, managers should consider the efficiency of discipline with respect to organization size. Will discipline be more effective in terms of preventing violations and promoting individual responsibility in the small or the large organization?

In a third area of study, researchers could study disciplinary process variables, such as intensity of punishment or proximity in time of punishment to the violation, in order to clarify their impact on controlling and preventing future problems. Each discipline organizing principle suggested in our models should receive careful examination for applicability to a specific situation before managers include them in their discipline program.

Fourth, the frequency of undesirable organizational behaviors (absenteeism, stealing and so forth) as independent moderating variables of the ability to achieve effective discipline should be clearly established. In a similar manner, further analysis could ascertain whether managers scoring relatively high on personality variables such as aggression, dominance and autonomy exhibit different disciplinary styles from those; for example, exhibiting a relatively high score on affiliation. More clearly, an analysis should be made of whether contingency methods apply in the administration of discipline.

A sixth direction for future examination of discipline involves the exploration of moral issues in discipline application. The underlying philosophy behind discipline is control over individuals. Fruitful investigation will seek to explain the moral limits of organizational discipline. It will acknowledge situations in which managers and subordinates have overstepped their authority or individual responsibility.

Finally, it must be determined whether the frequency of undesirable behavior in persons who have been disciplined previously is the same as for other personnel. Does knowing that another worker has been disciplined keep an employee in line? This perhaps is the most critical test of a discipline model. There is obviously little reason for applying discipline processes if the outcomes are negligible or negative in value.

Utilizing the dimensions and suggestions presented in this review, personnel administrators, other managers and management scholars will discover that the theory and practice of contemporary discipline is not obsolete in managing personnel. Emphasis should be placed on validating current principles of discipline and testing comprehensive motivation discipline models. The results of these efforts should lead to improved human and organizational performance.

Richard Discenza is an associate professor of production management and information systems at the University of Colorado, Colorado Springs. He is the co-author of Contemporary Supervision *(Random House, 1985). Howard L. Smith is an associate professor in the Department of Health Administration at the Medical College of Virginia in Richmond, VA.*

BIBLIOGRAPHY

Abrahamson, Lee H. *How to Develop and Administer an Effective Personnel Program* (Barrington, IL: Omega Center, 1981).

Armstrong, Michael. *Handbook of Personnel Management Practice* (New York: Nichols Pub., 1977).

Armstrong, Michaels, ed. *Personnel and Training Databook* (Philadelphia, PA: International Publication Service, 1982).

Austin, Charles F. *Management's Self-Inflicted Wounds: A Formula for Executive Self-Analysis* (New York: Holt, Rinehart and Winston, 1966).

Baker, Alton W. *Personnel Management in Small Plants* (Columbus, OH: Ohio State University College of Administrative Science, 1955).

Barber, David. *Basic Personnel Procedures* (Brookfield, VT: Brookfield Publishing Co., 1973).

Beach, Dale S. *Personnel: The Management of People at Work* (New York: Macmillan, 1980).

Beatty, Richard W. and Schneier, Craig E. *Personnel Administration: An Experiential Skill-Building Approach* (Reading, MA: Addison-Wesley, 1977).

Becker, Esther, ed. *Dictionary of Personnel and Industrial Relations* (New York: Philosophical Library Inc., 1958).

Bennett, Roger. *Managing Personnel & Performance* (Brookfield, VT: Brookfield Publishing Company, 1981).

Benton, Lewis. *Supervision and Management* (New York: McGraw-Hill, 1972).

Bittel, Lester R. *Improving Supervisory Performance* (New York: McGraw-Hill, 1976).

Blake, David H. et al. *Social Auditing: Evaluating the Impact of Corporate Programs* (New York: Praeger, 1976).

Brandon, Dick H. *Data Processing Organization & Manpower Planning* (New York: Van Nostrand Reinhold, 1974).

Broadwell, Martin M. *The Practice of Supervising: Making Experience Pay* (Reading, MA: Addison-Wesley, 1977).

Burack, Elmer H. *Personnel Management: Cases & Exercises* (St. Paul, MN: West Publishing Company, 1978).

Burack, Elmer H. *Personnel Management: A Human Resource System Approach* (New York: Wiley, 1982).

Burby, Raymond J. *Managing with People* (Reading, MA: Addison-Wesley, 1968).

Calhoun, R. *Cases in Personnel Management & Supervision* (Englewood Cliffs, NJ: Prentice-Hall, 1971).

Carlson, Robert D. and McHugh, James F. *Handbook of Personnel Administration Forms and Formats* (Englewood Cliffs, NJ: Prentice-Hall, 1978).

Carrell, Michael R. & Kuzmits, Frank E. *The Management of Human Resources* (Columbus, OH: Charles E. Merrill, 1981).

Carson, Charles R. *Managing Employee Honesty* (Stoneham, MA: Butterworth, 1977).

Cascio, Wayne. *Applied Psychology in Personnel Management* (Reston, VA: Reston Publishing Company, 1982).

Cayer, N. Joseph. *Managing Human Resources: An Introduction to Public Personnel Administration* (New York: St. Martins, 1980).

Cayer, N. Joseph. *Public Personnel Administration in the United States* (New York: St. Martins, 1975).

Chapman, Elwood N. *Supervisor's Survival Kit* (Chicago: Science Research Associates, 1981).

Chasnoff, Robert and Muniz, Peter. *Managing Human Resources: A Practical Guide* (Westfield, NJ: Laboratory for Applied Behavioral Science, 1981).

Cherrington, David J. *Personnel Management: Human Resources Management* (Dubuque, IA: William C. Brown, 1983).

Christie, Linda G. *Human Resources: A Hidden Profit Center* (Englewood Cliffs, NJ: Prentice-Hall, 1983).

Cohn, Theodore and Lindberg, Roy A. *Practical Personnel Policies for Small Business* (Boston, MA: CBI Pub., 1983).

Coleman, Charles J. *Personnel: An Open System Approach* (Waltham, MA: Little Brown & Company, 1979).

Crane, Donald P. *Personnel: The Management of Human Resources* (Boston, MA: Kent Publishing Company, 1982).

Cross, Michael. *U.S. Corporate Personnel Reduction Policies* (Brookfield, VT: Gower Publishing Ltd, 1982).

Cummings, Thomas G. and Molloy, Edmond S. *Improving Productivity and the Quality of Work Life* (New York: Praeger, 1977).

Danish, Steve, et al. *Helping Skills: A Basic Training Program* (New York: Human Science Press, 1980).

Davidson, William L. *How to Develop and Conduct Successful Employee Attitude Surveys* (Chicago: Dartnell Corporation, 1979).

Dessler, Gary. *Personnel Management* (Reston, VA: Reston, 1981).

De Spelder, Bruce E. *Ratios of Staff to Line Personnel* (Columbus, OH: Ohio State University College of Administrative Science, 1962).

Destnick, R. L. *Innovative Human Resource Management* (New York: American Management Association, 1972).

Destnick, Robert L. *The Expanding Role of the Human Resources Manager* (New York: American Management Association, 1979).

Destnick, Robert L. *Human Resource Management in the Multinational Company* (New York: Nichols Publishing, 1978).

Deutsch, Arnold. *The Human Resources Revolution: Communicate or Litigate* (New York: McGraw-Hill, 1979).

Dougherty, James L. *Union Free Management* (Chicago: Dartnell Corporation, 1972).

Dowling, William, ed. *Effective Management and the Behavioral Sciences: Conversations from Organizational Dynamics* (New York: American Management Association, 1978).

Dreher, George F. *Perspectives on Employee Staffing and Selection* (Homewood, IL: Richard D. Irwin, 1983).

DuBrin, Andrew. *Personnel and Human Resource Management* (New York: Van Nostrand Reinhold, 1980).

Dyer, B. *Personnel Systems and Records* (Brookfield, VT: Gower Publishing Ltd., 1979).

Ellis, C. R. *Personnel Practice: A Guide to Effective Supervision* (Philadelphia: International Publications Service, 1975).

Ellman, Edgar S. *Put It in Writing: A Complete Guide for Preparing Employee Policy Handbooks* (Boston, MA: CBI Pub., 1983).

Embry, Olice M. *Moving and Transferring Handbook* (Reading, MA: Addison-Wesley, 1975).

Famularo, Joseph J. *Handbook of Modern Personnel Administration* (New York: McGraw-Hill, 1972).

Farley, Jennie. *Affirmative Action and the Woman Worker: Guidelines for Personnel Management* (New York: American Management Association, 1979).

Farrow, Dawna. *Using Applied Psychology in Personnel Management* (Reston, VA: Reston, 1982).

Fuqua, Paul and Wilson, Jerry. *Security Investigator's Handbook* (Houston, TX: Gulf Publishing Company, 1979).

Genua, Robert L. *The Employer's Guide to Interviewing, Strategies and Tactics for Picking a Winner* (Englewood Cliffs: Prentice-Hall, 1979).

Glueck, William F. and Ivancevich, John M. *Personnel: A Diagnostic Approach* (Plano, TX: Business Publications Inc., 1982).

Grouch, W. W. *Guide for Modern Personnel Commissions* (Washington, DC: International Personnel Management Association, 1973).

Harris, O. Jeff. *How to Manage People at Work: A Short Course for Professionals* (New York: Wiley, 1977).

Jaffee, Cabot L. *Problems in Supervision: An In-Basket Training Exercise* (Reston, VA: Addison-Wesley, 1968).

Janger, Allen R. *The Personnel Function: Changing Objectives and Organizations* (New York: Conference Board, 1977).

Joyce R. D. *Encounter in Organizational Behavior: Problem Situations* (New York: Pergamon, 1974).

Jucius, Michael J. *Personnel Management* (Homewood, IL: Richard D. Irwin, 1979).

Karlins, Marvin. *The Human Use of Human Resources* (New York: McGraw-Hill, 1981).

Kaumeyer, Richard A. *Planning and Using a Total Personnel System* (New York: Van Nostrand Reinhold, 1981).

Keil E. C. *Performance Appraisal and the Manager* (New York: Lebhar-Friedman Books, 1977).

Kelly, Nelson L. *Personnel Management in Action: Skill Building Experiences* (St. Paul, MN: West Publishing Company, 1980).

Kellogg, Marion S. *Putting Management Theories to Work* (Houston, TX: Gulf Publishing Company, 1968).

Kellogg, Marion S. *Talking with Employees: A Guide for Managers* (Houston, TX: Gulf Publishing Company, 1979).

Kroeger, Louis, J. et al. *Public Personnel Administration: Progress and Prospects* (Washington, DC: International Personnel Management Association, 1968).

Kuzmits, Frank E. *Exercises in Personnel Management* (Columbus, OH: Charles E. Merrill, 1982).

Lawson J. W. and Smith, B. *How to Develop a Personnel Policy Manual* (Chicago: Dartnell Corporation, 1978).

Ledvinka, James. *Federal Regulation of Personnel and Human Resource Management* (New York: Van Nostrand Reinhold, 1982).

Lyons, T. P. *Personnel Function in a Changing Environment* (Woodstock, NY: Beekman Publications Inc., 1971).

McGregor, Douglas. *Human Side of Enterprise* (New York: McGraw-Hill, 1960).

Mathis, Robert L. and Jackson, John H. *Personnel: Contemporary Perspectives and Applications* (St. Paul, MN: West Publishing Company, 1982).

Megginson, Leon C. *Personnel and Human Resources Administration* (Homewood, IL: Richard D. Irwin, 1981).

Melucci, Richard J. *Modern Personnel Checklists* (Boston, MA: Warren Gorham & Lamont, Inc., 1982).

National Retail Merchants Association. *Cost Control Through Improved Personnel Practices* (New York: National Retail Merchants, 1979).

Norris, Carol. *OJT Personnel Clerk Resource Materials* (New York: McGraw-Hill, 1980).

Novit, Mitchell S. *Essentials of Personnel Management* (Englewood Cliffs, NJ: Prentice-Hall, 1979).

Oakley, Charles A. *Men at Work* (Salem, NH: Ayer Co., 1977).

Patten, Thomas H., Jr. *Classics of Personnel Management* (Durham, NC: Moore Publishing Company, 1979).

Pearlman, Kenneth and Schmidt, Frank L. *Contemporary Problems in Personnel* (New York: Wiley, 1983).

Pigors, Paul and Myers, Charles A. *Personnel Administration: A Point of View and a Method* (New York: McGraw-Hill, 1981).

Quick, Thomas. *Quick Solutions: 500 People Problems Managers Face and How to Solve Them* (New York: Wiley, 1987).

Robbins, Stephen P. *Personnel: The Management of Human Resources* (Englewood Cliffs, NJ: Prentice-Hall, 1982).

Roethlisberger, Fritz J. *Man-In-Organization: Essays of F. J. Roethlisberger* (Boston: Harvard University Press, 1968).

Roseman, Edward. *Confronting Nonpromotability: How to Manage a Stalled Career* (New York: American Management Association, 1977).

Roseman, Edward. *Managing Employee Turnover: A Positive Approach* (New York: American Management Association, 1981).

Rowland, Kendrith M. and Ferris, Gerald R. *Current Issues in Personnel Management* (Newton, MA: Allyn & Bacon, 1983).

Rowland, Kendrith M. and Ferris, Gerald R. *Personnel Management* (Newton, MA: Allyn & Bacon, 1982).

Roxe, Linda A. *Personnel Management for the Smaller Company: A Hands-On Manual* (New York: American Management Association, 1979).

Rush, Harold M. *Behavorial Science: Concepts and Management Application* (New York: Conference Board, 1969).

Sanford, Aubrey. *Human Relations: The Theory and Practice of Organizational Behavior* (Columbus, OH: Charles E. Merrill, 1977).

Sanzotta, Donald. *Motivational Theories and Applications for Managers* (New York: American Management Association, 1977).

Sayles, Leonard and Strauss, G. *Human Behavior in Organizations* (Englewood Cliffs, NJ: Prentice-Hall, 1966).

Sayles, Leonard and Strauss, George. *Managing Human Resources* (Englewood Cliffs, NJ: Prentice-Hall, 1981).

Schafritz, Jay M. *Dictionary of Personnel Management and Labor Relations* (New York: Facts On File Publications, 1986).

Scheer, Wilbert E. *Outside Influences on Personal Management* (Chicago: Dartnell Corporation, 1981).

Scheer, Wilbert E. *Personnel Administration Handbook* (Chicago: Dartnell Corporation, 1979).

Sibson, Robert E. *Increasing Employee Productivity* (New York: American Management Association, 1976).

Siegel, Laurence and Lane, Irving M. *Personnel and Organizational Psychology* (Homewood, IL: Richard D. Irwin, 1982).

Sikula, Andrew F. and McKenna, John F. *The Management of Human Resources: Personnel Text and Current Issues* (New York: Wiley, 1984).

Sikula, Andrew F. *Personnel Management: A Short Course for Professionals* (New York: Wiley, 1977).

Stahl, Glenn O. *Public Personnel Administration* (New York: Harper and Row, 1983).

Stanton, Erwin S. *Successful Personnel Recruiting and Selection: With EEO-Affirmative Action Guidelines* (New York: American Management Association, 1980).

Steiner, Gary A. *Creative Organization* (Chicago: University of Chicago Press, 1971).

Stockard, James G. *Rethinking People Management: A New Look at the Human Resources Function* (New York: American Management Association, 1980).

Stone, Thomas H. *Understand Personnel Management* (Hinsdale, IL: Dryden Press, 1982).

Strauss, George and Sayles, Leonard R. *Personnel: The Human Problem of Management* (Englewood Cliffs, NJ: Prentice-Hall, 1980).

Strohmer, Arthur F., Jr. *The Skills of Managing* (Reading, MA: Addison-Wesley, 1970).

Sweet, Donald H. *The Modern Employment Function* (Reading, MA: Addison-Wesley, 1973).

Tead, Ordway. *Human Nature and Management: Applications of Psychology to Executive Leadership* (Salem, NH: Ayer Co., 1977).

Van Fleet, James. *Twenty-Two Biggest Mistakes Managers Make and How to Correct Them* (Englewood Cliffs, NJ: Prentice-Hall, 1973).

Vervalin, Charles H. *Management and the Technical Professional* (Houston, TX: Gulf Publishing Company, 1981).

Walker, James W., and Gutteridge, Thomas G. *Career Planning Practices* (New York: American Management Association, 1979).

Werther, William and Davis, Keith. *Personnel Management* (New York: McGraw-Hill, 1981).

Wexley, Kenneth A. and Yukl, Gary A. *Organizational Behavior and Personal Psychology* (Homewood, IL: Richard E. Irwin, 1977).

Yoder, D. et al. *Handbook of Personnel Management and Labor Relations* (New York: McGraw-Hill, 1958).

Yoder, Dale and Staudohar, Paul D. *Personnel Management and Industrial Relations* (Englewood Cliffs, NJ: Prentice-Hall, 1982).

Yoder, Dale and Heneman, Herbert G. *Administration and Organization* (Washington, DC: Bureau of National Affairs, 1977).

INDEX